The Essential
GILBERT WHITE
of Selborne

Also available as Godine Country Classics:

A Countryman's Journal by Roy Barrette

Three Farms by Mark Kramer

A GODINE COUNTRY CLASSIC

The Essential GILBERT WHITE *of Selborne*

edited by H. J. Massingham
selected and introduced by Mark Daniel
wood engravings by Eric Ravilious

DAVID R. GODINE · PUBLISHER · BOSTON

This is a Godine Country Classic published in 1985 by
David R. Godine, Publisher, Inc.
306 Dartmouth Street
Boston, Massachusetts 02116

Library of Congress Cataloging in Publication Data

White, Gilbert, 1720–1793.
The essential Gilbert White of Selborne.

1. Natural history—England—Selbourne (Hampshire)—Early works to 1800. 2. White, Gilbert, 1720–1793. 3. Naturalists—England—Biography. I. Massingham, H. J. (Harold John), 1888–1952. II. Title.

QH138.S4W26 1985 508.422′74 84-48801
ISBN 0-87923-571-3 (pbk.)

First printing

Printed in the United States of America

CONTENTS

EDITOR'S NOTE

The only really substantial and representative selection of Gilbert White's work hitherto published is the Nonesuch Press's *The Writings of Gilbert White* edited by H.J. Massingham and illustrated by Eric Ravilious, published in two volumes in 1938. It is a beautiful book. The typography and the quality of the printing are exceptional, the decorations and the notes are a meticulous labour of love. That edition, however, was limited to eight hundred and fifty copies and is now very rare and valuable. To reproduce it in its entirety would be impossibly expensive. I have therefore abridged it, whilst retaining the original settings, the decorations and Massingham's erudite and compendious notes.

Inevitably, the condensation of those two heavy volumes into one has demanded some painful sacrifices. Some purists would argue that *The Natural History of Selborne* should have been left intact by merit of its status as a 'classic'. Such purists, however, will already own a complete copy of White's masterpiece. I have therefore not hesitated to excise such passages as reiterate material to be found elsewhere or are of merely specialised interest. I have retained almost all of the writings on swallows, although they fall into the latter category, because White's speculations about his own favourite birds seem to me to be important, curious and characteristic.

Some of the space saved has come from topping and tailing the letters. Like any correspondent, White was inclined to turn to new, stray subjects in his last paragraphs. Where such paragraphs are not of particular interest I have had no compunction about lopping them off.

The *Antiquities* are not much fun. They consist largely of a compilation of other men's historical researches and offer little more than a pedantic guidebook. I have thought it essential, however, to include some of them, for as I have made clear in the introduction, White thought them an indispensable half of his grand design – the portrait of the parish. Where Massingham edited mercifully, I have been ruthless. Of the three letters which I have left, two are of some interest to visitors to Selborne today and illustrate the general flavour of the work, while the third is instructive and amusing. In the tone of White's summary of William of

Wykeham's strictures, one can hear the quiet chuckle of the latter-day cleric.

I have included the *Naturalists Journal* for the last five years of White's life, for it is rich ground for delving. To select only such entries as appear curious or felicitous were to misrepresent White and the nature of the *Journal*. Massingham omitted the earlier years, quite rightly maintaining that the *Natural History* already draws on them heavily. For reasons of space I have had to remove the journal for 1788.

The recipients of the *Private Letters* which I have included were Gilbert's brother, the Rev. John White, his nephew and brother in law, Sam and Thomas Barker, and his favourite niece, Molly White. The letters to John White were written during the 1770s when he was chaplain to the garrison on Gibraltar. He shared with Gilbert a devotion to natural history, corresponded with Linnaeus and compiled a Natural History of Gilbratar, *Fauna Calpensis*.

The *Private letters* are valuable because they reveal much about White's personality. Whether writing about his vast circle of nephews and nieces (who eventually numbered 62) or brewing his own beer, they contain a lively, personal quality which is sometimes lacking from the formal letters of the *National History*. Thus to Sam Barker: 'Hay is become very scarce indeed! My rick is now almost as slender as the waste of a virgin: and it would have been much for the reputation of the last two brides that I have married, had their wastes been as slender.'

Whatever I have excluded, I must always be criticised by dedicated Whiteans. But the object throughout has been to offer for the first time in one reasonably priced volume a selection of the best of White's writings, for the newcomer to White and Selborne, for those who are familiar only with the *Natural History* and, indeed, for the single-minded White scholar when up a mountain or on a foreign beach.

I have appended notes on Eric Ravilious, who made the wood engravings which decorate the text so beautifully, and on H.J. Massingham whose dedicated and meticulous editing made this volume possible. My task has been merely to trim his edition.

M.D.

H.J. MASSINGHAM, (1888-1952)

Harold John Massingham was a great countryman in an age of great countrymen. Whilst working for the *New Age*, he numbered W.H. Davies, Ralph Hodgson and W. H. Hudson amongst his colleagues. Educated at Westminster and at Queen's College, Oxford, where illness prevented him from graduating, he contributed articles on natural history and literature to a wide range of publications, including *The Nation* and *The Athenaeum*. Inspired by an angry poem by Ralph Hodgson, Massingham set up the Plumage Group in order to stop the trade in bird feathers. He was later a member of the Board of Trade committee to implement the Importation of Plumage (Prohibition) Act of 1921. In the same year, he published his immensely popular and highly praised *Treasury of Seventeenth century Verse*. He was fascinated not only by natural history, but also by country crafts and practices and ancient forms of worship. He spent much of his time on his extensive walking tours in conversing with countrymen, gleaning information about skills and customs which might otherwise have been lost. These tours provided the material for *Wold Without End* (1932), *English Downland* (1936) and *Cotswold Country* (1937). One evening in 1937, he tripped over a dirty old feeding trough in the Upper Windrush valley and the resultant infection cost him a leg. His walking days over, he wrote regularly for *The Field* until 1951. *The English Countryman* (1942) is probably his most highly regarded work today, but no work gave him more pleasure and pride than his edition of *The Writings of Gilbert White* from which this selection is taken.

ERIC RAVILIOUS (1908-1942)

Eric Ravilious was a landscape watercolourist, woodcut engraver and lithographer. Born in 1908, he studied at Eastbourne and at the Royal College of Art (1922-1925). He won a travelling scholarship to Italy and returned to work with Edward Bawden on the mural in the Morley College refreshment rooms. His greatest gift, however, was for the evocation of the richly varied textures of the British landscape, and he seems to have preferred the raw media of wood and clay to smooth walls or canvas. He returned to the RCA in 1929 as an Instructor in Design, and not only illustrated a number of fine books, but also executed many designs for pottery and glass decoration. In 1940, he was appointed an official war artist. He painted many scenes in Norway, and much of his wartime work is to be found in the major public galleries. He was sent to Iceland in 1942, and was reported missing, presumed dead on an air patrol that same year.

Other Ravilious-decorated books include Nicholas Breton's *The Twelve Moneths* and Shakespeare's *Twelfth Night*, both of which were published by the Golden Cockerel Press. These, no less than the *Selborne*, illustrate his constant bid to attain subtle tones and contrasts in texture by the judicious use of black, white and ingenious patterned areas based on fifteenth-century *manière criblée* prints. Writing of Ravilious, Mr. David Bland, in his History of Book Illustration, says of the *Selborne*, 'One of the most delightful Nonesuch books, *The Writings of Gilbert White of Selborne*, appeared in 1938. It was the perfect book for an artist whose flair was not only for country subjects but also for small decorations.'

INTRODUCTION

> With the exception of Shakespeare, Milton and Wordsworth, there can hardly be another English man of letters to whom a larger body of comment and criticism has been devoted than Gilbert White. Considerably more than a hundred editions of him fill the shelves in the British Museum and the Bodleian, and papers relating to him are almost as many. What Thomas Aquinas was to the Church, Plutarch to biography, Chaucer to the mediaeval English spirit, Tennyson to the dreams of the nineteenth century, Gilbert White was and remains not merely to naturalists but to every student of a countryside which has only recently ceased to be the backbone of England. He is and always has been the Saturn of our green Olympiad...

Thus H.J. Massingham, himself a great countryman, in his introduction to the very rare Nonesuch Press edition of 1938 from which this new edition is gleaned.

White's stature has not diminished since Massingham wrote, nor have any rivals arisen. He stands alone in the history of literature and of science. Editions of his work proliferate, and it is clear that the evocative power of his writings is felt by readers who know neither Selborne nor England, for translations, particularly into the Japanese, abound. At the last count, *The Natural History of Selborne* was the fourth most published book in the English language. It is one of the very few works for which demand, so far from abating as is usual, has constantly grown throughout the world.

Why so specialised, so parochial a work should command such universal affection and respect has baffled, or at least defied the explanatory powers of, all his critics. Each seems to regard White's achievement in a different light and to value it for different reasons. As with a piece of music, but as with few other literary works, readers make *Selborne* their own. I enter the commentators lists not as a contender, for I have neither hope nor desire of an explanation of White's extraordinary appeal, but merely as an explorer of the problem, the man and achievement.

Long before I had read White, I had seen his world much as he saw it. I was brought up in Newton Valence, a tiny village at the westernmost corner of Selborne Common and once one of Gilbert White's curacies. My mother and I rode every day, through the orchids on Nore Hill, down to Dorton and the Lyths, to Farringdon, Hawkley, Prior's Dean or Empshott. By the time I was thirteen, I knew every square foot of White's wild parish. My route to Selborne was the same muddy path which he took on his pony.

The parish of Selborne has changed little since the end of the eighteenth century. Tarmac roads have been laid, but still follow the same courses, for Hampshire freestone lanes are deep-sunk and steep-sided and, in summer, cool green tunnels rich in wildlife. They have not changed in centuries. The downs of which the Hanger is the escarpment are now enclosed, but almost exclusively for agriculture, and frogged with copses that pre-date White. Some new houses have sprung up in Selborne, particularly at the North-East end of Gracious Street, but sensitive and wealthy landlords have ensured that it remains, to all intents and purposes, a one street village.

White's Norman church still stands, 'though much renovated, and its mighty yew tree (*Antiquities*, Letter V), reputed to be thirteen hundred years old. White measured its girth at twenty-three feet. It has since swelled to forty-one. The little green or 'plestor' (Letter XVIII) is untouched, 'though the maypole is gone, and White's house, 'The Wakes', is now the Gilbert White Museum. The house has been substantially extended, but the gardens are almost as he left them. On the other side of the street grow two of the four lindens which White planted to shut out the view of the butcher's shop and slaughterhouse.

There have been changes, of course, in the flora and fauna of the area, mostly, but not always, for the worse. Ravens, corncrakes, choughs, wrynecks and nightjars, for example, are not longer to be found, nor the greater hawks and falcons. The polecat and the pine marten have been driven from Southern England. Pond-life, as elsewhere in England, has suffered appalling depredations. Toads and frogs are now rare, and the discovery of a great crested newt would be a triumph indeed. Wildfowl had abandoned Newton pond by the time when I first visited it, jam-jar in hand. It quickly turned into an impenetrable bog of soggy reeds, capable of sustaining almost no aquatic life. Only in the last five years have villagers undertaken the Sisyphean task of clearing and restocking the pond from which White took so many of his specimens. On the other side of the coin, it is heartening to record that the siskin, the treecreeper, the nuthatch, the goldcrest and the various titmice are now, if not common, at least regularly observed. Many of the birds which White lists in the first and second letters to Daines Barrington are still to be found in season. Letter XLI remains a good rough guide to local flora, although as 'a short list of the more rare species', it exhibits White's relative lack of interest in wild flowers, for in the words of local naturalist Stephen Povey, Selborne remains 'unquestionably the richest parish in the country for wild flowers, particularly the orchidae'.

White's version of the natural world has a child-like quality. A child has favourite places and favourite flowers, returns from walks or rides with accounts of birds unrecognised or of curious animals. Everything is interesting, nothing marvellous. There is no twee wonder and no awe in White's writings. He accepts his surroundings, however curious. He neither anthropomorphises nor idealises, nor does he display that sense of superiority to 'brute creation' which characterises nineteenth-century naturalists. He is a *part* of his parish, no less than the swifts or Timothy the tortoise. No wonder, then, that no imitator has ever managed to recapture that authentic Whitean tone. Consciousness of any such end must inevitably destroy any chances of attaining it. A.C. Benson wrote of

White:

> This was thy daily task, to learn that man
> Is small, and not forget that man is great.

Nothing can tug at the exile's heart so hard as a typical entry plucked at random from White's journals. 'Sun chilly. Cold white dew,' 'Straw-berries, scarlet, cryed about. Straw-berries dry, and tasteless. Quail calls in the field next to the garden,' or, 'The mare lies out. St Foin begins to blow.' Rarely have poets sketched in such strong and simple lines a whole day, the sound, the smell, the feel of it. Yet White was no poet, no great innovative scientist. He was not acquainted with the great men of his age, ('though Alexander Pope presented him on his graduation in 1743 with a six-volume edition of his translation of *The Iliad*), nor was he renowned for his wit, eccentricity or simple flamboyance of character. Gilbert White was a country clergyman of the eighteenth century. He was, at first glance, exceptional in nothing. Such of his sermons as have survived are sturdy, commonplace and moderate in content and in tone. He was a charitable man, and evidently cared well for his parishioners. His account books show that he was liberal but not profligate with small presents to the poor and aged when their needs were great. He was, however, neither a notable philanthropist nor an ascetic. He liked his brandy and his table, his dancing and his travel. He was conspicuously unambitious, refusing all offers of promotion which might take him away from his own beloved Selborne, but he was not so high-minded as to turn down the living of Moreton Pinkney in Northamptonshire, a sinecure which demanded of him only that he ride up to the parish twice a year in order to collect his stipend. He was a scholar, and clearly a good one, but he left the care of academe to others more single-minded than he. Those Selborne men whose great grandparents must have known White well have received none but the most nebulous of traditions about him. He is remembered, if at all, as 'a pleasant man', 'a quiet man'. Edward Thomas, wrote a suitably negative – though far from pejorative – tribute, 'It is hard to find a flaw in the life he led.' He seems, in short, to have been exceptional only in that he was unexceptionable.

He was blessed, it is true, with a good brain, a ready wit, unfailing curiosity, a keen eye and an aural memory which would do credit to any musician, but these are, to greater or lesser degrees, the indispensable traits of any naturalist, and White's contributions to the science, though substantial, were by no means remarkable when compared with those of greater scholars of the past two centuries.

We look in vain to White's life for an explanation of his continued popularity and his enormous stature in the history of English thought and literature. He was born in Selborne in 1720. His father, John White, was a retired barrister who happened to be visiting his father, also called Gilbert White, but unlike his grandson, vicar of Selborne. We know little of John White and his wife. They lived for a while at Compton, near Guildford, then moved to East Harting, Sussex. It is uncertain whether they returned to Selborne before 1727, but in that year old Gilbert White died and the young Gilbert, who now had several brothers and sisters, was taken to live at 'The Wakes'.

Gilbert was the eldest of a large family of whom six feature prominently – directly or indirectly – in his works. The names of John, Thomas, Benjamin and Henry, all keen amateurs of science, occur often in White's journals and letters, as do those of his brothers in law, Henry Woods, gentleman and something of a naturalist, who married Rebecca White, and Anne White's husband, Thomas Barker of Lyndon Hall, Rutland, whose chief passion was astronomy. White's mother died in 1739, his father in 1758.

White attended Farnham and Basingstoke Grammar schools. The headmaster at Basingstoke was the Rev. Thomas Warton, whose two sons, Joseph and Thomas, were to become respectively headmaster of Winchester College and poet laureate. White alway remembered his acquaintance with these two, and the Wartons read his work with enthusiasm.

In 1740, White went up to Oriel College, Oxford. He evidently studied, but not to the exclusion of the usual pastimes of young country gentlemen. He kept a dog, a horse and a gun, and shot and fished whenever he could. The tone of outrage discernible in many a modern commentator's writings as they record this is unjustified. In the eighteenth century, ecology was unheard of and would have been considered gratuitous when explained. White has no sense of responsibility to something called 'nature', nor had he the oppidan habit of affining human emotions with the responses and instincts of animals and birds. There was a natural order of which he was a part. It is the unique fusion of this ancient, practical countryman's sensibility with the eighteenth century passion for precision and knowledge which distinguishes White's works from those of his predecessors and his successors.

It is notable, too, that White was equally dispassionate in his observations of human behaviour. The memorable accounts of the bee-eating idiot boy (Letter XXVII) and the leper (Letter XXXVII) manifest no greater sympathy and no less curiosity than that of the aged and brazen sow (Letter XXXIII), and there is something remarkable about the many entries in the Journals which describe the activities of men. What nineteenth century diarist would have written, as White did in the last entry of his life, 'Men wash their sheep'? The parallelism is impertinent. 'Sheepwashing begins' would be acceptable, but White's version, which gives equal grammatical status to both species, gives one the impression that, if sheep washed their men, he would record it with great interest but with no sense of affront.

This, of course, does not accord happily with our modern view of the 'nature lover'. Schooled by the Romantics, who wistfully strove to attain just such a 'fusion with the spirit of nature', we have come to expect the nature-lover to regard his world from a superior standpoint with sympathy and sentimental affection, much as a Victorian spinster might regard young children. We have even invented a very curious distinction betwen the 'human' and the 'natural'. In that sense, certainly, White was no nature-lover, but then, in that sense, neither is the gamekeeper or the huntsman. White rejoiced in his world, as a spaniel may rejoice to find new smells in the hedgerow, new birds and beasts to chase.

White took his MA degree in 1746, then took deacon's

orders and was appointed to the first of many curacies, at Swarraton and Bradley near Alresford. In 1751, he returned to Selborne as curate-in-charge for the ailing vicar. There followed a succession of appointments: Proctor to the University, Dean of Oriel, curate at Durley, Hampshire, at West Deane, Wiltshire and, always tending homeward, at Newton Valence. In 1756, he resumed the post of curate at Selborne. Although the appointment was to last only three years, it is clear from the extent of his planting and landscaping in the garden that he did not intend to leave 'The Wakes' again. For twenty-four years from 1761, he was curate at Faringdon, just two miles to the North-West of Selborne. He was easily able to fulfil his duties there without a change of address.

Two years after his appointment to Faringdon, indeed, White fulfilled a lifelong ambition. He bought 'The Wakes' which he had previously rented. Now nothing would induce him away from his village. Oxford friends repeatedly urged him to apply for vacant, more remunerative livings. He as consistently refused. The living of Selborne was in the gift of Magdalene College, Oxford (and remained so well into the 1960s), so White, an Oriel man, could never properly be called the vicar of Selborne, but, when the Faringdon curacy ended and White took up the vicar's duties in Selborne, there appear to have been no objection either from Oxford or from his parishioners.

Although White travelled extensively during these years, as far West as Devon, as far North as Shrewsbury, he suffered constant frustration as his list of observations and experiments grew. There were so few people with whom to discuss his discoveries (Letter X). A local peasant might confirm White's observations, but could not keep pace with the conjectural comparisons and speculations which his parson pours out in his letters. He was delighted, therefore, when he could visit London. His brother Benjamin had a Fleet Street bookshop and published books of natural history. Here White met much travelled men and men of science. Here, as last, he could test his ideas. Here, in 1767, he was introduced to Thomas Pennant, the zoologist, then preparing his great *British Zoology* for publication by Benjamin White.

Both men must have been overjoyed, for not only did they share an obsession but, while White lived in Southern downland, far from the sea, Pennant lived in Holywell, Flintshire, within reach of mountains, sea and rivers. They could thus compare findings from significantly diverse areas (Letter XIII). They immediately began to correspond.

Thomas Pennant (1726-1798) was in many ways more important than White in the history of the common disciplines. Although often somewhat harshly criticised by Whiteans, his works, as Sir William Jardine wrote, 'were much valued at the time of their publication, and contained the greater part of the knowledge of their times.' Unlike White, he wrote nothing which was not in time to be superseded or refined, but this in itself makes him nonetheless a distinguished and erudite scholar in an age renowned for its distinction and its erudition.

By any standards, let alone those of a gentleman and an amateur, the *corpus* of Pennant's work is enormous. On leaving Queen's College, Oxford where, like H.J. Massingham almost two hundred years later, he took no degree, he toured Cornwall and Ireland. These were just the first of many tours throughout the British Isles on which he kept detailed journals displaying an astonishing breadth and depth of knowledge. In 1755, he began his correspondence with Linnaeus, who sponsored and successfully lobbied for Pennant's election to the Royal Society of Upsala in 1757. The first part of Pennant's monumental *British Zoology* appeared in 1766. He then toured the Continent, discoursed with Voltaire at Ferney and with the naturalist Pallas in The Hague, and returned home to take up a fellowship of the Royal Society in London.

Besides the *British Zology*, Pennant's principal works in the field of Natural History are *The History of Quadrupeds* (1782) and *Arctic Zoology* (1784). His *Tour of Scotland* was very successful, and can take the lion's share of the credit for the boom in tourism to a country which had been regarded previously as hostile and unappealing. *The Journey from Chester to London* (1782) and *London* (1790) are still of interest to the modern reader.

Dr. Johnson, never one for unqualified expressions of approval, was surprisingly generous in his tribute to Pennant. 'He's a whig, sir, a sad dog,' he said, 'But he's the best traveller I ever read, he observes more things than anyone else does.'

This correspondence between Pennant and White forms the basis of *The Natural History*, but the original letters were very strictly edited and often expanded before they came to be published. The easy, familiar wit to be found in those of White's letters which were never intended for publication is barely perceptible in the formal published material. Many of the 'letters' in the book, too, were nothing of the sort. They were merely essays conceived in an eipistolary style with a 'Dear Sir' and an 'I am etc.' uncomfortably appended at the beginning and the end.

The idea of such a book was Daines Barrington's. Barrington, another bookshop acquaintance, was a Welsh barrister, later to become a judge. He had travelled very widely and was a naturalist of rather philosophical bent. He sent White the diary blank in which the first of the *Naturalist's Journals* was to be written and he suggested that White's copious notes might be knitted into a coherert history of the parish. White was not over-enthusiastic at first, but was encouraged by the publication of his papers on the Hirundines in the *Philosophical Transactions* of the Royal Society and at last White delivered the manuscript to his brother. In 1789, eighteen years after the initial suggestion, the book was published.

From the outset, it was well received, but it hardly changed its author's life at all. He continued about his daily business of baptising, marrying and burying, writing sermons and ministering to the poor. He continued to keep his journal, to brew beer, to experiment in his garden and to care for his two pets, Rover, the mongrel, and Timothy, the famous tortoise left to him by his aunt, Mrs. Snooke. He continued to write letters and to receive visitors, and every year we find him counting his nephews and nieces with a pride that keeps pace with their growing numbers. Towards the end of his life, his hearing and his eyesight began to fail, a sad business at the best of times, but, for a man who could write Letter XLII to Daines Barrington, short-sightedness must have been a particularly bitter affliction.

On 15 June 1793, White wrote the last entry in his journal and his last letter. Two days later, the doctor was called in from Alton. No-one knows what the illness was, White had been complaining of 'a bad nervous cough'. He died at 'The Wakes' on 26 June.

And that is all there is. It elucidates a little, but explains nothing.

The oldest and commonest explanation of any success, 'He was in the right place at the right time,' has a deal of validity. The right place White most certainly had for his hugely ambitious project. His ambition was, in essence, the total recreation of a parish with its history, geology, geography, its flora, its fauna, its men and its women. His dedication to this total vision explains why he so far delayed the work's publication, against the advice of his friends, in order to complete the *Antiquities*. Most readers have found this section to be a mere recapitulation of documents relating to Selborne's history, a compilation of others' researches, and it must be admitted that the greater part of the *Antiquities* makes very dreary reading, but White's dogged insistence on completing the work demonstrates more clearly than anything else both his resolve, as stated in the *Advertisement*, to lay before the public 'his idea of *parochial history*' and his refusal to see animal behaviour as a more or less important component of such a history than the conduct of the parish's human inhabitants. Had he searched the whole country over, he could not have selected a finer *locus* for such an enterprise. Selborne is small, has a long and intriguing history and is surrounded by a rare variety of geological formations and natural conditions, listed by White himself as 'Chalks, clays, sands, sheep-walks and downs, bogs, heaths, woodlands, and champaign fields'.

The time at which White wrote is also significant. His position in the history of his science is comparable with that of Malinowski in the history of anthropology. He took natural history into the field. The language of the science had been developed by assiduous classification and precise experiment. British sailors were now sending specimens of exotic species back from all over the globe. Scientists were kept fully occupied in distinguishing relations between one new species and another, naming them, recording distinctive physical traits. White learned in this tradition and read widely, but his greatest contribution to natural history lay not in his discovery of the harvest mouse or in the distinction of the three leaf warblers of Britain, but in his insistence that the naturalist must study 'the life and conversation of animals' and that he should rely upon his own observations, not upon the writings of others. He combined therefore the attitude of a seventeenth-century farmer with the discipline of the Enlightenment synthesist, or, which is another way of saying the same thing, the understanding of the peasant with the vocabulary of the scholar. In this, he is unique.

White stepped into his own back garden and observed familiar creatures closely and carefully. The quality of his observations has never been paralleled, nor the beauty of his concise syntax. His ingenuousness, his curiosity, his clear and above all Saxonic writing style and syntax, create a landscape we can walk through, observing as though a child. Latinate vocabulary and theoretical concepts convey little. By the very smallness of White's parish and by the use of words which were coined at the dawn of English history, we are given a vision of incomparable scope and grandeur. *To see a World in a Grain of Sand/And a Heaven in a Wild Flower* demands time and peace of mind. We can delve into White and pluck out a wild flower, a swallow, a fecund pig, a dozy tortoise, wherever we may be, and can study it as the thing itself. White does not guide our speculations.

Mark Daniel, 1983

THE NATURAL HISTORY OF SELBORNE

LETTER I

TO THOMAS PENNANT, ESQUIRE

The parish of Selborne lies in the extreme eastern corner of the county of Hampshire, bordering on the county of Sussex, and not far from the county of Surrey; is about fifty miles south-west of London, in latitude 51, and near midway between the towns of Alton and Petersfield. Being very large and extensive it abuts on twelve parishes, two of which are in Sussex, viz. Trotton and Rogate. If you begin from the south and proceed westward the adjacent parishes are Emshot, Newton Valence, Faringdon, Harteley Mauduit, Great Ward le ham,* Kingsley, Hedleigh, Bramshot, Trotton, Rogate, Lysse, and Greatham. The soils of this district are almost as various and diversified as the views and aspects. The high part to the southwest consists of a vast hill of chalk, rising three hundred feet above the village; and is divided into a sheep down, the high wood, and a long hanging wood called The Hanger. The covert of this eminence is altogether beech, the most lovely of all forest trees, whether we consider it's smooth rind or bark, it's glossy foliage, or graceful pendulous boughs. The down, or sheep-

* The modern Worldham.

walk, is a pleasing park-like spot, of about one mile by half that space, jutting out on the verge of the hill-country, where it begins to break down into the plains, and commanding a very engaging view, being an assemblage of hill, dale, wood-lands, heath, and water. The prospect is bounded to the south-east and east by the vast range of mountains called The Sussex Downs, by Guild-down near Guildford, and by the Downs round Dorking, and Ryegate in Surrey, to the north-east, which altogether, with the country beyond Alton and Farnham, form a noble and extensive outline.

At the foot of this hill, one stage or step from the uplands, lies the village, which consists of one single straggling street, three quarters of a mile in length, in a sheltered vale, and running parallel with The Hanger. The houses are divided from the hill by a vein of stiff clay* (good wheat-land), yet stand on a rock of white stone†, little in appearance removed from chalk; but seems so far from being calcarious, that it endures extreme heat. Yet that the freestone still preserves somewhat that is analogous to chalk, is plain from the beeches which descend as low as those rocks extend, and no farther, and thrive as well on them, where the ground is steep, as on the chalks.

The cart-way of the village divides, in a remarkable manner, two very incongruous soils. To the south-west is a rank clay,‡ that requires the labour of years to render it mellow; while the gardens to the north-east, and small enclosures behind, consist of a warm, forward, crumbling mould, called *black malm*,§ which seems highly saturated with vegetable and animal manure; and these may perhaps have been the original site of the town; while the woods and coverts might extend down to the opposite bank.

At each end of the village, which runs from south-east to north-west, arises a small rivulet: that at the north-west end frequently fails; but the other is a fine perennial spring, little

* Chalk marl, the stratum underneath the lowest series of the Chalk, composing The Hanger and Nore Hill.

† Chloritic marl, intermediate between the Upper Greensand and the Chalk. The *black malm* of the next paragraph is the lowest bed of the Upper Greensand.

‡ Also from the chalk marl.

§ Upper Greensand. So "white malm" and "white land". Clays.

influenced by drought or wet seasons, called Well-head.* This breaks out of some high grounds joining to Nore Hill, a noble chalk promontory, remarkable for sending forth two streams into two different seas. The one to the south becomes a branch of the Arun, running to Arundel, and so falling into the British channel: the other to the north, the Selborne stream, makes one branch of the Wey; and, meeting the Black-down stream at Hedleigh, and the Alton and Farnham stream at Tilford-bridge, swells into a considerable river, navigable at Godalming; from whence it passes to Guildford, and so into the Thames at Weybridge; and thus at the Nore into the German ocean.

Our wells, at an average, run to about sixty-three feet, and when sunk to that depth seldom fail; but produce a fine limpid water, soft to the taste, and much commended by those who drink the pure element, but which does not lather well with soap.

To the north-west, north and east of the village, is a range of fair enclosures, consisting of what is called a *white malm*, a sort of rotten or rubble stone, which, when turned up to the frost and rain, moulders to pieces, and becomes manure to itself.†

Still on to the north-east, and a step lower, is a kind of white land, neither chalk nor clay, neither fit for pasture nor for the plough, yet kindly for hops, which root deep into the freestone, and have their poles and wood for charcoal growing just at hand. This white soil produces the brightest hops.

As the parish still inclines down towards Wolmer-forest, at the juncture of the clays and sand‡ the soil becomes a wet, sandy

* *This spring produced, September* 14, 1781, *after a severe hot summer, and a preceding dry spring and winter, nine gallons of water in a minute, which is five hundred and forty in an hour, and twelve thousand nine hundred and sixty, or two hundred and sixteen hogsheads, in twenty-four hours, or one natural day. At this time many of the wells failed, and all the ponds in the vales were dry.* ⟨G. W.⟩

† *This soil produces good wheat and clover.* ⟨G. W.⟩

‡ Gault, lying between the Upper and Lower Greensand. The "hungry lean sand" is the topmost series of the Lower Greensand of Wolmer Forest. The chalk above The Hanger and on Nore Hill, smeared over as it is by Tertiary clay-with-flints, lies on the eastern verge of the great chalk mass that extends westward through Winchester into Salisbury Plain and south-westward from Salisbury across Cranborne Chase into Dorset as far as Beaminster. Selborne lies between the northern and southern tentacles of this chalk core, that of the North Downs travelling through Surrey and Kent to the cliffs of Dover and that of the South Downs leaving Hampshire at Butser Hill and reaching its Sussex termination at Beachy Head. Selborne's valley is a border chasm between the chalk and the Lower Greensand heights of Wolmer Forest, Hindhead, Holmbury and Leith Hills, and this accounts for the complexity of the strata which Gilbert White was the first to

loam, remarkable for timber, and infamous for roads. The oaks of Temple and Blackmoor stand high in the estimation of purveyors, and have furnished much naval timber; while the trees on the freestone grow large, but are what workmen call *shakey*, and so brittle as often to fall to pieces in sawing. Beyond the sandy loam the soil becomes an hungry lean sand, till it mingles with the forest; and will produce little without the assistance of lime and turnips.

unravel. The Weald clay, the third of the great strata of this region, and underneath the Lower Greensand, begins at Fernhurst, south of Selborne, and makes the Roman *Anderida Silva* and the Saxon *Andredsweald* of Sussex north of the South Downs.

LETTER II

TO THE SAME

In the court of Norton farm house, a manor farm to the north-west of the village, on the white malms, stood within these twenty years a *broad-leaved elm*, or *wych hazel*,* *ulmus folio latissimo scabro* of Ray, which, though it had lost a considerable leading bough in the great storm in the year 1703, equal to a moderate tree, yet, when felled, contained eight loads of timber; and, being too bulky for a carriage, was sawn off at seven feet above the butt, where it measured near eight feet in the diameter. This elm I mention to shew to what a bulk *planted elms* may attain; as this tree must certainly have been such from it's situation.

In the centre of the village, and near the church, is a square piece of ground surrounded by houses, and vulgarly called The Plestor.† In the midst of this spot stood, in old times, a vast oak,‡ with a short squat body, and huge horizontal arms extending almost to the extremity of the area. This venerable tree, surrounded with stone steps, and seats above them, was the delight of old and young, and a place of much resort in summer evenings; where the former sat in grave debate, while the latter frolicked and danced before them. Long might it have stood, had not the amazing tempest in 1703 overturned it at once, to the infinite regret of the inhabitants, and the vicar, who bestowed several pounds in setting it in it's place again: but all his care could not avail; the tree sprouted for a time, then withered and died. This oak I mention to shew to what a bulk *planted oaks* also may arrive: and planted this tree must certainly have been, as will appear from what will be said farther concerning this area, when we enter on the antiquities of Selborne.

On the Blackmoor estate there is a small wood called Losel's, of a few acres, that was lately furnished with a set of oaks of a

* Wych elm.

† See Letter X of the *Antiquities*, where an account is given of Sir Adam Gurdon's grant of The Plestor to Selborne Priory and of the charter for a market there.

‡ A sycamore, now dying, has taken its place.

peculiar growth and great value; they were tall and taper like firs, but standing near together had very small heads, only a little brush without any large limbs. About twenty years ago the bridge at the Toy, near Hampton Court, being much decayed, some trees were wanted for the repairs that were fifty feet long without bough, and would measure twelve inches diameter at the little end. Twenty such trees did a purveyor find in this little wood, with this advantage, that many of them answered the description at sixty feet. These trees were sold for twenty pounds apiece.

In the centre of this grove there stood an oak, which, though shapely and tall on the whole, bulged out into a large excrescence about the middle of the stem. On this a pair of ravens* had fixed their residence for such a series of years, that the oak was distinguished by the title of *The Raven-tree*. Many were the attempts of the neighbouring youths to get at this *eyry*: the difficulty whetted their inclinations, and each was ambitious of surmounting the arduous task. But, when they arrived at the swelling, it jutted out so in their way, and was so far beyond their grasp, that the most daring lads were awed, and acknowledged the undertaking to be too hazardous. So the ravens built on, nest upon nest, in perfect security, till the fatal day arrived in which the wood was to be levelled. It was in the month of February, when those birds usually sit. The saw was applied to the butt, the wedges were inserted into the opening, the woods echoed to the heavy blows of the beetle or mallet, the tree nodded to it's fall; but still the dam sat on. At last, when it gave way, the bird was flung from her nest; and, though her parental affection deserved a better fate, was whipped down by the twigs, which brought her dead to the ground.

* Long vanished from Selborne. "Near 40 Ravens have been playing about over the Hanger all day"—*Naturalist's Journal*, Feb. 14, 1781. The only place in Hampshire where the raven still breeds is the Isle of Wight, though several pairs still nest over the border on the Purbeck cliffs.

LETTER III

TO THE SAME

The fossil-shells of this district, and sorts of stone, such as have fallen within my observation, must not be passed over in silence. And first I must mention, as a great curiosity, a specimen that was plowed up in the chalky fields, near the side of the Down, and given to me for the singularity of it's appearance, which, to an incurious eye, seems like a petrified fish of about four inches long, the cardo passing for an head and mouth. It is in reality a *bivalve* of the *Linnæan Genus* of *Mytilus*, and the species of *Crista Galli*; called by Lister, *Rastellum;* by Rumphius, *Ostreum plicatum minus*; by D'Argenville, *Auris Porci*, s. *Crista Galli*;* and by those who make collections *cock's comb*. Though I applied to several such in London, I never could meet with an entire specimen; nor could I ever find in books any engraving from a perfect one. In the superb museum† at Leicester-house permission was given me to examine for this article; and, though I was disappointed as to the fossil, I was highly gratified with the sight of several of the shells themselves in high preservation. This bivalve is only known to inhabit the Indian ocean, where it fixes itself to a *zoophyte*, known by the name *Gorgonia*. The curious foldings of the suture the one into the other, the alternate flutings or grooves, and the curved form of my specimen being much easier expressed by the pencil than by words, I have caused it to be drawn and engraved.

Cornua Ammonis‡ are very common about this village. As we were cutting an inclining path§ up The Hanger, the labourers found them frequently on that steep, just under the soil, in the chalk, and of a considerable size. In the lane above Well-head, in

* Incorrect; the proper identification is *Ostrea vicordeana*.

† Sir Ashton Lever's; sold and its contents dispersed in 1806. See Letter XVIII to Barrington, in which the author makes a further reference to it.

‡ Ammonites.

§ This is the Bostal, branching from the foot of the Zig-Zag up through the hanging beech-wood to the crest of Selborne Common and Selborne Down. The author's eldest brother, Thomas, was the moving spirit of its construction in 1780.

the way to Emshot, they abound in the bank in a darkish sort of marl*; and are usually very small and soft: but in Clay's Pond,† a little farther on, at the end of the pit, where the soil is dug out for manure, I have occasionally observed them of large dimensions, perhaps fourteen or sixteen inches in diameter. But as these did not consist of firm stone, but were formed of a kind of *terra lapidosa*, or hardened clay, as soon as they were exposed to the rains and frost they mouldered away. These seemed as if they were a very recent production. In the chalk-pit, at the north-west end of The Hanger, large *nautili* are sometimes observed.

In the very thickest strata of our freestone, and at considerable depths, well-diggers often find large *scallops* or *pectines*, having both shells deeply striated, and ridged and furrowed alternately. They are highly impregnated with, if not wholly composed of, the stone of the quarry.

* The soil is as old as the pre-Roman cultivation of the chalk downs by the Celtic tribal communities.

† On the parish-boundary, in a field called Clays.

LETTER IV

TO THE SAME

As in a former letter the *freestone** of this place has been only mentioned incidentally, I shall here become more particular.

This stone is in great request for hearth-stones, and the beds of ovens: and in lining of lime-kilns it turns to good account; for the workmen use sandy loam instead of mortar; the sand of which fluxes,† and runs by the intense heat, and so cases over the whole face of the kiln with a strong vitrified coat like glass, that it is well preserved from injuries of weather, and endures thirty or forty years. When chiseled smooth, it makes elegant fronts for houses, equal in colour and grain to the Bath stone; and superior in one respect, that, when seasoned, it does not scale.‡ Decent chimney-pieces are worked from it of much closer and finer grain than Portland; and rooms are floored with it; but it proves rather too soft for this purpose. It is a freestone, cutting in all directions; yet has something of a grain parallel with the horizon, and therefore should not be *surbedded*,§ but laid in the same position that it grows in the quarry.|| On the ground abroad this fire-stone will not succeed for pavements, because, probably some degree of saltness prevailing within it, the rain tears the slabs to pieces.¶ Though this stone is too hard to be acted on by vinegar; yet both the white part, and even the *blue rag*,$ fer-

* The sandier element of the Upper Greensand. So later "forest-stone".

† *There may probably be also in the chalk itself that is burnt for lime a proportion of sand: for few chalks are so pure as to have none.* ⟨G. W.⟩

‡ The author is wrong here. The Bath stone (oolitic limestone) does not scale.

§ Set up edgewise, as are the top-stones or "toppers" of the majority of Cotswold dry-walls. "Taynton stone" is suitable for toppers because it is of oolitic limestone from the once-famous Taynton quarries near Burford.

|| *To* surbed *stone is to set it edgewise, contrary to the posture it had in the quarry, says Dr. Plot,* Oxfordsh., *p.* 77. *But* surbedding *does not succeed in our dry walls; neither do we use it so in ovens, though he says it is best for Teynton stone.* ⟨G. W.⟩

¶ "*Firestone is full of salts, and has no sulphur: must be close grained, and have no interstices. Nothing supports fire like salts; saltstone perishes exposed to wet and frost.*"—*Plot's* Staff., *p.* 152. ⟨G. W.⟩

$ The chalkier element of the Upper Greensand.

ments strongly in mineral acids. Though the white stone will not bear wet, yet in every quarry at intervals there are thin strata of *blue rag*, which resist rain and frost; and are excellent for pitching of stables, paths and courts, and for building of dry walls against banks; a valuable species of fencing, much in use in this village, and for mending of roads. This *rag* is rugged and stubborn, and will not hew to a smooth face; but is very durable: yet, as these strata are shallow and lie deep, large quantities cannot be procured but at considerable expense. Among the *blue rags* turn up some blocks tinged with a stain of *yellow* or *rust colour*, which seem to be nearly as lasting as the blue; and every now and then balls of a friable substance, like rust of iron, called *rust balls*.

In Wolmer Forest I see but one sort of stone, called by the workmen *sand*, or *forest-stone*. This is generally of the colour of rusty iron, and might probably be worked as iron ore; is very hard and heavy, and of a firm, compact texture, and composed of a small roundish crystalline grit, cemented together by a brown, terrene, ferruginous matter; will not cut without difficulty, nor easily strike fire with steel. Being often found in broad flat pieces, it makes good pavement for paths about houses, never becoming slippery in frost or rain; is excellent for dry walls, and is sometimes used in buildings. In many parts of that waste it lies scattered on the surface of the ground; but is dug on Weaver's Down, a vast hill on the eastern verge of that forest, where the pits are shallow, and the stratum thin. This stone is imperishable.*

From a notion of rendering their work the more elegant, and giving it a finish, masons chip this stone into small fragments about the size of the head of a large nail; and then stick the pieces into the wet mortar along the joints of their freestone walls: this embellishment† carries an odd appearance, and has occasioned strangers sometimes to ask us pleasantly, "whether we fastened our walls together with tenpenny nails."

* Non-porous.

† One of the delightful local mannerisms in architecture. It occurred principally in Surrey ("garnet-pointing"), and in Norfolk ("galletting"). Only in very recent times have geology and architecture been studied in intimate relation to one another, and here as elsewhere White foretold the knowledge of the future, as (*pace* Walter Johnson) he foreshadowed Lyell in his geological analysis of Selborne.

LETTER V

TO THE SAME

Among the singularities of this place the two rocky hollow lanes, the one to Alton, and the other to the forest, deserve our attention. These roads, running through the malm lands, are, by the traffick of ages, and the fretting of water, worn down through the first stratum of our freestone, and partly through the second; so that they look more like water-courses than roads; and are bedded with naked *rag* for furlongs together. In many places they are reduced sixteen or eighteen feet beneath the level of the fields; and after floods, and in frosts, exhibit very grotesque and wild appearances, from the tangled roots that are twisted among the strata, and from the torrents rushing down their broken sides; and especially when those cascades are frozen into icicles, hanging in all the fanciful shapes of frost-work. These rugged gloomy scenes affright the ladies when they peep down into them from the paths above, and make timid horsemen shudder while they ride along them; but delight the naturalist with their various botany, and particularly with their curious *filices** with which they abound.

* Ferns.

The manor of Selborne, was it strictly looked after, with all it's kindly aspects, and all it's sloping coverts, would swarm with game; even now hares, partridges, and pheasants abound; and in old days woodcocks were as plentiful. There are few quails, because they more affect open fields than enclosures; after harvest some few land-rails are seen.

The parish of Selborne, by taking in so much of the forest, is a vast district. Those who tread the bounds are employed part of three days in the business, and are of opinion that the outline, in all it's curves and indentings, does not comprise less than thirty miles.

The village stands in a sheltered spot, secured by The Hanger from the strong westerly winds. The air is soft, but rather moist from the effluvia of so many trees; yet perfectly healthy and free from agues...

We abound with poor; many of whom are sober and industrious, and live comfortably in good stone or brick cottages,* which are glazed, and have chambers above stairs: mud buildings we have none. Besides the employment from husbandry, the men work in hop gardens,† of which we have many; and fell and bark timber. In the spring and summer the women weed the corn; and enjoy a second harvest in September by hop picking. Formerly, in the dead months they availed themselves greatly by spinning wool, for making of *barragons*, a genteel corded stuff, much in vogue at that time for summer wear; and chiefly manufactured at Alton, a neighbouring town, by some of the people called Quakers: but from circumstances this trade is at an end.* The inhabitants enjoy a good share of health and longevity; and the parish swarms with children.

* *Since the passage above was written, I am happy in being able to say that the spinning employment is a little revived, to the no small comfort of the industrious housewife.* ⟨G.W.⟩

LETTER VI

TO THE SAME

Should I omit to describe with some exactness the forest of Wolmer,* of which three fifths perhaps lie in this parish, my account of Selborne would be very imperfect, as it is a district abounding with many curious productions, both animal and vegetable; and has often afforded me much entertainment both as a sportsman and as a naturalist.

The royal forest of Wolmer is a tract of land of about seven miles in length, by two and a half in breadth, running nearly from North to South, and is abutted on, to begin to the South, and so to proceed eastward, by the parishes of Greatham, Lysse, Rogate, and Trotton, in the county of Sussex; by Bramshot, Hedleigh, and Kingsley. This royalty consists entirely of sand covered with heath and fern; but is somewhat diversified with hills and dales, without having one standing tree in the whole extent. In the bottoms, where the waters stagnate, are many bogs, which formerly abounded with subterraneous trees; though Dr. Plot† says positively,‡ that "there never were any fallen trees hidden in the mosses of the southern counties". But he was mistaken: for I myself have seen cottages on the verge of this wild district, whose timbers consisted of a black hard wood, looking like oak, which the owners assured me they procured from the bogs by probing the soil with spits, or some such instruments: but the peat is so much cut out, and the moors have been so well examined, that none has been found of late.§ Besides the

* The Forest has ceased to be a natural treeless waste, partly through enclosure, partly through military occupation, but chiefly by the policy of planting conifers and turning the wilder parts of England into a gloomy, uniform, lifeless Black Forest.

† Author of two county histories, those of Oxfordshire and Staffordshire (1686), and, though inaccurate enough, an agreeable compost of folklore, family chronicles, ecclesiology, old wives' tales, natural history, gossip, and the farmer's year.

‡ *See his* Hist. of Staffordshire. ⟨G. W.⟩

§ *Old people have assured me, that on a winter's morning they have discovered these trees, in the bogs, by the hoar frost, which lay longer over the space where they were concealed, than on the surrounding morass. Nor does this seem to be a fanciful notion, but consistent with true philosophy. Dr. Hales saith, "That the warmth of the earth, at some depth under ground, has an influence in promoting a thaw, as well as the*

oak, I have also been shewn pieces of fossil-wood of a paler colour, and softer nature, which the inhabitants called fir: but, upon a nice examination, and trial by fire, I could discover nothing resinous in them; and therefore rather suppose that they were parts of a willow or alder, or some such aquatic tree.

This lonely domain is a very agreeable haunt for many sorts of wild fowls, which not only frequent it in the winter, but breed there in the summer; such as lapwings, snipes, wild-ducks, and, as I have discovered within these few years, teals.* Partridges in vast plenty are bred in good seasons on the verge of this forest, into which they love to make excursions: and in particular, in the dry summer of 1740 and 1741, and some years after, they swarmed to such a degree that parties of unreasonable sportsmen killed twenty and sometimes thirty brace in a day.

But there was a nobler species of game in this forest, now extinct, which I have heard old people say abounded much before shooting flying became so common, and that was the *heath-cock*, *black game*, or *grouse*. When I was a little boy I recollect one coming now and then to my father's table. The last pack remembered was killed about thirty-five years ago; and within these ten years one solitary *grey hen* was sprung by some beagles in beating for a hare. The sportsmen cried out, "A hen pheasant"; but a gentleman present, who had often seen grouse in the north of England, assured me that it was a greyhen.

Nor does the loss of our black game prove the only gap in the *Fauna Selborniensis*; for another beautiful link in the chain of

change of the weather from a freezing to a thawing state, is manifest, from this observation, viz. Nov. 29, 1731, *a little snow having fallen in the night, it was, by eleven the next morning, mostly melted away on the surface of the earth, except in several places in* Bushy-park, *where there were* drains *dug and covered with earth, on which the snow continued to lie, whether those drains were full of water or dry; as also where* elm-pipes *lay under ground: a plain proof this, that those drains intercepted the warmth of the earth from ascending from greater depths below them: for the snow lay where the drain had more than four feet of earth over it. It continued also to lie on thatch, tiles, and the tops of walls." See Hales's* Hæmastatics: p. 360. *Quere, Might not such observations be reduced to domestic use, by promoting the discovery of old obliterated drains and wells about houses; and in Roman stations and camps lead to the finding of pavements, baths and graves, and other hidden relics of curious antiquity*? ⟨G. W.⟩

* First discovered as a local (and English) breeding species by the author. The other birds mentioned still breed in the Forest, though in greatly diminished numbers. It is singular that he never mentions either the redshank or the tufted duck which may be considered our most plentiful breeding species to-day, the one on marshy ground, the other on the borders of parks.

beings is wanting, I mean the *red deer*, which toward the beginning of this century amounted to about five hundred head, and made a stately appearance. There is an old keeper, now alive, named Adams, whose great grandfather (mentioned in a perambulation taken in 1635) grandfather, father and self, enjoyed the head keepership of Wolmer forest in succession for more than an hundred years. This person assures me, that his father has often told him, that Queen Anne, as she was journeying on the Portsmouth road, did not think the forest of Wolmer beneath her royal regard. For she came out of the great road at Lippock,* which is just by, and, reposing herself on a bank smoothed for that purpose, lying about half a mile to the east of Wolmer-pond, and still called Queen's-bank, saw with great complacency and satisfaction the whole herd of red deer brought by the keepers along the vale before her, consisting then of about five hundred head. A sight this worthy the attention of the greatest sovereign! But he further adds that, by means of the *Waltham blacks*,† or, to use his own expression, as soon as they began *blacking*, they were reduced to about fifty head, and so continued decreasing till the time of the late Duke of Cumberland. It is now more than thirty years ago that his highness sent down an huntsman, and six yeomen-prickers, in scarlet jackets laced with gold, attended by the stag-hounds; ordering them to take every deer in this forest alive, and convey them in carts to Windsor. In the course of the summer they caught every stag, some of which showed extraordinary diversion: but, in the following winter, when the hinds were also carried off, such fine chases were exhibited as served the country people for matter of talk and wonder for years afterwards. I saw myself one of the yeomen-prickers single out a stag from the herd, and must confess that it was the most curious feat of activity I ever beheld, superior to anything in Mr. Astley's riding-school. The exertions made by the horse and deer much exceeded all my expectations; though the former greatly excelled the latter in speed. When the devoted deer was separated from his companions, they gave him, by their watches, law, as they called it, for twenty minutes; when, sounding their horns, the stop-dogs were permitted to pursue, and a most gallant scene ensued.

* Liphook. † Local deer-stealers. See Letter VII.

LETTER VII

TO THE SAME

Though large herds of deer do much harm to the neighbourhood, yet the injury to the morals of the people is of more moment than the loss of their crops. The temptation is irresistible; for most men are sportsmen by constitution: and there is such an inherent spirit for hunting in human nature, as scarce any inhibitions can restrain. Hence, towards the beginning of this century all this country was wild about deer-stealing. Unless he was a *hunter*, as they affected to call themselves, no young person was allowed to be possessed of manhood or gallantry. The *Waltham blacks* at length committed such enormities, that government was forced to interfere with that severe and sanguinary act called the *black act*,* which now comprehends more felonies than any law that ever was framed before. And, therefore, a late bishop of Winchester, when urged to restock Waltham-chase,† refused, from a motive worthy of a prelate, replying that "it had done mischief enough already".

Our old race of deer-stealers are hardly extinct yet: it was but

**Statute* 9 *Geo. I. c.* 22. ⟨G. W.⟩

† *This chase remains un-stocked to this day; the bishop was Dr. Hoadly.* ⟨G. W.⟩

a little while ago that, over their ale, they used to recount the exploits of their youth; such as watching the pregnant hind to her lair, and, when the calf was dropped, paring it's feet with a penknife to the quick to prevent it's escape, till it was large and fat enough to be killed; the shooting at one of their neighbours with a bullet in a turnip-field by moonshine, mistaking him for a deer; and the losing a dog in the following extraordinary manner:—Some fellows, suspecting that a calf new-fallen was deposited in a certain spot of thick fern, went, with a lurcher, to surprise it; when the parent-hind rushed out of the brake, and, taking a vast spring with all her feet close together, pitched upon the neck of the dog, and broke it short in two.

Another temptation to idleness and sporting was a number of rabbits, which possessed all the hillocks and dry places: but these being inconvenient to the huntsmen, on account of their burrows, when they came to take away the deer, they permitted the country people to destroy them all.

Such forests and wastes, when their allurements to irregularities are removed, are of considerable service to neighbourhoods that verge upon them, by furnishing them with peat and turf for their firing; with fuel for the burning their lime; and with ashes for their grasses; and by maintaining their geese and their stock of young cattle at little or no expense.

The manor-farm of the parish of Greatham has an admitted claim, I see, (by an old record taken from the Tower of London) of turning all live stock on the forest, at proper seasons, *bidentibus exceptis.** The reason, I presume, why sheep† are excluded, is, because, being such close grazers, they would pick out all the finest grasses, and hinder the deer from thriving.

Though (by statute 4 and 5 W. and Mary, c. 23) "to burn on any waste, between *Candlemas* and *Midsummer*, any grig,‡ ling, heath and furze, goss‡ or fern, is punishable with whipping and confinement in the house of correction"; yet, in this forest,

* *For this privilege the owner of that estate used to pay to the king annually seven bushels of oats.* ⟨G. W.⟩

† *In The Holt, where a full stock of fallow-deer has been kept up till lately, no sheep are admitted to this day.* ⟨G. W.⟩

‡ Goss, of course, is gorse; grig is a former dialect word for heather. There is a field in the Upper Windrush Valley of Gloucestershire which is still called "The Goss".

about March or April, according to the dryness of the season, such vast heath-fires are lighted up, that they often get to a masterless head, and, catching the hedges, have sometimes been communicated to the underwoods, woods, and coppices, where great damage has ensued. The plea for these burnings is, that, when the old coat of heath, &c. is consumed, young will sprout up, and afford much tender brouze for cattle; but, where there is large old furze, the fire, following the roots, consumes the very ground; so that for hundreds of acres nothing is to be seen but smother and desolation, the whole circuit round looking like the cinders of a volcano; and, the soil being quite exhausted, no traces of vegetation are to be found for years. These conflagrations, as they take place usually with a north-east or east wind, much annoy this village with their smoke, and often alarm the country; and, once in particular, I remember that a gentleman, who lives beyond Andover, coming to my house, when he got on the downs between that town and Winchester, at twenty-five miles distance, was surprised much with smoke and a hot smell of fire; and concluded that Alresford was in flames; but, when he came to that town, he then had apprehensions for the next village, and so on to the end of his journey.

On two of the most conspicuous eminences of this forest stand two *arbours* or *bowers*, made of the boughs of oaks; the one called Waldon-lodge, the other Brimstone-lodge: these the keepers renew annually on the feast of St. Barnabas, taking the old materials for a perquisite. The farm called Blackmoor,* in this parish, is obliged to find the posts and brush-wood for the former; while the farms at Greatham, in rotation, furnish for the latter; and are all enjoined to cut and deliver the materials at the spot. This custom I mention, because I look upon it to be of very remote antiquity.

* Ecclesiastically separated with Oakhanger from Selborne in 1867, and now spiritually so, being built over.

LETTER X*

TO THE SAME

August 4, 1767.

It has been my misfortune never to have had any neighbours whose studies have led them towards the pursuit of natural knowledge: so that, for want of a companion to quicken my industry and sharpen my attention, I have made but slender progress in a kind of information to which I have been attached from my childhood.

As to *swallows* (*hirundines rusticæ*) being found in a torpid state during the winter in the isle of Wight, or any part of this country, I never heard any such account worth attending to. But a clergyman, of an inquisitive turn, assures me, that, when he was a great boy, some workmen, in pulling down the battlements of a church tower early in the spring, found two or three *swifts* (*hirundines apodes*) among the rubbish, which were, at first appearance, dead; but, on being carried toward the fire, revived. He told me that, out of his great care to preserve them, he put them in a paper-bag, and hung them by the kitchen fire, where they were suffocated.

Another intelligent person has informed me that, while he was a schoolboy at Brighthelmstone, in Sussex, a great fragment of the chalk-cliff fell down one stormy winter on the beach; and that many people found *swallows* among the rubbish: but, on my questioning him whether he saw any of those birds himself; to my no small disappointment, he answered me in the negative; but that others assured him they did.†

* This is the first of the dated letters. The original one from which this version was abstracted had an introductory paragraph, omitted in the published text. The diffidence of the opening words is a little overdone, since no writer has ever received more support and encouragement at the hands of his visitors, neighbours, relations and correspondents in the pursuit of his vocation.

† Mr. E. M. Nicholson ably defends Gilbert White from the strictures cast by nearly all critics and editors, notably Grant Allen, upon his hesitation in rejecting the hibernation theory. This defence is just. Not only current but authoritative opinion favoured hibernation as opposed to migration, and White was bound to investigate before repudiating it. We are wise after the event, since migration is

Young broods of *swallows* began to appear this year on July the eleventh, and young *martins* (*hirundines urbicæ*) were then fledged in their nests. Both species will breed again once. For I see by my *fauna* of last year, that young broods came forth so late as September the eighteenth. Are not these late hatchings more in favour of hiding than migration? Nay, some young martins remained in their nests last year so late as September the twenty-ninth; and yet they totally disappeared with us by the fifth of October.

How strange is it that the *swift*, which seems to live exactly the same life with the *swallow* and *house-martin*, should leave us before the middle of August invariably! while the latter stay often till the middle of October; and once I saw numbers of house-martins on the seventh of November. The martins and *red-wing fieldfares** were flying in sight together; an uncommon assemblage of summer and winter-birds!

A little yellow bird† (it is either a species of the *alauda trivialis*, or rather perhaps of the *motacilla trochilus*) still continues to make a sibilous shivering noise in the tops of tall woods. The *stoparola*‡ of Ray (for which we have as yet no name in these parts) is called, in your *Zoology*, the *fly-catcher*. There is one circumstance characteristic of this bird, which seems to have escaped observation, and that is, it takes it's stand on the

only a very recently established certainty. Even Warde Fowler, less possessed with scientific Hubris than Grant Allen, is very severe with the author and talks of his enquiries into the facts as though he had slavishly adopted a classico-mediaeval fable derived straight out of the Bestiaries. Mr. Nicholson shows, on the contrary, that the seventeenth century naturalists were a majority in favour of migration, while their eighteenth century legatees, including Linnæus and Buffon, were a majority in favour of hibernation, either in hollow trees and caves or at the bottoms of lakes. Mr. Nicholson is the first living man to have brought out this very striking point. White never entertained any doubts of the truth of migration in general. In respect of the "Hirundines" he was misled by the appearances of many late parties of swallows or martins following earlier flocks from more northerly latitudes, by their desultory reluctant flight and habit of frequenting warm and sheltered retreats on their way.

* Redwing, an abbreviation of the older term.

† The wood-warbler. I have myself heard it singing in July. Obviously, White had not yet clearly distinguished the wood- from the willow-warbler (*Motacilla trochilus*), both of the same family and very alike except for the longer wings and slightly larger size of the former. They belong, of course, to quite a different family from the tree-pipit (*Alauda trivialis*). The distribution of the wood-warbler in Hampshire is irregular. See also Letters XVI and XIX to Pennant.

‡ The spotted flycatcher.

top of some stake or post, from whence it springs forth on it's prey, catching a fly in the air, and hardly ever touching the ground, but returning still to the same stand for many times together.

I perceive there are more than one species of the *motacilla trochilus*: Mr. Derham supposes, in Ray's *Philos. Letters*, that he has discovered three. In these there is again an instance of some very common birds that have as yet no English name.

Mr. Stillingfleet makes a question whether the *black-cap* (*motacilla atricapilla*) be a bird of passage or not: I think there is no doubt of it: for, in April, in the first fine weather, they come trooping, all at once, into these parts, but are never seen in the winter. They are delicate songsters.

Numbers of *snipes* breed every summer in some moory ground on the verge of this parish. It is very amusing to see the cock bird on wing at that time, and to hear his piping and humming notes.*

I have had no opportunity yet of procuring any of those mice† which I mentioned to you in town. The person that brought me the last says they are plenty in harvest, at which time I will take care to get more; and will endeavour to put the matter out of doubt, whether it be a non-descript species or not.

I suspect much there may be two species of water-rats.‡ Ray says, and Linnæus after him, that the water-rat is web-footed behind. Now I have discovered a rat on the banks of our little stream that is not web-footed, and yet is an excellent swimmer and diver: it answers exactly to the *mus amphibius* of Linnæus (See *Syst. Nat.*), which he says "*natat in fossis & urinatur*". I should be glad to procure one "*plantis palmatis*". Linnæus seems to be in a puzzle about his *mus amphibius*, and to doubt whether it differs from his *mus terrestris*; which if it be, as he allows, the "*mus agrestis capite grandi brachyuros*" of Ray, is widely different from the water-rat, both in size, make, and manner of life.

As to the *falco*, which I mentioned in town, I shall take the

* See also Letters XVI and XXXIX to Pennant.

† The harvest-mouse, which the author discovered as a separate British species.

‡ There is only one species, the water-vole. The error as to the webbed feet was common to eighteenth century naturalists.

liberty to send it down to you into Wales; presuming on your candour, that you will excuse me if it should appear as familiar to you as it is strange to me. Though mutilated "*qualem dices . . . antehac fuisse, tales cum sint reliquiæ!*"

It haunted a marshy piece of ground in quest of wild-ducks and snipes: but, when it was shot, had just knocked down a rook, which it was tearing in pieces. I cannot make it answer to any of our English hawks; neither could I find any like it at the curious exhibition of stuffed birds in Spring-Gardens. I found it nailed up at the end of a barn, which is the countryman's museum.

The parish I live in is a very abrupt, uneven country, full of hills and woods, and therefore full of birds.

LETTER XI

TO THE SAME

Selborne, *September* 9, 1767.

It will not be without impatience that I shall wait for your thoughts with regard to the *falco*; as to it's weight, breadth, &c. I wish I had set them down at the time: but, to the best of my remembrance, it weighed two pounds and eight ounces, and measured, from wing to wing, thirty-eight inches. It's *cere* and feet were yellow, and the circle of it's eyelids a bright yellow. As it had been killed some days, and the eyes were sunk, I could make no good observation on the colour of the pupils and the *irides*.

The most unusual birds I ever observed in these parts were a pair of *hoopoes* (*upupa*),* which came several years ago in the summer, and frequented an ornamented piece of ground, which joins to my garden, for some weeks. They used to march about in a stately manner, feeding in the walks, many times in the day; and seemed disposed to breed in my outlet;† but were frighted

* One was reported by the Hampshire Field Club in the county in 1936.

† What we should call the wild garden.

and persecuted by idle boys, who would never let them be at rest.

Three *gross-beaks** (*loxia coccothraustes*) appeared some years ago in my fields, in the winter; one of which I shot: since that, now and then one is occasionally seen in the same dead season.

A *cross-bill* (*loxia curvirostra*) was killed last year in this neighbourhood.

Our streams, which are small, and rise only at the end of the village, yield nothing but the *bull's-head* or *miller's-thumb* (*gobius fluviatilis capitatus*), the *trout* (*trutta fluviatilis*), the eel (*anguilla*), the *lampern* (*lampætra parva et fluviatilis*), and the *stickle-back* (*pisciculus aculeatus*).†

We are twenty miles from the sea, and almost as many from a great river, and therefore see but little of sea-birds. As to wild fowls, we have a few teams of *ducks* bred in the moors‡ where the snipes breed; and multitudes of *widgeons* and *teals* in hard weather frequent our lakes in the forest.

Having some acquaintance with a tame *brown owl*, I find that it casts up the fur of mice, and the feathers of birds in pellets, after the manner of hawks: when full, like a dog, it hides what it cannot eat.

The young of the barn-owl are not easily raised, as they want a constant supply of fresh mice: whereas the young of the brown owl will eat indiscriminately all that is brought; snails, rats, kittens, puppies, magpies, and any kind of carrion or offal.

The house-martins have eggs still, and squab-young. The last swift I observed was about the twenty-first of August; it was a straggler.

Red-starts, *fly-catchers*, *white-throats*, and *reguli non cristati*,§ still appear; but I have seen no *black-caps* lately.

I forgot to mention that I once saw, in Christ Church college

* The hawfinch, the very shy bird with a ponderous conical bill that has increased its numbers since White's time both at Selborne and elsewhere in the south of England.

† The three-spined stickleback, one of half a dozen British species.

‡ The marshier regions of Wolmer Forest. Thus, Moreton-in-the-Marsh means Moreton on the Boundary and Otmoor means Otmarsh.

§ The three leaf-warblers, chiff-chaff, willow- and wood-warblers, which White was the first to separate into distinct species.

quadrangle in Oxford, on a very sunny warm morning, a *house martin* flying about, and settling on the parapets, so late as the twentieth of November.

At present I know only two species of *bats*,* the common *vespertilio murinus* and the *vespertilio auritus*.

I was much entertained last summer with a tame bat, which would take flies out of a person's hand. If you gave it any thing to eat, it brought it's wings round before the mouth, hovering and hiding it's head in the manner of birds of prey when they feed. The adroitness it shewed in shearing off the wings of the flies, which were always rejected, was worthy of observation, and pleased me much. Insects seemed to be most acceptable, though it did not refuse raw flesh when offered: so that the notion, that bats go down chimnies and gnaw men's bacon, seems no improbable story. While I amused myself with this wonderful quadruped, I saw it several times confute the vulgar opinion, that bats when down on a flat surface cannot get on the wing again, by rising with great ease from the floor. It ran, I observed, with more dispatch than I was aware of; but in a most ridiculous and grotesque manner.

Bats drink on the wing, like swallows, by sipping the surface, as they play over pools and streams. They love to frequent waters, not only for the sake of drinking, but on account of insects, which are found over them in the greatest plenty. As I was going, some years ago, pretty late, in a boat from Richmond to Sunbury, on a warm summer's evening, I think I saw myriads of bats between the two places: the air swarmed with them all along the Thames, so that hundreds were in sight at a time.

I am, &c.

* *V. murinus* is a Continental species. The author is referring to the Pipistrelle and the Long-Eared Bat, two out of the fifteen British species.

LETTER XII

TO THE SAME

November 4, 1767.

SIR,

It gave me no small satisfaction to hear that the *falco** turned out an uncommon one. I must confess I should have been better pleased to have heard that I had sent you a bird that you had never seen before; but that, I find, would be a difficult task.

I have procured some of the mice† mentioned in my former letters, a young one and a female with young, both of which I have preserved in brandy. From the colour, shape, size, and manner of nesting, I make no doubt but that the species is non-descript. They are much smaller, and more slender, than the *mus domesticus medius* of Ray; and have more of the squirrel or dormouse colour: their belly is white; a straight line along their sides divides the shades of their back and belly. They never enter into houses; are carried into ricks and barns with the sheaves; abound in harvest; and build their nests amidst the straws of the corn above the ground, and sometimes in thistles. They breed as many as eight at a litter, in a little round nest composed of the blades of grass or wheat.

One of these nests I procured this autumn, most artificially platted, and composed of the blades of wheat; perfectly round, and about the size of a cricket-ball; with the aperture so ingeniously closed, that there was no discovering to what part it belonged. It was so compact and well filled, that it would roll across the table without being discomposed, though it contained eight little mice that were naked and blind. As this nest was perfectly full, how could the dam come at her litter respectively so as to administer a teat to each? perhaps she opens different places for that purpose, adjusting them again when the business is over: but she could not possibly be contained herself in the ball with her young, which moreover would be daily increasing in bulk. This wonderful procreant cradle, an elegant instance of the

* *This hawk proved to be the* falco peregrinus; *a variety.* ⟨G. W.⟩

† Harvest-mice.

efforts of instinct, was found in a wheat-field suspended in the head of a thistle.

A gentleman, curious in birds, wrote me word that his servant had shot one last January, in that severe weather, which he believed would puzzle me. I called to see it this summer, not knowing what to expect: but, the moment I took it in hand, I pronounced it the male *garrulus bohemicus* or German silk-tail,* from the five peculiar crimson tags or points which it carries at the ends of five of the short remiges. It cannot, I suppose, with any propriety, be called an English bird: and yet I see, by Ray's *Philosoph. Letters*, that great flocks of them, feeding on haws, appeared in this kingdom in the winter of 1685.

The mention of haws puts me in mind that there is a total failure of that wild fruit, so conducive to the support of many of the winged nation. For the same severe weather, late in the spring, which cut off all the produce of the more tender and curious trees, destroyed also that of the more hardy and common.

Some birds, haunting with the missel-thrushes, and feeding on the berries of the yew-tree, which answered to the description of the *merula torquata* or *ring-ouzel*, were lately seen in this neighbourhood. I employed some people to procure me a specimen, but without success. See Letter VIII.

Query—Might not *Canary* birds† be naturalized to this climate, provided their eggs were put, in the spring, into the nests of some of their congeners, as goldfinches, greenfinches, &c.? Before winter perhaps they might be hardened, and able to shift for themselves.

About ten years ago I used to spend some weeks yearly at Sunbury,‡ which is one of those pleasant villages lying on the Thames, near Hampton-court. In the autumn, I could not help being much amused with those myriads of the swallow kind which assemble in those parts. But what struck me most was, that, from the time they began to congregate, forsaking the

* The Waxwing, an irregular winter visitor that appears in rushes during certain years, perhaps owing to a failure in the food-supply (berries) of its native home in Scandinavia. In 1936 it was reported at Burton and Basingstoke in the county. (See *Papers and Proceedings of the Hampshire Field Club*, 1936, p. 273.)

† The Serin Finch of south Europe, an olive-green, brown and yellow bird related to the canary and visiting south-east England as a rare wanderer.

‡ On a visit to his friend since Oriel days, John Mulso, the Vicar (1746-60), and later the Vicar of Witney, where White visited him.

chimnies and houses, they roosted every night in the osier-beds of the aits of that river. Now this resorting towards that element, at that season of the year, seems to give some countenance to the northern opinion (strange as it is) of their retiring under water. A Swedish naturalist* is so much persuaded of that fact, that he talks, in his calendar of *Flora*, as familiarly of the swallow's going under water in the beginning of September, as he would of his poultry going to roost a little before sunset.

An observing gentleman in London writes me word that he saw an house-martin, on the twenty-third of last October, flying in and out of it's nest in the Borough. And I myself, on the twenty-ninth of last October (as I was travelling through Oxford), saw four or five swallows hovering round and settling on the roof of the county-hospital.

Now is it likely that these poor little birds† (which perhaps had not been hatched but a few weeks) should, at that late season of the year, and from so midland a county, attempt a voyage to Goree or Senegal, almost as far as the equator?‡

I acquiesce entirely in your opinion—that, though most of the swallow kind may migrate, yet that some do stay behind and hide with us during the winter.

As to the short-winged soft-billed birds, which come trooping in such numbers in the spring, I am at a loss even what to suspect about them. I watched them narrowly this year, and saw them abound till about Michaelmas, when they appeared no longer. Subsist they cannot openly among us, and yet elude the eyes of the inquisitive: and, as to their hiding, no man pretends to have found any of them in a torpid state in the winter. But with regard to their migration, what difficulties attend that supposition! that such feeble bad fliers (who the summer long never flit but from hedge to hedge) should be able to traverse vast seas and continents in order to enjoy milder seasons amidst the regions of Africa!§

* A. M. Berger. *Calendarium Floræ* (1756) was Englished in 1761.

† They certainly reach South Africa.

‡ *See Adanson's* Voyage to Senegal. ⟨G. W.⟩

§ Coleridge's note in his copy of *Selborne*: "Surely from Dover to Calais and from Gibraltar (or even Toulon) to the coast of Barbary, cannot be called a traverse of *vast seas.*" This is a foolish note, since elsewhere White himself says that migrating birds seek the narrowest passages across to the Continent. What he means are the Atlantic and Indian Oceans.

LETTER XIII

TO THE SAME

Selborne, *Jan.* 22, 1768.

SIR,

As in one of your former letters you expressed the more satisfaction from my correspondence on account of my living in the most southerly county; so now I may return the compliment, and expect to have my curiosity gratified by your living much more to the North.

For many years past I have observed that towards Christmas vast flocks of chaffinches* have appeared in the fields; many more, I used to think, than could be hatched in any one neighbourhood. But, when I came to observe them more narrowly, I was amazed to find that they seemed to me to be almost all hens. I communicated my suspicions to some intelligent neighbours, who, after taking pains about the matter, declared that they also thought them all mostly females; at least fifty to one. This extraordinary occurrence brought to my mind the remark of Linnæus; that "before winter all their hen chaffinches migrate through Holland into Italy". Now I want to know, from some curious person in the north, whether there are any large flocks of these finches with them in the winter, and of which sex they mostly consist? For, from such intelligence, one might be able to judge whether our female flocks migrate from the other end of the island, or whether they come over to us from the continent.

We have, in the winter, vast flocks of the common linnets; more, I think, than can be bred in any one district. These, I observe, when the spring advances, assemble on some tree in the sunshine, and join all in a gentle sort of chirping,† as if they were about to break up their winter quarters and betake themselves to their proper summer homes. It is well known, at least, that the

* Hence *Fringilla coelebs*. Mr. Nicholson has an interesting note on this passage, the explanation given being the readier tendency of the females to migrate owing to the territorial needs of the males and to more sedentary habits.

† These belling choruses are one of the delights of English country.

swallows and the fieldfares do congregate with a gentle twittering before they make their respective departure.

You may depend on it that the bunting,* *emberiza miliaria*, does not leave this country in the winter. In January 1767 I saw several dozen of them, in the midst of a severe frost, among the bushes on the downs near Andover: in our woodland enclosed district it is a rare bird.

Wagtails,† both white and yellow, are with us all the winter. Quails crowd to our southern coast, and are often killed in numbers by people that go on purpose.

Mr. Stillingfleet, in his Tracts, says that "if the wheatear (*œnanthe*) does not quit England, it certainly shifts places; for about harvest they are not to be found, where there was before great plenty of them". This well accounts for the vast quantities that are caught about that time on the south downs near Lewes, where they are esteemed a delicacy. There have been shepherds, I have been credibly informed, that have made many pounds in a season by catching them in traps. And though such multitudes are taken, I never saw (and I am well acquainted with those parts) above two or three at a time: for they are never gregarious. They may perhaps migrate in general; and, for that purpose, draw towards the coast of Sussex in autumn: but that they do not all withdraw I am sure; because I see a few stragglers in many counties, at all times of the year, especially about warrens and stone quarries.

I have no acquaintance, at present, among the gentlemen of the navy: but have written to a friend, who was a sea-chaplain in the late war, desiring him to look into his minutes, with respect to birds that settled on their rigging during their voyage up or down the channel. What Hasselquist‡ says on that subject is remarkable: there were little short-winged birds frequently com-

* White means the corn bunting, a bird of open and arable land, and so uncommon in wooded Selborne. His statement is too round. The corn bunting is a partial migrant. He might have meant the cirl bunting, common in the parish—I have heard it singing in the churchyard. But he failed to identify this bird, probably because it has considerably increased in the neighbourhood since his time.

† The author is speaking of the pied and the grey wagtails. The white is a winter visitor that very occasionally nests here; the yellow, which is becoming less abundant, goes abroad in the autumn. It is commonest in the valleys of Stour, Avon and Test (*Ornithological Report for the County of Hampshire*, 1936).

‡ A pupil of Linnæus.

ing on board his ship all the way from our channel quite up to the Levant, especially before squally weather.

What you suggest, with regard to Spain, is highly probable. The winters of Andalusia* are so mild, that, in all likelihood, the soft-billed birds that leave us at that season may find insects sufficient to support them there.

Some young man, possessed of fortune, health, and leisure, should make an autumnal voyage into that kingdom; and should spend a year there, investigating the natural history of that vast country. Mr. Willughby† passed through that kingdom on such an errand; but he seems to have skirted along in a superficial manner and an ill humour, being much disgusted at the rude dissolute manners of the people.

I have no friend left now at Sunbury to apply to about the swallows roosting on the aits of the Thames: nor can I hear any more about those birds which I suspected were *merulæ torquatæ*.

As to the small mice, I have farther to remark, that though they hang their nests for breeding up amidst the straws of the standing corn, above the ground; yet I find that, in the winter, they burrow deep in the earth, and make warm beds of grass: but their grand rendezvous seems to be in corn-ricks, into which they are carried at harvest. A neighbour housed an oat-rick lately, under the thatch of which were assembled near an hundred, most of which were taken; and some I saw. I measured them; and found that, from nose to tail,‡ they were just two inches and a quarter, and their tails just two inches long. Two of them, in a scale, weighed down just one copper halfpenny, which is about the third of an ounce avoirdupois: so that I suppose they are the smallest quadrupeds in this island. A full-grown *mus medius domesticus* weighs, I find, one ounce lumping weight, which is more than six times as much as the mouse above; and measures from nose to rump four inches and a quarter, and the same in it's tail...

* As a matter of fact, bitter winds are more prevalent in Spain than even the mistral elsewhere along the Mediterranean. This, rather than the reason given by Mr. Nicholson (competition with native birds), may be why our migrants do not linger there.

† *See Ray's* Travels, *p.* 466. ⟨G. W.⟩

‡ Harting in his Edition says that the tail, being prehensile, is very serviceable for running up and down the straw and in building the nest.

LETTER XV

TO THE SAME

Selborne, *March* 30, 1768.

DEAR SIR,

Some intelligent country people have a notion that we have, in these parts, a species of the *genus mustelinum*, besides the weasel, stoat, ferret, and polecat; a little reddish beast, not much bigger than a field mouse, but much longer, which they call a *cane*.* This piece of intelligence can be little depended on; but farther inquiry may be made.

A gentleman in this neighbourhood had two milkwhite rooks in one nest. A booby of a carter, finding them before they were able to fly, threw them down and destroyed them, to the regret of the owner, who would have been glad to have preserved such a curiosity in his rookery. I saw the birds myself nailed against the end of a barn, and was surprised to find that their bills, legs, feet, and claws were milkwhite.

A shepherd saw, as he thought, some white larks on a down above my house this winter: were not these the *emberiza nivalis*, the snow-flake† of the *Brit. Zool.*? No doubt they were.

A few years ago I saw a cock bullfinch in a cage, which had been caught in the fields after it was come to it's full colours. In about a year it began to look dingy; and, blackening every succeeding year, it became coal-black at the end of four. It's chief food was hempseed. Such influence has food on the colour of animals! The pied and mottled colours of domesticated animals are supposed to be owing to high, various, and unusual food.

I had remarked, for years, that the root of the cuckoo-pint (*arum*) was frequently scratched out of the dry banks of hedges, and eaten in severe snowy weather. After observing, with some exactness, myself, and getting others to do the same, we found

* The female weasel, smaller than the male. The ferret is not a wild animal. The author may have intended the *pine-marten*, exterminated from the south of England in the nineteenth century.

† The snow bunting, a winter visitor except in the Scottish mountains, where it nests. There was a considerable influx along the east coast of Hampshire in 1936.

it was the thrush kind that searched it out. The root of the *arum* is remarkably warm and pungent.

Our flocks of female chaffinches have not yet forsaken us. The blackbirds and thrushes are very much thinned down by that fierce weather in January.

In the middle of February I discovered, in my tall hedges, a little bird* that raised my curiosity: it was of that yellow-green colour that belongs to the *salicaria* kind, and, I think, was soft-billed. It was no *parus*; and was too long and too big for the golden-crowned wren, appearing most like the largest willow-wren. It hung sometimes with it's back downwards, but never continuing one moment in the same place. I shot at it, but it was so desultory that I missed my aim.

I wonder that the stone curlew, *charadrius oedicnemus*, should be mentioned by the writers as a rare bird: it abounds in all the campaign parts of Hampshire and Sussex, and breeds, I think, all the summer, having young ones, I know, very late in the autumn. Already they begin clamouring in the evening. They cannot, I think, with any propriety, be called, as they are by Mr. Ray, "*circa aquas versantes*"; for with us, by day at least, they haunt only the most dry, open, upland fields and sheep walks, far removed from water: what they may do in the night I cannot say. Worms are their usual food, but they also eat toads and frogs.

I can shew you some good specimens of my *new mice*. Linnæus perhaps would call the species *mus minimus*.

* Some editors suggest the chiff-chaff, others the siskin. The latter is much more likely to be correct, because the description is decidely siskinian, and for a chiff-chaff to arrive in the middle of February after severe weather would be most unusual. By "desultory" the author means fitful in movement.

LETTER XVI

TO THE SAME

Selborne, *April* 18, 1768.

DEAR SIR,

The history of the stone curlew,* *charadrius oedicnemus*, is as follows. It lays it's eggs, usually two, never more than three, on the bare ground, without any nest, in the field; so that the countryman, in stirring his fallows, often destroys them. The young run immediately from the egg like partridges, &c. and are withdrawn to some flinty field by the dam, where they sculk among the stones, which are their best security; for their feathers are so exactly of the colour of our grey spotted flints, that the most exact observer, unless he catches the eye of the young bird, may be eluded. The eggs are short and round; of a dirty white, spotted with dark bloody blotches. Though I might not be able, just when I pleased, to procure you a bird, yet I could shew you them almost any day; and any evening you may hear them round the village, for they make a clamour which may be heard a mile. *Oedicnemus* is a most apt and expressive name for them, since their legs seem swoln† like those of a gouty man. After harvest I have shot them before the pointers in turnip-fields.

I make no doubt but there are three species of the *willow-wrens*:‡ two I know perfectly; but have not been able yet to procure the third. No two birds can differ more in their notes, and that constantly, than those two that I am acquainted with; for the one has a joyous, easy, laughing note; the other a harsh loud chirp. The former is every way larger, and three quarters of an

* A fine piece of original observation. See also Letters XXI and XXXIII to Pennant and Letter LIX to Barrington.

† Hence the local name, "Thick-knee".

‡ White soon identified the third species, the wood-warbler of the "high beechen tops". He was the first to separate and distinguish the three species. It is curious that a letter so acute and first-hand in discovery and expressive in communicating it, should commit the vulgar error (lower down) of accusing "willow-wrens" of being garden pests. Perhaps he confused them with the young of the garden-warbler, which they somewhat resemble, birds that are keen fruitarians. "Smallest willow-wren" (still lower down) is the chiff-chaff, "middle" the willow-warbler.

inch longer, and weighs two drams and an half; while the latter weighs but two: so the songster is one fifth heavier than the chirper. The chirper (being the first summer-bird of passage that is heard, the wryneck sometimes excepted) begins his two notes in the middle of March, and continues them through the spring and summer till the end of August, as appears by my journals. The legs of the larger of these two are flesh-coloured; of the less, black.

The *grasshopper-lark* began his sibilous note in my fields last Saturday. Nothing can be more amusing than the whisper of this little bird, which seems to be close by though at an hundred yards distance; and, when close at your ear, is scarce any louder than when a great way off. Had I not been a little acquainted with insects, and known that the grasshopper kind is not yet hatched, I should have hardly believed but that it had been a *locusta* whispering in the bushes. The country people laugh when you tell them that it is the note of a bird. It is a most artful creature, sculking in the thickest part of a bush; and will sing at a yard distance, provided it be concealed. I was obliged to get a person to go on the other side of the hedge where it haunted; and then it would run, creeping like a mouse, before us for an hundred yards together, through the bottom of the thorns; yet it would not come into fair sight: but in a morning early, and when undisturbed, it sings on the top of a twig, gaping and shivering with it's wings. Mr. Ray himself had no knowledge of this bird, but received his account from Mr. Johnson, who apparently confounds it with the *reguli non cristati*, from which it is very distinct. See Ray's *Philos. Letters*, p. 108.

The fly-catcher (*stoparola*) has not yet appeared: it usually breeds in my vine. The *redstart* begins to sing: it's note is short and imperfect, but is continued till about the middle of June. The *willow-wrens* (the smaller sort) are horrid pests in a garden, destroying the pease, cherries, currants, &c.; and are so tame that a gun will not scare them.

A LIST *of the* SUMMER BIRDS *of* PASSAGE *discovered in this neighbourhood, ranged somewhat in the Order in which they appear:*

	Linnæi Nomina.
Smallest willow-wren,	*Motacilla trochilus:*
Wryneck,	*Jynx torquilla:*

House-swallow,	*Hirundo rustica:*
Martin,	*Hirundo urbica:*
Sand-martin,	*Hirundo riparia:*
Cuckoo,	*Cuculus canorus:*
Nightingale,	*Motacilla luscinia:*
Blackcap,	*Motacilla atricapilla:*
Whitethroat,	*Motacilla sylvia:*
Middle willow-wren,	*Motacilla trochilus:*
Swift,	*Hirundo apus:*
Stone curlew,?	*Charadrius oedicnemus?*
Turtle-dove,?	*Turtur aldrovandi?*
Grasshopper-lark,	*Alauda trivialis:*
Landrail,	*Rallus crex:*
Largest willow-wren,	*Motacilla trochilus:*
Redstart,	*Motacilla phœnicurus:*
Goatsucker, or fern-owl,	*Caprimulgus europæus:*
Fly-catcher,	*Muscicapa grisola.*

My countrymen talk much of a bird that makes a clatter with it's bill against a dead bough, or some old pales, calling it a jar-bird. I procured one to be shot in the very fact; it proved to be the *sitta europæa* (*the nuthatch*). Mr. Ray says that the less spotted *woodpecker* does the same. This noise may be heard a furlong or more.

Now is the only time to ascertain the short-winged summer birds; for, when the leaf is out, there is no making any remarks on such a restless tribe; and, when once the young begin to appear, it is all confusion: there is no distinction of genus, species, or sex.

In breeding-time snipes play over the moors, piping and humming: they always hum as they are descending. Is not their hum ventriloquous like that of the turkey? Some suspect it is made by their wings.*

This morning I saw the golden-crowned wren, whose crown glitters like burnished gold. It often hangs like a titmouse, with it's back downwards.

Yours, &c. &c.

* The question is still undecided. See also Letters X and XXXIX to Pennant.

LETTER XVII

TO THE SAME

Selborne, *June* 18, 1768.

DEAR SIR,

On Wednesday last arrived your agreeable letter of June the 10th. It gives me great satisfaction to find that you pursue these studies still with such vigour, and are in such forwardness with regard to reptiles and fishes.

The reptiles, few as they are, I am not acquainted with, so well as I could wish, with regard to their natural history. There is a degree of dubiousness and obscurity attending the propagation of this class of animals, something analogous to that of the *cryptogamia* in the sexual system of plants: and the case is the same with regard to some of the fishes; as the eel, &c.

The method in which toads procreate and bring forth seems to be very much in the dark. Some authors say that they are viviparous: and yet Ray classes them among his oviparous animals;* and is silent with regard to the manner of their bringing forth. Perhaps they may be ἔσω μὲν ᾠοτόκοι, ἔξω δὲ ζωοτόκοι, as is known to be the case with the viper.

The copulation of frogs (or at least the appearance of it; for Swammerdam† proves that the male has no *penis intrans*) is notorious to every body: because we see them sticking upon each others backs for a month together in the spring: and yet I never saw, or read, of toads being observed in the same situation. It is strange that the matter with regard to the venom of toads‡ has not been yet settled. That they are not noxious to some animals is plain: for ducks, buzzards, owls, stone curlews, and snakes, eat them, to my knowledge, with impunity. And I well remember the time, but was not eye-witness to the fact (though numbers of persons were) when a quack, at this village, ate a toad to make the country-people stare; afterwards he drank oil.

* Toads are oviparous, producing spawn in strings on the surface of ponds.

† An astute Dutch biologist of the seventeenth century.

‡ Toads are not poisonous but exude a self-protective acid secretion from the skin.

I have been informed also, from undoubted authority, that some ladies (ladies you will say of peculiar taste) took a fancy to a toad, which they nourished summer after summer, for many years, till he grew to a monstrous size, with the maggots which turn to flesh flies. The reptile used to come forth every evening from an hole under the garden-steps; and was taken up, after supper, on the table to be fed. But at last a tame raven, kenning him as he put forth his head, gave him such a severe stroke with his horny beak as put out one eye. After this accident the creature languished for some time and died.

I need not remind a gentleman of your extensive reading of the excellent account there is from Mr. Derham, in Ray's *Wisdom of God in the Creation* (p. 365), concerning the migration of frogs from their breeding ponds. In this account he at once subverts that foolish opinion of their dropping from the clouds in rain;* shewing that it is from the grateful coolness and moisture of those showers that they are tempted to set out on their travels, which they defer till those fall. Frogs are as yet in their tadpole state; but, in a few weeks, our lanes, paths, fields, will swarm for a few days with myriads of those emigrants, no larger than my little finger nail. Swammerdam gives a most accurate account of the method and situation in which the male impregnates the spawn of the female. How wonderful is the œconomy of Providence with regard to the limbs of so vile a reptile! While it is an *aquatic* it has a fish-like tail, and no legs: as soon as the legs sprout, the tail drops off as useless, and the animal betakes itself to the land!

Merret,† I trust, is widely mistaken when he advances that the *rana arborea* is an English reptile; it abounds in Germany and Switzerland.

It is to be remembered that the *salamandra aquatica* of Ray (the water-newt or eft) will frequently bite at the angler's bait, and is often caught on his hook. I used to take it for granted that the *salamandra aquatica* was hatched, lived, and died, in the water. But John Ellis, Esq. F.R.S. (the coralline Ellis)‡ asserts, in a

* This is still believed in remote country districts and I heard of an instance the other day.

† Christopher Merret, a seventeenth century Fellow of White's College, Oriel, and a systematist in natural history.

‡ Ellis substantiated the animal being of corals in the middle of the century.

letter to the Royal Society, dated June the 5th, 1766, in his account of the *mud inguana*, an amphibious *bipes* from South Carolina, that the water-eft, or newt, is only the *larva* of the land-eft, as tadpoles are of frogs. Lest I should be suspected to misunderstand his meaning, I shall give it in his own words. Speaking of the *opercula* or coverings to the gills of the *mud inguana*, he proceeds to say that "The form of these pennated coverings approach very near to what I have some time ago observed in the *larva* or *aquatic* state of our *English lacerta*, known by the name of eft, or newt; which serve them for coverings to their gills, and for fins to swim with while in this state; and which they lose, as well as the fins of their tails, when they *change* their state and *become land animals*, as I have observed, by keeping them alive for some time myself."

Linnæus, in his *Systema Naturæ*, hints at what Mr. Ellis advances more than once.

Providence has been so indulgent to us as to allow of but one venomous reptile of the serpent kind in these kingdoms, and that is the viper. As you propose the good of mankind to be an object of your publications, you will not omit to mention common sallad-oil as a sovereign remedy against the bite of the viper. As to the blind worm (*anguis fragilis*, so called because it snaps in sunder with a small blow), I have found, on examination, that it is perfectly innocuous. A neighbouring yeoman (to whom I am indebted for some good hints) killed and opened a female viper about the twenty-seventh of May: he found her filled with a chain of eleven eggs, about the size of those of a blackbird; but none of them were advanced so far towards a state of maturity as to contain any rudiments of young. Though they are oviparous, yet they are viviparous also, hatching their young within their bellies, and then bringing them forth. Whereas snakes* lay chains of eggs every summer in my melon beds, in spite of all that my people can do to prevent them; which eggs do not hatch till the spring following, as I have often experienced. Several intelligent folks assure me that they have seen the viper open her mouth and admit her helpless young down her throat† on sudden surprises, just as the female opossum does her brood into the

* Grass-snakes.

† Still unproved or disproved.

pouch under her belly, upon the like emergencies; and yet the London viper-catchers insist on it, to Mr. Barrington, that no such thing ever happens. The serpent kind eat, I believe, but once in a year; or, rather, but only just at one season of the year. Country people talk much of a water-snake, but, I am pretty sure, without any reason; for the common snake (*coluber natrix*) delights much to sport in the water, perhaps with a view to procure frogs and other food.

I cannot well guess how you are to make out your twelve species of reptiles,* unless it be by the various species, or rather varieties, of our *lacerti*, of which Ray enumerates five. I have not had opportunity of ascertaining these; but remember well to have seen, formerly, several beautiful green *lacerti* on the sunny sandbanks near Farnham, in Surrey; and Ray admits there are such in Ireland.

* We have only half as many, and but two lizards, the sand-lizard and the common lizard.

LETTER XVIII

TO THE SAME

Selborne, *July* 27, 1768.

DEAR SIR,

I received your obliging and communicative letter of June the 28th, while I was on a visit at a gentleman's house, where I had neither books to turn to, nor leisure to sit down, to return you an answer to many queries, which I wanted to resolve in the best manner that I am able.

A person, by my order, has searched our brooks, but could find no such fish as the *gasterosteus pungitius*: he found the *gasterosteus aculeatus* in plenty. This morning, in a basket, I packed a little earthen pot full of wet moss, and in it some sticklebacks, male and female; the females big with spawn; some lamperns; some bulls heads; but I could procure no minnows. This basket will be in Fleet-street by eight this evening; so I hope Mazel* will have them fresh and fair to-morrow morning. I gave some directions, in a letter, to what particulars the engraver should be attentive.

Finding, while I was on a visit, that I was within a reasonable distance of Ambresbury, I sent a servant over to that town, and procured several living specimens of loaches, which he brought, safe and brisk, in a glass decanter. They were taken in the gullies that were cut for watering the meadows. From these fishes (which measured from two to four inches in length) I took the following description: "The loach, in it's general aspect, has a pellucid appearance: it's back is mottled with irregular collections of small black dots, not reaching much below the *linea lateralis*, as are the back and tail fins: a black line runs from each eye down to the nose; it's belly is of a silvery white; the upper jaw projects beyond the lower, and is surrounded with six feelers, three on each side: it's pectoral fins are large, it's ventral much smaller; the fin behind it's anus small; it's dorsal fin large,

* Peter Mazel engraved the plates both for Pennant's *British Zoology* and of the Church and the Plestor in the first edition of *Selborne*.

containing eight spines; it's tail, where it joins to the tail-fin, *remarkably broad*, without any taperness, so as to be characteristic of this genus: the tail-fin is broad, and square at the end. From the breadth and muscular strength of the tail it appears to be an active nimble fish."

In my visit I was not very far from Hungerford, and did not forget to make some inquiries concerning the wonderful method of curing cancers by means of toads. Several intelligent persons, both gentry and clergy, do, I find, give a great deal of credit to what was asserted in the papers: and I myself dined with a clergyman who seemed to be persuaded that what is related is matter of fact; but, when I came to attend to his account, I thought I discerned circumstances which did not a little invalidate the woman's story of the manner in which she came by her skill. She says of herself "that, labouring under a virulent cancer, she went to some church where there was a vast crowd: on going into a pew, she was accosted by a strange clergyman; who, after expressing compassion for her situation, told her that if she would make such an application of living toads as is mentioned she would be well". Now is it likely that this unknown gentleman should express so much tenderness for this single sufferer, and not feel any for the many thousands that daily languish under this terrible disorder? Would he not have made use of this invaluable nostrum for his own emolument; or, at least, by some means of publication or other, have found a method of making it public for the good of mankind? In short, this woman (as it appears to me) having set up for a cancer-doctress, finds it expedient to amuse the country with this dark and mysterious relation.

The water-eft has not, that I can discern, the least appearance of any gills;* for want of which it is continually rising to the surface of the water to take in fresh air. I opened a big-bellied one indeed, and found it full of spawn. Not that this circumstance at all invalidates the assertion that they are *larvæ*: for the *larvæ* of insects are full of eggs, which they exclude the instant they enter their last state...

* Gills occur only among the young, as is proper to amphibians, whose remote ancestors were purely aquatic.

LETTER XIX

TO THE SAME

Selborne, *Aug*. 17, 1768.

DEAR SIR,

I have now, past dispute, made out three distinct species of the willow-wrens (*motacillæ trochili*) which *constantly* and *invariably* use distinct notes. But, at the same time, I am obliged to confess that I know nothing of your willow-lark.* In my letter of April the 18th, I had told you peremptorily that I knew your willow-lark, but had not seen it then: but, when I came to procure it, it proved, in all respects, a very *motacilla trochilus*; only that it is a size larger than the two other, and the yellow-green of the whole upper part of the body is more vivid, and the belly of a clearer white. I have specimens of the three sorts now lying before me; and can discern that there are three gradations of sizes, and that the least has black legs, and the other two flesh-coloured ones. The yellowest bird is considerably the largest, and has it's quill-feathers and secondary feathers tipped with white, which the others have not. This last haunts only the tops of trees in high beechen woods, and makes a sibilous grasshopper-like noise, now and then, at short intervals, shivering a little with it's wings when it sings; and is, I make no doubt now, the *regulus non cristatus* of Ray; which he says "*cantat voce stridulâ locustæ*". Yet this great ornithologist never suspected that there were three species.

* Brit. Zool. *edit*. 1776, *octavo*, *p*. 381. ⟨G. W.⟩

LETTER XX

TO THE SAME

Selborne, *October* 8, 1768.

It is, I find, in *zoology* as it is in *botany*: all nature is so full, that that district produces the greatest variety which is the most examined. Several birds, which are said to belong to the north only, are, it seems, often in the south. I have discovered this summer three species of birds with us, which writers mention as only to be seen in the northern counties. The first that was brought me (on the 14th of May), was the sandpiper,* *tringa hypoleucus*: it was a cock bird, and haunted the banks of some ponds near the village; and, as it had a companion, doubtless intended to have bred near that water. Besides, the owner has told me since, that, on recollection, he has seen some of the same birds round his ponds in former summers.

The next bird that I procured (on the 21st of May) was a male red-backed butcher bird,† *lanius collurio*. My neighbour, who shot it, says that it might easily have escaped his notice, had not the outcries and chattering of the white-throats and other small birds drawn his attention to the bush where it was: it's craw was filled with the legs and wings of beetles.

The next rare birds (which were procured for me last week) were some ring-ousels,‡ *turdi torquati*.

This week twelve months a gentleman from London, being with us, was amusing himself with a gun, and found, he told us, on an old yew hedge where there were berries, some birds like blackbirds, with rings of white round their necks: a neighbouring farmer also at the same time observed the same; but, as no specimens were procured, little notice was taken. I mentioned

* The common sandpiper. It very rarely breeds in the south, though its sweet-toned whistle is common among northern lochs. Small flocks or single birds both of the common and green sandpipers visit the county, usually in the summer.

† Not a northern bird at all, and locally distributed over south-east England.

‡ In the south (except on Dartmoor) only a passage migrant from northern and north midland uplands and becoming steadily more scarce. Seven other letters refer to the ring-ousel: XXI, XXIV, XXV, XXVI, XXXI, XXXVIII to Pennant and VII to Barrington.

this circumstance to you in my letter of November the 4th, 1767: (you however paid but small regard to what I said, as I had not seen these birds myself): but last week the aforesaid farmer, seeing a large flock, twenty or thirty of these birds, shot two cocks and two hens: and says, on recollection, that he remembers to have observed these birds again last spring, about Lady-day, as it were, on their return to the north. Now perhaps these ousels are not the ousels of the north of England, but belong to the more northern parts of Europe; and may retire before the excessive rigor of the frosts in those parts; and return to breed in the spring, when the cold abates. If this be the case, here is discovered a new bird of winter passage, concerning whose migrations the writers are silent: but if these birds should prove the ousels of the north of England, then here is a migration disclosed within our own kingdom never before remarked. It does not yet appear whether they retire beyond the bounds of our island to the south; but it is most probable that they usually do, or else one cannot suppose that they would have continued so long unnoticed in the southern counties. The ousel is larger than a blackbird, and feeds on haws; but last autumn (when there were no haws) it fed on yew-berries: in the spring it feeds on ivy-berries, which ripen only at that season, in March and April.

I must not omit to tell you (as you have been so lately on the study of reptiles) that my people, every now and then of late, draw up with a bucket of water from my well, which is 63 feet deep, a large black warty lizard* with a fin-tail and yellow belly. How they first came down at that depth, and how they were ever to have got out thence without help, is more than I am able to say.

My thanks are due to you for your trouble and care in the examination of a buck's head. As far as your discoveries reach at present, they seem much to corroborate my suspicions; and I hope Mr. ——† may find reason to give his decision in my favour; and then, I think, we may advance this extraordinary provision of nature as a new instance of the wisdom of God in the creation.

* The Great Crested Newt.

† The surgeon John Hunter.

As yet I have not quite done with my history of the *oedicnemus*, or stone-curlew; for I shall desire a gentleman in Sussex* (near whose house these birds congregate in vast flocks in the autumn) to observe nicely when they leave him, (if they do leave him) and when they return again in the spring: I was with this gentleman lately, and saw several single birds.

* John Woods of Chilgrove, near Chichester. His brother, Henry, married the author's sister, Rebecca.

LETTER XXI

TO THE SAME

Selborne, *Nov.* 28, 1768.

DEAR SIR,

With regard to the *oedicnemus*, or stone-curlew, I intend to write very soon* to my friend near Chichester, in whose neighbourhood these birds seem most to abound; and shall urge him to take particular notice when they begin to congregate, and afterwards to watch them most narrowly whether they do not withdraw themselves during the dead of the winter. When I have obtained information with respect to this circumstance, I shall have finished my history of the *stone-curlew*; which I hope will prove to your satisfaction, as it will be, I trust, very near the truth. This gentleman, as he occupies a large farm of his own, and is abroad early and late, will be a very proper spy upon the motions of these birds: and besides, as I have prevailed on him to buy the *Naturalist's Journal*† (with which he is much delighted), I shall expect that he will be very exact in his dates. It is very extraordinary, as you observe, that a bird so common with us should never straggle to you.

And here will be the properest place to mention, while I think of it, an anecdote which the above-mentioned gentleman told me when I was last at his house; which was that, in a warren joining to his outlet, many daws (*corvi monedulæ*) build every year in the rabbit-burrows under ground. The way he and his brothers used to take their nests, while they were boys, was by listening at the mouths of the holes; and, if they heard the young ones cry, they twisted the nest out with a forked stick. Some water-fowls (viz. the puffins) breed, I know, in that manner; but I should never have suspected the daws of building in holes on the flat ground.

* Mr. Nicholson points out that the passage has been transposed from a former letter. The ring-ousels would all have gone by November. It is an example of the traffic of dates and passages from the original to the published letters.

† Printed in 1767 and presented by Barrington to the author who recorded his observations in it. See my prefatory note to the *Naturalist's Journal* in Volume II.

Another very unlikely spot is made use of by daws as a place to breed in, and that is Stonehenge. These birds deposit their nests in the interstices between the upright and the impost stones of that amazing work of antiquity: which circumstance alone speaks the prodigious height of the upright stones, that they should be tall enough to secure those nests from the annoyance of shepherd-boys, who are always idling round that place.

One of my neighbours last Saturday, November the 26th, saw a martin in a sheltered bottom: the sun shone warm, and the bird was hawking briskly after flies. I am now perfectly satisfied that they do not all leave this island in the winter.

You judge very right, I think, in speaking with reserve and caution concerning the cures done by toads: for, let people advance what they will on such subjects, yet there is such a propensity in mankind towards deceiving and being deceived, that one cannot safely relate any thing from common report, especially in print, without expressing some degree of doubt and suspicion.

Your approbation, with regard to my new discovery of the migration of the ring-ousel, gives me satisfaction; and I find you concur with me in suspecting that they are foreign birds which visit us. You will be sure, I hope, not to omit to make inquiry whether your ring-ousels leave your rocks in the autumn. What puzzles me most, is the very short stay they make with us; for in about three weeks they are all gone. I shall be very curious to remark whether they will call on us at their return in the spring, as they did last year.

I want to be better informed with regard to ichthyology. If fortune had settled me near the sea-side, or near some great river, my natural propensity would soon have urged me to have made myself acquainted with their productions: but as I have lived mostly in inland parts, and in an upland district, my knowledge of fishes extends little farther than to those common sorts which our brooks and lakes produce.

I am, &c.

LETTER XXII

TO THE SAME

Selborne, *Jan.* 2, 1769.

DEAR SIR,

As to the peculiarity of jackdaws building with us under the ground in rabbit-burrows, you have, in part, hit upon the reason; for, in reality, there are hardly any towers or steeples in all this country. And perhaps, Norfolk excepted,* Hampshire and Sussex are as meanly furnished with churches as almost any counties in the kingdom. We have many livings of two or three hundred pounds a year, whose houses of worship make little better appearance than dovecots. When I first saw Northamptonshire, Cambridgeshire and Huntingdonshire, and the fens of Lincolnshire, I was amazed at the number of spires which presented themselves in every point of view. As an admirer of prospects, I have reason to lament this want in my own country; for such objects are very necessary ingredients in an elegant landscape.†

What you mention with respect to reclaimed toads raises my curiosity. An ancient author, though no naturalist, has well remarked that "*Every kind of beasts, and of birds, and of serpents, and things in the sea, is tamed, and hath been tamed, of mankind*".‡

It is a satisfaction to me to find that a green lizard§ has actually been procured for you in Devonshire;|| because it corroborates my discovery, which I made many years ago, of the same

* White knew nothing of Norfolk churches. With the exception of Northants and Lincolnshire, and setting aside the fifteenth century towers of Somerset, the interiors of Devon, and the Norman doorways of the south Midlands, Norfolk is probably the first county in England for the beauty and richness of its churches, especially in the fifteenth century when the cloth-trade was at its zenith.

† The voice of the eighteenth century. I have little doubt myself that the wonderful broach spires of the Fens were deliberately built in relation to the values of the landscape. It is hardly true, however, as Mr. Nicholson says, that spires are "best developed" in the plains. The tallest existing spire, Salisbury's, and one still higher but long fallen, Malmesbury's, were both built in upland country, and the same is true of the Nene Valley spires. They were built where they could command the widest area of country, whether in the plain or among the hills.

‡ *James*, chap. iii. 7. ⟨G. W.⟩

§ This must have been the sand-lizard, the green being a European species.

|| Staying at the Rectory of the Rev. Nathan Wells, of East Allington.

sort, on a sunny sandbank near Farnham, in Surrey. I am well acquainted with the south hams of Devonshire; and can suppose that district, from it's southerly situation, to be a proper habitation for such animals in their best colours.

Since the ring-ousels of your vast mountains do certainly not forsake them against winter,* our suspicions that those which visit this neighbourhood about Michaelmas are not English birds, but driven from the more northern parts of Europe by the frosts, are still more reasonable; and it will be worth your pains to endeavour to trace from whence they come, and to inquire why they make so very short a stay.

In your account of your error with regard to the two species of herons, you incidentally gave me great entertainment in your description of the heronry at Cressi-hall; which is a curiosity I never could manage to see. Fourscore nests of such a bird on one tree is a rarity which I would ride half as many miles† to have a sight of. Pray be sure to tell me in your next whose seat Cressi-hall is, and near what town it lies.‡ I have often thought that those vast extents of fens have never been sufficiently explored. If half a dozen gentlemen, furnished with a good strength of water-spaniels, were to beat them over for a week, they would certainly find more species.

There is no bird, I believe, whose manners I have studied more than that of the *caprimulgus* (the goat-sucker), as it is a wonderful and curious creature: but I have always found that though sometimes it may chatter as it flies, as I know it does, yet in general it utters it's jarring note sitting on a bough; and I have for many an half hour watched it as it sat with it's under mandible quivering, and particularly this summer. It perches usually on a bare twig, with it's head lower than it's tail, in an attitude well expressed by your draughtsman in the folio *British Zoology*. This bird is most punctual in beginning it's song exactly at the close of day; so exactly that I have known it strike up more than once or twice just at the report of the Portsmouth evening gun,

* An error of Pennant's. Ring-ousels migrate south and south-east from the Welsh mountains, the Lakes and the Pennines and the Peak of Derbyshire. From Dartmoor they also go south in autumn.

† A more telling example of the author's inexhaustible curiosity than if he had said double as many miles.

‡ *Cressi-hall is near Spalding, in Lincolnshire.* ⟨G. W.⟩

which we can hear when the weather is still. It appears to me past all doubt that it's notes are formed by organic impulse, by the powers of the parts of it's windpipe, formed for sound, just as cats pur.* You will credit me, I hope, when I assure you that, as my neighbours were assembled in an hermitage† on the side of a steep hill where we drink tea, one of these churn-owls came and settled on the cross of that little straw edifice and began to chatter, and continued his note for many minutes: and we were all struck with wonder to find that the organs of that little animal, when put in motion, gave a sensible vibration to the whole building! This bird also sometimes makes a small squeak, repeated four or five times; and I have observed that to happen when the cock has been pursuing the hen in a toying way through the boughs of a tree.

It would not be at all strange if your bat, which you have procured, should prove a new one, since five species‡ have been found in a neighbouring kingdom. The great sort that I mentioned is certainly a non-descript. I saw but one this summer, and that I had no opportunity of taking.

Your account of the *Indian-grass* was entertaining. I am no angler myself; but inquiring of those that are, what they supposed that part of their tackle to be made of? they replied "of the intestines of a silkworm".

Though I must not pretend to great skill in entomology, yet I cannot say that I am ignorant of that kind of knowledge: I may now and then perhaps be able to furnish you with a little information.

The vast rains ceased with us much about the same time as with you, and since we have had delicate weather. Mr. Barker, who has measured the rain for more than thirty years, says, in a late letter, that more has fallen this year than in any he ever attended to; though, from July 1763 to January 1764, more fell than in any seven months of this year.

* A passage is omitted here from the original letter, correcting one of Pennant's numerous errors.

† The wig-wam-like structure on the slope of The Hanger (see notes to later references) is frequently mentioned in the *Private Letters*. So apt and minute is the author's description of the nightjar that the hermitage must surely have served as a "hide" for purposes of observation.

‡ Now twelve.

LETTER XXIII

TO THE SAME

Selborne, *February* 28, 1769.

DEAR SIR,

It is not improbable that the Guernsey lizard and our green lizards may be specifically the same; all that I know is, that, when some years ago many Guernsey lizards were turned loose in Pembroke college garden, in the university of Oxford, they lived a great while, and seemed to enjoy themselves very well, but never bred. Whether this circumstance will prove any thing either way I shall not pretend to say.

I return you thanks for your account of Cressi-hall; but recollect, not without regret, that in June 1746 I was visiting for a week together at Spalding, without ever being told that such a curiosity was just at hand. Pray send me word in your next what sort of tree it is that contains such a quantity of herons' nests; and whether the heronry consists of a whole grove or wood, or only of a few trees.

It gave me satisfaction to find we accorded so well about the *caprimulgus*: all I contended for was to prove that it often chatters sitting as well as flying; and therefore the noise was voluntary, and from organic impulse, and not from the resistance of the air against the hollow of it's mouth and throat.

If ever I saw any thing like actual migration, it was last Michaelmas-day. I was travelling, and out early in the morning: at first there was a vast fog; but, by the time that I was got seven or eight miles from home towards the coast, the sun broke out into a delicate warm day. We were then on a large heath or common, and I could discern, as the mist began to break away, great numbers of swallows (*hirundines rusticæ*) clustering on the stunted shrubs and bushes, as if they had roosted there all night. As soon as the air became clear and pleasant they all were on the wing at once;* and, by a placid and easy flight, proceeded on

* The reverse is true. It was not discovered for 150 years that swallows migrate in small parties, and in so relaxed, desultory and lingering a fashion that the length of time in which Nature kept her secret is not surprising.

southward towards the sea: after this I did not see any more flocks, only now and then a straggler.

I cannot agree with those persons that assert that the swallow kind disappear some and some gradually, as they come, for the bulk of them seem to withdraw at once: only some stragglers stay behind a long while, and do never, there is the greatest reason to believe, leave this island. Swallows seem to lay themselves up, and to come forth in a warm day, as bats do continually of a warm evening, after they have disappeared for weeks. For a very respectable gentleman assured me that, as he was walking with some friends under Merton-wall on a remarkably hot noon, either in the last week in December or the first week in January, he espied three or four swallows huddled together on the moulding of one of the windows of that college. I have frequently remarked that swallows are seen later at Oxford than elsewhere: is it owing to the vast massy buildings of that place, to the many waters round it, or to what else?

When I used to rise in a morning last autumn, and see the swallows and martins clustering on the chimnies and thatch of the neighbouring cottages, I could not help being touched with a secret delight, mixed with some degree of mortification: with delight, to observe with how much ardour and punctuality those poor little birds obeyed the strong impulse towards migration, or hiding, imprinted on their minds by their great Creator; and with some degree of mortification, when I reflected that, after all our pains and inquiries, we are yet not quite certain to what regions they do migrate, and are still farther embarrassed to find that some do not actually migrate at all.

These reflections made so strong an impression on my imagination, that they became productive of a composition that may perhaps amuse you for a quarter of an hour when next I have the honour of writing to you.

LETTER XXV

TO THE SAME

Selborne, *Aug*. 30, 1769.

DEAR SIR,

It gives me satisfaction to find that my account of the *ousel migration* pleases you. You put a very shrewd question when you ask me how I know that their autumnal migration is southward? Was not candour and openness the very life of natural history, I should pass over this query just as a sly commentator does over a crabbed passage in a classic; but common ingenuousness obliges me to confess, not without some degree of shame, that I only reasoned in that case from analogy. For as all other autumnal birds migrate from the northward to us, to partake of our milder winters, and return to the northward again when the rigorous cold abates, so I concluded that the ring-ousels did the same, as well as their congeners the fieldfares; and especially as ring-ousels are known to haunt cold mountainous countries: but I have good reason to suspect since that they may come to us from the westward; because I hear, from very good authority, that they breed on Dartmoor; and that they forsake that wild district about the time that our visitors appear, and do not return till late in the spring.

I have taken a great deal of pains about your *salicaria* and mine, with a white stroke over it's eye and a tawny rump. I have surveyed it alive and dead, and have procured several specimens; and am perfectly persuaded myself (and trust you will soon be convinced of the same) that it is no more nor less than the *passer arundinaceus minor* of Ray. This bird, by some means or other, seems to be entirely omitted in the *British Zoology*; and one reason probably was because it is so strangely classed in Ray, who ranges it among his *picis affines*. It ought no doubt to have gone among his *aviculæ caudâ unicolore*, and among your slender-billed small birds of the same division. Linnæus might with great propriety have put it into his genus of *motacilla*; and the *motacilla salicaria* of his *fauna suecica* seems to come the nearest to it. It is no uncommon bird, haunting the sides of ponds and rivers where there is covert, and the reeds and sedges of moors. The country people in some places call it the *sedge-bird.* It sings incessantly night and day during the breeding-time, imitating the note of a sparrow, a swallow, a sky-lark; and has a strange hurrying manner in it's song. My specimens correspond most minutely to the description of your *fen salicaria* shot near Revesby. Mr. Ray has given an excellent characteristic of it when he says, "*Rostrum & pedes in hâc aviculâ multò majores sunt quâm pro corporis ratione.*" See letter May 29, 1769.

I have got you the egg of an *oedicnemus*, or stone-curlew, which was picked up in a fallow on the naked ground: there were two; but the finder inadvertently crushed one with his foot before he saw them.

When I wrote to you last year on reptiles, I wish I had not forgot to mention the faculty that snakes have of stinking *se defendendo.* I know a gentleman* who kept a tame snake, which was in it's person as sweet as any animal while in good humour and unalarmed; but as soon as a stranger, or a dog or cat, came in, it fell to hissing, and filled the room with such nauseous effluvia as rendered it hardly supportable. Thus the squnck, or stonck, of Ray's *Synop. Quadr.* is an innocuous and sweet animal; but, when pressed hard by dogs and men, it can eject such a most pestilent and fetid smell and excrement, that nothing can be more horrible.

A gentleman sent me lately a fine specimen† of the *lanius minor cinerascens cum maculâ in scapulis albâ, Raii;* which is a bird that, at the time of your publishing your two first volumes of *British Zoology*, I find you had not seen. You have described it well from *Edwards*'s drawing.

* Sampson Newberg of Devon.

† The woodchat, a very occasional visitor of the shrike genus, and a larger relation of the butcher-bird.

LETTER XXVI

TO THE SAME

Selborne, *December* 8, 1769.

DEAR SIR,

I was much gratified by your communicative letter on your return from Scotland, where you spent, I find, some considerable time, and gave yourself good room to examine the natural curiosities of that extensive kingdom, both those of the islands, as well as those of the highlands. The usual bane of such expeditions is hurry; because men seldom allot themselves half the time they should do: but, fixing on a day for their return, post from place to place, rather as if they were on a journey that required dispatch, than as philosophers investigating the works of nature. You must have made, no doubt, many discoveries, and laid up a good fund of materials for a future edition of the *British Zoology*; and will have no reason to repent that you have bestowed so much pains on a part of Great-Britain that perhaps was never so well examined before.

It has always been matter of wonder to me that fieldfares, which are so congenerous to thrushes and blackbirds, should never chuse to breed in England: but that they should not think even the highlands cold and northerly, and sequestered enough, is a circumstance still more strange and wonderful. The ring-ousel, you find, stays in Scotland the whole year round;* so that we have reason to conclude that those migrators that visit us for a short space every autumn do not come from thence.

And here, I think, will be the proper place to mention that those birds were most punctual again in their migration this autumn, appearing, as before, about the 30th of September: but their flocks were larger than common, and their stay protracted somewhat beyond the usual time. If they came to spend the whole winter with us, as some of their congeners do, and then left us, as they do, in spring, I should not be so much struck with the occurrence, since it would be similar to that of the other

* Another Pennant error.

winter birds of passage; but when I see them for a fortnight at Michaelmas, and again for about a week in the middle of April, I am seized with wonder, and long to be informed whence these travellers come, and whither they go, since they seem to use our hills merely as an inn or baiting place.*

Your account of the greater brambling, or snow-fleck,† is very amusing; and strange it is that such a short-winged bird should delight in such perilous voyages over the northern ocean! Some country people in the winter time have every now and then told me that they have seen two or three white larks on our downs; but, on considering the matter, I begin to suspect that these are some stragglers of the birds we are talking of, which sometimes perhaps may rove so far to the southward.

It pleases me to find that white hares‡ are so frequent on the Scottish mountains, and especially as you inform me that it is a distinct species; for the quadrupeds of Britain are so few, that every new species is a great acquisition.

The eagle-owl, could it be proved to belong to us, is so majestic a bird, that it would grace our *fauna* much. I never was informed before where wild-geese§ are known to breed.

You admit, I find, that I have proved your *fen-salicaria* to be the lesser reed-sparrow of Ray: and I think you may be secure that I am right; for I took very particular pains to clear up that matter, and had some fair specimens; but, as they were not well preserved, they are decayed already. You will, no doubt, insert it in it's proper place in your next edition. Your additional plates will much improve your work.

De Buffon, I know, has described the water shrew-mouse:|| but still I am pleased to find you have discovered it in Lincolnshire, for the reason I have given in the article of the white hare.

As a neighbour was lately plowing in a dry chalky field, far removed from any water, he turned out a water-rat, that was curiously laid up in an *hybernaculum* artificially formed of grass

* To bait = "to stop at an inn" (*Oxford Dict.*).

† The snow bunting. Present in the south of England during severe winters.

‡ The blue or mountain hare with a white coat in winter.

§ The Grey Lag Goose. "Now it nests only in Scotland and some of the Hebridean islands" (T. A. Coward). Two flocks were reported over the county by the Hampshire Field Club in 1936.

|| Widely distributed.

and leaves. At one end of the *burrow* lay above a gallon of potatoes regularly stowed, on which it was to have supported itself for the winter. But the difficulty with me is how this *amphibius mus* came to fix it's winter station at such a distance from the water. Was it determined in it's choice of that place by the mere accident of finding the potatoes which were planted there; or is it the constant practice of the aquatic-rat to forsake the neighbourhood of the water in the colder months?

Though I delight very little in analogous reasoning, knowing how fallacious it is with respect to natural history; yet, in the following instance, I cannot help being inclined to think it may conduce towards the explanation of a difficulty that I have mentioned before, with respect to the invariable early retreat of the *hirundo apus*, or swift, so many weeks before it's congeners; and that not only with us, but also in Andalusia, where they also begin to retire about the beginning of August.

The great large bat*† (which by the by is at present a nondescript in England, and what I have never been able yet to procure) retires or migrates very early in the summer: it also ranges very high for it's food, feeding in a different region of the air; and that is the reason I never could procure one. Now this is exactly the case with the swifts; for they take their food in a more exalted region than the other species, and are very seldom seen hawking for flies near the ground, or over the surface of the water. From hence I would conclude that these *hirundines*, and the larger bats, are supported by some sorts of high-flying gnats, scarabs, or *phalænæ*, that are of short continuance; and that the short stay of these strangers is regulated by the defect of their food.

By my journal it appears that curlews‡ clamoured on to October the thirty-first; since which I have not seen or heard any. Swallows were observed on to November the third.

* *The little bat appears almost every month in the year; but I have never seen the large ones till the end of April, nor after July. They are most common in June, but never in any plenty: are a rare species with us.* ⟨G. W.⟩

† The noctule, discovered by the author.

‡ White never met the common curlew, a bird of the coast and inland moors. He means the stone curlew.

LETTER XXVII

TO THE SAME

Selborne, *Feb.* 22, 1770.

DEAR SIR,

Hedge-hogs abound in my gardens and fields. The manner in which they eat their roots of the plantain in my grass-walks is very curious: with their upper mandible, which is much longer than their lower, they bore under the plant, and so eat the root off upwards, leaving the tuft of leaves untouched. In this respect they are serviceable, as they destroy a very troublesome weed; but they deface the walks in some measure by digging little round holes. It appears, by the dung that they drop upon the turf, that beetles are no inconsiderable part of their food. In June last I procured a litter of four or five young hedge-hogs, which appeared to be about five or six days old; they, I find, like puppies, are born blind, and could not see when they came to my hands. No doubt their spines are soft and flexible at the time of their birth, or else the poor dam would have but a bad time of it in the critical moment of parturition: but it is plain that they soon harden; for these little pigs had such stiff prickles on their backs and sides as would easily have fetched blood, had they not been handled with caution. Their spines are quite white at this age; and they have little hanging ears, which I do not remember to be discernible in the old ones. They can, in part, at this age draw their skin down over their faces; but are not able to contract themselves into a ball, as they do, for the sake of defence, when full grown. The reason, I suppose, is, because the curious muscle that enables the creature to roll itself up in a ball was not then arrived at it's full tone and firmness.* Hedge-hogs make a deep and warm *hybernaculum* with leaves and moss, in which they conceal themselves for the winter: but I never could find that they stored in any winter provision, as some quadrupeds certainly do.

* Bell recalls a hedgehog deliberately falling ten feet on stones without injury, owing to being rolled up in a ball.

I have discovered an anecdote* with respect to the fieldfare (*turdus pilaris*), which I think is particular enough: this bird, though it sits on trees in the day-time, and procures the greatest part of it's food from whitethorn hedges; yea, moreover, builds on very high trees; as may be seen by the *fauna suecica*; yet always appears with us to roost on the ground. They are seen to come in flocks just before it is dark, and to settle and nestle among the heath on our forest. And besides, the larkers, in dragging their nets by night, frequently catch them in the wheat-stubbles; while the bat-fowlers, who take many red-wings in the hedges, never entangle any of this species. Why these birds, in the matter of roosting, should differ from all their congeners, and from themselves also with respect to their proceedings by day, is a fact for which I am by no means able to account.

I have somewhat to inform you of concerning the *moose-deer*; but in general foreign animals fall seldom in my way: my little intelligence is confined to the narrow sphere of my own observations at home.

* Not a tale but a record in the raw.

LETTER XXVIII

TO THE SAME

Selborne, *March* 1770.

On Michaelmas-day 1768 I managed to get a sight of the female moose belonging to the duke of Richmond, at Goodwood; but was greatly disappointed, when I arrived at the spot, to find that it died, after having appeared in a languishing way for some time, on the morning before. However, understanding that it was not stripped, I proceeded to examine this rare quadruped: I found it in an old green-house, slung under the belly and chin by ropes, and in a standing posture; but, though it had been dead for so short a time, it was in so putrid a state that the stench was hardly supportable. The grand distinction between this deer, and any other species that I have ever met with, consisted in the strange length of it's legs; on which it was tilted up much in the manner of the birds of the *grallæ* order. I measured it, as they do an horse, and found that, from the ground to the wither, it was just five feet four inches; which height answers exactly to sixteen hands, a growth that few horses arrive at: but then, with this length of legs, it's neck was remarkably short, no more than twelve inches; so that, by straddling with one foot forward and the other backward, it grazed on the plain ground, with the greatest difficulty, between it's legs: the ears were vast and lopping, and as long as the neck; the head was about twenty inches long, and ass-like; and had such a redundancy of upper lip as I never saw before, with huge nostrils. The lip, travellers say, is esteemed a dainty dish in North America. It is very reasonable to suppose that this creature supports itself chiefly by browsing of trees, and by wading after water plants; towards which way of livelihood the length of legs and great lip must contribute much. I have read somewhere that it delights in eating the *nymphæa*, or water-lily. From the fore-feet to the belly behind the shoulder it measured three feet and eight inches: the length of the legs before and behind consisted a great deal in the *tibia*, which was strangely long; but, in my haste to get out of the stench, I forgot to measure that joint exactly. It's scut seemed to be about an inch long; the colour was a grizzly black; the mane about four inches long; the fore-hoofs were upright and shapely, the hind flat and splayed. The spring before it was only two years old, so that most probably it was not then come to it's growth. What a vast tall beast must a full grown stag be! I have been told some arrive at ten feet and an half! This poor creature had at first a female companion of the same species, which died the spring before. In the same garden was a young stag, or red deer, between whom and this moose it was hoped that there might have been a breed; but their inequality of height must have always been a bar to any commerce of the amorous kind. I should have been glad to have examined the teeth, tongue, lips, hoofs, &c. minutely; but the putrefaction precluded all farther curiosity. This animal, the keeper told me, seemed to enjoy itself best in the extreme frost of the former winter. In the house they shewed me the horn of a male moose, which had no front-antlers, but only a broad palm with some snags on the edge. The noble owner of the dead moose proposed to make a skeleton of her bones.

Please to let me hear if my female moose corresponds with that you saw; and whether you think still that the American moose and European elk are the same creature.* I am,

With the greatest esteem, &c.

* They are.

LETTER XXIX

TO THE SAME

Selborne, *May* 12, 1770.

DEAR SIR,

Last month we had such a series of cold turbulent weather, such a constant succession of frost, and snow, and hail, and tempest, that the regular migration or appearance of the summer birds was much interrupted. Some did not shew themselves (at least were not heard) till weeks after their usual time; as the *black-cap* and *white-throat*; and some have not been heard yet, as the *grasshopper-lark* and largest *willow-wren*. As to the *fly-catcher*, I have not seen it; it is indeed one of the latest, but should appear about this time: and yet, amidst all this meteorous strife and war of the elements, two swallows discovered themselves as long ago as the eleventh of April, in frost and snow; but they withdrew quickly, and were not visible again for many days. House-martins, which are always more backward than swallows, were not observed till May came in.

Among the *monogamous* birds several are to be found, after pairing-time, single, and of each sex: but whether this state of celibacy* is matter of choice or necessity, is not so easily discoverable. When the house-sparrows deprive my martins of their nests, as soon as I cause one to be shot, the other, be it cock or hen, presently procures a mate, and so for several times following.

I have known a dove-house infested by a pair of white owls, which made great havock among the young pigeons: one of the owls was shot as soon as possible; but the survivor readily found a mate, and the mischief went on. After some time the new pair were both destroyed, and the annoyance ceased.†

Another instance I remember of a sportsman, whose zeal for the increase of his game being greater than his humanity, after

* Birds, that is to say, which have failed to secure nesting sites. They fill up any losses among the nesting pairs.

† It is rare for barn-owls to feed upon other birds, a commoner prey of the tawny owl. Waterton in his *Essays* champions them altogether from bird-eating.

pairing-time he always shot the cock-bird of every couple of partridges upon his grounds; supposing that the rivalry of many males interrupted the breed: he used to say, that, though he had widowed the same hen several times, yet he found she was still provided with a fresh paramour, that did not take her away from her usual haunt.

Again; I knew a lover of setting, an old sportsman, who has often told me that soon after harvest he has frequently taken small coveys of partridges, consisting of cock-birds alone; these he pleasantly used to call old bachelors.

There is a propensity belonging to common house-cats that is very remarkable; I mean their violent fondness for fish, which appears to be their most favourite food: and yet nature in this instance seems to have planted in them an appetite that, unassisted, they know not how to gratify: for of all quadrupeds cats are the least disposed towards water; and will not, when they can avoid it, deign to wet a foot, much less to plunge into that element.

Quadrupeds that prey on fish are amphibious: such is the otter, which by nature is so well formed for diving, that it makes great havock among the inhabitants of the waters. Not supposing that we had any of those beasts in our shallow brooks, I was much pleased to see a male otter brought to me, weighing twenty-one pounds, that had been shot on the bank of our stream below the Priory, where the rivulet divides the parish of Selborne from Harteley-wood.

LETTER XXXI

TO THE SAME

Selborne, *Sept.* 14, 1770.

DEAR SIR,

You saw, I find, the ring-ousels again among their native crags; and are farther assured that they continue resident in those cold regions the whole year. From whence then do our ring-ousels migrate so regularly every September, and make their appearance again, as if in their return, every April? They are more early this year than common, for some were seen at the usual hill on the fourth of this month.

An observing Devonshire gentleman tells me that they frequent some parts of Dartmoor, and breed there; but leave those haunts about the end of September or beginning of October, and return again about the end of March.

Another intelligent person assures me that they breed in great abundance all over the Peak of Derby, and are called there *Tor-ousels*; withdraw in October and November, and return in spring. This information seems to throw some light on my new migration.

Scopoli's* new work (which I have just procured) has it's merit in ascertaining many of the birds of the *Tirol* and *Carniola*. Monographers, come from whence they may, have, I think, fair pretence to challenge some regard and approbation from the lovers of natural history; for, as no man can alone investigate all the works of nature, these partial writers may, each in their department, be more accurate in their discoveries, and freer from errors, than more general writers; and so by degrees may pave the way to an universal correct natural history. Not that Scopoli is so circumstantial and attentive to the life and conversation of his birds as I could wish: he advances some false facts; as when he says of the *hirundo urbica* that "*pullos extra nidum non nutrit*". This assertion I know to be wrong from repeated observation this summer; for house-martins do feed their young flying,

* *Annus Primus Historico-Naturalis.* ⟨G. W.⟩

though it must be acknowledged not so commonly as the house-swallow; and the feat is done in so quick a manner as not to be perceptible to indifferent observers. He also advances some (I was going to say) improbable facts; as when he says of the woodcock that "*pullos rostro portat fugiens ab hoste*".* But candour forbids me to say absolutely that any fact is false, because I have never been witness to such a fact. I have only to remark that the long unweildy bill of the woodcock is perhaps the worst adapted of any among the winged creation for such a feat of natural affection.

I am, &c.

* Scopoli was right. In case of danger, the mother bird does carry her young either between the thighs or by the feet. Ornithologists bandy argument as to which method is adopted. Coward sensibly suggested both methods. When birds are regarded once more as living beings, instead of biological automata, as they are now, it will be granted that members of the same species can and do perform the same act in different ways. But that day is not yet. The serene open-mindedness of the author is very noticeable in this passage, a jewel on the forehead of science, which it is only too ready to barter for dogma. But he cherished it always.

LETTER XXXV

TO THE SAME

Selborne, 1771.

DEAR SIR,

Happening to make a visit to my neighbour's peacocks, I could not help observing that the trains of those magnificent birds appear by no means to be their tails; those long feathers growing not from their *uropygium*, but all up their backs. A range of short brown stiff feathers, about six inches long, fixed in the *uropygium*, is the real tail, and serves as the *fulcrum* to prop the train, which is long and top-heavy, when set on end. When the train is up, nothing appears of the bird before but it's head and neck; but this would not be the case were those long feathers fixed only in the rump, as may be seen by the turkey-cock when in a strutting attitude. By a strong muscular vibration these birds can make the shafts of their long feathers clatter like the swords of a sword-dancer; they then trample very quick with their feet, and run backwards towards the females.

I should tell you that I have got an uncommon *calculus ægogropila*, taken out of the stomach of a fat ox; it is perfectly round, and about the size of a large Seville orange; such are, I think, usually flat.

LETTER XXXVI

TO THE SAME

Sept. 1771.

DEAR SIR,

The summer through I have seen but two of that large species of bat* which I call *vespertilio altivolans*, from it's manner of feeding high in the air: I procured one of them, and found it to be a male; and made no doubt, as they accompanied together, that the other was a female: but, happening in an evening or two to procure the other likewise, I was somewhat disappointed, when it appeared to be also of the same sex. This circumstance, and the great scarcity of this sort, at least in these parts, occasions some suspicions in my mind whether it is really a species, or whether it may not be the male part of the more known species, one of which may supply many females; as is known to be the case in sheep, and some other quadrupeds. But this doubt can only be cleared by a farther examination, and some attention to the sex, of more specimens: all that I know at present is, that my two were amply furnished with the parts of generation much resembling those of a boar.

In the extent of their wings they measured fourteen inches and an half; and four inches and an half from the nose to the tip of the tail: their heads were large, their nostrils bilobated, their shoulders broad and muscular; and their whole bodies fleshy and plump. Nothing could be more sleek and soft than their fur, which was of a bright chesnut colour; their maws were full of food, but so macerated that the quality could not be distinguished; their livers, kidnies, and hearts, were large, and their bowels covered with fat. They weighed each, when entire, full one ounce and one drachm. Within the ear there was somewhat of a peculiar structure† that I did not understand perfectly; but refer it to the observation of the curious anatomist. These creatures sent forth a very rancid and offensive smell.

* The noctule.
† The *tragus*. Vestigiary in man. See Harting's Edition.

LETTER XXXVII

TO THE SAME

Selborne, 1771.

DEAR SIR,

On the twelfth of July I had a fair opportunity of contemplating the motions of the *caprimulgus*, or fern-owl, as it was playing round a large oak that swarmed with *scarabæi solstitiales*, or fern-chafers. The powers of it's wing were wonderful, exceeding, if possible, the various evolutions and quick turns of the swallow genus. But the circumstance that pleased me most was, that I saw it distinctly, more than once, put out it's short leg while on the wing, and, by a bend of the head, deliver somewhat into it's mouth. If it takes any part of it's prey with it's foot, as I have now the greatest reason to suppose it does these chafers, I no longer wonder at the use of it's middle toe, which is curiously furnished with a serrated claw.

Swallows and martins, the bulk of them I mean, have forsaken us sooner this year than usual; for, on September the twenty-second, they rendezvoused in a neighbour's walnut-tree, where it seemed probable they had taken up their lodging for the night. At the dawn of the day, which was foggy, they arose all together in infinite numbers, occasioning such a rushing from the strokes of their wings against the hazy air, as might be heard to a considerable distance: since that no flock has appeared, only a few stragglers.

Some swifts staid late, till the twenty-second of August—a rare instance! for they usually withdraw within the first week.*†

On September the twenty-fourth three or four ring-ousels appeared in my fields for the first time this season: how punctual are these visitors in their autumnal and spring migrations!

* *See Letter LII to Mr. Barrington.* ⟨G. W.⟩

† In our generation, the swift certainly leaves us later in the month. But we have rifled only fragments of Nature's huge store-room of secrets. Why has the swift decided to go abroad a fortnight later than it did 160 years ago?

LETTER XXXIX

TO THE SAME

Dear Sir,

Selborne, *Nov.* 9, 1773.

As you desire me to send you such observations as may occur, I take the liberty of making the following remarks, that you may, according as you think me right or wrong, admit or reject what I here advance, in your intended new edition of the *British Zoology*.

The osprey was shot about a year ago at Frinsham-pond, a great lake, at about six miles from hence, while it was sitting on the handle of a plough and devouring a fish: it used to precipitate itself into the water, and so take it's prey by surprise.

A great ash-coloured butcher-bird* was shot last winter in Tisted-park, and a red-backed butcher-bird at Selborne: they are *raræ aves* in this county.

Crows go in pairs the whole year round.

Cornish choughs† abound, and breed on Beachy-head and on all the cliffs of the Sussex coast.

The common wild-pigeon, or stock-dove,‡ is a bird of passage in the south of England, seldom appearing till towards the end

* The Great Grey Shrike, a winter visitor to the east coast in sparse numbers.

† Long exterminated from Sussex, and very rare nowadays even on Cornish cliffs, its headquarters. See Letter VII to Barrington.

‡ Both wood-pigeon (ring-dove) and stock-dove (without the wing-bar) breed with us.

of November; is usually the latest winter-bird of passage. Before our beechen woods were so much destroyed we had myriads of them, reaching in strings for a mile together as they went out in a morning to feed. They leave us early in spring; where do they breed?

The people of Hampshire and Sussex call the missel-bird the storm-cock, because it sings early in the spring in blowing showery weather; it's song often commences with the year: with us it builds much in orchards.

A gentleman assures me he has taken the nests of ring-ousels on Dartmoor: they build in banks on the sides of streams.

Titlarks* not only sing sweetly as they sit on trees, but also as they play and toy about on the wing; and particularly while they are descending, and sometimes as they stand on the ground.

Adanson's testimony seems to me to be a very poor evidence that European swallows migrate during our winter to Senegal: he does not talk at all like an ornithologist; and probably saw only the swallows of that country,† which I know build within Governor O'Hara's hall against the roof. Had he known European swallows, would he not have mentioned the species?

The *house-swallow* washes by dropping into the water as it flies: this species appears commonly about a week before the *house-martin*, and about ten or twelve days before the *swift*.

In 1772 there were young house-martins in their nest till October the twenty-third.‡

The *swift* appears about *ten* or *twelve* days later than the *house-swallow*: viz. about the twenty-fourth or twenty-sixth of April.

Whin-chats and *stone-chatters* stay with us the whole year.§

Some wheat-ears continue with us the winter through.

Wagtails, all sorts, remain with us all the winter.

Bulfinches, when fed on hempseed, often become wholly black.||

* This is the tree-pipit, a distinct species from the meadow-pipit.

† Nevertheless, Adanson was right.

‡ House-martins have been known exceptionally to rear four broods in a season. Sir William Beach-Thomas gives an example.

§ True for the stonechat but not for the whinchat. The yellow wagtail is also a summer migrant.

|| Coleridge in the notes to his copy of *Selborne* says that he saw a canary at Göttingen "changed to a light black" by hempseed.

We have vast flocks of *female* chaffinches all the winter, with hardly any males among them.

When you say that in breeding-time the cock-snipes make a bleating noise, and I a drumming (perhaps I should have rather said an humming), I suspect we mean the same thing. However, while they are playing about on the wing they certainly make a loud piping with their mouths: but whether that bleating or humming is ventriloquous, or proceeds from the motion of their wings, I cannot say; but this I know, that when this noise happens the bird is always descending, and his wings are violently agitated.

Soon after the lapwings have done breeding they congregate, and, leaving the moors and marshes, betake themselves to downs and sheep-walks.

Two years ago last spring the little auk* was found alive and unhurt, but fluttering and unable to rise, in a lane a few miles from Alresford, where there is a great lake: it was kept awhile, but died.

I saw young teals taken alive in the ponds of Wolmer-forest in the beginning of July† last, along with flappers, or young wild-ducks.

Speaking of the *swift*, that page says "*it's drink the dew*"; whereas it should be "it drinks on the wing"; for all the swallow kind sip their water as they sweep over the face of pools or rivers: like Virgil's bees, they drink flying; "*flumina summa libant*". In this method of drinking perhaps this genus may be peculiar.

Of the sedge-bird be pleased to say it sings most part of the night; it's notes are hurrying, but not unpleasing, and imitative of several birds; as the sparrow, swallow, sky-lark. When it happens to be silent in the night, by throwing a stone or clod into the bushes where it sits you immediately set it a singing; or in other words, though it slumbers sometimes, yet as soon as it is awakened it reassumes it's song.

* Doubtless driven inland by sea gales.

† This date does not tally with the one given in a letter to John White of June 26, 1773 in which is written: "Some boys killed lately at Oakhanger-ponds some flappers or young wild-ducks; among the rest they took some young teals alive." The earlier date is certainly the correct one.

LETTER XL

TO THE SAME

Selborne, *Sept.* 2, 1774.

Dear Sir,

Before your letter arrived, and of my own accord, I had been remarking and comparing the tails of the male and female swallow, and this ere any young broods appeared; so that there was no danger of confounding the dams with their *pulli*: and besides, as they were then always in pairs, and busied in the employ of nidification, there could be no room for mistaking the sexes, nor the individuals of different chimnies the one for the other. From all my observations, it constantly appeared that each sex has the long feathers in it's tail that give it that forked shape; with this difference, that they are longer in the tail of the male than in that of the female.

Nightingales, when their young first come abroad, and are helpless, make a plaintive and a jarring noise; and also a snapping or cracking, pursuing people along the hedges as they walk: these last sounds seem intended for menace and defiance.

The grasshopper-lark chirps* all night in the height of summer.

Swans turn white the second year, and breed the third.

Weasels prey on moles, as appears by their being sometimes caught in mole-traps.

Sparrow-hawks sometimes breed in old crows' nests, and the kestril in churches and ruins.

There are supposed to be two sorts of eels in the island of Ely. The threads sometimes discovered in eels are perhaps their young: the generation of eels is very dark and mysterious.†

* The grasshopper-warbler's song is like the fly-fisher's reel when he is casting, so that the abrupt impression of "chirp" is not apposite. But White is here delivering information to the unworthy Pennant by the load, and so his memoranda lack the exquisite precision of his description of the same bird in Letter XVI. The grasshopper-warbler breeds chiefly in north-east Hampshire, but only in small numbers.

† Even more mysterious though less dark now that their miraculous voyages to their spawning grounds in the Sargasso Sea, and the transformation of the larvae on their journey back to a home they have never seen, are known. The common eel is our only species and the "threads" are parasitic worms.

Hen-harriers breed on the ground, and seem never to settle on trees.

When redstarts shake their tails they move them horizontally, as dogs do when they fawn: the tail of a wagtail, when in motion, bobs up and down like that of a jaded horse.*

Hedge-sparrows have a remarkable flirt with their wings in breeding-time; as soon as frosty mornings come they make a very piping plaintive noise.

Many birds which become silent about Midsummer reassume their notes again in September; as the thrush, blackbird,† woodlark,‡ willow-wren, &c.; hence August is by much the most mute month, the spring, summer, and autumn through. Are birds induced to sing again because the temperament of autumn resembles that of spring?

Linnæus ranges plants geographically; palms inhabit the tropics, grasses the temperate zones, and mosses and lichens the polar circles; no doubt animals may be classed in the same manner with propriety.§

House-sparrows build under eaves in the spring; as the weather becomes hotter they get out for coolness, and nest in plum-trees and apple-trees. These birds have been known sometimes to build in rooks' nests, and sometimes in the forks of boughs under rooks' nests.

As my neighbour was housing a rick he observed that his dogs devoured all the little red mice|| that they could catch, but rejected the common mice; and that his cats ate the common mice, refusing the red.

Red-breasts sing all through the spring, summer, and autumn. The reason that they are called autumn songsters is, because in the two first seasons their voices are drowned and lost in the general chorus; in the latter their song becomes distinguishable. Many songsters of the autumn seem to be the young cock red-breasts of that year: notwithstanding the prejudices in their

* No poet could rival so inspired a comparison, in which observation and imagination become one. The same may be said of "the temperament of autumn" lower down.

† The blackbird does not resume its song after the moult.

‡ "Numerous in N.E. Hants." (*Hampshire Field Club Papers*, vol. XIII, p. 272.)

§ This modest line anticipates the whole principle of modern zoology.

|| Harvest-mice.

favour, they do much mischief* in gardens to the summer-fruits.†

The titmouse, which early in February begins to make two quaint notes, like the whetting of a saw, is the marsh titmouse:‡ the great titmouse sings with three cheerful joyous notes, and begins about the same time.

Wrens sing all the winter through, frost excepted.§

House-martins came remarkably late this year both in Hampshire and Devonshire: is this circumstance for or against either hiding or migration?

Most birds drink sipping at intervals; but pigeons take a long continued draught, like quadrupeds.

Notwithstanding what I have said in a former letter, no grey crows were ever known to breed on Dartmoor; it was my mistake.

The appearance and flying of the *scarabæus solstitialis*, or fern-chafer, commence with the month of July, and cease about the end of it. These scarabs are the constant food of *caprimulgi*, or fern owls, through that period. They abound on the chalky downs and in some sandy districts, but not in the clays.

In the garden of the Black-bear inn in the town of Reading is a stream or canal running under the stables and out into the fields on the other side of the road: in this water are many carps, which lie rolling about in sight, being fed by travellers, who amuse themselves by tossing them bread: but as soon as the weather grows at all severe these fishes are no longer seen, because they retire under the stables, where they remain till the return of spring. Do they lie in a torpid state? if they do not, how are they supported?

* Robins are harmless in a garden, though they do take a few of my Alpine strawberries.

† *They eat also the berries of the ivy, the honey-suckle, and the* euonymus europæus, *or spindle-tree.* ⟨G. W.⟩

‡ The "saw-sharpener" is the great titmouse or oxeye. Mr. Nicholson suggests that the marsh-tit is here confused with the willow-tit, which has only recently been given specific rank and is more abundant at Selborne than the marsh-tit. In north-eastern Hampshire the reverse is true. The "whetting of a saw" applies to the great tit, and the "three cheerful joyous notes" more closely fit both the marsh- and the willow-tits.

§ Wrens will often sing in a crisp dry frost and under a sun that gilds without warming the hedgerows.

The note of the white-throat,* which is continually repeated, and often attended with odd gesticulations on the wing, is harsh and displeasing. These birds seem of a pugnacious disposition; for they sing with an erected crest and attitudes of rivalry and defiance; are shy and wild in breeding-time, avoiding neighbourhoods, and haunting lonely lanes and commons; nay even the very tops of the Sussex-downs, where there are bushes and covert; but in July and August they bring their broods into gardens and orchards, and make great havock among the summer-fruits.

The black-cap has in common a full, sweet, deep, loud, and wild pipe; yet that strain is of short continuance, and his motions are desultory; but when that bird sits calmly and engages in song in earnest, he pours forth very sweet, but inward melody, and expresses great variety of soft and gentle modulations, superior perhaps to those of any of our warblers, the nightingale excepted.

Black-caps mostly haunt orchards and gardens; while they warble their throats are wonderfully distended.

The song of the redstart is superior, though somewhat like that of the white-throat: some birds have a few more notes than others. Sitting very placidly on the top of a tall tree in a village, the cock sings from morning to night: he affects neighbourhoods, and avoids solitude, and loves to build in orchards and about houses; with us he perches on the vane of a tall maypole.

The fly-catcher is of all our summer birds the most mute and the most familiar; it also appears the last of any. It builds in a vine, or a sweetbriar, against the wall of an house, or in the hole of a wall, or on the end of a beam or plate, and often close to the post of a door where people are going in and out all day long. This bird does not make the least pretension to song,† but uses a little inward wailing note when it thinks it's young in danger from cats or other annoyances: it breeds but once, and retires early.

Selborne parish alone can and has exhibited at times more than half the birds that are ever seen in all Sweden; the former

* Voluble, excitable, impetuous, but hardly "displeasing", though the melody is more than a little throaty.

† Nevertheless, the flycatcher has a very faint "inward" song.

has produced more than one hundred and twenty species, the latter only two hundred and twenty-one. Let me add also that it has shewn near half the species that were ever known in Great-Britain.*†

On a retrospect, I observe that my long letter carries with it a quaint and magisterial air, and is very sententious; but, when I recollect that you requested stricture and anecdote, I hope you will pardon the didactic manner for the sake of the information it may happen to contain.

* *Sweden* 221, *Great-Britain* 252 *species.* <G. W.>

† The list now numbers 499, but nearly half of these are no more entitled to be on it than many men to be found in the Honours List.

LETTER XLI

TO THE SAME

It is matter of curious inquiry to trace out how those species of soft-billed birds, that continue with us the winter through, subsist during the dead months. The imbecility of birds seems not to be the only reason why they shun the rigour of our winters; for the robust *wry-neck* (so much resembling the hardy race of *wood-peckers*) migrates, while the feeble little *golden-crowned wren*, that shadow of a bird, braves our severest frosts without availing himself of houses or villages, to which most of our winter-birds crowd in distressful seasons, while this keeps aloof in fields and woods; but perhaps this may be the reason why they may often perish, and why they are almost as rare as any bird we know.

I have no reason to doubt but that the soft-billed birds, which winter with us, subsist chiefly on insects in their *aurelia* state. All the species of *wagtails* in severe weather haunt shallow streams near their spring-heads, where they never freeze; and, by wading, pick out the aurelias of the genus of* *Phryganeæ*, &c.

Hedge-sparrows frequent sinks and gutters in hard weather, where they pick up crumbs and other sweepings: and in mild weather they procure worms, which are stirring every month in the year, as any one may see that will only be at the trouble of taking a candle to a grass-plot on any mild winter's night. Red-breasts and wrens in the winter haunt out-houses, stables, and barns, where they find spiders and flies that have laid themselves up during the cold season. But the grand support of the soft-billed birds in winter is that infinite profusion of *aureliæ* of the *lepidoptera ordo*, which is fastened to the twigs of trees and their trunks; to the pales and walls of gardens and buildings; and is found in every cranny and cleft of rock or rubbish, and even in the ground itself.

Every species of titmouse winters with us; they have what I call a kind of intermediate bill between the hard and the soft,

* *See Derham's* Physico-theology, *p.* 235. ⟨G. W.⟩

between the Linnæan genera of *fringilla* and *motacilla*. One species alone spends it's whole time in the woods and fields, never retreating for succour in the severest seasons to houses and neighbourhoods; and that is the delicate long-tailed titmouse, which is almost as minute as the golden-crowned wren: but the blue titmouse, or nun (*parus cæruleus*), the cole-mouse (*parus ater*), the great black-headed titmouse (*fringillago*), and the marsh titmouse (*parus palustris*), all resort, at times, to buildings; and in hard weather particularly. The great titmouse, driven by stress of weather, much frequents houses; and, in deep snows, I have seen this bird, while it hung with it's back downwards (to my no small delight and admiration), draw straws lengthwise from out the eaves of thatched houses, in order to pull out the flies that were concealed between them, and that in such numbers that they quite defaced the thatch, and gave it a ragged appearance.*

The blue *titmouse*, or *nun*, is a great frequenter of houses, and a general devourer. Besides insects, it is very fond of flesh; for it frequently picks bones on dunghills: it is a vast admirer of suet, and haunts butchers' shops. When a boy, I have known twenty in a morning caught with snap mouse-traps, baited with tallow or suet. It will also pick holes in apples left on the ground, and be well entertained with the seeds on the head of a sunflower. The blue, marsh, and great titmice will, in very severe weather, carry away barley and oat straws from the sides of ricks.

How the *wheat-ear* and *whin-chat*† support themselves in winter cannot be so easily ascertained, since they spend their time on wild heaths and warrens: the former especially, where there are stone quarries: most probably it is that their maintenance arises from the *aureliæ* of the *lepidoptera ordo*,‡ which furnish them with a plentiful table in the wilderness.

I am, &c.

* Owing to the decline of agriculture and the consequent reversion of arable to pasture, the same problem more acutely confronts the contemporary thatcher who, much reduced in numbers, is compelled to spend the most of his time in repairing thatched roofs that would have lasted twice as long if lack of colour had not abandoned them to the birds.

† Both migrants. The former is a diminishing species in Hampshire.

‡ Namely butterflies and moths in the chrysalid stage.

LETTER XLIII

TO THE SAME

A pair of *honey-buzzards*,* *buteo apivorus, sive vespivorus Raii*, built them a large shallow nest, composed of twigs and lined with dead beechen leaves, upon a tall slender beech near the middle of Selborne-hanger, in the summer of 1780. In the middle of the month of June a bold boy climbed this tree, though standing on so steep and dizzy a situation, and brought down an egg, the only one in the nest, which had been sat on for some time, and contained the embrio of a young bird. The egg was smaller, and not so round as those of the common buzzard; was dotted at each end with small red spots, and surrounded in the middle with a broad bloody zone.†

The hen-bird was shot, and answered exactly to Mr. Ray's

* Egg-collectors exterminated this fine hawk as an English breeding species. Mr. Nicholson, prince of observers as he is, has a laughable note here. He quotes another entry from the *Naturalist's Journal* of June, 1781: "The male still haunts about the Hanger, and on sunny mornings soars above the hill to inhale the coolness of the upper air." His own comment is as follows: "As a modern observer would say, to make the fact of his holding territory there as conspicuous as possible to prospective rivals and a prospective mate." Of course, in enjoying the soaring bird, we were forgetting that men of science have to make a living.

† The honey-buzzard's egg is much darker, rounder and more richly smeared and blotched with mahogany than the common buzzard's.

description of that species; had a black *cere*, short thick legs, and a long tail. When on the wing this species may be easily distinguished from the *common buzzard* by it's hawk-like appearance, small head, wings not so blunt, and longer tail. This specimen contained in it's craw some limbs of frogs and many grey snails without shells. The *irides* of the eyes of this bird were of a beautiful bright yellow colour.

About the tenth of July in the same summer a pair of *sparrow-hawks* bred in an old crow's nest on a low beech in the same hanger; and as their brood, which was numerous, began to grow up, became so daring and ravenous, that they were a terror to all the dames in the village that had chickens or ducklings under their care. A boy climbed the tree, and found the young so fledged that they all escaped from him; but discovered that a good house had been kept: the larder was well-stored with provisions; for he brought down a young blackbird, jay, and house-martin, all clean picked, and some half devoured. The old birds had been observed to make sad havock for some days among the new-flown swallows and martins, which, being but lately out of their nests, had not acquired those powers and command of wing that enable them, when more mature, to set such enemies at defiance.

LETTER XLIV

TO THE SAME

Selborne, *Nov*. 30, 1780.

DEAR SIR,

Every incident that occasions a renewal of our correspondence will ever be pleasing and agreeable to me.

As to the wild *wood-pigeon*,* the *oenas*, or *vinago*, of Ray, I am much of your mind; and see no reason for making it the origin of the common *house-dove*: but suppose those that have advanced that opinion may have been misled by another appellation, often given to the *oenas*, which is that of *stock-dove*.

Unless the stock-dove in the winter varies greatly in manners from itself in summer, no species seems more unlikely to be domesticated, and to make an *house-dove*. We very rarely see the latter settle on trees at all, nor does it ever haunt the woods; but the former, as long as it stays with us, from November perhaps to February, lives the same wild life with the *ring-dove*, *palumbus torquatus*; frequents coppices and groves, supports itself chiefly by mast, and delights to roost in the tallest beeches. Could it be known in what manner stock-doves build, the doubt would be settled with me at once, provided they construct their nests on trees, like the *ring-dove*, as I much suspect they do.

You received, you say, last spring a *stock-dove* from Sussex; and are informed that they sometimes breed in that country. But why did not your correspondent determine the place of it's nidification, whether on rocks, cliffs, or trees? If he was not an adroit ornithologist I should doubt the fact, because people with us perpetually confound the *stock-dove* with the *ring-dove*.

For my own part, I readily concur with you in supposing that house-doves are derived from the *small blue rock-pigeon*, for

* The name is used in its descriptive, not its specific sense, which applies to the ring-dove. Stock-doves breed in rabbit-burrows, holes in trees, rock-fissures, squirrel dreys, ruins and cathedrals, never in tree-tops like the ring-dove. In deriving the domesticated pigeon from the rock-dove, the author shows great prescience.

many reasons. In the first place the wild stock-dove is manifestly larger than the common house-dove, against the usual rule of domestication, which generally enlarges the breed. Again, those two remarkable *black spots* on the remiges of each wing of the stock-dove, which are so characteristic of the species, would not, one should think, be totally lost by it's being reclaimed; but would often break out among its descendants. But what is worth an hundred arguments is, the instance you give in Sir Roger Mostyn's house-doves in Caernarvonshire; which, though tempted by plenty of food and gentle treatment, can never be prevailed on to inhabit their cote for any time; but, as soon as they begin to breed, betake themselves to the fastnesses of Ormshead, and deposit their young in safety amidst the inaccessible caverns, and precipices of that stupendous promontory.

Naturam expellas furcâ . . . tamen usque recurret.

I have consulted a sportsman, now in his seventy-eighth year, who tells me that fifty or sixty years back, when the beechen woods were much more extensive than at present, the number of wood-pigeons was astonishing; that he has often killed near twenty in a day; and that with a long wild-fowl piece he has shot seven or eight at a time on the wing as they came wheeling over his head: he moreover adds, which I was not aware of, that often there were among them little parties of small *blue doves*, which he calls *rockiers*. The food of these numberless emigrants was beech-mast and some acorns; and particularly barley, which they collected in the stubbles. But of late years, since the vast increase of turnips, that vegetable has furnished a great part of their support in hard weather; and the holes they pick in these roots greatly damage the crop. From this food their flesh has contracted a rancidness which occasions them to be rejected by nicer judges of eating, who thought them before a delicate dish. They were shot not only as they were feeding in the fields, and especially in snowy weather, but also at the close of the evening, by men who lay in ambush among the woods and groves to kill them as they came in to roost.* These are the principal cir-

* *Some old sportsmen say that the main part of these flocks used to withdraw as soon as the heavy Christmas frosts were over.* ⟨G. W.⟩

cumstances relating to this wonderful *internal* migration, which with us takes place towards the end of November, and ceases early in the spring. Last winter we had in Selborne high wood about an hundred of these doves; but in former times the flocks were so vast, not only with us but all the district round, that on mornings and evenings they traversed the air, like rooks, in strings, reaching for a mile together. When they thus rendezvoused here by thousands, if they happened to be suddenly roused from their roost-trees on an evening,

Their rising all at once was like the sound
Of thunder heard remote.——

It will by no means be foreign to the present purpose to add, that I had a relation in this neighbourhood who made it a practice, for a time, whenever he could procure the eggs of a *ring-dove*, to place them under a pair of doves that were sitting in his own pigeon-house; hoping thereby, if he could bring about a coalition, to enlarge his breed, and teach his own doves to beat out into the woods and to support themselves by mast: the plan was plausible, but something always interrupted the success; for though the birds were usually hatched, and sometimes grew to half their size, yet none ever arrived at maturity. I myself have seen these foundlings in their nest displaying a strange ferocity of nature, so as scarcely to bear to be looked at, and snapping with their bills by way of menace. In short, they always died, perhaps for want of proper sustenance: but the owner thought that by their fierce and wild demeanour they frighted their foster-mothers, and so were starved.

Virgil, as a familiar occurrence, by way of simile, describes a dove haunting the cavern of a rock in such engaging numbers, that I cannot refrain from quoting the passage: and John Dryden has rendered it so happily in our language, that without farther excuse I shall add his translation also.

Qualis speluncâ subitò commota Columba,
Cui domus, et dulces latebroso in pumice nidi,
Fertur in arva volans, plausumque exterrita pennis
Dat tecto ingentem—mox aere lapsa quieto,
Radit iter liquidum, celeres neque commovet alas.

As when a dove her rocky hold forsakes,
Rous'd, in a fright her sounding wings she shakes;
The cavern rings with clattering:—out she flies,
And leaves her callow care, and cleaves the skies:
At first she flutters:—but at length she springs
To smoother flight, and shoots upon her wings.

I am, &c.

LETTER I

TO THE HONOURABLE DAINES BARRINGTON*

Selborne, *June* 30, 1769.

DEAR SIR,

When I was in town last month I partly engaged that I would sometime do myself the honour to write to you on the subject of natural history: and I am the more ready to fulfil my promise, because I see you are a gentleman of great candour, and one that will make allowances; especially where the writer professes to be an *out-door naturalist*, one that takes his observations from the subject itself, and not from the writings of others.

The following is a LIST *of the* SUMMER BIRDS *of* PASSAGE *which I have discovered in this neighbourhood, ranged somewhat in the order in which they appear:*†

	RAII NOMINA	USUALLY APPEARS ABOUT
1. Wryneck,	*Jynx, sive torquilla:*	The middle of March: harsh note.
2. Smallest willow-wren,	*Regulus non cristatus:*	March 23: chirps till September.
3. Swallow,	*Hirundo domestica:*	April 13.
4. Martin,	*Hirundo rustica:*	Ditto.

* See p. 4.

† Out of the list, 2 is the chiff-chaff, 9 the willow-warbler, 14 the grasshopper-warbler, 18 the wood-warbler, 20 the common flycatcher. The nightingale and turtle-dove are now separated from the Passerine Order. By "white wagtail", White means the pied wagtail. The ring-ousel, woodcock and wheatear are summer migrants, and the common snipe is a resident species, as are stock-dove, mallard, pochard, teal and hawfinch ("gros-beak"). The less reed-sparrow is the sedge-warbler, and the "wood-pigeon" is the stock dove. The crossbill and waxwing are occasional visitors in winter and autumn, and the yellow wagtail and whin-chat leave us in the autumn. The "wild-goose" may belong to any of five or six species. The "Wild-Swan" is the Whooper Swan, and it is interesting that the *Hampshire Field Club Papers* reported six of them in the county (on the Beaulieu River) in 1936.

	RAII NOMINA	USUALLY APPEARS ABOUT
5. Sand-martin,	*Hirundo riparia:*	April 13.
6. Black-cap,	*Atricapilla:*	Ditto: a sweet wild note.
7. Nightingale,	*Luscinia:*	Beginning of April.
8. Cuckoo,	*Cuculus:*	Middle of April.
9. Middle willow-wren,	*Regulus non cristatus:*	Ditto: a sweet plaintive note.
10. White-throat,	*Ficedulæ affinis:*	Ditto: mean note; sings on till September.
11. Red-start,	*Ruticilla:*	Ditto: more agreeable song.
12. Stone-curlew,	*Oedicnemus:*	End of March: loud nocturnal whistle.
13. Turtle-dove,	*Turtur:*	
14. Grasshopper-lark,	*Alauda minima locustæ voce:*	Middle April: a small sibilous note, till the end of July.
15. Swift,	*Hirundo apus:*	About April 27.
16. Less reed-sparrow,	*Passer arundinaceus minor:*	A sweet polyglot, but hurrying: it has the notes of many birds.
17. Land-rail,	*Ortygometra:*	A loud harsh note, crex, crex.
18. Largest willow-wren,	*Regulus non cristatus:*	*Cantat voce stridulâ locustæ;* end of April, on the tops of high beeches.
19. Goatsucker, or fern-owl	*Caprimulgus:*	Beginning of May: chatters by night with a singular noise.
20. Fly-catcher,	*Stoparola:*	May 12. A very mute bird: this is the latest summer bird of passage.

This assemblage of curious and amusing birds belongs to ten several genera of the Linnæan system; and are all of the *ordo* of *passeres* save the *jynx* and *cuculus*, which are *picæ*, and the *charadrius* (*oedicnemus*) and *rallus* (*ortygometra*), which are *gallæ*.

These birds, as they stand numerically, belong to the following Linnæan genera:

1.	*Jynx:*	13. *Columba:*
2, 6, 7, 9, 10, 11, 16, 18.	*Motacilla:*	17. *Rallus:*
3, 4, 5, 15.	*Hirundo:*	19. *Caprimulgus:*
8.	*Cuculus:*	14. *Alauda:*
12.	*Charadrius:*	20. *Muscicapa.*

Most soft-billed birds live on insects, and not on grain and seeds; and therefore at the end of summer they retire: but the following soft-billed birds, though insect-eaters, stay with us the year round:

	RAII NOMINA	
Redbreast, Wren,	*Rubecula:* *Passer troglodytes:*	These frequent houses; and haunt out-buildings in the winter: eat spiders.
Hedge-sparrow,	*Curruca:*	Haunt sinks for crumbs and other sweepings.
White-wagtail, Yellow wagtail, Grey wagtail,	*Motacilla alba:* *Motacilla flava:* *Motacilla cinerea:*	These frequent shallow rivulets near the spring heads, where they never freeze: eat the aureliæ of Phryganea. The smallest birds that walk.
Wheat-ear,	*Oenanthe:*	Some of these are to be seen with us the winter through.
Whin-chat, Stone-chatter,	*Oenanthe secunda:* *Oenanthe tertia:*	
Golden-crowned wren,	*Regulus cristatus:*	This is the smallest British bird: haunts the tops of tall trees; stays the winter through.

A LIST *of the* WINTER BIRDS *of* PASSAGE *round this neighbourhood, ranged somewhat in the order in which they appear:* *

	RAII NOMINA	
1. Ring-ousel,	*Merula torquata:*	This is a new migration, which I have lately discovered about Michaelmas week, and again about the fourteenth of March.
2. Redwing,	*Turdus iliacus:*	About old Michaelmas.
3. Fieldfare,	*Turdus pilaris:*	Though a percher by day, roosts on the ground.
4. Royston-crow,	*Cornix cinerea:*	Most frequent on downs.
5. Woodcock,	*Scolopax:*	Appears about old Michaelmas.
6. Snipe,	*Gallinago minor:*	Some snipes constantly breed with us.
7. Jack-snipe,	*Gallinago minima:*	
8. Wood-pigeon,	*Oenas*:	Seldom appears till late: not in such plenty as formerly.
9. Wild-swan,	*Cygnus ferus:*	On some large waters.
10. Wild-goose,	*Anser ferus:*	

* It is very singular that the Starling does not appear in this list. The bird is, next to the house-sparrow, the most abundant species in England, and the vast winter flocks, performing their sky-writing in perfect order against the sunset clouds before they rain down to roost in wood or reedy broad or Thames ait or river sallows, are a familiar evidence of its incalculable numbers. The starling has increased enormously since the era of the game-laws in the mid-nineteenth century and pheasant-preserving in the twentieth, owing to the relentless persecution of birds of prey. The consequence of this vested interest is that the bird is now a nuisance to man and bird alike, and there can be no doubt at all that Gilbert White's day saw it in tens where ours sees it in thousands. But winter flocking is its germinal characteristic, and it must have been noticeably present in eighteenth-century Selborne.

	RAII NOMINA	
11. Wild-duck,	*Anas torquata minor:*	On our lakes and streams.
12. Pochard,	*Anas fera fusca:*	
13. Wigeon,	*Penelope:*	
14. Teal, breeds with us in Wolmer-forest,	*Querquedula:*	
15. Gross-beak,	*Coccothraustes:*	These are only wanderers that appear occasionally, and are not observant of any regular migration.
16. Cross-bill,	*Loxia:*	
17. Silk-tail,	*Garrulus bohemicus:*	

These birds, as they stand numerically, belong to the following Linnæan genera:

1, 2, 3,	*Turdus:*	9, 10, 11, 12, 13, 14,	*Anas:*
4,	*Corvus:*	15, 16,	*Loxia:*
5, 6, 7,	*Scolopax:*	17,	*Ampelis.*
8,	*Columba:*		

Birds that sing in the night are but few.

	RAII NOMINA	
Nightingale,	*Luscinia:*	"In shadiest covert hid." MILTON.
Woodlark,	*Alauda arborea:*	Suspended in mid air.
Less reed-sparrow,	*Passer arundinaceus minor:*	Among reeds and willows.

I should now proceed to such birds as continue to sing after Midsummer, but, as they are rather numerous, they would exceed the bounds of this paper: besides, as this is now the season for remarking on that subject, I am willing to repeat my observations on some birds concerning the continuation of whose song I seem at present to have some doubt.

I am, &c.

LETTER II

TO THE SAME

Selborne, *Nov*. 2, 1769.

DEAR SIR,

When I did myself the honour to write to you about the end of last June on the subject of natural history, I sent you a list of the summer-birds of passage which I have observed in this neighbourhood; and also a list of the winter-birds of passage: I mentioned besides those soft-billed birds that stay with us the winter through in the south of England, and those that are remarkable for singing in the night.

According to my proposal, I shall now proceed to such birds (singing birds strictly so called) as continue in full song till after Midsummer; and shall range them somewhat in the order in which they first begin to open as the spring advances.

	RAII NOMINA	
1. Wood-lark,	*Alauda arborea:*	In January, and continues to sing through all the summer and autumn.
2. Song-thrush,	*Turdus simpliciter dictus:*	In February and on to August, reassume their song in autumn.
3. Wren,	*Passer troglodytes:*	All the year, hard frost excepted.
4. Redbreast,	*Rubecula:*	Ditto.
5. Hedge-sparrow,	*Curruca:*	Early in February to July the 10th.
6. Yellowhammer,	*Emberiza flava:*	Early in February, and on through July to August the 21st.
7. Skylark,	*Alauda vulgaris:*	In February, and on to October.

	RAII NOMINA	
8. Swallow,	*Hirundo domestica:*	From April to September.
9. Black-cap,	*Atricapilla:*	Beginning of April to July 13th.
10. Titlark,*	*Alauda pratorum:*	From middle of April to July the 16th.
11. Blackbird,	*Merula vulgaris:*	Sometimes in February and March, and so on to July the twenty-third; reassumes in autumn.
12. White-throat,	*Ficedulæ affinis*:	In April and on to July 23.
13. Goldfinch,	*Carduelis:*	April, and through to September 16.
14. Greenfinch,	*Chloris:*	On to July and August 2.
15. Less reed-sparrow,	*Passer arundinaceus minor:*	May, on to beginning of July.
16. Common linnet,	*Linaria vulgaris:*	Breeds and whistles on till August; reassumes it's note when they begin to congregate in October, and again early before the flocks separate.

Birds that cease to be in full song, and are usually silent at or before Midsummer:

17. Middle willow-wren,	*Regulus non cristatus:*	Middle of June: begins in April.
18. Redstart,	*Ruticilla:*	Ditto: begins in May.
19. Chaffinch,	*Fringilla:*	Beginning of June: sings first in February.
20. Nightingale,	*Luscinia:*	Middle of June: sings first in April.

* The meadow-pipit is here confused with the tree-pipit.

Birds that sing for a short time, and very early in the spring:

	RAII NOMINA	
21. Missel-bird,	*Turdus viscivorus:*	January the 2d, 1770, in February. Is called in Hampshire and Sussex the storm-cock, because it's song is supposed to forebode windy wet weather: is the largest singing bird we have.
22. Great titmouse, or ox-eye,*	*Fringillago:*	In February, March, April: reassumes for a short time in September.

Birds that have somewhat of a note or song, and yet are hardly to be called singing birds:

23. Golden-crowned wren,	*Regulus cristatus:*	It's note as minute as it's person; frequents the tops of high oaks and firs: the smallest British bird.
24. Marsh titmouse,	*Parus palustris:*	Haunts great woods: two harsh sharp notes.
25. Small willow-wren,	*Regulus non cristatus:*	Sings in March, and on to September.
26. Largest ditto,	*Ditto:*	*Cantat voce stridulâ locustæ;* from end of April to August.
27. Grasshopper-lark,	*Alauda minima voce locustæ:*	Chirps all night, from the middle of April to the end of July.

* Oxeye, as we say to-day. No. 24 may be the willow-tit. No. 25 is the chiffchaff; No. 26 the wood-warbler; No. 27 the grasshopper-warbler; No. 28 the house-martin, and No. 30 the corn-bunting.

	RAII NOMINA	
28. Martin,	*Hirundo agrestis:*	All the breeding time; from May to September.
29. Bullfinch,	*Pyrrhula:*	
30. Bunting,	*Emberiza alba:*	From the end of January to July.

All singing birds, and those that have any pretensions to song, not only in Britain, but perhaps the world through, come under the Linnæan *ordo* of *passeres*.

The above-mentioned birds, as they stand numerically, belong to the following Linnæan genera.

1, 7, 10, 27.	*Alauda:*	8, 28.	*Hirundo.*
2, 11, 21.	*Turdus:*	13, 16, 19.	*Fringilla.*
3, 4, 5, 9, 12, 15, 17, 18, 20, 23, 25, 26.	*Motacilla:*	22, 24.	*Parus.*
6, 30.	*Emberiza:*	14, 29.	*Loxia.*

Birds that sing as they fly* are but few.

	RAII NOMINA	
Skylark,	*Alauda vulgaris:*	Rising, suspended, and falling.
Titlark,†	*Alauda pratorum:*	In it's descent; also sitting on trees, and walking on the ground.
Woodlark,	*Alauda arborea:*	Suspended; in hot summer nights all night long.
Blackbird,	*Merula:*	Sometimes from bush to bush.
White-throat,	*Ficedulæ affinis:*	Uses when singing on the wing odd jerks and gesticulations.
Swallow,	*Hirundo domestica:*	In soft sunny weather.
Wren,	*Passer troglodytes:*	Sometimes from bush to bush.

* The list can be considerably lengthened.

† By 'titlark,' the author here intends the tree-pipit, which he did not distinguish from the meadow-pipit, possibly because the meadow-pipit also sings in and slides down the air. But whereas the tree-pipit takes the air from a tree, the meadow-pipit rises to sing from the ground.

Birds that breed most early in these parts:

	RAII NOMINA	
Raven,	*Corvus:*	Hatches in February and March.
Song-thrush,	*Turdus:*	In March.
Blackbird,	*Merula:*	In March.
Rook,	*Cornix frugilega:*	Builds the beginning of March.
Woodlark,	*Alauda arborea:*	Hatches in April.
Ring-dove,	*Palumbus torquatus:*	Lays the beginning of April.

All birds that continue in full song till after Midsummer appear to me to breed more than once.

Most kinds of birds seem to me to be wild and shy somewhat in proportion to their bulk; I mean in this island, where they are much pursued and annoyed: but in Ascension Island, and many other desolate places, mariners have found fowls so unacquainted with an human figure, that they would stand still to be taken; as is the case with boobies, &c. As an example of what is advanced, I remark that the *golden-crested wren* (the smallest British bird) will stand unconcerned till you come within three or four yards of it, while the *bustard* (*otis*), the largest British land fowl, does not care to admit a person within so many furlongs.*

I am, &c.

* Hardly surprising when it was hunted until it became extinct.

LETTER III

TO THE SAME

Selborne, *Jan.* 15, 1770.

DEAR SIR,

It was no small matter of satisfaction to me to find that you were not displeased with my little *methodus* of birds. If there was any merit in the sketch, it must be owing to it's punctuality. For many months I carried a list in my pocket of the birds that were to be remarked, and, as I rode or walked about my business, I noted each day the continuance or omission of each bird's song: so that I am as sure of the certainty of my facts as a man can be of any transaction whatsoever.

I shall now proceed to answer the several queries which you put in your two obliging letters, in the best manner that I am able. Perhaps Eastwick, and it's environs, where you heard so very few birds, is not a woodland country, and therefore not stocked with such songsters. If you will cast your eye on my last letter, you will find that many species continued to warble after the beginning of July.

The titlark and yellowhammer breed late, the latter very late; and therefore it is no wonder that they protract their song: for I lay it down as a maxim in ornithology, that as long as there is any incubation going on there is music.* As to the redbreast and wren,† it is well known to the most incurious observer that they whistle the year round, hard frost excepted; especially the latter.

It was not in my power to procure you a black-cap, or a less reed-sparrow, or sedge-bird, alive. As the first is undoubtedly, and the last, as far as I can yet see, a summer bird of passage,

* Mr. Nicholson fully subscribes in his note upon this passage to the contemporary fashion in ornithology for declaring all song to be territorial. This dogma ignores both social and migratory singing. Swallows, linnets, goldfinches and other birds frequently sing when their "territories" are deserted for the season, while robins, wrens and thrushes will sing in winter when there is no competition for small holdings. The horrid heresy must also be dared that birds do sometimes forget their biology and sing for the joy of the day, the song and the life beating within them.

† The wren often sings in a hard frost

they would require more nice and curious management in a cage than I should be able to give them: they are both distinguished songsters. The note of the former has such a wild sweetness that it always brings to my mind those lines in a song in *As You Like It*.

And tune his merry note
Unto the *wild* bird's throat.

SHAKESPEARE.

The latter has a surprising variety of notes resembling the song of several other birds; but then it has also an hurrying manner, not at all to it's advantage: it is notwithstanding a delicate polyglot.*

It is new to me that titlarks in cages sing in the night; perhaps only caged birds do so. I once knew a tame redbreast in a cage that always sang as long as candles were in the room; but in their wild state no one supposes they sing in the night.

I should be almost ready to doubt the fact, that there are to be seen much fewer birds in July than in any former month, notwithstanding so many young are hatched daily. Sure I am that it is far otherwise with respect to the *swallow tribe*, which increases prodigiously as the summer advances: and I saw, at the time mentioned, many hundreds of young wagtails on the banks of the Cherwell, which almost covered the meadows. If the matter appears as you say in the other species, may it not be owing to the dams being engaged in incubation, while the young are concealed by the leaves?

Many times have I had the curiosity to open the stomachs of *woodcocks* and *snipes*; but nothing ever occurred that helped to explain to me what their subsistence might be: all that I could ever find was a soft mucus, among which lay many pellucid small gravels.

I am, &c.

* A term adopted from White's brother, John.

LETTER IV

TO THE SAME

Selborne, *Feb.* 19, 1770.

Dear Sir,

Your observation that "the *cuckoo* does not deposit it's egg indiscriminately in the nest of the first bird that comes in it's way, but probably looks out a nurse in some degree congenerous, with whom to intrust it's young", is perfectly new to me; and struck me so forcibly, that I naturally fell into a train of thought that led me to consider whether the fact was so, and what reason there was for it. When I came to recollect and inquire, I could not find that any cuckoo had ever been seen in these parts, except in the nest of the *wagtail*, the *hedge-sparrow*, the *titlark*, the *white-throat*, and the *redbreast*, all soft-billed insectivorous birds. The excellent Mr. Willughby mentions the nest of the *palumbus* (*ring-dove*), and of the *fringilla* (*chaffinch*), birds that subsist on acorns and grains, and such hard food: but then he does not mention them as of his own knowledge; but says afterwards that he saw himself a *wagtail* feeding a cuckoo. It appears hardly possible that a soft-billed bird should subsist on the same food with the hard-billed: for the former have thin membranaceous stomachs suited to their soft food; while the latter, the granivorous tribe, have strong muscular gizzards, which, like mills, grind, by the help of small gravels and pebbles, what is swallowed. This proceeding of the cuckoo, of dropping it's eggs as it were by chance, is such a monstrous outrage on maternal affection, one of the first great dictates of nature; and such a violence on instinct; that, had it only been related of a bird in the Brasils, or Peru, it would never have merited our belief. But yet, should it farther appear that this simple bird, when divested of that natural *στοργὴ* that seems to raise the kind in general above themselves, and inspire them with extraordinary degrees of cunning and address, may be still endued with a more enlarged faculty of discerning what species are suitable and congenerous nursing-mothers for it's disregarded eggs and young, and may deposit them only under *their* care, this would be adding wonder to wonder, and instancing, in a fresh manner, that the methods of Providence are not subjected to any mode or rule, but astonish us in new lights, and in various and changeable appearances.*

What was said by a very ancient and sublime writer concerning the defect of natural affection in the ostrich, may be well applied to the bird we are talking of:

"*She is hardened against her young ones, as though they were not her's:*

"*Because God hath deprived her of wisdom, neither hath he imparted to her understanding.*"†

Query. Does each female cuckoo lay but one egg in a season, or does she drop several in different nests according as opportunity offers?

I am, &c.

* The promiscuous or rather polyandrous cuckoo lays from half to a full score of eggs in a season, and each hen-cuckoo lays her eggs in the nests of one species only within a given area. In one beat the bird will choose the robin; in the adjacent belt another cuckoo will choose the dunnock, and so on.

† *Job xxxix.* 16, 17. 〈G. W.〉

LETTER V

TO THE SAME

Selborne, *April* 12, 1770.

DEAR SIR,

I heard many birds of several species sing last year after Midsummer; enough to prove that the summer solstice is not the period that puts a stop to the music of the woods. The yellowhammer no doubt persists with more steadiness than any other; but the woodlark, the wren, the redbreast, the swallow, the white-throat, the goldfinch, the common linnet, are all undoubted instances of the truth of what I advanced.

If this severe season does not interrupt the regularity of the summer migrations, the blackcap will be here in two or three days. I wish it was in my power to procure you one of those songsters; but I am no birdcatcher; and so little used to birds in a cage, that I fear if I had one it would soon die for want of skill in feeding.

Was your reed-sparrow, which you kept in a cage, the thick-billed reed-sparrow of the *Zoology*, p. 320; or was it the less reed-sparrow of Ray, the *sedge-bird* of Mr. Pennant's last publication, p. 16?

As to the matter of long-billed birds growing fatter in moderate frosts, I have no doubt within myself what should be the reason. The thriving at those times appears to me to arise altogether from the gentle check which the cold throws upon insensible perspiration.* The case is just the same with blackbirds, &c.; and farmers and warreners observe, the first, that their hogs fat more kindly at such times, and the latter that their rabbits are never in such good case as in a gentle frost. But when frosts are severe, and of long continuance, the case is soon altered; for then a want of food soon overbalances the repletion occasioned by a checked perspiration. I have observed, moreover, that some human constitutions are more inclined to plumpness in winter than in summer.

* This is an old wives' tale.

When birds come to suffer by severe frost, I find that the first that fail and die are the redwing-fieldfares, and then the song-thrushes.

You wonder, with good reason, that the hedge-sparrows, &c. can be induced at all to sit on the egg of the cuckoo without being scandalized at the vast disproportioned size of the supposititious egg;* but the brute creation, I suppose, have very little idea of size, colour, or number. For the common hen, I know, when the fury of incubation is on her, will sit on a single shapeless stone instead of a nest full of eggs that have been withdrawn: and, moreover, a hen-turkey, in the same circumstances, would sit on in the empty nest till she perished with hunger.

I think the matter might be easily determined whether a cuckoo lays one or two eggs, or more, in a season, by opening a female during the laying-time. If more than one was come down out of the ovary, and advanced to a good size, doubtless then she would that spring lay more than one.

I will endeavour to get a hen, and to examine.

Your supposition that there may be some natural obstruction in singing birds while they are mute, and that when this is removed the song recommences, is new and bold: I wish you could discover some good grounds for this suspicion.

I was glad you were pleased with my specimen of the *caprimulgus*, or fern-owl; you were, I find, acquainted with the bird before.

When we meet I shall be glad to have some conversation with you concerning the proposal you make of my drawing up an account of the animals in this neighbourhood. Your partiality towards my small abilities persuades you, I fear, that I am able to do more than is in my power: for it is no small undertaking for a man unsupported and alone to begin a natural history from his own autopsia! Though there is endless room for observation in the field of nature, which is boundless, yet investigation (where a man endeavours to be sure of his facts) can make

* White evidently failed to observe that the cuckoo's egg is only a trifle larger than are those of its victimized foster-mother. When I was at Abbotsbury two years ago, I hit upon an authentic example of a marsh-warbler ejecting a cuckoo's egg and piercing it with the sharp bill. If other birds of the same and other species exhibited the same combination of sagacity with resentment, the cuckoo would become extinct.

but slow progress; and all that one could collect in many years would go into a very narrow compass.

Some extracts from your ingenious "Investigations of the difference between the present temperature of the air in Italy," &c. have fallen in my way; and gave me great satisfaction: they have removed the objections that always arose in my mind whenever I came to the passages which you quote. Surely the judicious Virgil, when writing a didactic poem for the region of Italy, could never think of describing freezing rivers, unless such severity of weather pretty frequently occurred!

P.S. Swallows appear amidst snows and frost.

LETTER VI

TO THE SAME

Selborne, *May* 21, 1770.

DEAR SIR,

The severity and turbulence of last month so interrupted the regular process of summer migration, that some of the birds do but just begin to shew themselves, and others are apparently thinner than usual; as the white-throat, the black-cap, the redstart, the fly-catcher. I well remember that after the very severe spring in the year 1739-40 summer birds of passage were very scarce. They come probably hither with a south-east wind, or when it blows between those points;* but in that unfavourable year the winds blowed the whole spring and summer through from the opposite quarters. And yet amidst all these disadvantages two swallows, as I mentioned in my last, appeared this year as early as the eleventh of April amidst frost and snow; but they withdrew again for a time.

I am not pleased to find that some people seem so little satisfied with Scopoli's new publication;† there is room to expect great things from the hands of that man, who is a good naturalist: and one would think that an history of the birds of so distant and southern a region as Carniola would be new and interesting. I could wish to see that work, and hope to get it sent down. Dr. Scopoli is physician to the wretches that work in the quicksilver mines of that district.

When you talked of keeping a reed-sparrow,‡ and giving it seeds, I could not help wondering; because the reed-sparrow which I mentioned to you (*passer arundinaceus minor Raii*) is a soft-billed bird; and most probably migrates hence before winter; whereas the bird you kept (*passer torquatus Raii*) abides all the year, and is a thick-billed bird. I question whether the latter

* "We now know that migrating birds prefer a wind on the beam rather than one astern." Note by Warde Fowler in his Edition.

† *This work he calls his* Annus Primus Historico-Naturalis. ⟨G. W.⟩

‡ The "soft-billed" is the sedge-warbler, the "thick-billed" the reed-bunting.

be much of a songster; but in this matter I want to be better informed. The former has a variety of hurrying notes, and sings all night. Some part of the song of the former, I suspect, is attributed to the latter. We have plenty of the soft-billed sort; which Mr. Pennant had entirely left out of his *British Zoology*, till I reminded him of his omission. See *British Zoology* last published, p. 16.*

I have somewhat to advance on the different manners in which different birds fly and walk; but as this is a subject that I have not enough considered, and is of such a nature as not to be contained in a small space, I shall say nothing further about it at present.†

No doubt the reason why the sex of birds in their first plumage is so difficult to be distinguished is, as you say, "because they are not to pair and discharge their parental functions till the ensuing spring." As colours seem to be the chief external sexual distinction in many birds, these colours do not take place till sexual attachments begin to obtain. And the case is the same in quadrupeds; among whom, in their younger days, the sexes differ but little: but, as they advance to maturity, horns and shaggy manes, beards and brawny necks, &c. &c. strongly discriminate the male from the female. We may instance still farther in our own species, where a beard and stronger features are usually characteristic of the male sex: but this sexual diversity does not take place in earlier life; for a beautiful youth shall be so like a beautiful girl that the difference shall not be discernible;‡

Quem si puellarum insereres choro,
Mirè sagaces falleret hospites
Discrimen obscurum, solutis
Crinibus, ambiguoque vultu.

HOR.

* *See Letter XXV to Mr. Pennant.* ⟨G. W.⟩
† *See Letter XLII to Mr. Barrington.* ⟨G. W.⟩
‡ A characteristic letter in the sense of the original mind laying and hatching a clutch of new ideas which posterity was to rear.

LETTER VII

TO THE SAME

Ringmer, near Lewes, *Oct*. 8, 1770.

DEAR SIR,

I am glad to hear that Kuckalm is to furnish you with the birds of Jamaica; a sight of the *hirundines* of that hot and distant island would be a great entertainment to me.

The *Anni* of Scopoli are now in my possession; and I have read the *Annus Primus* with satisfaction: for though some parts of this work are exceptionable, and he may advance some mistaken observations; yet the ornithology of so distant a country as Carniola is very curious. Men that undertake only one district are much more likely to advance natural knowledge than those that grasp at more than they can possibly be acquainted with: every kingdom, every province, should have it's own *monographer*.

The reason perhaps why he mentions nothing of Ray's *Ornithology* may be the extreme poverty and distance of his country, into which the works of our great naturalist may have never yet found their way. You have doubts, I know, whether this Ornithology is genuine, and really the work of Scopoli: as to myself, I think I discover strong tokens of authenticity; the style corresponds with that of his *Entomology*; and his characters of his

Ordines and Genera are many of them new, expressive, and masterly. He has ventured to alter some of the Linnæan *genera* with sufficient shew of reason.

It might perhaps be mere accident that you saw so many swifts and no swallows at Staines; because, in my long observation of those birds, I never could discover the least degree of rivalry or hostility between the species.

Ray remarks that birds of the *gallinæ order*, as cocks and hens, partridges, and pheasants, &c. are *pulveratrices*, such as dust themselves, using that method of cleansing their feathers, and ridding themselves of their vermin. As far as I can observe, many birds that dust themselves never wash: and I once thought that those birds that wash themselves would never dust; but here I find myself mistaken; for common house-sparrows are great *pulveratrices*, being frequently seen grovelling and wallowing in dusty roads; and yet they are great washers. Does not the skylark dust?

Query. Might not Mahomet and his followers take one method of purification from these *pulveratrices*? because I find from travellers of credit, that if a strict mussulman is journeying in a sandy desert where no water is to be found, at stated hours he strips off his clothes, and most scrupulously rubs his body over with sand or dust.

A countryman told me he had found a young *fern-owl* in the nest of a small bird on the ground; and that it was fed by the little bird. I went to see this extraordinary phenomenon, and found that it was a young cuckoo hatched in the nest of a titlark: it was become vastly too big for it's nest, appearing

— — — — — in tenui re
Majores pennas nido extendisse — —

and was very fierce and pugnacious, pursuing my finger, as I teazed it, for many feet from the nest, and sparring and buffetting with it's wings like a game-cock. The dupe of a dam appeared at a distance, hovering about with meat in it's mouth, and expressing the greatest solicitude.

In July I saw several cuckoos skimming over a large pond; and found, after observation, that they were feeding on the *libellulæ*, or *dragon-flies*; some of which they caught as they settled on the weeds, and some as they were on the wing. Notwithstanding what Linnæus says, I cannot be induced to believe that they are birds of prey.*

This district affords some birds that are hardly ever heard of at Selborne. In the first place considerable flocks of *cross-beaks* (*loxiæ curvirostræ*) have appeared this summer in the pine-groves belonging to this house; the *water-ousel*† is said to haunt the mouth of the Lewes river, near Newhaven; and the *Cornish chough*‡ builds, I know, all along the chalky cliffs of the Sussex shore.

I was greatly pleased to see little parties of *ring-ousels* (my newly discovered migraters) scattered, at intervals, all along the Sussex downs from Chichester to Lewes. Let them come from whence they will, it looks very suspicious that they are cantoned along the coast in order to pass the channel when severe weather advances. They visit us again in April, as it should seem, in their return; and are not to be found in the dead of winter. It is remarkable that they are very tame, and seem to have no manner of apprehensions of danger from a person with a gun. There are bustards§ on the wide downs near Brighthelmstone. No doubt you are acquainted with the Sussex downs: the prospects and rides round Lewes are most lovely!

As I rode along near the coast I kept a very sharp look out in the lanes and woods, hoping I might, at this time of the year, have discovered some of the summer short-winged birds of passage crowding towards the coast in order for their departure: but it was very extraordinary that I never saw|| a redstart, white-throat, black-cap, uncrested wren, fly-catcher, &c. And I remember to have made the same remark in former years, as I usually

* A gamekeeper I once talked with near Selborne assured me that the cuckoo changed into a hawk during the winter. The error about a bird that is purely insectivorous is no doubt due partly to its disappearance in the autumn and partly to its hawk-like appearance on the wing. The cuckoo looks half-way to a hawk.

† The dipper, long vanished from the Sussex Ouse. The crossbill is more frequently seen than in White's day because it frequents the gloomy, foreign-looking woodlands of conifers planted by the Forestry Commission and hostile to the peculiarly English appearance of the Selborne neighbourhood.

‡ See note to Letter XXXIX to Pennant.

§ The Great Bustard (*otis tarda*) was exterminated by 1840, partly by enclosure, partly by a wantonly destructive "sport", partly by encroachment upon its breeding grounds, but chiefly by egg-collectors.

|| Plainly because he was too late in the season.

come to this place annually about this time. The birds most common along the coast at present are the stone-chatters, whinchats,* buntings, linnets, some few wheat-ears, titlarks, &c. Swallows and house-martins abound yet, induced to prolong their stay by this soft, still, dry season.

A land tortoise, which has been kept for thirty years in a little walled court belonging to the house where I now am visiting,† retires under ground about the middle of November, and comes forth again about the middle of April. When it first appears in the spring it discovers very little inclination towards food; but in the height of summer grows voracious: and then as the summer declines it's appetite declines; so that for the last six weeks in autumn it hardly eats at all. Milky plants, such as lettuces, dandelions, sowthistles, are it's favourite dish. In a neighbouring village one was kept till by tradition it was supposed to be an hundred years old. An instance of vast longevity in such a poor reptile!

* It is doubtful whether White knew the whinchat. He certainly did not know that it was a summer migrant, and all his allusions to it are suspicious.

† At the house of his aunt, Rebecca Snooke, at Ringmer, near Lewes.

LETTER VIII

TO THE SAME

Selborne, *Dec.* 20, 1770.

DEAR SIR,

The birds that I took for *aberdavines** were reed-sparrows (*passeres torquati*).

There are doubtless many home internal migrations within this kingdom that want to be better understood: witness those vast flocks of hen chaffinches that appear with us in the winter without hardly any cocks among them. Now was there a due proportion of each sex, it should seem very improbable that any one district should produce such numbers of these little birds; and much more when only one half of the species appears: therefore we may conclude that the *fringillæ cælebes*, for some good purposes, have a peculiar migration of their own in which the sexes part. Nor should it seem so wonderful that the intercourse of sexes in this species of birds should be interrupted in winter; since in many animals, and particularly in bucks and does, the sexes herd separately, except at the season when commerce is necessary for the continuance of the breed. For this matter of the chaffinches see *Fauna Suecica*, p. 85, and *Systema Naturæ*, p. 318. I see every winter vast flights of hen chaffinches, but none of cocks.

Your method of accounting for the periodical motions of the British singing birds, or birds of flight, is a very probable one; since the matter of food is a great regulator of the actions and proceedings of the brute creation: there is but one that can be set in competition with it, and that is love.† But I cannot quite

* The older name for the siskin. White refers to a deleted passage in the fifth letter to Barrington in which he mentions having seen siskins. He forgets that the passage has been struck out of his text. His reason for removing what he wrote in the original MS. was his later discovery that the birds were reed-buntings and not siskins. He is thus referring the reader to a previous observation that no longer exists. Since he did not find out his own error until nearly a year after the present, eighth letter is dated, the modern reader is given a speaking illustration of the modifications of the MSS. in the printed text. It is one of the services conferred by Mr. Nicholson's edition of Selborne that he examines these differences in some detail.

† See my *Introduction*.

acquiesce with you in one circumstance when you advance that, "when they have thus feasted, they again separate into small parties of five or six, and get the best fare they can within a certain district, having no inducement to go in quest of fresh-turned earth." Now if you mean that the business of congregating is quite at an end from the conclusion of wheat-sowing to the season of barley and oats, it is not the case with us; for larks and chaffinches, and particularly linnets, flock and congregate as much in the very dead of winter as when the husbandman is busy with his ploughs and harrows.

Sure there can be no doubt but that woodcocks* and fieldfares leave us in the spring, in order to cross the seas, and to retire to some districts more suitable to the purpose of breeding. That the former pair before they retire, and that the hens are forward with egg, I myself, when I was a sportsman, have often experienced. It cannot indeed be denied but that now and then we hear of a woodcock's nest, or young birds, discovered in some part or other of this island: but then they are always mentioned as rarities, and somewhat out of the common course of things: but as to redwings and fieldfares, no sportsman or naturalist has ever yet, that I could hear, pretended to have found the nest or young of those species in any part of these kingdoms.† And I the more admire at this instance as extraordinary, since, to all appearance, the same food in summer as well as in winter might support them here which maintains their congeners, the blackbirds and thrushes, did they chuse to stay the summer through. From hence it appears that it is not food alone which determines some species of birds with regard to their stay or departure. Fieldfares and redwings disappear sooner or later according as the warm weather comes on earlier or later. For I well remember, after that dreadful winter‡ 1739-40, that cold north-east winds continued to blow on through April and May, and that these kinds of birds (what few remained of them) did not depart as usual, but were seen lingering about till the beginning of June...

* Many remain to nest, but the author is less in fault than he appears, since an increase in nesting pairs has taken place since his death.

† Harting in his Edition gives examples of redwings and fieldfares nesting in Britain, but these and similar reports have all been discredited.

‡ When the Thames was frozen over.

LETTER IX

TO THE SAME

Fyfield, near Andover, *Feb.* 12, 1771.

Dear Sir,

You are, I know, no great friend to migration;* and the well attested accounts from various parts of the kingdom seem to justify you in your suspicions, that at least many of the swallow kind do not leave us in the winter, but lay themselves up like insects and bats, in a torpid state, and slumber away the more uncomfortable months till the return of the sun and fine weather awakens them.

But then we must not, I think, deny migration in general; because migration certainly does subsist in some places, as my brother in Andalusia has fully informed me. Of the motions of these birds he has ocular demonstration, for many weeks together, both spring and fall: during which periods myriads of the swallow kind traverse the Straits from north to south, and from south to north, according to the season. And these vast migrations consist not only of *hirundines* but also of *bee-birds*, *hoopoes*, *oro pendolos*, or *golden thrushes*,† &c. &c. and also many of our *soft-billed summer-birds of passage*; and moreover of birds which never leave us, such as all the various sorts of hawks and kites. Old Belon,‡ two hundred years ago, gives a curious account of the incredible armies of hawks and kites which he saw in the spring-time traversing the Thracian Bosphorus from Asia to Europe. Besides the above mentioned, he remarks that the procession is swelled by whole troops of eagles and vultures.

Now it is no wonder that birds residing in Africa should retreat before the sun as it advances, and retire to milder regions, and especially birds of prey, whose blood being heated with hot animal food, are more impatient of a sultry climate: but then I

* See note to Letter X to Pennant.

† Golden orioles, a bird of the thrush family that in England escapes the gun only to be robbed of its eggs by the collector on the very rare occasions when it attempts to nest here. One was reported in the county in 1936.

‡ The sixteenth century author of a *History of Birds*.

cannot help wondering why kites and hawks, and such hardy birds as are known to defy all the severity of England, and even of Sweden and all north Europe, should want to migrate from the south of Europe, and be dissatisfied with the winters of Andalusia.*

It does not appear to me that much stress may be laid on the difficulty and hazard that birds must run in their migrations, by reason of vast oceans, cross winds, &c.; because, if we reflect, a bird may travel from England to the equator without launching out and exposing itself to boundless seas, and that by crossing the water at Dover, and again at Gibraltar. And I with the more confidence advance this obvious remark, because my brother has always found that some of his birds, and particularly the swallow kind, are very sparing of their pains in crossing the Mediterranean: for when arrived at Gibraltar, they do not

> ——— Rang'd in figure wedge their way,
> —————— And set forth
> Their airy caravan high over seas
> Flying, and over lands with mutual wing
> Easing their flight: ————
>
> MILTON.

but scout and hurry along in little detached parties of six or seven in a company; and sweeping low, just over the surface of the land and water, direct their course to the opposite continent at the narrowest passage they can find. They usually slope across the bay to the south-west, and so pass over opposite to Tangier, which, it seems, is the narrowest space.†

In former letters we have considered whether it was probable that woodcocks in moon-shiny nights cross the German ocean from Scandinavia. As a proof that birds of less speed may pass that sea, considerable as it is, I shall relate the following incident, which, though mentioned to have happened so many years ago, was strictly matter of fact:—As some people were shooting in the parish of Trotton, in the county of Sussex, they killed a duck in that dreadful winter 1708-9, with a silver collar

* Because a bird nests at the northernmost limit of its range.

† It took another 150 years before the routes of birds and their methods of flight on migration received so precise an account.

about it's neck,*† on which were engraven the arms of the king of Denmark. This anecdote the rector of Trotton at that time has often told to a near relation of mine; and, to the best of my remembrance, the collar was in the possession of the rector.

At present I do not know any body near the sea-side that will take the trouble to remark at what time of the moon woodcocks first come: if I lived near the sea myself I would soon tell you more of the matter. One thing I used to observe when I was a sportsman, that there were times in which woodcocks were so sluggish and sleepy that they would drop again when flushed just before the spaniels, nay just at the muzzle of a gun that had been fired at them: whether this strange laziness was the effect of a recent fatiguing journey I shall not presume to say.

Nightingales not only never reach Northumberland and Scotland, but also, as I have been always told, Devonshire and Cornwall. In those two last counties we cannot attribute the failure of them to the want of warmth: the defect in the west is rather a presumptive argument that these birds come over to us from the continent at the narrowest passage, and do not stroll so far westward.‡

Let me hear from your own observation whether skylarks do not dust. I think they do: and if they do, whether they wash also.§

The *alauda pratensis*‖ of Ray was the poor dupe that was educating the booby of a cuckoo mentioned in my letter of October last.

Your letter came too late for me to procure a ring-ousel for Mr. Tunstal during their autumnal visit; but I will endeavour to get him one when they call on us again in April. I am glad that you and that gentleman saw my Andalusian birds; I hope they answered your expectation. Royston, or grey crows, are winter birds that come much about the same time with the wood-

* *I have read a like anecdote of a swan.* ⟨G. W.⟩

† Harting in his Edition (1874) maintained that this bird was a cormorant, the birds, trained for fishing, having collars attached to their necks. This is an absurdity. Not even an eighteenth century sportsman would confuse a cormorant with a duck, and ducks do cross the North Sea from Denmark in large numbers.

‡ Mr. Nicholson says that the nightingale has "slightly extended" its range in modern times.

§ Coleridge's Note. "Skylarks dust, but do not wash."

‖ The meadow-pipit.

cock: they, like the fieldfare and redwing, have no apparent reason for migration; for as they fare in the winter like their congeners, so might they in all appearance in the summer. Was not Tenant, when a boy, mistaken? did he not find a missel-thrush's nest, and take it for the nest of a fieldfare?

The stock-dove, or wood-pigeon, *œnas Raii*, is the last winter bird of passage which appears with us; and is not seen till towards the end of November: about twenty years ago they abounded in the district of Selborne; and strings of them were seen morning and evening that reached a mile or more: but since the beechen woods have been greatly thinned they are much decreased in number. The ring-dove, *palumbus Raii*, stays with us the whole year, and breeds several times through the summer.

Before I received your letter of October last I had just remarked in my journal that the trees were unusually green. This uncommon verdure lasted on late into November; and may be accounted for from a late spring, a cool and moist summer; but more particularly from vast armies of chafers, or tree-beetles, which, in many places, reduced whole woods to a leafless naked state. These trees shot again at Midsummer, and then retained their foliage till very late in the year.

My musical friend,* at whose house I am now visiting, has tried all the owls that are his near neighbours with a pitch-pipe set at concert-pitch, and finds they all hoot in B flat. He will examine the nightingales next spring.

I am, &c. &c.

* The Rev. Henry White of Fyfield, Hampshire, White's brother. He wrote log-books which give a very prosaic account of his farming activities.

LETTER X

TO THE SAME

Selborne, *Aug*. 1, 1771.

DEAR SIR,

From what follows, it will appear that neither owls nor cuckoos keep to one note. A friend remarks that many (most) of his owls hoot in B flat;* but that one went almost half a note below A. The pipe he tried their notes by was a common half-crown pitch-pipe, such as masters use for tuning of harpsichords; it was the common London pitch.

A neighbour of mine, who is said to have a nice ear, remarks that the owls about this village hoot in three different keys, in G flat, or F sharp, in B flat and A flat. He heard two hooting to each other, the one in A flat, and the other in B flat. *Query*: Do these different notes proceed from different species, or only from various individuals? The same person finds upon trial that the note of the cuckoo (of which we have but one species) varies in different individuals; for, about Selborne wood, he found they were mostly in D: he heard two sing together, the one in D, the other in D sharp, who made a disagreeable concert: he afterwards heard one in D sharp, and about Wolmer-forest some in C. As to nightingales, he says that their notes are so short, and their transitions so rapid, that he cannot well ascertain their key. Perhaps in a cage, and in a room, their notes may be more distinguishable. This person has tried to settle the notes of a swift, and of several other small birds, but cannot bring them to any criterion.

As I have often remarked that redwings are some of the first birds that suffer with us in severe weather, it is no wonder at all

* Many attempts have been made to render bird-music into musical notation (see Wichert: *Evolution of Bird Song*) but fruitlessly. On the other hand, individual birds will sing a bar that can be so rendered, and I have a blackbird in my garden that sings a complete human tune-passage which day after day he will repeat in the same order and pitch of the notes.

that they retreat from Scandinavian winters: and much more the *ordo* of *grallæ*, who, all to a bird, forsake the northern parts of Europe at the approach of winter. "*Grallæ tanquam conjuratæ unanimiter in fugam se conjiciunt; ne earum unicam quidem inter nos habitantem invenire possimus; ut enim æstate in australibus degere nequeunt ob defectum lumbricorum, terramque siccam; ita nec in frigidis ob eandem causam,*" says Ekmarck the Swede, in his ingenious little treatise called *Migrationes Avium*, which by all means you ought to read while your thoughts run on the subject of migration. See *Amœnitates Academicæ*, vol. 4, p. 565.

Birds may be so circumstanced as to be obliged to migrate in one country and not in another: but the *grallæ*, (which procure their food from marshes and boggy grounds) must in winter forsake the more northerly parts of Europe, or perish for want of food.

I am glad you are making inquiries from Linnæus concerning the woodcock: it is expected of him that he should be able to account for the motions and manner of life of the animals of his own *Fauna*.

Faunists, as you observe, are too apt to acquiesce in bare descriptions, and a few synonyms: the reason is plain; because all that may be done at home in a man's study, but the investigation of the life and conversation of animals, is a concern of much more trouble and difficulty, and is not to be attained but by the active and inquisitive, and by those that reside much in the country.

Foreign systematics are, I observe, much too vague in their specific differences; which are almost universally constituted by one or two particular marks, the rest of the description running in general terms. But our countryman, the excellent Mr. Ray, is the only describer that conveys some precise idea in every term or word, maintaining his superiority over his followers and imitators in spite of the advantage of fresh discoveries and modern information...

LETTER XI

TO THE SAME

Selborne, *Feb.* 8, 1772.

DEAR SIR,

When I ride about in the winter, and see such prodigious flocks of various kinds of birds, I cannot help admiring at these congregations, and wishing that it was in my power to account for those appearances almost peculiar to the season. The two great motives which regulate the proceedings of the brute creation are love and hunger; the former incites animals to perpetuate their kind, the latter induces them to preserve individuals: whether either of these should seem to be the ruling passion in the matter of congregating is to be considered. As to love, that is out of the question at a time of the year when that soft passion is not indulged: besides, during the amorous season, such a jealousy prevails between the male birds that they can hardly bear to be together in the same hedge or field. Most of the singing and elation of spirits of that time seem to me to be the effect of rivalry and emulation: and it is to this spirit of jealousy that I chiefly attribute the equal dispersion of birds in the spring over the face of the country.

Now as to the business of food: as these animals are actuated by instinct to hunt for necessary food, they should not, one would suppose, crowd together in pursuit of sustenance at a time when it is most likely to fail; yet such associations do take place in hard weather chiefly, and thicken as the severity increases. As some kind of self-interest and self-defence is no doubt the motive for the proceeding, may it not arise from the helplessness of their state in such rigorous seasons; as men crowd together, when under great calamities, though they know not why? Perhaps approximation may dispel some degree of cold; and a crowd may make each individual appear safer from the ravages of birds of prey and other dangers.*

If I admire when I see how much congenerous birds love to

* See my *Introduction*.

congregate, I am the more struck when I see incongruous ones in such strict amity.* If we do not much wonder to see a flock of rooks usually attended by a train of daws, yet it is strange that the former should so frequently have a flight of starlings for their satellites. Is it because rooks have a more discerning scent than their attendants, and can lead them to spots more productive of food? Anatomists say that rooks, by reason of two large nerves which run down between the eyes into the upper mandible, have a more delicate feeling in their beaks than other round-billed birds, and can grope for their meat when out of sight. Perhaps then their associates attend them on the motive of interest, as greyhounds wait on the motions of their finders; and as lions are said to do on the yelpings of jackalls. Lapwings and starlings sometimes associate.

* There are many singular examples of friendly partnership between individual birds of widely different genera.

LETTER XIII

TO THE SAME

April 12, 1772.

DEAR SIR,

While I was in Sussex last autumn my residence was at the village near Lewes,* from whence I had formerly the pleasure of writing to you. On the first of November I remarked that the old tortoise,† formerly mentioned, began first to dig the ground in order to the forming it's hybernaculum, which it had fixed on just beside a great tuft of hepaticas. It scrapes out the ground with it's fore-feet, and throws it up over it's back with it's hind; but the motion of it's legs is ridiculously slow, little exceeding the hour-hand of a clock; and suitable to the composure of an animal said to be a whole month in performing one feat of copulation. Nothing can be more assiduous than this creature night and day in scooping the earth, and forcing it's great body into the cavity; but, as the noons of that season proved unusually warm and sunny, it was continually interrupted, and called forth by the heat in the middle of the day; and though I continued there till the thirteenth of November, yet the work remained unfinished. Harsher weather, and frosty mornings, would have quickened it's operations. No part of it's behaviour ever struck me more than the extreme timidity it always expresses with regard to rain; for though it has a shell that would secure it against the wheel of a loaded cart, yet does it discover as much solicitude about rain as a lady dressed in all her best attire, shuffling away on the first sprinklings, and running it's head up in a corner. If attended to, it becomes an excellent weather-glass; for as sure as it walks elate, and as it were on tiptoe, feeding with great earnestness in a morning, so sure will it rain before night. It is totally a diurnal animal, and never pretends to stir after it becomes dark. The tortoise, like other reptiles, has an arbitrary stomach as well as lungs; and can refrain

* At Ringmer.

† See Letters VII and L to Barrington.

from eating as well as breathing for a great part of the year. When first awakened it eats nothing; nor again in the autumn before it retires: through the height of the summer it feeds voraciously, devouring all the food that comes in it's way. I was much taken with it's sagacity in discerning those that do it kind offices: for, as soon as the good old lady* comes in sight who has waited on it for more than thirty years, it hobbles towards it's benefactress with aukward alacrity; but remains inattentive to strangers. Thus not only "*the ox knoweth his owner, and the ass his master's crib*,"† but the most abject reptile and torpid of beings distinguishes the hand that feeds it, and is touched with the feelings of gratitude!

I am, &c. &c.

P.S. In about three days after I left Sussex the tortoise retired into the ground under the hepatica.

* Mrs. Snooke. Timothy came to Selborne after her death in 1780.

† *Isaiah* i. 3. 〈G. W.〉

LETTER XIV

TO THE SAME

Selborne, *March* 26, 1773.

DEAR SIR,

The more I reflect on the στοργη of animals, the more I am astonished at it's effects. Nor is the violence of this affection more wonderful than the shortness of it's duration. Thus every hen is in her turn the virago of the yard, in proportion to the helplessness of her brood; and will fly in the face of a dog or a sow in defence of those chickens, which in a few weeks she will drive before her with relentless cruelty.

This affection sublimes the passions, quickens the invention, and sharpens the sagacity of the brute creation. Thus an hen, just become a mother, is no longer that placid bird she used to be, but with feathers standing on end, wings hovering, and clocking note, she runs about like one possessed. Dams will throw themselves in the way of the greatest danger in order to avert it from their progeny. Thus a partridge will tumble along before a sportsman in order to draw away the dogs from her helpless covey.* In the time of nidification the most feeble birds will assault the most rapacious. All the hirundines of a village are up in arms at the sight of an hawk, whom they will persecute till he leaves that district. A very exact observer has often remarked that a pair of ravens nesting in the rock of Gibraltar would suffer no vulture or eagle to rest near their station, but would drive them from the hill with an amazing fury: even the blue thrush† at the season of breeding would dart out from the clefts of the rocks to chase away the kestril, or the sparrow-hawk. If you stand near the nest of a bird that has young, she will not be induced to betray them by an inadvertent fondness, but will

* Mr. Nicholson says that this decoying of the enemy away from the brood is "unintentional". But how can he or anybody tell to what extent the paroxysms are genuine and to what extent counterfeit? Surely it is more likely that the one was a development of the other. The mechanist theory is so anxious to deny intelligence to animals that it is frequently unable to employ it in observing them.

† The rock-thrush of Southern Europe.

wait about at a distance with meat in her mouth for an hour together.

Should I farther corroborate what I have advanced above by some anecdotes which I probably may have mentioned before in conversation, yet you will, I trust, pardon the repetition for the sake of the illustration.

The flycatcher of the *Zoology* (the *stoparola* of Ray) builds every year in the vines that grow on the walls of my house. A pair of these little birds had one year inadvertently placed their nest on a naked bough, perhaps in a shady time, not being aware of the inconvenience that followed. But an hot sunny season coming on before the brood was half fledged, the reflection of the wall became insupportable, and must inevitably have destroyed the tender young, had not affection suggested an expedient, and prompted the parent-birds to hover over the nest all the hotter hours, while with wings expanded, and mouths gaping for breath, they screened off the heat from their suffering offspring.

A farther instance I once saw of notable sagacity in a willow-wren, which had built in a bank in my fields. This bird a friend and myself had observed as she sat in her nest; but were particularly careful not to disturb her, though we saw she eyed us with some degree of jealousy. Some days after as we passed that way we were desirous of remarking how this brood went on; but no nest could be found, till I happened to take up a large bundle of long green moss, as it were, carelessly thrown over the nest in order to dodge the eye of any impertinent intruder.

A still more remarkable mixture of sagacity and instinct occurred to me one day as my people were pulling off the lining of an hotbed, in order to add some fresh dung. From out of the side of this bed leaped an animal with great agility that made a most grotesque figure; nor was it without great difficulty that it could be taken; when it proved to be a large white-bellied field-mouse* with three or four young clinging to her teats by their mouths and feet. It was amazing that the desultory and rapid motions of this dam should not oblige her litter to quit their hold, especially when it appeared that they were so young as to be both naked and blind!

* Doubtless the long-tailed field-mouse.

To these instances of tender attachment, many more of which might be daily discovered by those that are studious of nature, may be opposed that rage of affection, that monstrous perversion of the *στοργη*, which induces some females of the brute creation to devour their young because their owners have handled them too freely, or removed them from place to place! Swine, and sometimes the more gentle race of dogs and cats, are guilty of this horrid and preposterous murder. When I hear now and then of an abandoned mother that destroys her offspring, I am not so much amazed; since reason perverted, and the bad passions let loose, are capable of any enormity: but why the parental feelings of brutes, that usually flow in one most uniform tenor, should sometimes be so extravagantly diverted, I leave to abler philosophers than myself to determine.*

I am, etc.

* The author answers his own question in this eloquent passage by the phrase "rage of affection", induced by fear.

LETTER XV

TO THE SAME

Selborne, *July* 8, 1773.

DEAR SIR,

Some young men went down lately to a pond on the verge of Wolmer-forest to hunt flappers, or young wild-ducks, many of which they caught, and, among the rest, some very minute yet well-fledged wild-fowls alive, which upon examination I found to be teals. I did not know till then that teals ever bred in the south of England, and was much pleased with the discovery: this I look upon as a great stroke in natural history.

We have had, ever since I can remember, a pair of white owls that constantly breed under the eaves* of this church. As I have paid good attention to the manner of life of these birds during their season of breeding, which lasts the summer through, the following remarks may not perhaps be unacceptable:—About an hour before sunset (for then the mice begin to run) they sally forth in quest of prey, and hunt all round the hedges of meadows and small enclosures for them, which seem to be their only food. In this irregular country we can stand on an eminence and see them beat the fields over like a setting-dog, and often drop down

* A good example of the author's acuteness of observation, and of his timelessness for the reader. He teaches us that a pair of human eyes with a mind behind them do count for something, even in an age of science, apparatus and machines.

in the grass or corn. I have minuted these birds with my watch for an hour together, and have found that they return to their nests, the one or the other of them, about once in five minutes; reflecting at the same time on the adroitness that every animal is possessed of as far as regards the well being of itself and offspring. But a piece of address, which they shew when they return loaded, should not, I think, be passed over in silence.—As they take their prey with their claws, so they carry it in their claws to their nest: but, as the feet are necessary in their ascent under the tiles they constantly perch first on the roof of the chancel, and shift the mouse from their claws to their bill, that the feet may be at liberty to take hold of the plate on the wall as they are rising under the eaves.

White owls seem not (but in this I am not positive) to hoot* at all: all that clamorous hooting appears to me to come from the wood kinds. The white owl does indeed snore and hiss in a tremendous manner; and these menaces well answer the intention of intimidating: for I have known a whole village up in arms on such an occasion, imagining the church-yard to be full of goblins and spectres. White owls also often scream horribly as they fly along; from this screaming probably arose the common people's imaginary species of *screech-owl*, which they superstitiously think attends the windows of dying persons. The plumage of the remiges of the wings of every species of owl that I have yet examined is remarkably soft and pliant. Perhaps it may be necessary that the wings of these birds should not make much resistance or rushing, that they may be enabled to steal through the air unheard upon a nimble and watchful quarry.

While I am talking of owls, it may not be improper to mention what I was told by a gentleman of the county of Wilts. As they were grubbing a vast hollow pollard-ash that had been the mansion of owls for centuries, he discovered at the bottom a mass of matter that at first he could not account for. After some examination, he found that it was a congeries of the bones of mice (and perhaps of birds and bats) that had been heaping together for ages, being cast up in pellets out of the crops of many generations of inhabitants. For owls cast up the bones, fur, and

* I have heard the barn owl hoot in a tone that might easily deceive one who heard it without having seen the bird as coming from the tawny owl.

feathers, of what they devour, after the manner of hawks. He believes, he told me, that there were bushels of this kind of substance.

When brown owls hoot their throats swell as big as an hen's egg. I have known an owl of this species live a full year without any water. Perhaps the case may be the same with all birds of prey. When owls fly they stretch out their legs behind them as a balance to their large heavy heads: for as most nocturnal birds have large eyes and ears they must have large heads to contain them. Large eyes I presume are necessary to collect every ray of light, and large concave ears to command the smallest degree of sound or noise.

I am, &c.

It will be proper to premise here that the sixteenth, eighteenth, twentieth, and twenty-first letters have been published already in the *Philosophical Transactions:* but as nicer observation has furnished several corrections and additions, it is hoped that the republication of them will not give offence; especially as these sheets would be very imperfect without them, and as they will be new to many readers who had no opportunity of seeing them when they made their first appearance.

The *hirundines* are a most inoffensive, harmless, entertaining, social, and useful tribe of birds: they touch no fruit in our gardens; delight, all except one species, in attaching themselves to our houses; amuse us with their migrations, songs, and marvellous agility; and clear our outlets from the annoyances of gnats and other troublesome insects. Some districts in the south seas, near Guiaquil,*† are desolated, it seems, by the infinite swarms of venomous mosquitoes, which fill the air, and render those coasts insupportable. It would be worth inquiring whether any species of *hirundines* is found in those regions. Whoever contemplates the myriads of insects that sport in the sun-beams of a summer evening in this country, will soon be convinced to what a degree our atmosphere would be choaked with them was it not for the friendly interposition of the swallow tribe.

* *See Ulloa's* Travels. ⟨G. W.⟩

† Viz. Guayaquil, the town in Ecuador.

Many species of birds have their peculiar *lice*; but the *hirundines* alone seem to be annoyed with *dipterous* insects, which infest every species, and are so large, in proportion to themselves, that they must be extremely irksome and injurious to them. These are the *hippoboscæ hirundinis,** with narrow subulated† wings, abounding in every nest; and are hatched by the warmth of the bird's own body during incubation, and crawl about under it's feathers.

A *species* of them is familiar to horsemen in the south of England under the name of *forest-fly*; and to some of *side-fly*, from it's running sideways like a crab. It creeps under the tails, and about the groins, of horses, which, at their first coming out of the north, are rendered half frantic by the tickling sensation; while our own breed little regards them.

The curious Réaumur‡ discovered the large eggs, or rather *pupæ*, of these flies as big as the flies themselves, which he hatched in his own bosom. Any person that will take the trouble to examine the old nests of either species of swallows may find in them the black shining cases or skins of the *pupæ* of these insects: but for other particulars, too long for this place, we refer the reader to *l'Histoire d'Insectes* of that admirable entomologist. Tom. iv, pl. 11.

* Viz. *Hippobosca equina*, Linnæus. They are large gnats.

† Viz. awl-shaped.

‡ Réaumur (1683-1757) is an admirable example of the enquiring spirit before the era of specialization. He peered about his native France asking why, hopping like the flea he was interested in from object to object, caring for all these things and illuminating many of them by his eager and discerning mind.

LETTER XVI

TO THE SAME

Selborne, *Nov*. 20, 1773.

DEAR SIR,

In obedience to your injunctions I sit down to give you some account of the house-martin, or martlet; and, if my monography of this little domestic and familiar bird should happen to meet with your approbation, I may probably soon extend my inquiries to the rest of the British *hirundines*—the swallow, the swift, and the bank-martin.

A few house-martins begin to appear about the sixteenth of April; usually some few days later than the swallow. For some time after they appear the hirundines in general pay no attention to the business of nidification, but play and sport about, either to recruit from the fatigue of their journey, if they do migrate at all, or else that their blood may recover it's true tone and texture after it has been so long benumbed by the severities of winter. About the middle of May, if the weather be fine, the martin begins to think in earnest of providing a mansion for it's family. The crust or shell of this nest seems to be formed of such dirt or loam as comes most readily to hand, and is tempered and wrought together with little bits of broken straws to render it tough and tenacious. As this bird often builds against a perpendicular wall without any projecting ledge under, it requires it's utmost efforts to get the first foundation firmly fixed, so that it may safely carry the superstructure. On this occasion the bird not only clings with it's claws, but partly supports itself by strongly inclining it's tail against the wall, making that a fulcrum; and thus steadied it works and plasters the materials into the face of the brick or stone. But then, that this work may not, while it is soft and green, pull itself down by it's own weight, the provident architect has prudence and forbearance enough not to advance her work too fast; but by building only in the morning, and by dedicating the rest of the day to food and amusement, gives it sufficient time to dry and harden. About half an inch seems to be a sufficient layer for a day. Thus careful workmen when they build mud-walls (informed at first perhaps by this little bird) raise but a moderate layer at a time, and then desist; lest the work should become top-heavy, and so be ruined by it's own weight. By this method in about ten or twelve days is formed an hemispheric nest with a small aperture towards the top, strong, compact, and warm; and perfectly fitted for all the purposes for which it was intended. But then nothing is more common than for the house-sparrow, as soon as the shell is finished, to seize on it as it's own, to eject the owner, and to line it after it's own manner.

After so much labour is bestowed in erecting a mansion, as Nature seldom works in vain, martins will breed on for several years together in the same nest,* where it happens to be well sheltered and secure from the injuries of weather. The shell or crust of the nest is a sort of rustic-work full of knobs and protuberances on the outside: nor is the inside of those that I have examined smoothed with any exactness at all; but is rendered soft and warm, and fit for incubation, by a lining of small straws, grasses, and feathers; and sometimes by a bed of moss interwoven with wool. In this nest they tread, or engender, frequently during the time of building; and the hen lays from three to five white eggs.

At first when the young are hatched, and are in a naked and helpless condition, the parent birds, with tender assiduity, carry out what comes away from their young. Was it not for this affectionate cleanliness the nestlings would soon be burnt up, and destroyed in so deep and hollow a nest, by their own caustic excrement. In the quadruped creation the same neat precaution is made use of; particularly among dogs and cats, where the dams lick away what proceeds from their young. But in birds there seems to be a particular provision, that the dung of nestlings is enveloped in a tough kind of jelly, and therefore is the easier conveyed off without soiling or daubing. Yet, as nature is cleanly in all her ways, the young perform this office for themselves in a little time by thrusting their tails out at the aperture of their nest. As the young of small birds presently arrive at

* And when that nest is past usage, they will providently demolish its fabric in the building of another, especially in these days of tarred roads, when building material is hard to come by.

their ἡλικία, or full growth, they soon become impatient of confinement, and sit all day with their heads out at the orifice, where the dams, by clinging to the nest, supply them with food from morning to night. For a time the young are fed on the wing by their parents; but the feat is done by so quick and almost imperceptible a slight, that a person must have attended very exactly to their motions before he would be able to perceive it. As soon as the young are able to shift for themselves, the dams immediately turn their thoughts to the business of a second brood: while the first flight, shaken off and rejected by their nurses, congregate in great flocks, and are the birds that are seen clustering and hovering on sunny mornings and evenings round towers and steeples, and on the roofs of churches and houses. These congregatings usually begin to take place about the first week in August; and therefore we may conclude that by that time the first flight is pretty well over. The young of this species do not quit their abodes all together; but the more forward birds get abroad some days before the rest. These approaching the eaves of buildings, and playing about before them, make people think that several old ones attend one nest.* They are often capricious in fixing on a nesting-place, beginning many edifices, and leaving them unfinished; but when once a nest is completed in a sheltered place, it serves for several seasons. Those which breed in a ready finished house get the start in hatching of those that build new by ten days or a fortnight. These industrious artificers are at their labours in the long days before four in the morning: when they fix their materials they plaster them on with their chins, moving their heads with a quick vibratory motion. They dip and wash as they fly sometimes in very hot weather, but not so frequently as swallows. It has been observed that martins usually build to a north-east or north-west aspect, that the heat of the sun may not crack and destroy their nests: but instances are also remembered where they bred for many years in vast abundance in an hot stifled inn-yard, against a wall facing to the south.

Birds in general are wise in their choice of situation: but in this

* Edmund Selous was one of the first, if not the first, to observe that these adult young actually do feed their brethren in the "procreant cradle". In this, they resemble the young of the moorhen.

neighbourhood every summer is seen a strong proof to the contrary at an house without eaves in an exposed district, where some martins build year by year in the corners of the windows. But, as the corners of these windows (which face to the south-east and south-west) are too shallow, the nests are washed down every hard rain; and yet these birds drudge on to no purpose from summer to summer, without changing their aspect or house. It is a piteous sight to see them labouring when half their nest is washed away and bringing dirt . . . "*generis lapsi sarcire ruinas.*"* Thus is instinct a most wonderful unequal faculty; in some instances so much above reason, in other respects so far below it! Martins love to frequent towns,† especially if there are great lakes and rivers at hand; nay they even affect the close air of London. And I have not only seen them nesting in the Borough, but in even the Strand and Fleet-street; but then it was obvious from the dinginess of their aspect that their feathers partook of the filth of that sooty atmosphere. Martins are by far the least agile of the four species; their wings and tails are short, and therefore they are not capable of such surprising turns and quick and glancing evolutions as the swallow. Accordingly they make use of a placid easy motion in a middle region of the air, seldom mounting to any great height, and never sweeping long together over the surface of the ground or water. They do not wander far for food, but affect sheltered districts, over some lake, or under some hanging wood, or in some hollow vale, especially in windy weather. They breed the latest of all the swallow kind: in 1772 they had nestlings on to October the twenty-first, and are never without unfledged young as late as Michaelmas.

As the summer declines the congregating flocks increase in numbers daily by the constant accession of the second broods; till at last they swarm in myriads upon myriads round the villages on the Thames, darkening the face of the sky as they frequent the aits of that river, where they roost. They retire, the bulk of them I mean, in vast flocks together about the beginning of October: but have appeared of late years in a considerable flight in this

* From Virgil's Georgics, as is the quotation in Letter XVIII to Barrington.

† Hardly, nowadays, and they are much less abundant even in the more remote villages. In the more secluded hamlets of the South Midlands and the West Country, I have constantly received information from the villagers about the decrease of the house-martins' nests under the cottage eaves.

neighbourhood, for one day or two, as late as November the third and sixth, after they were supposed to have been gone for more than a fortnight. They therefore withdraw with us the latest of any species. Unless these birds are very short-lived indeed, or unless they do not return to the district where they are bred,* they must undergo vast devastations some how, and some where; for the birds that return yearly bear no manner of proportion to the birds that retire.

House-martins are distinguished from their congeners by having their legs covered with soft downy feathers down to their toes. They are no songsters; but twitter in a pretty inward soft manner in their nests. During the time of breeding they are often greatly molested with fleas.

I am, &c.

* They constantly do, unless circumstances are unfavourable.

LETTER XVIII

TO THE SAME

Selborne, *Jan.* 29, 1774.

DEAR SIR,

The house-swallow, or chimney-swallow, is undoubtedly the first comer* of all the British *hirundines*; and appears in general on or about the thirteenth of April, as I have remarked from many years observation. Not but now and then a straggler is seen much earlier: and, in particular, when I was a boy I observed a swallow for a whole day together on a sunny warm Shrove Tuesday; which day could not fall out later than the middle of March, and often happened early in February.

It is worth remarking that these birds are seen first about lakes and mill-ponds; and it is also very particular, that if these early visitors happen to find frost and snow, as was the case of the two dreadful springs of 1770 and 1771, they immediately withdraw for a time. A circumstance this much more in favour of hiding than migration; since it is much more probable that a bird should retire to it's hybernaculum just at hand, than return for a week or two only to warmer latitudes.

The swallow, though called the chimney-swallow, by no means builds altogether in chimnies, but often within barns and out-houses against the rafters; and so she did in Virgil's time:

> — — — — Antè
> Garrula quàm tignis nidos suspendat hirundo.

In Sweden she builds in barns, and is called *ladu swala*, the barn-swallow. Besides, in the warmer parts of Europe there are no chimnies to houses, except they are *English-built*: in these countries she constructs her nest in porches, and gate-ways, and galleries, and open halls.

Here and there a bird may affect some odd, peculiar place; as we have known a swallow build down the shaft of an old well,

* The sand-martin is the first to come, as the author himself acknowledged sixteen years later. The earliest date of arrival in Hampshire in 1936 was March 7th.

through which chalk had been formerly drawn up for the purpose of manure: but in general with us this *hirundo* breeds in chimnies,* and loves to haunt those stacks where there is a constant fire, no doubt for the sake of warmth. Not that it can subsist in the immediate shaft where there is a fire; but prefers one adjoining to that of the kitchen, and disregards the perpetual smoke of that funnel, as I have often observed with some degree of wonder.

Five or six or more feet down the chimney does this little bird begin to form her nest about the middle of May, which consists, like that of the house-martin, of a crust or shell composed of dirt or mud, mixed with short pieces of straw to render it tough and permanent; with this difference, that whereas the shell of the martin is nearly hemispheric, that of the swallow is open at the top, and like half a deep dish: this nest is lined with fine grasses, and feathers which are often collected as they float in the air.

Wonderful is the address which this adroit bird shews all day long in ascending and descending with security through so narrow a pass. When hovering over the mouth of the funnel, the vibrations of her wings acting on the confined air occasion a rumbling like thunder. It is not improbable that the dam submits to this inconvenient situation so low in the shaft, in order to secure her broods from rapacious birds, and particularly from owls, which frequently fall down chimnies, perhaps in attempting to get at these nestlings.

The swallow lays from four to six white eggs, dotted with red specks; and brings out her first brood about the last week in June, or the first week in July. The progressive method by which the young are introduced into life is very amusing: first, they emerge from the shaft with difficulty enough, and often fall down into the rooms below: for a day or so they are fed on the chimney-top, and then are conducted to the dead leafless bough of some tree, where, sitting in a row, they are attended with great assiduity, and may then be called *perchers*. In a day or two more they become *flyers*, but are still unable to take their own food; therefore they play about near the place where the dams are hawking for flies; and, when a mouthful is collected, at a certain signal

* Hardly ever nowadays. Swallows have retired from houses to outhouses. The modern cylindrical chimney is unfavourable to their nidification.

given, the dam and the nestling advance, rising towards each other, and meeting at an angle; the young one all the while uttering such a little quick note of gratitude and complacency, that a person must have paid very little regard to the wonders of Nature that has not often remarked this feat.

The dam betakes herself immediately to the business of a second brood as soon as she is disengaged from her first; which at once associates with the first broods of *house-martins*; and with them congregates, clustering on sunny roofs, towers, and trees. This hirundo brings out her second brood towards the middle and end of August.

All the summer long is the swallow a most instructive pattern of unwearied industry and affection; for, from morning to night, while there is a family to be supported, she spends the whole day in skimming close to the ground, and exerting the most sudden turns and quick evolutions. Avenues, and long walks under hedges, and pasture-fields, and mown meadows where cattle graze, are her delight, especially if there are trees interspersed; because in such spots insects most abound. When a fly is taken a smart snap from her bill is heard, resembling the noise at the shutting of a watch-case; but the motion of the mandibles are too quick for the eye.

The swallow, probably the male bird, is the *excubitor* to house-martins, and other little birds, announcing the approach of birds of prey. For as soon as an hawk appears, with a shrill alarming note he calls all the swallows and martins about him; who pursue in a body, and buffet and strike their enemy till they have driven him from the village, darting down from above on his back, and rising in a perpendicular line in perfect security. This bird also will sound the alarm, and strike at cats when they climb on the roofs of houses, or otherwise approach the nests. Each species of hirundo drinks as it flies along, sipping the surface of the water; but the swallow alone, in general, *washes* on the wing, by dropping into a pool for many times together: in very hot weather house-martins and bank-martins dip and wash a little.

The swallow is a delicate songster, and in soft sunny weather sings both perching and flying; on trees in a kind of concert, and on chimney tops: is also a bold flyer, ranging to distant downs and commons even in windy weather, which the other species seem much to dislike; nay, even frequenting exposed sea-port towns, and making little excursions over the salt water. Horsemen on wide downs are often closely attended by a little party of swallows for miles together, which plays before and behind them, sweeping around, and collecting all the sculking insects that are roused by the trampling of the horses feet: when the wind blows hard, without this expedient, they are often forced to settle to pick up their lurking prey.

This species feeds much on little *coleoptera*, as well as on gnats and flies; and often settles on dug ground, or paths, for gravels to grind and digest it's food. Before they depart, for some weeks, to a bird, they forsake houses and chimnies, and roost in trees; and usually withdraw about the beginning of October; though some few stragglers may appear on at times till the first week in November.*

Some few pairs haunt the new and open streets of London next the fields, but do not enter, like the house-martin, the close and crowded parts of the city.

Both male and female are distinguished from their congeners by the length and forkedness of their tails. They are undoubtedly the most nimble of all the species: and when the male pursues the female in amorous chase, they then go beyond their usual speed, and exert a rapidity almost too quick for the eye to follow.

After this circumstantial detail of the life and discerning *στοργη* of the swallow, I shall add, for your farther amusement, an anecdote or two not much in favour of her sagacity:—

A certain swallow built for two years together on the handles of a pair of garden-shears, that were stuck up against the boards in an out-house, and therefore must have her nest spoiled whenever that implement was wanted: and, what is stranger still, another bird of the same species built it's nest on the wings and body of an owl that happened by accident to hang dead and dry from the rafter of a barn. This owl, with the nest on it's wings, and with eggs in the nest, was brought as a curiosity worthy the

* Mr. Nicholson remarks that they have now been recorded for every month in the year, "exceptionally surviving a very mild winter in England". White, therefore, was not so far wrong in toying with the idea that some of them spent the winter in holes, crannies and caves, since the winterers in England would naturally seek the most concealed and sheltered retreats for roosting.

most elegant private museum in Great-Britain. The owner, struck with the oddity of the sight, furnished the bringer with a large shell, or conch, desiring him to fix it just where the owl hung: the person did as he was ordered, and the following year a pair, probably the same pair, built their nest in the conch, and laid their eggs.

The owl and the conch make a strange grotesque appearance, and are not the least curious specimens in that wonderful collection of art and nature.*

Thus is instinct in animals, taken the least out of it's way, an undistinguishing, limited faculty; and blind to every circumstance that does not immediately respect self-preservation, or lead at once to the propagation or support of their species.†

I am,

With all respect, &c. &c.

* *Sir Ashton Lever's Musæum.* ⟨G. W.⟩

† See my *Introduction.*

LETTER XX

TO THE SAME

Selborne, *Feb.* 26, 1774.

DEAR SIR,

The sand-martin, or bank-martin, is by much the least of any of the British *hirundines*; and, as far as we have ever seen, the smallest known hirundo: though Brisson asserts that there is one much smaller, and that is the *hirundo esculenta.**

But it is much to be regretted that it is scarce possible for any observer to be so full and exact as he could wish in reciting the circumstances attending the life and conversation of this little bird, since it is *fera naturâ*, at least in this part of the kingdom, disclaiming all domestic attachments, and haunting wild heaths and commons where there are large lakes: while the other species, especially the swallow and house-martin, are remarkably gentle and domesticated, and never seem to think themselves safe but under the protection of man.

Here are in this parish, in the sand-pits and banks of the lakes of Wolmer-forest, several colonies of these birds; and yet they are never seen in the village; nor do they at all frequent the cottages that are scattered about in that wild district.† The only instance I ever remember where this species haunts any building is at the town of Bishop's Waltham, in this county, where many sand-martins nestle and breed in the scaffold-holes of the back-wall of William of Wykeham's stables: but then this wall stands in a very sequestered and retired enclosure, and faces upon a large and beautiful lake. And indeed this species seems so to delight in large waters, that no instance occurs of their abounding, but near vast pools or rivers: and in particular it has been remarked that they swarm in the banks of the Thames in some places below London-bridge.

* The edible swift.

† The reason for this is not dislike of the human neighbourhood so much as lack of suitable nesting sites. Sand-martins still breed in Wolmer Forest, a noisy, militarized, built-up area at the present time.

It is curious to observe with what different degrees of architectonic skill Providence has endowed birds of the same genus, and so nearly correspondent in their general mode of life! for while the swallow and the house-martin discover the greatest address in raising and securely fixing crusts or shells of loam as cunabula for their young, the bank-martin terebrates a round and regular hole in the sand or earth, which is serpentine, horizontal, and about two feet deep. At the inner end of this burrow does this bird deposit, in a good degree of safety, her rude nest, consisting of fine grasses and feathers, usually goose-feathers, very inartificially laid together.

Perseverance will accomplish any thing: though at first one would be disinclined to believe that this weak bird, with her soft and tender bill and claws, should ever be able to bore the stubborn sand-bank without entirely disabling herself: yet with these feeble instruments have I seen a pair of them make great dispatch: and could remark how much they had scooped that day by the fresh sand which ran down the bank, and was of a different colour from that which lay loose and bleached in the sun.

In what space of time these little artists are able to mine and finish these cavities I have never been able to discover, for reasons given above; but it would be a matter worthy of observation, where it falls in the way of any naturalist to make his remarks.* This I have often taken notice of, that several holes of different depths are left unfinished at the end of the summer. To imagine that these beginnings were intentionally made in order to be in the greater forwardness for next spring, is allowing perhaps too much foresight and *rerum prudentia* to a simple bird. May not the cause of these *latebræ* being left unfinished arise from their meeting in those places with strata too harsh, hard, and solid, for their purpose, which they relinquish, and go to a fresh spot that works more freely? Or may they not in other places fall in with a soil as much too loose and mouldering, liable to flounder,† and threatening to overwhelm them and their labours?

One thing is remarkable—that, after some years, the old holes

* Mr. Nicholson gives examples of a twenty-inches tunnel excavated within two days and a four-feet tunnel within sixteen.

† A striking example of the author's power of vitalizing his descriptions.

are forsaken and new ones bored; perhaps because the old habitations grow foul and fetid from long use, or because they may so abound with fleas as to become untenantable. This species of swallow moreover is strangely annoyed with fleas: and we have seen fleas, bed-fleas* (*pulex irritans*), swarming at the mouths of these holes, like bees on the stools of their hives.

The following circumstance should by no means be omitted—that these birds do *not* make use of their caverns by way of hybernacula, as might be expected; since banks so perforated have been dug out with care in the winter, when nothing was found but empty nests.

The sand-martin arrives much about the same time with the swallow, and lays, as she does, from four to six white eggs. But as this species is *cryptogame*, carrying on the business of nidification, incubation, and the support of it's young in the dark, it would not be so easy to ascertain the time of breeding, were it not for the coming forth of the broods, which appear much about the time, or rather somewhat earlier than those of the swallow. The nestlings are supported in common like those of their congeners, with gnats and other small insects; and sometimes they are fed with *libellulæ* (dragon-flies) almost as long as themselves. In the last week in June we have seen a row of these sitting on a rail near a great pool as *perchers*; and so young and helpless, as easily to be taken by hand: but whether the dams ever feed them on the wing, as swallows and house-martins do, we have never yet been able to determine; nor do we know whether they pursue and attack birds of prey.†

When they happen to breed near hedges and enclosures, they are dispossessed of their breeding holes by the house-sparrow, which is on the same account a fell adversary to house-martins.

These *hirundines* are no songsters, but rather mute, making only a little harsh noise when a person approaches their nests. They seem not to be of a sociable turn, never with us congregregating with their congeners in the autumn. Undoubtedly they breed a second time, like the house-martin and swallow; and withdraw about Michaelmas.

Though in some particular districts they may happen to

* Not actually bed-fleas but separate species closely allied to them.

† They do both, just like their congeners.

abound, yet in the whole, in the south of England at least, is this much the rarest species. For there are few towns or large villages but what abound with house-martins; few churches, towers, or steeples, but what are haunted by some swifts; scarce a hamlet or single cottage-chimney that has not it's swallow; while the bank-martins, scattered here and there, live a sequestered life among some abrupt sand-hills, and in the banks of some few rivers.

These birds have a peculiar manner of flying; flitting about with odd jerks, and vacillations, not unlike the motions of a butterfly. Doubtless the flight of all *hirundines* is influenced by, and adapted to, the peculiar sort of insects which furnish their food. Hence it would be worth inquiry to examine what particular genus of insects affords the principal food of each respective species of swallow.

Notwithstanding what has been advanced above, some few sand-martins, I see, haunt the skirts of London, frequenting the dirty pools in Saint George's-Fields, and about White-Chapel. The question is where these build, since there are no banks or bold shores in that neighbourhood: perhaps they nestle in the scaffold holes of some old or new deserted building. They dip and wash as they fly sometimes, like the house-martin and swallow.

Sand-martins differ from their congeners in the diminutiveness of their size, and in their colour, which is what is usually called a mouse-colour. Near Valencia, in Spain, they are taken, says Willughby, and sold in the markets for the table; and are called by the country people, probably from their desultory jerking manner of flight, *Papilion de Montagna.*

LETTER XXI

TO THE SAME

Selborne, *Sept.* 28, 1774.

Dear Sir,

As the *swift* or *black-martin* is the largest of the British *hirundines*, so is it undoubtedly the latest comer. For I remember but one instance of it's appearing before the last week in April: and in some of our late frosty, harsh springs, it has not been seen till the beginning of May. This species usually arrives in pairs.

The swift, like the sand-martin, is very defective in architecture, making no crust, or shell, for it's nest; but forming it of dry grasses and feathers, very rudely and inartificially put together. With all my attention to these birds, I have never been able once to discover one in the act of collecting or carrying in materials: so that I have suspected (since their nests are exactly the same) that they sometimes usurp upon the house-sparrows, and expel them, as sparrows do the house and sand-martin; well remembering that I have seen them squabbling together at the entrance of their holes; and the sparrows up in arms, and much-disconcerted at these intruders. And yet I am assured, by a nice observer* in such matters, that they do collect feathers for their nests in Andalusia; and that he has shot them with such materials in their mouths.

Swifts, like sand-martins, carry on the business of nidification quite in the dark, in crannies of castles, and towers, and steeples, and upon the tops of the walls of churches under the roof; and therefore cannot be so narrowly watched as those species that build more openly: but, from what I could ever observe, they begin nesting about the middle of May; and I have remarked, from eggs taken, that they have sat hard by the ninth of June. In general they haunt tall buildings, churches, and steeples, and breed only in such: yet in this village some pairs frequent the lowest and meanest cottages, and educate their young under

* John White, the author's brother, while in Gibraltar.

those thatched roofs. We remember but one instance where they breed out of buildings; and that is in the sides of a deep chalk-pit near the town of Odiham, in this county, where we have seen many pairs entering the crevices, and skimming and squeaking round the precipices.

As I have regarded these amusive birds with no small attention, if I should advance something new and peculiar with respect to them, and different from all other birds, I might perhaps be credited; especially as my assertion is the result of many years exact observation. The fact that I would advance is, that swifts *tread*, or copulate, on the wing: and I would wish any nice observer, that is startled at this supposition, to use his own eyes, and I think he will soon be convinced. In another *class* of animals, viz. the *insect*, nothing is so common as to see the different species of many genera in conjunction as they fly. The swift is almost continually on the wing; and as it never settles on the ground, on trees, or roofs, would seldom find opportunity for amorous rites, was it not enabled to indulge them in the air. If any person would watch these birds of a fine morning in May, as they are sailing round at a great height from the ground, he would see, every now and then, one drop on the back of another, and both of them sink down together for many fathoms with a loud piercing shriek. This I take to be the juncture when the business of generation is carrying on.

As the swift eats, drinks, collects materials for it's nest, and, as it seems, propagates on the wing; it appears to live more in the air than any other bird, and to perform all functions there save those of sleeping and incubation.*

This *hirundo*† differs widely from it's congeners in laying invariably but *two* eggs‡ at a time, which are milk-white, long, and peaked at the small end; whereas the other species lay at each brood from *four* to *six*. It is a most alert bird, rising very early, and retiring to roost very late; and is on the wing in the height of summer at least sixteen hours. In the longest days it does not withdraw to rest till a quarter before nine in the evening, being

* Swifts do also sleep in the air.

† Is now separated from swallows and martins because of its distinctive anatomical differences from them.

‡ Not infrequently three.

the latest of all day birds. Just before they retire whole groups of them assemble high in the air, and squeak, and shoot about with wonderful rapidity. But this bird is never so much alive as in sultry thundry weather, when it expresses great alacrity, and calls forth all it's powers. In hot mornings several, getting together in little parties, dash round the steeples and churches, squeaking as they go in a very clamorous manner: these, by nice observers, are supposed to be males, serenading their sitting hens; and not without reason, since they seldom squeak till they come close to the walls or eaves, and since those within utter at the same time a little inward note of complacency.

When the hen has sat hard all day, she rushes forth just as it is almost dark, and stretches and relieves her weary limbs, and snatches a scanty meal for a few minutes, and then returns to her duty of incubation. Swifts, when wantonly and cruelly shot while they have young, discover a little lump of insects in their mouths, which they pouch and hold under their tongue. In general they feed in a much higher district than the other species; a proof that gnats and other insects do also abound to a considerable height in the air: they also range to vast distances; since loco-motion is no labour to them, who are endowed with such wonderful powers of wing. Their powers seem to be in proportion to their leavers; and their wings are longer in proportion than those of almost any other bird. When they mute, or ease themselves in flight, they raise their wings, and make them meet over their backs.

At some certain times in the summer I had remarked that swifts were hawking very low for hours together over pools and streams; and could not help inquiring into the object of their pursuit that induced them to descend so much below their usual range. After some trouble, I found that they were taking *phryganeæ*, *ephemeræ*, and *libellulæ* (cadew-flies, may-flies, and dragon-flies) that were just emerged out of their aurelia state. I then no longer wondered that they should be so willing to stoop for a prey that afforded them such plentiful and succulent nourishment.

They bring out their young about the middle or latter end of July: but as these never become perchers, nor, that ever I could discern, are fed on the wing by their dams, the coming forth of the young is not so notorious as in the other species.

On the thirtieth of last June I untiled the eaves of an house where many pairs build, and found in each nest only *two* squab, naked *pulli*: on the eighth of July I repeated the same inquiry, and found they had made very little progress towards a fledged state, but were still naked and helpless. From whence we may conclude that birds whose way of life keeps them perpetually on the wing would not be able to quit their nest till the end of the month. Swallows and martins, that have numerous families, are continually feeding them every two or three minutes; while swifts, that have but two young to maintain, are much at their leisure, and do not attend on their nests for hours together.

Sometimes they pursue and strike at hawks that come in their way; but not with that vehemence and fury that swallows express on the same occasion. They are out all day long in wet days, feeding about, and disregarding still rain: from whence two things may be gathered; first, that many insects abide high in the air, even in rain; and next, that the feathers of these birds must be well preened to resist so much wet. Windy, and particularly windy weather with heavy showers, they dislike; and on such days withdraw, and are scarce ever seen.

There is a circumstance respecting the *colour* of swifts, which seems not to be unworthy our attention. When they arrive in the spring they are all over of a glossy, dark soot-colour, except their chins, which are white; but, by being all day long in the sun and air, they become quite weather-beaten and bleached before they depart, and yet they return glossy again in the spring.* Now, if they pursue the sun into lower latitudes, as some suppose, in order to enjoy a perpetual summer, why do they not return bleached? Do they not rather perhaps retire to rest for a season, and at that juncture moult and change their feathers, since all other birds are known to moult soon after the season of breeding?

Swifts are very anomalous in many particulars, dissenting from all their congeners not only in the number of their young, but in breeding but *once* in a summer; whereas all the other British *hirundines* breed invariably *twice*. It is past all doubt that swifts can breed but once, since they withdraw in a short time after the flight of their young, and some time before their con-

*Swifts moult in their winter quarters in Africa.

geners bring out their second broods. We may here remark, that, as swifts breed but *once* in a summer, and only *two* at a time, and the other *hirundines twice*, the latter, who lay from four to six eggs, increase at an average five times as fast as the former.

But in nothing are swifts more singular than in their early retreat. They retire, as to the main body of them, by the tenth of August, and sometimes a few days sooner: and every straggler invariably withdraws by the twentieth, while their congeners, all of them, stay till the beginning of October; many of them all through that month, and some occasionally to the beginning of November. This early retreat is mysterious and wonderful, since that time is often the sweetest season in the year. But, what is more extraordinary, they begin to retire still earlier in the most southerly parts of Andalusia, where they can be no ways influenced by any defect of heat; or, as one might suppose, defect of food. Are they regulated in their motions with us by a failure of food, or by a propensity to moulting, or by a disposition to rest after so rapid a life, or by what? This is one of those incidents in natural history that not only baffles our searches, but almost eludes our guesses!*

These hirundines never perch on trees or roofs, and so never congregate with their congeners. They are fearless while haunting their nesting places, and are not to be scared with a gun; and are often beaten down with poles and cudgels as they stoop to go under the eaves. Swifts are much infested with those pests to the genus called *hippoboscæ hirundinis*; and often wriggle and scratch themselves, in their flight, to get rid of that clinging annoyance.

Swifts are no songsters, and have only one harsh screaming note; yet there are ears to which it is not displeasing, from an agreeable association of ideas, since that note never occurs but in the most lovely summer weather.

They never settle on the ground but through accident; and when down can hardly rise, on account of the shortness of their legs and the length of their wings: neither can they walk, but only crawl; but they have a strong grasp with their feet, by which they cling to walls. Their bodies being flat they can enter a very narrow crevice; and where they cannot pass on their bellies they will turn up edgewise.

* As it does to-day.

The particular formation of the foot discriminates the swift from all the British *hirundines*; and indeed from all other known birds, the *hirundo melba*, or great white-bellied swift of Gibraltar, excepted; for it is so disposed as to carry "*omnes quatuor digitos anticos*" all it's four toes forward; besides the least toe, which should be the back-toe, consists of one bone alone, and the other three only of two apiece. A construction most rare and peculiar, but nicely adapted to the purposes in which their feet are employed. This, and some peculiarities attending the nostrils and under mandible, have induced a discerning* naturalist to suppose that this *species* might constitute a *genus per se*.†

In London a party of swifts frequents the Tower, playing and feeding over the river just below the bridge: others haunt some of the churches of the Borough next the fields; but do not venture, like the *house-martin*, into the close crowded part of the town.

The Swedes have bestowed a very pertinent name on this swallow, calling it *ring swala*,‡ from the perpetual *rings* or circles that it takes round the scene of it's nidification.

Swifts feed on *coleoptera*, or small beetles with hard cases over their wings, as well as on the softer insects; but it does not appear how they can procure gravel to grind their food, as swallows do, since they never settle on the ground. Young ones, over-run with *hippoboscæ*, are sometimes found, under their nests, fallen to the ground: the number of vermin rendering their abode insupportable any longer. They frequent in this village several abject cottages; yet a succession still haunts the same unlikely roofs: a good proof this that the same birds return to the same spots. As they must stoop very low to get up under these humble eaves, cats lie in wait, and sometimes catch them on the wing.

On the fifth of July, 1775, I again untiled part of a roof over the nest of a swift. The dam sat in the nest; but so strongly was she affected by natural στοργη for her brood, which she supposed to be in danger, that, regardless of her own safety, she would not

* *John Antony Scopoli, of Carniola, M.D.* ⟨G. W.⟩

† Not however by Linnæus, who classed the *Cypseli* with the *Hirundines*.

‡ Folklore derives the name "swallow" from the birds flying round the Cross on Calvary and crying "Svala, Svala" (Console! Console!)

stir, but lay sullenly by them, permitting herself to be taken in hand. The squab young we brought down and placed on the grass-plot, where they tumbled about, and were as helpless as a new-born child. While we contemplated their naked bodies, their unwieldy disproportioned abdomina, and their heads, too heavy for their necks to support, we could not but wonder when we reflected that these shiftless beings in a little more than a fortnight would be able to dash through the air almost with the inconceivable swiftness of a meteor; and perhaps, in their emigration, must traverse vast continents and oceans as distant as the equator. So soon does Nature advance small birds to their ἡλικια, or state of perfection; while the progressive growth of men and large quadrupeds is slow and tedious!

I am, &c.

LETTER XXII

TO THE SAME

Selborne, *Sept.* 13, 1774.

Dear Sir,

By means of a straight cottage-chimney I had an opportunity this summer of remarking, at my leisure, how swallows ascend and descend through the shaft: but my pleasure, in contemplating the address with which this feat was performed to a considerable depth in the chimney, was somewhat interrupted by apprehensions lest my eyes might undergo the same fate with those of Tobit.*†

Perhaps it may be some amusement to you to hear at what times the different species of hirundines arrived this spring in three very distant counties of this kingdom. With us the swallow was seen first on April the 4th, the swift on April the 24th, the bank-martin on April the 12th, and the house-martin not till April the 30th. At South Zele,‡ Devonshire, swallows did not arrive till April the 25th; swifts, in plenty, on May the 1st; and house-martins not till the middle of May. At Blackburn,§ in Lancashire, swifts were seen April the 28th, swallows April the 29th, house-martins May the 1st. Do these different dates, in such distant districts, prove any thing for or against migration?

* *Tobit*, ii, 10. 〈G. W.〉

† "The same night also I returned from the burial and slept by the wall of my courtyard, being polluted, and my face was uncovered. And I knew not that there were sparrows (swallows) in the wall, and mine eyes being open, the sparrows muted warm dung into mine eyes, and a whiteness came into mine eyes, and I went to the physicians, but they helped me not." (*Tobit*, ii, 10.)

‡ The author must have received these reports from his friend, Sampson Newbery, whose father was the Vicar of South Zele, and from his brother, John, who became Vicar of Blackburn in 1772. The reference to a date succeeding that of the present letter in the one preceding it is a further example of how arbitrary and inconsequent were the datings of the *Selborne Letters*.

§ John White became Vicar of Blackburn in 1772, after his return from Gibraltar. See note to entry of Oct. 7, 1789, in the *Naturalist's Journal*.

A farmer, near Weyhill,* fallows his land with two teams of asses; one of which works till noon, and the other in the afternoon. When these animals have done their work, they are penned all night, like sheep, on the fallow. In the winter they are confined and foddered in a yard, and make plenty of dung.

Linnæus says that hawks "*paciscuntur inducias cum avibus, quamdiu cuculus cuculat*": but it appears to me that, during that period, many little birds are taken and destroyed by birds of prey, as may be seen by their feathers left in lanes and under hedges.

The *missel-thrush* is, while breeding, fierce and pugnacious, driving such birds as approach it's nest, with great fury, to a distance. The Welch call it *pen y llwyn*, the head or master of the coppice. He suffers no magpie, jay, or blackbird, to enter the garden where he haunts; and is, for the time, a good guard to the new-sown legumens. In general he is very successful in the defence of his family: but once I observed in my garden, that several magpies came determined to storm the nest of a missel-thrush: the dams defended their mansion with great vigour, and fought resolutely *pro aris et focis*; but numbers at last prevailed, they tore the nest to pieces, and swallowed the young alive.

In the season of nidification the wildest birds are comparatively tame. Thus the *ring-dove* breeds in my fields, though they are continually frequented; and the missel-thrush, though most shy and wild in the autumn and winter, builds in my garden close to a walk where people are passing all day long.†

Wall-fruit abounds with me this year; but my grapes, that used to be forward and good, are at present backward beyond all precedent: and this is not the worst of the story; for the same ungenial weather, the same black cold solstice, has injured the more necessary fruits of the earth, and discoloured and blighted our wheat. The crop of hops promises to be very large.

Frequent returns of deafness incommode me sadly, and half disqualify me for a naturalist; for, when those fits are upon me,

* There are many references to Weyhill in Henry White's unpublished Log-Books. It was near Fyfield, Henry White's living, and one of the most famous fairs in the South of England.

† Bell notes more than a century later (1877) that the two species were still breeding on the same sites.

I lose all the pleasing notices and little intimations arising from rural sounds; and May is to me as silent and mute with respect to the notes of birds, &c. as August. My eyesight is, thank God, quick and good; but with respect to the other sense, I am, at times, disabled:

And Wisdom at one entrance quite shut out.

LETTER XXIII

TO THE SAME

Selborne, *June* 8, 1775.

DEAR SIR,

On September the 21st, 1741, being then on a visit, and intent on field-diversions, I rose before daybreak: when I came into the enclosures, I found the stubbles and clover-grounds matted all over with a thick coat of cobweb, in the meshes of which a copious and heavy dew hung so plentifully that the whole face of the country seemed, as it were, covered with two or three setting-nets drawn one over another. When the dogs attempted to hunt, their eyes were so blinded and hoodwinked that they could not proceed, but were obliged to lie down and scrape the incumbrances from their faces with their fore-feet, so that, finding my sport interrupted, I returned home musing in my mind on the oddness of the occurrence.

As the morning advanced the sun became bright and warm, and the day turned out one of those most lovely ones which no season but the autumn produces; cloudless, calm, serene, and worthy of the South of France itself.

About nine an appearance very unusual began to demand our attention, a shower of cobwebs falling from very elevated regions, and continuing, without any interruption, till the close of the day. These webs were not single filmy threads, floating in the air in all directions, but perfect flakes or rags; some near an inch broad, and five or six long, which fell with a degree of velocity that shewed they were considerably heavier than the atmosphere.

On every side as the observer turned his eyes might he behold a continual succession of fresh flakes falling into his sight, and twinkling like stars as they turned their sides towards the sun.

How far this wonderful shower extended would be difficult to say; but we know that it reached Bradley,* Selborne, and

* The author's uncle, the Rev. Charles White, was the vicar in 1775.

Alresford, three places which lie in a sort of a triangle, the shortest of whose sides is about eight miles in extent.

At the second of those places there was a gentleman* (for whose veracity and intelligent turn we have the greatest veneration) who observed it the moment he got abroad; but concluded that, as soon as he came upon the hill above his house, where he took his morning rides, he should be higher than this meteor, which he imagined might have been blown, like *Thistle-down*, from the common above: but, to his great astonishment, when he rode to the most elevated part of the down, 300 feet above his fields, he found the webs in appearance still as much above him as before; still descending into sight in a constant succession, and twinkling in the sun, so as to draw the attention of the most incurious.

Neither before nor after was any such fall observed; but on this day the flakes hung in the trees and hedges so thick, that a diligent person sent out might have gathered baskets full.

The remark that I shall make on these cobweb-like appearances, called *gossamer*, is, that, strange and superstitious as the notions about them were formerly, nobody in these days doubts but that they are the real production of small spiders, which swarm in the fields in fine weather in autumn, and have a power of shooting out webs from their tails so as to render themselves buoyant, and lighter than air.† But why these apterous insects should *that day* take such a wonderful aërial excursion, and why their webs should at once become so gross and material as to be considerably more weighty than air, and to descend with precipitation, is a matter beyond my skill. If I might be allowed to hazard a supposition, I should imagine that those filmy threads, when first shot, might be entangled in the rising dew, and so drawn up, spiders and all, by a brisk evaporation into the region where clouds are formed: and if the spiders have a power of coiling and thickening their webs in the air, as Dr. Lister‡ says they have, [see his Letters to Mr. Ray] then, when they were become heavier than the air, they must fall.

* Gilbert's father, John White.

† *Coleridge's Note*. "Permit me to observe, as a certain yet hitherto unnoticed etymology of this word, that it [gossamer] is 'God's Dame's Hair', and in Monkish Latin . . . called *Fila Marniael*."

‡ Queen Anne's court physician.

Every day in fine weather, in autumn chiefly, do I see those spiders shooting out their webs and mounting aloft: they will go off from your finger if you will take them into your hand. Last summer one alighted on my book as I was reading in the parlour; and, running to the top of the page, and shooting out a web, took it's departure from thence. But what I most wondered at was, that it went off with considerable velocity in a place where no air was stirring; and I am sure that I did not assist it with my breath. So that these little crawlers seem to have, while mounting, some loco-motive power without the use of wings, and to move in the air faster than the air itself.

LETTER XXIV*

TO THE SAME

Selborne, *Aug*. 15, 1775.

Dear Sir,

There is a wonderful spirit of sociality in the brute creation, independent of sexual attachment: the congregating of gregarious birds in the winter is a remarkable instance.

Many horses, though quiet with company, will not stay one minute in a field by themselves: the strongest fences cannot restrain them. My neighbour's horse will not only not stay by himself abroad, but he will not bear to be left alone in a strange stable without discovering the utmost impatience, and endeavouring to break the rack and manger with his fore feet. He has been known to leap out at a stable-window, through which dung was thrown, after company; and yet in other respects is remarkably quiet. Oxen and cows will not fatten by themselves; but will neglect the finest pasture that is not recommended by society. It would be needless to instance in sheep, which constantly flock together.

But this propensity seems not to be confined to animals of the same species; for we know a doe, still alive, that was brought up from a little fawn with a dairy of cows; with them it goes a-field, and with them it returns to the yard. The dogs of the house take no notice of this deer, being used to her; but, if strange dogs come by, a chase ensues; while the master smiles to see his favourite securely leading her pursuers over hedge, or gate, or stile, till she returns to the cows, who, with fierce lowings and menacing horns, drive the assailants quite out of the pasture.

Even the great disparity of kind and size does not always prevent social advances and mutual fellowship. For a very intelligent and observant person has assured me that, in the former part of his life, keeping but one horse, he happened also on a

* This letter was published in Barrington's *Miscellanies*. Rightly, since it anticipates Kropotkin's *Mutual Aid*. See Letter XI to Barrington. The quotation at the end is from *Paradise Lost*.

time to have but one solitary hen. These two incongruous animals spent much of their time together in a lonely orchard, where they saw no creature but each other. By degrees an apparent regard began to take place between these two sequestered individuals. The fowl would approach the quadruped with notes of complacency, rubbing herself gently against his legs: while the horse would look down with satisfaction, and move with the greatest caution and circumspection, lest he should trample on his diminutive companion. Thus, by mutual good offices, each seemed to console the vacant hours of the other: so that Milton, when he puts the following sentiment in the mouth of Adam, seems to be somewhat mistaken:

Much less can *bird* with *beast*, or fish with fowl,
So well converse, nor with the ox the ape.

I am, &c.

LETTER XXV

TO THE SAME

Selborne, *Oct.* 2, 1775.

Dear Sir,

We have two gangs or hordes of gypsies which infest the south and west of England, and come round in their circuit two or three times in the year. One of these tribes calls itself by the noble name of Stanley, of which I have nothing particular to say; but the other is distinguished by an appellative somewhat remarkable—As far as their harsh gibberish can be understood, they seem to say that the name of their clan is Curleople:* now the termination of this word is apparently Grecian: and as Mezeray and the gravest historians all agree that these vagrants did certainly migrate from Egypt and the East, two or three centuries ago, and so spread by degrees over Europe, may not this family-name, a little corrupted, be the very name they brought with them from the Levant? It would be matter of some curiosity, could one meet with an intelligent person among them, to inquire whether, in their jargon, they still retain any Greek words: the Greek radicals will appear in hand, foot, head, water, earth, &c. It is possible that amidst their cant and corrupted dialect many mutilated remains of their native language might still be discovered.

With regard to those peculiar people, the gypsies, one thing is very remarkable, and especially as they come from warmer climates; and that is, that while other beggars lodge in barns, stables, and cow-houses, these sturdy savages seem to pride themselves in braving the severities of winter, and in living *sub dio* the whole year round. Last September was as wet a month as ever was known; and yet during those deluges did a young gypsy-girl lie-in in the midst of one of our hop-gardens, on the cold ground, with nothing over her but a piece of blanket extended on

* The gipsies, "diddecoys" as they are called in some country dialects, reached England from India about the reign of Henry VII. But, though Sanskrit was their speech, the intercourse between India and Greece left its mark upon the latter many centuries after the conquests of Alexander.

a few hazel-rods bent hoop fashion, and stuck into the earth at each end, in circumstances too trying for a cow in the same condition: yet within this garden there was a large hop-kiln, into the chambers of which she might have retired, had she thought shelter an object worthy her attention.

Europe itself, it seems, cannot set bounds to the rovings of these vagabonds; for Mr. Bell,* in his return from Peking, met a gang of these people on the confines of Tartary, who were endeavouring to penetrate those deserts and try their fortune in China.†

Gypsies are called in French, *Bohémiens*; in Italian and modern Greek, *Zingani*.‡

* John Bell's book, published in 1763, is *Travels from St. Petersburg in Russia to Various Parts of Asia.*

† *See Bell's* Travels in China. ⟨G. W.⟩

‡ *Coleridge's Note.* "The Zingani in Calabria and Apulia are not gypsies, but Christian Greeks with a very strange religion."

LETTER XXVI *

TO THE SAME

Selborne, *Nov.* 1, 1775.

Dear Sir,

Hîc . . . tædæ pingues, hic plurimus ignis
Semper, et assiduâ postes fuligine nigri.

I shall make no apology for troubling you with the detail of a very simple piece of domestic œconomy, being satisfied that you think nothing beneath your attention that tends to utility: the matter alluded to is the use of *rushes* instead of candles, which I am well aware prevails in many districts besides this; but as I know there are countries also where it does not obtain, and as I have considered the subject with some degree of exactness, I shall proceed in my humble story, and leave you to judge of the expediency.

The proper species of *rush* for this purpose seems to be the *juncus conglomeratus*, or common soft rush, which is to be found in most moist pastures, by the sides of streams, and under hedges. These rushes are in best condition in the height of summer; but may be gathered, so as to serve the purpose well, quite on to autumn. It would be needless to add that the largest and longest are best. Decayed labourers, women, and children, make it their business to procure and prepare them. As soon as they are cut they must be flung into water, and kept there; for otherwise they will dry and shrink, and the peel will not run. At first a person would find it no easy matter to divest a rush of it's peel or rind, so as to leave one regular, narrow, even rib from top to bottom that may support the pith: but this, like other feats, soon becomes familiar even to children; and we have seen an old woman, stone-blind, performing this business with great dispatch, and seldom failing to strip them with the nicest regularity. When these *junci* are thus far prepared, they must lie out on the grass to be bleached, and take the dew for some nights, and afterwards be dried in the sun.

* This letter is a notable example of the universality of the author's interests and knowledge, so long as they were parochial.

Some address is required in dipping these rushes in the scalding fat or grease; but this knack also is to be attained by practice. The careful wife of an industrious Hampshire labourer obtains all her fat for nothing; for she saves the scummings of her bacon-pot for this use; and, if the grease abounds with salt, she causes the salt to precipitate to the bottom, by setting the scummings in a warm oven. Where hogs are not much in use, and especially by the sea-side, the coarser animal-oils will come very cheap. A pound of common grease may be procured for four pence; and about six pounds of grease will dip a pound of rushes; and one pound of rushes may be bought for one shilling: so that a pound of rushes, medicated and ready for use, will cost three shillings. If men that keep bees will mix a little wax with the grease, it will give it a consistency, and render it more cleanly, and make the rushes burn longer: mutton-suet would have the same effect.

A good rush, which measured in length two feet four inches and an half, being minuted, burnt only three minutes short of an hour: and a rush still of greater length has been known to burn one hour and a quarter.

These rushes give a good clear light. Watch-lights (coated with tallow), it is true, shed a dismal one, "darkness visible"; but then the wicks of those have *two* ribs of the rind, or peel, to support the pith, while the wick of the dipped rush has but *one*. The *two* ribs are intended to impede the progress of the flame and make the candle last.

In a pound of dry rushes, avoirdupois, which I caused to be weighed and numbered, we found upwards of one thousand six hundred individuals. Now suppose each of these burns, one with another, only half an hour, then a poor man will purchase eight hundred hours of light, a time exceeding thirty-three entire days, for three shillings. According to this account each rush, before dipping, costs $\frac{1}{33}$ of a farthing, and $\frac{1}{11}$ afterwards. Thus a poor family will enjoy $5\frac{1}{2}$ hours of comfortable light for a farthing. An experienced old housekeeper assures me that one pound and an half of rushes completely supplies his family the year round, since working people burn no candle in the long days, because they rise and go to bed by daylight.

Little farmers use rushes much in the short days, both morning and evening, in the dairy and kitchen; but the very poor, who are always the worst œconomists, and therefore must continue very poor, buy an halfpenny candle every evening, which, in their blowing open rooms, does not burn much more than two hours. Thus have they only two hours light for their money instead of eleven.

While on the subject of rural œconomy, it may not be improper to mention a pretty implement of housewifery that we have seen no where else; that is, little neat besoms which our foresters make from the stalks of the *polytricum commune*, or *great golden maiden-hair*, which they call *silk-wood*, and find plenty in the bogs. When this moss is well combed and dressed, and divested of it's outer skin, it becomes of a beautiful bright-chesnut colour; and, being soft and pliant, is very proper for the dusting of beds, curtains, carpets, hangings, &c. If these besoms were known to the brush-makers in town, it is probable they might come much in use for the purpose above-mentioned.*

I am, &c.

* *A besom of this sort is to be seen in Sir Ashton Lever's Museum.* 〈G. W.〉

LETTER XXVII

TO THE SAME

Selborne, *Dec.* 12, 1775.

DEAR SIR,

We had in this village more than twenty years ago an idiot-boy, whom I well remember, who, from a child, shewed a strong propensity to bees; they were his food, his amusement, his sole object. And as people of this cast have seldom more than one point in view, so this lad exerted all his few faculties on this one pursuit. In the winter he dosed away his time, within his father's house, by the fire side, in a kind of torpid state, seldom departing from the chimney-corner; but in the summer he was all alert, and in quest of his game in the fields, and on sunny banks. Honey-bees, humble-bees, and wasps, were his prey wherever he found them: he had no apprehensions from their stings, but would seize them *nudis manibus*, and at once disarm them of their weapons, and suck their bodies for the sake of their honey-bags. Sometimes he would fill his bosom between his shirt and his skin with a number of these captives; and sometimes would confine them in bottles. He was a very *merops apiaster, or bee-bird*; and very injurious to men that kept bees; for he would slide into their bee-gardens, and, sitting down before the stools, would rap with his fingers on the hives, and so take the bees as they came out. He has been known to overturn hives for the sake of honey, of which he was passionately fond. Where metheglin* was making he would linger round the tubs and vessels, begging a draught of what he called *bee-wine*. As he ran about he used to make a humming noise with his lips, resembling the buzzing of bees. This lad was lean and sallow, and of a cadaverous complexion; and, except in his favourite pursuit, in which he was wonderfully adroit, discovered no manner of understanding. Had his capacity been better, and directed to the same object, he had perhaps abated much of our wonder at the feats of a more modern exhibiter of bees: and we may justly say of him now,

> ——————————— Thou,
> Had thy presiding star propitious shone,
> Should'st Wildman† be ————.

When a tall youth he was removed from hence to a distant village, where he died, as I understand, before he arrived at manhood.

I am, &c.

* The rural version up to comparatively recent times (before the Machine Age destroyed all the local industries) of the Saxon mead. It used to be made in a farmhouse not far from Poole Harbour up to the time of the War.

† Author of *A Treatise on the Management of Bees*, 1768.

LETTER XXVIII

TO THE SAME

Selborne, *Jan.* 8, 1776.

DEAR SIR,

It is the hardest thing in the world to shake off superstitious prejudices: they are sucked in as it were with our mother's milk; and, growing up with us at a time when they take the fastest hold and make the most lasting impressions, become so interwoven into our very constitutions, that the strongest good sense is required to disengage ourselves from them. No wonder therefore that the lower people retain them their whole lives through, since their minds are not invigorated by a liberal education, and therefore not enabled to make any efforts adequate to the occasion.

Such a preamble seems to be necessary before we enter on the superstitions of this district, lest we should be suspected of exaggeration in a recital of practices too gross for this enlightened age.

But the people of Tring, in Hertfordshire, would do well to remember, that no longer ago than the year 1751, and within twenty miles of the capital, they seized on two superannuated wretches, crazed with age, and overwhelmed with infirmities, on a suspicion of witchcraft; and, by trying experiments,* drowned them in a horse-pond.

In a farm-yard near the middle of this village stands, at this day, a row of pollard-ashes, which, by the seams and long cicatrices down their sides, manifestly shew that, in former times, they have been cleft asunder. These trees, when young and flexible, were severed and held open by wedges, while ruptured children, stripped naked, were pushed through the apertures, under a persuasion that, by such a process, the poor babes would be cured of their infirmity. As soon as the operation was over, the tree, in the suffering part, was plastered with loam, and carefully swathed up. If the parts coalesced and soldered together, as usu-

*No doubt a traditional survival of the archaic trial by water.

ally fell out, where the feat was performed with any adroitness at all, the party was cured; but, where the cleft continued to gape, the operation, it was supposed, would prove ineffectual. Having occasion to enlarge my garden not long since, I cut down two or three such trees, one of which did not grow together.

We have several persons now living in the village, who, in their childhood, were supposed to be healed by this superstitious ceremony, derived down perhaps from our Saxon ancestors, who practised it before their conversion to Christianity.*

At the south corner of the Plestor, or area, near the church, there stood, about twenty-years ago, a very old grotesque hollow pollard-ash, which for ages had been looked on with no small veneration as a *shrew-ash.* Now a shrew-ash is an ash whose twigs or branches, when gently applied to the limbs of cattle, will immediately relieve the pains which a beast suffers from the running of a *shrew-mouse* over the part affected: for it is supposed that a shrew-mouse is of so baneful and deleterious a nature, that wherever it creeps over a beast, be it horse, cow, or sheep, the suffering animal is afflicted with cruel anguish, and threatened with the loss of the use of the limb. Against this accident, to which they were continually liable, our provident forefathers always kept a shrew-ash at hand, which, when once medicated, would maintain it's virtue for ever. A shrew-ash was made thus:†—Into the body of the tree a deep hole was bored with an auger, and a poor devoted shrew-mouse was thrust in alive, and plugged in, no doubt, with several quaint incantations long since forgotten. As the ceremonies necessary for such a consecration are no longer understood, all succession is at an end, and no such tree is known to subsist in the manor, or hundred.

As to that on the Plestor

The late vicar stubb'd and burnt it,

* The practice probably comes down from the Bronze Age. The Long Stone at Minchinhampton, near Stroud, has a hole through it into which up to recent years children were passed for rickets. The opening was the portal to the House of the Dead, and perhaps the idea originated from that of rebirth, the passage through the stone being from a ceremonial death to a ceremonial rebirth or, in later times, from sickness to health. Sacred tree and sacred stone were closely associated in archaic ritual, and both being repositories of the living dead, the sick were passed through a *divine* body, in tree or stone form.

† *For a similar practice, see Plot's* Staffordshire. ⟨G. W.⟩

when he was way-warden,* regardless of the remonstrances of the by-standers, who interceded in vain for it's preservation, urging it's power and efficacy, and alledging that it had been

Religione patrum multos servata per annos.

I am, &c.

* The "way-warden" was one of the pre-Enclosure officials of the old manorial village-community. The Enclosures were later at Selborne than in many other parts, and squatter's rights survived at Oakhanger as late as the present generation.

LETTER XXXI

TO THE SAME

Selborne, *April* 29, 1776.

DEAR SIR,

On August the 4th, 1775, we surprised a large viper, which seemed very heavy and bloated, as it lay in the grass basking in the sun. When we came to cut it up, we found that the abdomen was crowded with young, fifteen in number; the shortest of which measured full seven inches, and were about the size of full-grown earth-worms. This little fry issued into the world with the true viper-spirit about them, shewing great alertness as soon as disengaged from the belly of the dam: they twisted and wriggled about, and set themselves up, and gaped very wide when touched with a stick, shewing manifest tokens of menace and defiance, though as yet they had no manner of fangs that we could find, even with the help of our glasses.

To a thinking mind nothing is more wonderful than that early instinct which impresses young animals with the notion of the situation of their natural weapons, and of using them properly in their own defence, even before those weapons subsist or are formed. Thus a young cock will spar at his adversary before his spurs are grown; and a calf or a lamb will push with their heads before their horns are sprouted. In the same manner did these young adders attempt to bite before their fangs were in being. The dam however was furnished with very formidable ones, which we lifted up (for they fold down when not used) and cut them off with the point of our scissars.

There was little room to suppose that this brood had ever been in the open air before; and that they were taken in for refuge, at the mouth of the dam, when she perceived that danger was approaching; because then probably we should have found them somewhere in the neck, and not in the abdomen.

LETTER XXXII

TO THE SAME

Castration has a strange effect: it emasculates both man, beast, and bird, and brings them to a near resemblance of the other sex. Thus eunuchs have smooth unmuscular arms, thighs, and legs; and broad hips, and beardless chins, and squeaking voices. Gelt-stags and bucks have hornless heads, like hinds and does. Thus wethers have small horns, like ewes; and oxen large bent horns, and hoarse voices when they low, like cows: for bulls have short straight horns; and though they mutter and grumble in a deep tremendous tone, yet they low in a shrill high key. Capons have small combs and gills, and look pallid about the head, like pullets; they also walk without any parade, and hover chickens like hens. Barrow-hogs have also small tusks like sows.

Thus far it is plain that the deprivation of *masculine vigour* puts a stop to the growth of those parts or appendages that are looked upon as it's insignia. But the ingenious Mr. Lisle,* in his book on husbandry, carries it much farther; for he says that the loss of those insignia alone has sometimes a strange effect on the ability itself: he had a boar so fierce and venereous, that, to prevent mischief, orders were given for his tusks to be broken off. No sooner had the beast suffered this injury than his powers forsook him, and he neglected those females to whom before he was passionately attached, and from whom no fences could restrain him.

* Connected by marriage with the Vicar of Selborne in 1784.

LETTER XXXIII

TO THE SAME

The natural term of an hog's life is little known, and the reason is plain—because it is neither profitable nor convenient to keep that turbulent animal to the full extent of it's time: however, my neighbour, a man of substance, who had no occasion to study every little advantage to a nicety, kept an half-bred Bantam-sow, who was as thick as she was long, and whose belly swept on the ground till she was advanced to her seventeenth year; at which period she shewed some tokens of age by the decay of her teeth and the decline of her fertility.

For about ten years this prolific mother produced two litters in the year of about ten at a time, and once above twenty at a litter; but, as there were near double the number of pigs to that of teats, many died. From long experience in the world this female was grown very sagacious and artful:—when she found occasion to converse with a boar she used to open all the intervening gates, and march, by herself, up to a distant farm where one was kept; and when her purpose was served would return by the same means. At the age of about fifteen her litters began to be reduced to four or five; and such a litter she exhibited when in her fatting-pen. She proved, when fat, good bacon, juicy, and tender; the rind, or sward, was remarkably thin. At a moderate computation she was allowed to have been the fruitful parent of three hundred pigs: a prodigious instance of fecundity in so large a quadruped! She was killed in spring 1775.

I am, &c.

LETTER XXXIV

TO THE SAME

Selborne, *May* 9, 1776.

DEAR SIR,

— — — — — — — admorunt ubera tigres.

We have remarked in a former letter how much incongruous animals, in a lonely state, may be attached to each other from a spirit of sociality; in this it may not be amiss to recount a different motive which has been known to create as strange a fondness.

My friend had a little helpless *leveret* brought to him, which the servants fed with milk in a spoon, and about the same time his cat kittened and the young were dispatched and buried. The hare was soon lost, and supposed to be gone the way of most fondlings, to be killed by some dog or cat. However, in about a fortnight, as the master was sitting in his garden in the dusk of the evening, he observed his cat, with tail erect, trotting towards him, and calling with little short inward notes of complacency, such as they use towards their kittens, and something gamboling after, which proved to be the leveret that the cat had supported with her milk, and continued to support with great affection.*

Thus was a graminivorous animal nurtured by a carnivorous and predaceous one!

Why so cruel and sanguinary a beast as a cat, of the ferocious genus of *Feles*, the *murium leo*, as Linnæus calls it, should be affected with any tenderness towards an animal which is it's natural prey, is not so easy to determine.

This strange affection probably was occasioned by that desiderium, those tender maternal feelings, which the loss of her kittens had awakened in her breast; and by the complacency and ease she derived to herself from the procuring her teats to be drawn, which were too much distended with milk, till, from

* The *Naturalist's Journal* gives another and similar example of a cat giving suck to three young squirrels.

habit, she became as much delighted with this foundling as if it had been her real offspring.

This incident is no bad solution of that strange circumstance which grave historians as well as the poets assert, of exposed children being sometimes nurtured by female wild beasts that probably had lost their young. For it is not one whit more marvellous that Romulus and Remus, in their infant state, should be nursed by a she-wolf, than that a poor little sucking leveret should be fostered and cherished by a bloody grimalkin.

— — — — viridi fœtam Mavortis in antro
Procubuisse lupam: geminos huic ubera circum
Ludere pendentes pueros, et lambere matrem
Impavidos: illam tereti cervice reflexam
Mulcere alternos, et corpora fingere linguâ.*

* From the *Aeneid*.

LETTER XXXV

TO THE SAME

Selborne, *May* 20, 1777.

DEAR SIR,

Lands that are subject to frequent inundations are always poor; and probably the reason may be because the worms are drowned. The most insignificant insects and reptiles are of much more consequence, and have much more influence in the œconomy of Nature, than the incurious are aware of; and are mighty in their effect, from their minuteness, which renders them less an object of attention; and from their numbers and fecundity. Earth-worms, though in appearance a small and despicable link in the chain of Nature, yet, if lost, would make a lamentable chasm. For, to say nothing of half the birds, and some quadrupeds which are almost entirely supported by them, worms seem to be the great promoters of vegetation,* which would proceed but lamely without them, by boring, perforating, and loosening the soil, and rendering it pervious to rains and the fibres of plants, by drawing straws and stalks of leaves and twigs into it; and, most of all, by throwing up such infinite numbers of lumps of earth called worm-casts, which, being their excrement, is a fine manure for grain and grass. Worms probably provide new soil for hills and slopes where the rain washes the earth away; and they affect slopes, probably to avoid being flooded. Gardeners and farmers express their detestation of worms; the former because they render their walks unsightly, and make them much work: and the latter because, as they think, worms eat their green corn. But these men would find that the earth without worms would soon become cold, hard-bound, and void of fermentation; and consequently steril: and besides, in favour of worms, it should be hinted that green corn, plants, and

* This letter anticipates Darwin's discoveries of the part played by earthworms in the economy of Nature. Though Darwin was aware of White's contribution to the subject, he acknowledged it in very airy fashion, under his breath, so to speak. Yet from this one brief letter, the quintessence of the Darwinian papers can be extracted.

flowers, are not so much injured by them as by many species of *coleoptera* (scarabs), and *tipulæ* (long-legs) in their larva, or grub-state; and by unnoticed myriads of small shell-less snails, called slugs, which silently and imperceptibly make amazing havoc in the field and garden.*

These hints we think proper to throw out in order to set the inquisitive and discerning to work.

A good monography of worms would afford much entertainment and information at the same time, and would open a large and new field in natural history. Worms work most in the spring; but by no means lie torpid in the dead months; are out every mild night in the winter, as any person may be convinced that will take the pains to examine his grass-plots with a candle; are hermaphrodites,† and much addicted to venery, and consequently very prolific.

I am, &c.

* *Farmer Young, of Norton-farm, says that this spring* (1777) *about four acres of his wheat in one field was entirely destroyed by* slugs, *which swarmed on the blades of corn, and devoured it as fast as it sprang.* ⟨G. W.⟩

† First discovered by the author.

LETTER XXXVI

TO THE SAME

Selborne, *Nov.* 22, 1777.

DEAR SIR,

You cannot but remember that the twenty-sixth and twenty-seventh of last March were very hot days; so sultry that every body complained and were restless under those sensations to which they had not been reconciled by gradual approaches.

This sudden summer-like heat was attended by many summer coincidences; for on those two days the thermometer rose to sixty-six in the shade; many species of insects revived and came forth; some bees swarmed in this neighbourhood; the old tortoise, near Lewes, in Sussex, awakened and came forth out of it's dormitory; and, what is most to my present purpose, many *house-swallows* appeared and were very alert in many places, and particularly at Cobham, in Surrey.

But as that short warm period was succeeded as well as preceded by harsh severe weather, with frequent frosts and ice, and cutting winds, the insects withdrew, the tortoise retired again into the ground, and the swallows were seen no more until the tenth of April, when, the rigour of the spring abating, a softer season began to prevail.

Again: it appears by my journals for many years past that *house-martins* retire, to a bird, about the beginning of October; so that a person not very observant of such matters would conclude that they had taken their last farewell: but then it may be seen in my diaries also that considerable flocks have discovered themselves again in the first week of November, and often on the fourth day of that month only *for one day*; and that not as if they were in actual migration, but playing about at their leisure and feeding calmly,* as if no enterprize of moment at all agitated their spirits. And this was the case in the beginning of this very

* Warde Fowler in his and L. C. Miall's Edition of *Selborne* (1901) justly calls attention to the author's perception of the leisureliness of autumnal migration.

month; for, on the fourth of November, more than twenty house-martins, which, in appearance, had all departed about the seventh of October, were seen again, for that *one morning only*, sporting between my fields and the Hanger, and feasting on insects which swarmed in that sheltered district. The preceding day was wet and blustering, but the fourth was dark and mild, and soft, the wind at south-west, and the thermometer at $58'\frac{1}{2}$; a pitch not common at that season of the year. Moreover, it may not be amiss to add in this place, that whenever the thermometer is above 50 the bat comes flitting out in every autumnal and winter-month.

From all these circumstances laid together, it is obvious that torpid insects, reptiles, and quadrupeds, are awakened from their profoundest slumbers by a little untimely warmth; and therefore that nothing so much promotes this death-like stupor as a defect of heat. And farther, it is reasonable to suppose that two whole species, or at least many individuals of those two species, of British *hirundines*, do never leave this island at all, but partake of the same benumbed state: for we cannot suppose that, after a month's absence, house-martins can return from southern regions to appear for *one* morning in November, or that house-swallows should leave the districts of Africa to enjoy, in March, the transient summer of a *couple* of days.

I am, &c.

LETTER XXXVII*

TO THE SAME

Selborne, *Jan.* 8, 1778.

DEAR SIR,

There was in this village several years ago a miserable pauper, who, from his birth, was afflicted with a leprosy, as far as we are aware of a singular kind, since it affected only the palms of his hands and the soles of his feet. This scaly eruption usually broke out twice in the year, at the spring and fall; and, by peeling away, left the skin so thin and tender that neither his hands or feet were able to perform their functions; so that the poor object was half his time on crutches, incapable of employ, and languishing in a tiresome state of indolence and inactivity. His habit was lean, lank, and cadaverous. In this sad plight he dragged on a miserable existence, a burden to himself and his parish, which was obliged to support him till he was relieved by death at more than thirty years of age.

The good women, who love to account for every defect in children by the doctrine of longing, said that his mother felt a violent propensity for oysters, which she was unable to gratify; and that the black rough scurf on his hands and feet were the shells of that fish. He knew his parents, neither of which were lepers; his father in particular lived to be far advanced in years.

In all ages the leprosy has made dreadful havock among mankind. The Israelites seem to have been greatly afflicted with it from the most remote times; as appears from the peculiar and repeated injunctions given them in the Levitical law.† Nor was the rancour of this foul disorder much abated in the last period of their commonwealth, as may be seen in many passages of the New Testament.

Some centuries ago this horrible distemper prevailed all

* This letter is eloquent not only of the wide scope and diversity of knowledge acquired by a country parson who confined his observations to his own parish, but of their social value by virtue of their intimacy.

† *See Leviticus, chap.* xiii *and* xiv. ⟨G. W.⟩

Europe over; and our forefathers were by no means exempt, as appears by the large provision made for objects labouring under this calamity. There was an hospital for female lepers in the diocese of Lincoln, a noble one near Durham, three in London and Southwark, and perhaps many more in or near our great towns and cities. Moreover, some crowned heads, and other wealthy and charitable personages, bequeathed large legacies to such poor people as languished under this hopeless infirmity.

It must therefore, in these days, be, to an humane and thinking person, a matter of equal wonder and satisfaction, when he contemplates how nearly this pest is eradicated, and observes that a leper now is a rare sight. He will, moreover, when engaged in such a train of thought, naturally inquire for the reason. This happy change perhaps may have originated and been continued from the much smaller quantity of salted meat and fish now eaten in these kingdoms; from the use of linen next the skin; from the plenty of better bread; and from the profusion of fruits, roots, legumes, and greens, so common in every family. Three or four centuries ago, before there were any enclosures, sown-grasses, field-turnips, or field-carrots, or hay, all the cattle which had grown fat in summer, and were not killed for winter-use, were turned out soon after Michaelmas to shift as they could through the dead months; so that no fresh meat could be had in winter or spring. Hence the marvellous account of the vast stores of salted flesh found in the larder of the eldest Spencer* in the days of Edward the Second, even so late in the spring as the third of May. It was from magazines like these that the turbulent barons supported in idleness their riotous swarms of retainers ready for any disorder or mischief. But agriculture is now arrived at such a pitch of perfection, that our best and fattest meats are killed in the winter; and no man need eat salted flesh, unless he prefers it, that has money to buy fresh.

One cause of this distemper might be, no doubt, the quantity of wretched fresh and salt fish consumed by the commonalty at all seasons as well as in lent; which our poor now would hardly be persuaded to touch.

The use of linen changes, shirts or shifts, in the room of sordid and filthy woollen, long worn next the skin, is a matter of neat-

* *Viz. six hundred bacons, eighty carcasses of beef, and six hundred muttons.* ⟨G. W.⟩

ness comparatively modern; but must prove a great means of preventing cutaneous ails. At this very time woollen instead of linen prevails among the poorer Welch, who are subject to foul eruptions.

The plenty of good wheaten bread that now is found among all ranks of people in the south, instead of that miserable sort which used in old days to be made of barley or beans, may contribute not a little to the sweetening their blood and correcting their juices; for the inhabitants of mountainous districts, to this day, are still liable to the itch and other cutaneous disorders, from a wretchedness and poverty of diet.

As to the produce of a garden, every middle-aged person of observation may perceive, within his own memory, both in town and country, how vastly the consumption of vegetables is increased. Green-stalls in cities now support multitudes in a comfortable state, while gardeners get fortunes. Every decent labourer also has his garden, which is half his support, as well as his delight; and common farmers provide plenty of beans, peas, and greens, for their hinds to eat with their bacon; and those few that do not are despised for their sordid parsimony, and looked upon as regardless of the welfare of their dependants. Potatoes have prevailed in this little district, by means of premiums, within these twenty years only; and are much esteemed here now by the poor, who would scarce have ventured to taste them in the last reign.

Our Saxon ancestors certainly had some sort of cabbage, because they call the month of February *sprout-cale*; but, long after their days, the cultivation of gardens was little attended to. The religious, being men of leisure, and keeping up a constant correspondence with Italy, were the first people among us that had gardens and fruit-trees in any perfection, within the walls of their abbies* and priories. The barons neglected every pursuit that did not lead to war or tend to the pleasure of the chase.

It was not till gentlemen took up the study of horticulture themselves that the knowledge of gardening made such hasty advances. Lord Cobham, Lord Ila, and Mr. Waller of Beacons-

* "*In* monasteries *the lamp of knowledge continued to burn, however dimly. In them men of business were formed for the state: the art of writing was cultivated by the* monks*; they were the only proficients in mechanics*, gardening, *and architecture*." *See Dalrymple's* Annals of Scotland. <G. W.>

field, were some of the first people of rank that promoted the elegant science of ornamenting without despising the superintendence of the kitchen quarters and fruit walls.

A remark made by the excellent Mr. Ray in his Tour of Europe at once surprises us, and corroborates what has been advanced above; for we find him observing, so late as his days, that "the Italians use several herbs for sallets, which *are not yet* or have not been but *lately* used in England, viz. *selleri* (celery) which is nothing else but the sweet smallage; the young shoots whereof, with a little of the head of the root cut off, they eat raw with oil and pepper". And farther he adds "*curled endive* blanched is much used beyond seas; and, for a raw sallet, seemed to excel lettuce itself". Now this journey was undertaken no longer ago than in the year 1663.

I am, &c.

LETTER XXXVIII

TO THE SAME

Fortè puer, comitum seductus ab agmine fido,
Dixerat, ecquis adest? et, adest, responderat echo.
Hic stupet; utque aciem partes divisit in omnes;
Voce, veni, clamat magna. Vocat illa vocantem.*

Selborne, *Feb.* 12, 1778.

DEAR SIR,

In a district so diversified as this, so full of hollow vales and hanging woods, it is no wonder that echoes should abound. Many we have discovered that return the cry of a pack of dogs, the notes of a hunting-horn, a tunable ring of bells, or the melody of birds, very agreeably: but we were still at a loss for a polysyllabical, articulate echo, till a young gentleman, who had parted from his company in a summer evening walk, and was calling after them, stumbled upon a very curious one in a spot where it might least be expected. At first he was much surprised, and could not be persuaded but that he was mocked by some boy; but, repeating his trials in several languages, and finding his respondent to be a very adroit polyglot, he then discerned the deception.

This echo in an evening, before rural noises cease, would repeat ten syllables most articulately and distinctly, especially if quick dactyls were chosen. The last syllables of

Tityre, tu patulæ recubans . . .

were as audibly and intelligibly returned as the first: and there is no doubt, could trial have been made, but that at midnight, when the air is very elastic, and a dead stillness prevails, one or two syllables more might have been obtained; but the distance rendered so late an experiment very inconvenient.

Quick dactyls, we observed, succeeded best; for when we

* Ovid's *Metamorphoses*.

came to try it's powers in slow, heavy, embarrassed spondees of the same number of syllables,

Monstrum horrendum, informe, ingens . . .

we could perceive a return but of four or five.

All echoes have some one place to which they are returned stronger and more distinct than to any other; and that is always the place that lies at right angles with the object of repercussion, and is not too near, nor too far off. Buildings, or naked rocks, re-echo much more articulately than hanging wood or vales; because in the latter the voice is as it were entangled, and embarrassed in the covert, and weakened in the rebound.

The true object of this echo, as we found by various experiments, is the stone-built, tiled hop-kiln in Gally-lane, which measures in front 40 feet, and from the ground to the eaves 12 feet. The true *centrum phonicum*, or just distance, is one particular spot in the King's-field, in the path to Nore-hill, on the very brink of the steep balk above the hollow cart way. In this case there is no choice of distance; but the path, by meer contingency, happens to be the lucky, the identical spot, because the ground rises or falls so immediately, if the speaker either retires or advances, that his mouth would at once be above or below the object.

We measured this polysyllabical echo with great exactness, and found the distance to fall very short of Dr. Plot's rule for distinct articulation: for the Doctor, in his history of Oxfordshire, allows 120 feet for the return of each syllable distinctly: hence this echo, which gives ten distinct syllables, ought to measure 400 yards, or 120 feet to each syllable; whereas our distance is only 258 yards, or near 75 feet, to each syllable. Thus our measure falls short of the Doctor's, as five to eight: but then it must be acknowledged that this candid philosopher was convinced afterwards, that some latitude must be admitted of in the distance of echoes according to time and place.

When experiments of this sort are making, it should always be remembered that weather and the time of day have a vast influence on an echo; for a dull, heavy, moist air deadens and clogs the sound; and hot sunshine renders the air thin and weak, and deprives it of all it's springiness; and a ruffling wind quite defeats the whole. In a still, clear, dewy evening the air is most elastic; and perhaps the later the hour the more so.

Echo has always been so amusing to the imagination, that the poets have personified her; and in their hands she has been the occasion of many a beautiful fiction. Nor need the gravest man be ashamed to appear taken with such a phænomenon, since it may become the subject of philosophical or mathematical inquiries.

One should have imagined that echoes, if not entertaining, must at least have been harmless and inoffensive; yet Virgil advances a strange notion, that they are injurious to bees. After enumerating some probable and reasonable annoyances, such as prudent owners would wish far removed from their bee-gardens, he adds

——————— aut ubi concava pulsu
Saxa sonant, vocisque offensa resultat imago.

This wild and fanciful assertion will hardly be admitted by the philosophers of these days; especially as they all now seem agreed that insects are not furnished with any organs of hearing* at all. But if it should be urged, that though they cannot *hear* yet perhaps they may *feel* the repercussions of sounds, I grant it is possible they may. Yet that these impressions are distasteful or hurtful, I deny, because bees, in good summers, thrive well in my outlet, where the echoes are very strong: for this village is another Anathoth,† a place of *responses* or *echoes*. Besides, it does not appear from experiment that bees are in any way capable of being affected by sounds: for I have often tried my own with a large speaking-trumpet held close to their hives, and with such an exertion of voice as would have haled a ship at the distance of a mile, and still these insects pursued their various employments undisturbed, and without shewing the least sensibility or resentment.

Some time since it's discovery this echo is become totally silent, though the object, or hop-kiln, remains: nor is there any

* The auditory organs of many insects are highly developed: viz. in crickets, grasshoppers, gnats, locusts, etc. The stridulation of grasshoppers is a song of love to the females and of rivalry to other suitors.

† *Joshua*, xxi, 18; *Isaiah*, x, 30. Oddly enough, Mr. Nicholson is the first editor of Gilbert White to make these references.

mystery in this defect; for the field between is planted as an hop-garden, and the voice of the speaker is totally absorbed and lost among the poles and entangled foliage of the hops. And when the poles are removed in autumn the disappointment is the same; because a tall quick-set hedge, nurtured up for the purpose of shelter to the hop ground, entirely interrupts the impulse and repercussion of the voice: so that till those obstructions are removed no more of it's garrulity can be expected.

Should any gentleman of fortune think an echo in his park or outlet a pleasing incident, he might *build* one at little or no expense. For whenever he had occasion for a new barn, stable, dog-kennel, or the like structure, it would be only needful to erect this building on the gentle declivity of an hill, with a like rising opposite to it, at a few hundred yards distance; and perhaps success might be the easier ensured could some canal, lake, or stream, intervene. From a seat at the *centrum phonicum* he and his friends might amuse themselves sometimes of an evening with the prattle of this loquacious nymph;* of whose complacency and decent reserve more may be said than can with truth of every individual of her sex; since she is — — — —

— — — — — — quæ nec *reticere* loquenti,
Nec *prior* ipsa *loqui* didicit resonabilis echo.

I am, &c.

* A passage which reveals the ornamental habit of mind of the eighteenth century country gentleman more graphically than any amount of history.

LETTER XXXIX

TO THE SAME

Selborne, *May* 13, 1778.

DEAR SIR,

Among the many singularities attending those amusing birds the *swifts*, I am now confirmed in the opinion that we have every year the same number of pairs invariably; at least the result of my inquiry has been exactly the same for a long time past. The swallows and martins are so numerous, and so widely distributed over the village, that it is hardly possible to recount them; while the swifts, though they do not all build in the church, yet so frequently haunt it, and play and rendezvous round it, that they are easily enumerated. The number that I constantly find are *eight pairs*; about half of which reside in the church, and the rest build in some of the lowest and meanest thatched cottages. Now as these eight pairs, allowance being made for accidents, breed yearly eight pairs more, what becomes annually of this increase; and what determines every spring which pairs shall visit us, and reoccupy their ancient haunts?

Ever since I have attended to the subject of ornithology, I have always supposed that that sudden reverse of affection, that strange ἀντιστοργη, which immediately succeeds in the feathered kind to the most passionate fondness, is the occasion of an equal dispersion of birds over the face of the earth.* Without this provision one favourite district would be crowded with inhabitants, while others would be destitute and forsaken. But the parent birds seem to maintain a jealous superiority, and to oblige the young to seek for new abodes: and the rivalry of the males, in many kinds, prevents their crowding the one on the other. Whether the swallows and house-martins return in the same exact number annually is not easy to say...

LETTER XL

TO THE SAME

Selborne, *June* 2, 1778.

Dear Sir,

The standing objection to botany has always been, that it is a pursuit* that amuses the fancy and exercises the memory, without improving the mind or advancing any real knowledge: and, where the science is carried no farther than a mere systematic classification, the charge is but too true. But the botanist that is desirous of wiping off this aspersion should be by no means content with a list of names; he should study plants philosophically, should investigate the laws of vegetation, should examine the powers and virtues of efficacious herbs, should promote their cultivation; and graft the gardener, the the planter, and the husbandman, on the phytologist. Not that system is by any means to be thrown aside; without system the field of Nature would be a pathless wilderness; but system should be subservient to, not the main object of, pursuit.

Vegetation is highly worthy of our attention; and in itself is of the utmost consequence to mankind, and productive of many of the greatest comforts and elegancies of life. To plants we owe timber, bread, beer, honey, wine, oil, linen, cotton, &c. what not only strengthens our hearts, and exhilarates our spirits, but what secures us from inclemencies of weather and adorns our persons. Man, in his true state of nature, seems to be subsisted by spontaneous vegetation:† in middle climes, where grasses prevail, he mixes some animal food with the produce of the field and garden: and it is towards the polar extremes only that, like his kindred bears and wolves, he gorges himself with flesh alone, and is driven, to what hunger has never been known to compel the very beasts, to prey on his own species.‡

* White had already progressed from his own age of "what" to that of the future which asked "why".

† Viz., man in the Old Stone Age was a food-gatherer and not a planter before the earliest civilizations (*circa* 6000 B.C.).

‡ *See the late Voyages to the South-seas.* ⟨G. W.⟩

The productions of vegetation have had a vast influence on the commerce of nations, and have been the great promoters of navigation, as may be seen in the articles of sugar, tea, tobacco, opium, ginseng, betel, paper, &c. As every climate has it's peculiar produce, our natural wants bring on a mutual intercourse; so that by means of trade each distant part is supplied with the growth of every latitude. But, without the knowledge of plants and their culture, we must have been content with our hips and haws, without enjoying the delicate fruits of India and the salutiferous* drugs of Peru.

Instead of examining the minute distinctions of every various species of each obscure genus, the botanist should endeavour to make himself acquainted with those that are useful. You shall see a man readily ascertain every herb of the field, yet hardly know wheat from barley, or at least one sort of wheat or barley from another.

But of all sorts of vegetation the *grasses* seem to be most neglected; neither the farmer nor the grazier seem to distinguish the annual from the perennial, the hardy from the tender, nor the succulent and nutritive from the dry and juiceless.

The study of grasses would be of great consequence to a northerly, and grazing kingdom. The botanist that could improve the swerd of the district where he lived would be an useful member of society: to raise a thick turf on a naked soil would be worth volumes of systematic knowledge; and he would be the best commonwealth's man that could occasion the growth of "*two blades of grass* where *one* alone was seen before".†

I am, &c.

* A Whited word like his "terebrates".

† If White had been alive to-day, he would have seen one blade of grass where two were seen before and in an age with a scientific knowledge of growing three where one was before. See my *Introduction.*

LETTER XLI

TO THE SAME

Selborne, *July* 3, 1778.

DEAR SIR,

In a district so diversified with such a variety of hill and dale, aspects, and soils, it is no wonder that great choice of plants should be found. Chalks, clays, sands, sheep-walks and downs, bogs, heaths, woodlands, and champaign fields, cannot but furnish an ample *Flora*. The deep rocky lanes abound with *filices*, and the pastures and moist woods with *fungi*. If in any branch of botany we may seem to be wanting, it must be in the large aquatic plants, which are not to be expected on a spot far removed from rivers, and lying up amidst the hill country at the spring heads. To enumerate all the plants that have been discovered within our limits would be a needless work; but a short list of the more rare, and the spots where they are to be found,* may be neither unacceptable nor unentertaining:—

Helleborus fœtidus, stinking hellebore, bear's foot, or setterwort, all over the High-wood and Coney-croft-hanger: this continues a great branching plant the winter through, blossoming about January, and is very ornamental in shady walks and shrubberies. The good women give the leaves powdered to children troubled with worms; but it is a violent remedy, and ought to be administered with caution.

Helleborus viridis,† green hellebore,—in the deep stony lane on the left hand just before the turning to Norton-farm, and at the top of Middle Dorton under the hedge: this plant dies down to the ground early in autumn, and springs again about February, flowering almost as soon as it appears above ground.

* Mr. Nicholson has an extremely useful note here of which the following is a condensed version. Shrubwood, now beech, is the eastern spur of the Hanger; King's Field is towards Nore Hill with High-Wood on the crest; Coneycroft Hanger is opposite; the stony lane is the old road to Alton; Dorton lies between the Church and the old Priory with the meadows of Short and Long Lith; the church-litten is the churchyard and Grange Farm is in Gracious Street, at the north end of the village.

† This rather than *H. fœtidus* is commonly called Bear's Foot. Both, like Old Man's Beard, are plants of the chalk and the limestone.

Vaccinium oxycoccos, creeping bilberries, or cranberries,—in the bogs of Bin's-pond;

Vaccinium myrtillus, whortle, or bilberries,—on the dry hillocks of Woolmer-forest;

Drosera rotundifolia, round-leaved sundew.
——— *longifolia*, long-leaved ditto. } In the bogs of Bin's-pond.

Comarum palustre, purple comarum, or marsh cinque foil,—in the bogs of Bin's-pond;

Hypericum androsæmum, Tutsan, St. John's Wort,—in the stony, hollow lanes;

Vinca minor, less periwinkle,—in Selborne-hanger and Shrubwood;

Monotropa hypopithys, yellow monotropa, or bird's nest,—in Selborne-hanger under the shady beeches, to whose roots it seems to be parasitical—at the north-west end of the Hanger;

Chlora perfoliata, *Blackstonia perfoliata*, *Hudsoni*, perfoliated yellow-wort,—on the banks in the King's-field;

Paris quadrifolia, herb Paris, true-love, or one-berry,—in the Church-litten-coppice;

Chrysosplenium oppositifolium, opposite golden saxifrage,—in the dark and rocky hollow lanes;

Gentiana amarella, autumnal gentian, or fellwort,—on the Zig-zag and Hanger;

Lathræa squammaria, tooth-wort,—in the Church-litten-coppice under some hazels near the foot-bridge, in Trimming's garden hedge, and on the dry wall opposite Grange-yard;

Dipsacus pilosus, small teasel,—in the Short and Long Lith.

Lathyrus sylvestris, narrow-leaved, or wild lathyrus,—in the bushes at the foot of the Short Lith, near the path;

Ophrys spiralis, ladies traces,*—in the Long Lith, and towards the south-corner of the common;

Ophrys nidus avis, birds' nest ophrys,†—in the Long Lith un-

* We say Tresses to-day.

† Viz., bird's nest orchis. Nearly all these plants mentioned by White are to be found to-day, but more easily on the oolitic limestone of the south-west and Midlands than on the chalk. Extract from the *Naturalist's Journal* of May 24, 1774: "This curious plant was found in bloom in the long Lythe among the dead leaves under the thickest beeches, and also among some bushes at Dorton." In the Cotswolds, I have seen it on sites exactly as White describes, but never among beeches. The "helleborine" mentioned is doubtless the white, not the red (*cephalanthera rubra*), an extremely rare plant.

der the shady beeches among the dead leaves; in Great Dorton among the bushes, and on the Hanger plentifully;

Serapias latifolia, helleborine,—in the High-wood under the shady beeches;

Daphne laureola, spurge laurel,—in Selborne-Hanger and the High-wood;

Daphne mezereum, the mezereon,—in Selborne-Hanger among the shrubs at the south-east end above the cottages.

Lycoperdon tuber, truffles,—in the Hanger and High-wood.

Sambucus ebulus, dwarf elder, walwort, or danewort,—among the rubbish and ruined foundations of the Priory.*

Of all the propensities of plants none seem more strange than their different periods of blossoming. Some produce their flowers in the winter, or very first dawnings of spring; many when the spring is established; some at midsummer, and some not till autumn. When we see the *helleborus fœtidus* and *helleborus niger* blowing at Christmas, the *helleborus hyemalis* in January, and the *helleborus viridis* as soon as ever it emerges out of the ground, we do not wonder, because they are kindred plants that we expect should keep pace the one with the other. But other congenerous vegetables differ so widely in their time of flowering that we cannot but admire. I shall only instance at present in the *crocus sativus*, the vernal, and the autumnal crocus, which have such an affinity, that the best botanists only make them varieties of the same *genus*, of which there is only one *species*; not being able to discern any difference in the *corolla*, or in the internal structure. Yet the *vernal crocus* expands it's flowers by the beginning of March at farthest, and often in very rigorous weather; and cannot be retarded but by some violence offered; while the *autumnal* (the Saffron) defies the influence of the spring and summer, and will not blow till most plants begin to fade and run to seed. This circumstance is one of the wonders of the creation, little noticed, because a common occurrence: yet ought not to be overlooked on account of it's being familiar, since it would be as difficult to be explained as the most stupendous phænomenon in nature.

* The passage from here to the end of the letter occurs in the MS., but not in the first edition.

Say, what impels, amidst surrounding snow
Congeal'd, the *crocus*' flamy bud to glow?
Say, what retards, amidst the summer's blaze,
Th' *autumnal bulb*, till pale, declining days?
The God of Seasons; whose pervading power
Controls the sun, or sheds the fleecy shower:
He bids each flower his quick'ning word obey;
Or to each lingering bloom enjoins delay.*

* *Coleridge's Note*. "A noble paraphrase of 'I don't know'."

LETTER XLII*

TO THE SAME

Omnibus animalibus reliquis certus et uniusmodi, et in suo cuique genere incessus est: aves solæ vario meatu feruntur, et in terrâ, et in äere.

PLIN. *Hist. Nat.* lib. x. cap. 38.

Selborne, *Aug.* 7, 1778.

DEAR SIR,

A good ornithologist should be able to distinguish birds by their air as well as by their colours and shape; on the ground as well as on the wing, and in the bush as well as in the hand. For, though it must not be said that every *species* of birds has a manner peculiar to itself, yet there is somewhat in most *genera* at least, that at first sight discriminates them, and enables a judicious observer to pronounce upon them with some certainty. Put a bird in motion

— — Et vera incessu patuit — — — —.

Thus *kites* and *buzzards* sail round in circles with wings expanded and motionless; and it is from their gliding manner that

* It might well be said that this and the following letter give the finest descriptions of the voices and motions of birds ever written.

the former are still called in the north of England *gleads*, from the Saxon verb *glidan*, to glide. The *kestrel*, or *wind-hover*, has a peculiar mode of hanging in the air in one place, his wings all the while being briskly agitated. *Hen-harriers* fly low over heaths or fields of corn, and beat the ground regularly like a pointer or setting-dog. *Owls* move in a buoyant manner, as if lighter than the air; they seem to want ballast. There is a peculiarity belonging to *ravens* that must draw the attention even of the most incurious—they spend all their leisure time in striking and cuffing each other on the wing in a kind of playful skirmish; and, when they move from one place to another, frequently turn on their backs with a loud croak, and seem to be falling to the ground. When this odd gesture betides them, they are scratching themselves with one foot, and thus lose the center of gravity.* *Rooks* sometimes dive and tumble in a frolicksome manner; *crows* and *daws* swagger in their walk; *wood-peckers* fly *volatu undoso*, opening and closing their wings at every stroke, and so are always rising or falling in curves. All of this genus use their tails, which incline downward, as a support while they run up trees. *Parrots*, like all other hooked-clawed birds, walk aukwardly, and make use of their bill as a third foot, climbing and descending with ridiculous caution. All the *gallinæ* parade and walk gracefully, and run nimbly; but fly with difficulty, with an impetuous whirring, and in a straight line. *Magpies* and *jays* flutter with powerless wings, and make no dispatch; *herons* seem incumbered with too much sail for their light bodies; but these vast hollow wings are necessary in carrying burdens, such as large fishes, and the like; *pigeons*, and particularly the sort called *smiters*, have a way of clashing their wings the one against the other over their backs with a loud snap; another variety called *tumblers* turn themselves over in the air. Some birds have movements peculiar to the season of love: thus *ring-doves*, though strong and rapid at other times, yet in the spring hang about on the wing in a toying and playful manner; thus the *cock-snipe*, while breeding, forgetting his former flight, fans the air like the wind-hover; and the *green-finch* in particular exhibits such languishing and faul-

* I have often seen ravens perform this antic on Bindon Hill, near Lulworth. It is done in pure sportiveness and exhilaration of spirits, and is not accidental as White suggests.

tering gestures as to appear like a wounded and dying bird; the *king-fisher* darts along like an arrow; *fern-owls*, or *goat-suckers*, glance* in the dusk over the tops of trees like a meteor; *starlings* as it were swim along, while *missel-thrushes* use a wild and desultory flight; *swallows* sweep over the surface of the ground and water, and distinguish themselves by rapid turns and quick evolutions; *swifts* dash round in circles; and the *bank-martin* moves with frequent vacillations like a butterfly. Most of the small birds fly by jerks, rising and falling as they advance. Most small birds hop; but *wagtails* and *larks* walk, moving their legs alternately. *Skylarks* rise and fall perpendicularly as they sing; *woodlarks* hang poised in the air; and *titlarks* rise and fall in large curves, singing in their descent. The *white-throat* uses odd jerks and gesticulations over the tops of hedges and bushes. All the *duck-kind* waddle; *divers* and *auks* walk as if fettered, and stand erect on their tails: these are the *compedes* of Linnæus. *Geese* and *cranes*, and most wild-fowls, move in figured flights, often changing their position. The secondary *remiges* of *Tringæ*, *wild-ducks*, and some others, are very long, and give their wings, when in motion, an hooked appearance. *Dabchicks*, *moor-hens*, and *coots*, fly erect, with their legs hanging down, and hardly make any dispatch; the reason is plain, their wings are placed too forward out of the true center of gravity; as the legs of *auks* and *divers* are situated too backward.

* Mr. Nicholson would replace this by "glide". "Glance" is a precise and imaginative impression; "glide" an ornithological exactitude.

LETTER XLIII

TO THE SAME

Selborne, *Sept*. 9, 1778.

DEAR SIR,

From the motion of birds, the transition is natural enough to their notes and language, of which I shall say something. Not that I would pretend to understand their language like the *vizier*; who, by the recital of a conversation which passed between two owls, reclaimed a sultan,* before delighting in conquest and devastation; but I would be thought only to mean that many of the winged tribes have various sounds and voices adapted to express their various passions, wants, and feelings; such as anger, fear, love, hatred, hunger, and the like. All species are not equally eloquent; some are copious and fluent as it were in their utterance, while others are confined to a few important sounds: no bird, like the fish kind, is quite mute, though some are rather silent. The language of birds is very ancient, and, like other ancient modes of speech, very elliptical; little is said, but much is meant and understood.†

* *See* Spectator, *Vol.* vii, *No.* 512. ⟨G. W.⟩

† A passage of the utmost brilliance in intuitively grasping a scientific truth unknown in the author's day.

The notes of the eagle-kind are shrill and piercing; and about the season of nidification much diversified, as I have been often assured by a curious observer* of Nature, who long resided at Gibraltar, where eagles abound. The notes of our *hawks* much resemble those of the king of birds. *Owls* have very expressive notes; they hoot in a fine vocal sound, much resembling the *vox humana*, and reducible by a pitch-pipe to a musical key. This note seems to express complacency and rivalry among the males: they use also a quick call and an horrible scream;† and can snore and hiss† when they mean to menace. *Ravens*, besides their loud croak, can exert a deep and solemn note that makes the woods to echo; the amorous sound of a *crow* is strange and ridiculous; *rooks*, in the breeding season, attempt sometimes in the gaiety of their hearts to sing, but with no great success; the *parrot*-kind have many modulations of voice, as appears by their aptitude to learn human sounds; *doves* coo in an amorous and mournful manner, and are emblems of despairing lovers; the *woodpecker* sets up a sort of loud and hearty laugh; the *fern-owl*, or *goat-sucker*, from the dusk till day-break, serenades his mate with the clattering of castanets. All the tuneful *passeres* express their complacency by sweet modulations, and a variety of melody. The *swallow*, as has been observed in a former letter, by a shrill alarm bespeaks the attention of the other *hirundines*, and bids them be aware that the hawk is at hand. Aquatic and gregarious birds, especially the nocturnal, that shift their quarters in the dark, are very noisy and loquacious; as cranes, wild-geese, wild-ducks, and the like: their perpetual clamour prevents them from dispersing and losing their companions.

In so extensive a subject, sketches and outlines are as much as can be expected; for it would be endless to instance in all the infinite variety of the feathered nation. We shall therefore confine the remainder of this letter to the few domestic fowls of our yards, which are most known, and therefore best understood. And first the *peacock*, with his gorgeous train, demands our attention; but, like most of the gaudy birds, his notes are grating and shocking to the ear: the yelling of cats, and the braying of an ass, are not more disgustful. The voice of the *goose* is trumpet-like,

* John White.

† This applies to the barn owl only.

and clanking; and once saved the Capitol at Rome, as grave historians assert: the hiss also of the *gander* is formidable and full of menace, and "protective of his young". Among *ducks** the sexual distinction of voice is remarkable; for, while the *quack* of the female is loud and sonorous, the voice of the *drake* is inward and harsh, and feeble, and scarce discernible. The cock *turkey* struts and gobbles to his mistress in a most uncouth manner; he hath also a pert and petulant note when he attacks his adversary. When a hen *turkey* leads forth her young brood she keeps a watchful eye; and if a bird of prey appear, though ever so high in the air, the careful mother announces the enemy with a little inward moan, and watches him with a steady and attentive look; but, if he approach, her note becomes earnest and alarming, and her outcries are redoubled.

No inhabitants of a yard seem possessed of such a variety of expression and so copious a language as common poultry. Take a chicken of four or five days old, and hold it up to a window where there are flies, and it will immediately seize it's prey, with little twitterings of complacency; but if you tender it a wasp or a bee, at once it's note becomes harsh, and expressive of disapprobation and a sense of danger. When a pullet is ready to lay she intimates the event by a joyous and easy soft note. Of all the occurrences of their life that of *laying* seems to be the most important; for no sooner has a hen disburdened herself, than she rushes forth with a clamorous kind of joy, which the cock and the rest of his mistresses immediately adopt. The tumult is not confined to the family concerned, but catches from yard to yard, and spreads to every homestead within hearing, till at last the whole village is in an uproar. As soon as a hen becomes a mother her new relation demands a new language; she then runs clocking and screaming about, and seems agitated as if possessed. The father of the flock has also a considerable vocabulary; if he finds food, he calls a favourite concubine to partake; and if a bird of prey passes over, with a warning voice he bids his family beware. The gallant *chanticleer* has, at command, his amorous phrases and his terms of defiance. But the sound by which he is best known is his *crowing*: by this he has been distinguished

* The author here refers to our familiar wild duck or mallard, and not to other species of ducks.

in all ages as the countryman's clock or larum, as the watchman that proclaims the divisions of the night. Thus the poet elegantly styles him:

— — — the crested cock, whose clarion sounds
The silent hours.*

A neighbouring gentleman one summer had lost most of his chickens by a sparrow-hawk, that came gliding down between a faggot pile and the end of his house to the place where the coops stood. The owner, inwardly vexed to see his flock thus diminishing, hung a setting net adroitly between the pile and the house, into which the caitif dashed, and was entangled. Resentment suggested the law of retaliation; he therefore clipped the hawk's wings, cut off his talons, and, fixing a cork on his bill, threw him down among the brood-hens. Imagination cannot paint the scene that ensued; the expressions that fear, rage, and revenge, inspired, were new, or at least such as had been unnoticed before: the exasperated matrons upbraided, they execrated, they insulted, they triumphed. In a word, they never desisted from buffetting their adversary till they had torn him in an hundred pieces.

* From *Paradise Lost*. But Chaucer's *The Nun's Priest's Tale* is nearer in imaginative likeness to the whole passage.

LETTER XLVI

TO THE SAME

Selborne.

— — — resonant arbusta — — — — —

There is a steep abrupt pasture field interspersed with furze close to the back of this village, well known by the name of the Short Lithe, consisting of a rocky dry soil, and inclining to the afternoon sun. This spot abounds with the *gryllus campestris*, or *field-cricket*; which, though frequent in these parts, is by no means a common insect in many other counties.

As their cheerful summer cry cannot but draw the attention of a naturalist, I have often gone down to examine the œconomy of these *grylli*, and study their mode of life: but they are so shy and cautious that it is no easy matter to get a sight of them; for, feeling a person's footsteps as he advances, they stop short in the midst of their song,* and retire backward nimbly into their burrows, where they lurk till all suspicion of danger is over.

At first we attempted to dig them out with a spade, but without any great success; for either we could not get to the bottom of the hole, which often terminated under a great stone; or else, in breaking up the ground, we inadvertently squeezed the poor insect to death. Out of one so bruised we took a multitude of eggs, which were long and narrow, of a yellow colour, and covered with a very tough skin. By this accident we learned to distinguish the male from the female; the former of which is shining black, with a golden stripe across his shoulders; the latter is more dusky, more capacious about the abdomen, and carries a long sword-shaped weapon at her tail, which probably is the instrument with which she deposits her eggs in crannies and safe receptacles.

Where violent methods will not avail, more gentle means will

* Among grasshoppers, the male fiddles on the thigh of the hind leg; with crickets, the horny ridge is under the wing.

often succeed; and so it proved in the present case; for, though a spade be too boisterous and rough an implement, a pliant stalk of grass, gently insinuated into the caverns, will probe their windings to the bottom, and quickly bring out the inhabitant; and thus the humane inquirer may gratify his curiosity without injuring the object of it. It is remarkable that, though these insects are furnished with long legs behind, and brawny thighs for leaping, like grasshoppers; yet when driven from their holes they shew no activity, but crawl along in a shiftless manner, so as easily to be taken: and again, though provided with a curious apparatus of wings, yet they never exert them when there seems to be the greatest occasion. The males only make that shrilling noise perhaps out of rivalry and emulation, as is the case with many animals which exert some sprightly note during their breeding time: it is raised by a brisk friction of one wing against the other. They are solitary beings, living singly male or female, each as it may happen; but there must be a time when the sexes have some intercourse, and then the wings may be useful perhaps during the hours of night. When the males meet they will fight fiercely, as I found by some which I put into the crevices of a dry stone wall, where I should have been glad to have made them settle. For though they seemed distressed by being taken out of their knowledge, yet the first that got possession of the chinks would seize on any that were obtruded upon them with a vast row of serrated fangs. With their strong jaws, toothed like the shears of a lobster's claws, they perforate and round their curious regular cells, having no fore-claws to dig, like the mole-cricket. When taken in hand I could not but wonder that they never offered to defend themselves, though armed with such formidable weapons. Of such herbs as grow before the mouths of their burrows they eat indiscriminately; and on a little platform, which they make just by, they drop their dung; and never, in the day time, seem to stir more than two or three inches from home. Sitting in the entrance of their caverns they chirp all night as well as day from the middle of the month of May to the middle of July; and in hot weather, when they are most vigorous, they make the hills echo; and, in the stiller hours of darkness, may be heard to a considerable distance. In the beginning of the season their notes are more faint and inward; but become louder as the summer advances, and so die away again by degrees.

Sounds do not always give us pleasure according to their sweetness and melody; nor do harsh sounds always displease. We are more apt to be captivated or disgusted with the associations which they promote, than with the notes themselves. Thus the shrilling of the *field-cricket*, though sharp and stridulous, yet marvellously delights some hearers, filling their minds with a train of summer ideas of everything that is rural, verdurous, and joyous.

About the tenth of March the crickets appear at the mouths of their cells, which they then open and bore, and shape very elegantly. All that ever I have seen at that season were in their pupa state, and had only the rudiments of wings, lying under a skin or coat, which must be cast before the insect can arrive at it's perfect state;* from whence I should suppose that the old ones of last year do not always survive the winter. In August their holes begin to be obliterated, and the insects are seen no more till spring.

Not many summers ago I endeavoured to transplant a colony to the terrace in my garden, by boring deep holes in the sloping turf. The new inhabitants stayed some time, and fed and sung; but wandered away by degrees, and were heard at a farther distance every morning; so that it appears that on this emergency they made use of their wings in attempting to return to the spot from which they were taken.

One of these crickets, when confined in a paper cage and set in the sun, and supplied with plants moistened with water, will feed and thrive, and become so merry and loud as to be irksome in the same room where a person is sitting: if the plants are not wetted it will die.

* *We have observed that they cast these skins in April, which are then seen lying at the mouths of their holes.* ⟨G. W.⟩

LETTER XLVII

TO THE SAME

Selborne.

DEAR SIR,

Far from all resort of mirth
Save the cricket on the hearth.
MILTON'S *Il Penseroso.*

While many other insects must be sought after in fields and woods, and waters, the *gryllus domesticus*, or *house-cricket*, resides altogether within our dwellings, intruding itself upon our notice whether we will or no. This species delights in new-built houses, being, like the spider, pleased with the moisture of the walls; and besides, the softness of the mortar enables them to burrow and mine between the joints of the bricks or stones, and to open communications from one room to another. They are particularly fond of kitchens and bakers' ovens, on account of their perpetual warmth.

Tender insects that live abroad either enjoy only the short period of one summer, or else doze away the cold uncomfortable months in profound slumbers; but these, residing as it were in a torrid zone, are always alert and merry: a good Christmas fire is to them like the heats of the dog-days. Though they are frequently heard by day, yet is their natural time of motion only in the night. As soon as it grows dusk, the chirping increases, and they come running forth, and are from the size of a flea to that of their full stature. As one should suppose, from the burning atmosphere which they inhabit, they are a thirsty race, and shew a great propensity for liquids, being found frequently drowned in pans of water, milk, broth, or the like. Whatever is moist they affect: and therefore often gnaw holes in wet woollen stockings and aprons that are hung to the fire: they are the housewife's barometer, foretelling her when it will rain; and are prognostic sometimes, she thinks, of ill or good luck; of the death of a near relation, or the approach of an absent lover. By being the constant companions of her solitary hours they naturally become the objects of her superstition. These crickets are not only very thirsty, but very voracious; for they will eat the scummings of pots, and yeast, salt, and crumbs of bread; and any kitchen offal or sweepings. In the summer we have observed them to fly, when it became dusk, out of the windows, and over the neighbouring roofs. This feat of activity accounts for the sudden manner in which they often leave their haunts, as it does for the method by which they come to houses where they were not known before. It is remarkable, that many sorts of insects seem never to use their wings but when they have a mind to shift their quarters and settle new colonies. When in the air they move "*volatu undoso*", in waves or curves, like *wood-peckers*, opening and shutting their wings at every stroke, and so are always rising or sinking.

When they increase to a great degree, as they did once in the house where I am now writing, they become noisome pests, flying into the candles, and dashing into people's faces; but may be blasted and destroyed by gunpowder discharged into their crevices and crannies. In families, at such times, they are, like Pharaoh's plague of frogs,—"in their bedchambers, and upon their beds, and in their ovens, and in their kneading-troughs."* Their shrilling noise is occasioned by a brisk attrition of their wings. Cats catch hearth-crickets, and, playing with them as they do with mice, devour them. Crickets may be destroyed, like wasps, by phials half filled with beer, or any liquid, and set in their haunts; for, being always eager to drink, they will crowd in till the bottles are full.

* *Exod.* viii, 3. ⟨G. W.⟩

LETTER XLVIII

TO THE SAME

Selborne.

How diversified are the modes of life not only of incongruous but even of congenerous animals; and yet their specific distinctions are not more various than their propensities. Thus, while the *field-cricket* delights in sunny dry banks, and the *house-cricket* rejoices amidst the glowing heat of the kitchen hearth or oven, the *gryllus gryllo talpa* (the *mole-cricket*), haunts moist meadows, and frequents the sides of ponds and banks of streams, performing all it's functions in a swampy wet soil. With a pair of fore-feet, curiously adapted to the purpose, it burrows and works under ground like the mole, raising a ridge as it proceeds, but seldom throwing up hillocks.

As *mole-crickets* often infest gardens by the sides of canals, they are unwelcome guests to the gardener, raising up ridges in their subterraneous progress, and rendering the walks unsightly. If they take to the kitchen quarters, they occasion great damage among the plants and roots, by destroying whole beds of cabbages, young legumes, and flowers. When dug out they seem very slow and helpless, and make no use of their wings by day; but at night they come abroad, and make long excursions, as I have been convinced by finding stragglers, in a morning, in improbable places. In fine weather, about the middle of April, and just at the close of day, they begin to solace themselves with a low, dull, jarring note, continued for a long time without interruption, and not unlike the chattering of the fern-owl, or goat-sucker, but more inward.

About the beginning of May they lay their eggs, as I was once an eye-witness: for a gardener at an house, where I was on a visit, happening to be mowing, on the 6th of that month, by the side of a canal, his scythe struck too deep, pared off a large piece of turf, and laid open to view a curious scene of domestic œconomy:

———— ingentem lato dedit ore fenestram:
Apparet domus intus, et atria longa patescunt:
Apparent ——— penetralia.*

There were many caverns and winding passages leading to a kind of chamber, neatly smoothed and rounded, and about the size of a moderate snuff-box. Within this secret nursery were deposited near an hundred eggs of a dirty yellow colour, and enveloped in a tough skin, but too lately excluded to contain any rudiments of young, being full of a viscous substance. The eggs lay but shallow, and within the influence of the sun, just under a little heap of fresh-moved mould, like that which is raised by ants.

When *mole-crickets* fly they move "*cursu undoso*", rising and falling in curves, like the other species mentioned before. In different parts of this kingdom people call them *fen-crickets*, *churr-worms*, and *eve-churrs*,† all very apposite names.

Anatomists, who have examined the intestines of these insects, astonish me with their accounts; for they say that, from the structure, position, and number of their stomachs, or maws, there seems to be good reason to suppose that this and the two former species *ruminate* or *chew* the *cud*‡ like many quadrupeds!

* From the *Æneid.*

† Also applied to the fern-owl or nightjar, viz: Meredith's "the brown eve-jar".

‡ The food is masticated in the gizzard, behind the crop.

LETTER L

TO THE SAME

Selborne, *April* 21, 1780.

DEAR SIR,

The old Sussex tortoise,* that I have mentioned to you so often, is become my property. I dug it out of it's winter dormitory in March last, when it was enough awakened to express it's resentments by hissing; and, packing it in a box with earth, carried it eighty miles in post-chaises. The rattle and hurry of the journey so perfectly roused it that, when I turned it out on a border, it walked twice down to the bottom of my garden; however, in the evening, the weather being cold, it buried itself in the loose mould, and continues still concealed.

As it will be under my eye,† I shall now have an opportunity of enlarging my observations on it's mode of life, and propensities;

* White sent a delightful autobiography of Timothy to his friend, John Mulso's sister, Hester (the blue-stocking, Mrs. Chapone), who had written some verses on the patriarch. See Letter XII to Molly White in Vol. 2. See also Letters VII and XIII of this series and the *Naturalist's Journal* for March, 1781. Timothy's shell is preserved in the British Museum. Some editors print the second half of this letter at the end of the *Antiquities*, possibly on account of Timothy's longevity.

† Timothy had been recently removed from Mrs. Snooke's house (the author's aunt) at Ringmer to The Wakes at Selborne.

and perceive already that, towards the time of coming forth, it opens a breathing place in the ground near it's head, requiring, I conclude, a freer respiration, as it becomes more alive. This creature not only goes under the earth from the middle of November to the middle of April, but sleeps great part of the summer; for it goes to bed in the longest days at four in the afternoon, and often does not stir in the morning till late. Besides, it retires to rest for every shower; and does not move at all in wet days.

When one reflects on the state of this strange being, it is a matter of wonder to find that Providence should bestow such a profusion of days, such a seeming waste of longevity, on a reptile that appears to relish it so little as to squander more than two thirds of it's existence in a joyless stupor, and be lost to all sensation for months together in the profoundest of slumbers.

Because we call this creature an abject reptile, we are too apt to undervalue his abilities, and depreciate his powers of instinct. Yet he is, as Mr. Pope says of his lord,

——— Much too wise to walk into a well:

and has so much discernment as not to fall down an haha; but to stop and withdraw from the brink with the readiest precaution.

Though he loves warm weather he avoids the hot sun; because his thick shell, when once heated, would, as the poet says of solid armour—"scald with safety". He therefore spends the more sultry hours under the umbrella of a large cabbage-leaf, or amidst the waving forests of an asparagus-bed.

But as he avoids heat in the summer, so, in the decline of the year, he improves the faint autumnal beams, by getting within the reflection of a fruit-wall; and, though he never has read that planes inclining to the horizon receive a greater share of warmth,* he inclines his shell, by tilting it against the wall, to collect and admit every feeble ray.

Pitiable seems the condition of this poor embarrassed reptile: to be cased in a suit of ponderous armour, which he cannot lay

* *Several years ago a book was written entitled* Fruit-walls improved by inclining them to the horizon*: in which the author has shewn, by calculation, that a much greater number of the rays of the sun will fall on such walls than on those which are perpendicular.* ⟨G. W.⟩

aside; to be imprisoned, as it were, within his own shell, must preclude, we should suppose, all activity and disposition for enterprise. Yet there is a season of the year (usually the beginning of June) when his exertions are remarkable. He then walks on tiptoe, and is stirring by five in the morning; and, traversing the garden, examines every wicket and interstice in the fences, through which he will escape if possible: and often has eluded the care of the gardener, and wandered to some distant field. The motives that impel him to undertake these rambles seem to be of the amorous kind: his fancy then becomes intent on sexual attachments, which transport him beyond his usual gravity, and induce him to forget for a time his ordinary solemn deportment.

While I was writing this letter, a moist and warm afternoon, with the thermometer at 50, brought forth troops of *shell-snails;* and, at the same juncture, the *tortoise* heaved up the mould and put out it's head; and the next morning came forth, as it were raised from the dead; and walked about till four in the afternoon. This was a curious coincidence! a very amusing occurrence! to see such a similarity of feelings between the two φερεοικοι! for so the Greeks called both the *shell-snail* and the *tortoise.*

Summer birds are, this cold and backward spring, unusually late: I have seen but one swallow yet. This conformity with the weather convinces me more and more that they sleep in the winter.

LETTER LI

TO THE SAME

Selborne, *Sept*. 3, 1781.

I have now read your miscellanies through with much care and satisfaction; and am to return you my best thanks for the honourable mention made in them of me as a naturalist, which I wish I may deserve.

In some former letters I expressed my suspicions that many of the house-martins do not depart in the winter far from this village. I therefore determined to make some search about the south-east end of the hill, where I imagined they might slumber out the uncomfortable months of winter. But supposing that the examination would be made to the best advantage in the spring, and observing that no martins had appeared by the 11th of April last; on that day I employed some men to explore the shrubs and cavities of the suspected spot. The persons took pains, but without any success; however, a remarkable incident occurred in the midst of our pursuit—while the labourers were at work a house-martin, the first that had been seen this year, came down the village in the sight of several people, and went at once into a nest, where it stayed a short time, and then flew over the houses; for some days after no martins were observed, not till the 16th of April, and then only a pair. Martins in general were remarkably late this year.

LETTER LII

TO THE SAME

Selborne, *Sept.* 9, 1781.

I have just met with a circumstance respecting swifts, which furnishes an exception to the whole tenor of my observations ever since I have bestowed any attention on that species of hirundines. Our swifts, in general, withdrew this year about the first day of August, all save one pair, which in two or three days was reduced to a single bird. The perseverance of this individual made me suspect that the strongest of motives, that of an attachment to her young, could alone occasion so late a stay. I watched therefore till the twenty-fourth of August, and then discovered that, under the eaves of the church, she attended upon two young, which were fledged, and now put out their white chins from a crevice. These remained till the twenty-seventh, looking more alert every day, and seeming to long to be on the wing. After this day they were missing at once; nor could I ever observe them with their dam coursing round the church in the act of learning to fly, as the first broods evidently do. On the thirty-first I caused the eaves to be searched, but we found in the nest only two callow, dead, stinking swifts, on which a second nest had been formed. This double nest was full of the black shining cases of the *hippoboscæ hirundinis*.

The following remarks on this unusual incident are obvious. The first is, that though it may be disagreeable to swifts to remain beyond the beginning of August, yet that they can subsist longer is undeniable. The second is, that this uncommon event, as it was owing to the loss of the first brood, so it corroborates my former remark, that swifts breed regularly but once; since, was the contrary the case, the occurrence above could neither be new nor rare.

P.S. One swift was seen at Lyndon,* in the county of Rutland, in 1782, so late as the third of September.

* See the *Naturalist's Journal* for September, 1781. The information was doubtless received from Thomas Barker, who married the author's sister.

LETTER LIII

TO THE SAME

As I have sometimes known you make inquiries about several kinds of insects, I shall here send you an account of one sort which I little expected to have found in this kingdom. I had often observed that one particular part of a vine growing on the walls of my house was covered in the autumn with a black dust-like appearance, on which the flies fed eagerly; and that the shoots and leaves thus affected did not thrive; nor did the fruit ripen. To this substance I applied my glasses; but could not discover that it had any thing to do with animal life, as I at first expected: but, upon a closer examination behind the larger boughs, we were surprised to find that they were coated over with husky shells, from whose sides proceeded a cotton-like substance, surrounding a multitude of eggs. This curious and uncommon production put me upon recollecting what I have heard and read concerning the *coccus* vitis viniferæ* of Linnæus, which, in the south of Europe, infests many vines, and is an horrid and loathsome pest. As soon as I had turned to the accounts given of this insect, I saw at once that it swarmed on my vine; and did not appear to have been at all checked by the preceding winter, which had been uncommonly severe.

Not being then at all aware that it had any thing to do with England, I was much inclined to think that it came from Gibraltar among the many boxes and packages of plants and birds which I had formerly received from thence; and especially as the vine infested grew immediately under my study-window, where I usually kept my specimens. True it is that I had received nothing from thence for some years: but as insects, we know, are conveyed from one country to another in a very unexpected manner, and have a wonderful power of maintaining their existence till they fall into a *nidus* proper for their support and increase, I cannot but suspect still that these *cocci* came to me originally from Andalusia. Yet, all the while, candour obliges me to con-

* *Pulvinaria vitis.*

fess that Mr. Lightfoot* has written me word that he once, and but once, saw these insects on a vine at Weymouth in Dorsetshire; which, it is here to be observed, is a sea-port town to which the *coccus* might be conveyed by shipping.

As many of my readers may possibly never have heard of this strange and unusual insect, I shall here transcribe a passage from a natural history of Gibraltar, written by the Reverend John White, late vicar of Blackburn in Lancashire, but not yet published:—

"In the year 1770 a vine, which grew on the east-side of my house, and which had produced the finest crops of grapes for years past, was suddenly overspread on all the woody branches with large lumps of a white fibrous substance resembling spiders' webs, or rather raw cotton. It was of a very clammy quality, sticking fast to every thing that touched it, and capable of being spun into long threads. At first I suspected it to be the product of spiders, but could find none. Nothing was to be seen connected with it but many *brown oval husky shells*, which by no means looked like insects, but rather resembled bits of the dry bark of the vine. The tree had a plentiful crop of grapes set, when this pest appeared upon it; but the fruit was manifestly injured by this foul incumbrance. It remained all the summer, still increasing, and loaded the woody and bearing branches to a vast degree. I often pulled off great quantities by handfuls; but it was so slimy and tenacious that it could by no means be cleared. The grapes never filled to their natural perfection, but turned watery and vapid. Upon perusing the works afterwards of M. de Réaumur, I found this matter perfectly described and accounted for. Those husky shells, which I had observed, were no other than the *female coccus*, from whose sides this cotton-like substance exudes, and serves as a covering and security for their eggs."

To this account I think proper to add, that, though the female *cocci* are stationary, and seldom remove from the place to which they stick, yet the male is a winged insect; and that the black dust which I saw was undoubtedly the excrement of the females, which is eaten by ants as well as flies. Though the utmost severity of our winter did not destroy these insects, yet the attention

* F.L.S. and F.R.S. Mr. Nicholson gives interesting details of the fellow-traveller with Pennant through Scotland and the Hebrides.

of the gardener in a summer or two has entirely relieved my vine from this filthy annoyance.

As we have remarked above that insects are often conveyed from one country to another in a very unaccountable manner, I shall here mention an emigration of small *aphides*, which was observed in the village of Selborne no longer ago than August the 1st, 1785.

At about three o'clock in the afternoon of that day, which was very hot, the people of this village were surprised by a shower of *aphides*, or *smother-flies*, which fell in these parts. Those that were walking in the street at that juncture found themselves covered with these insects, which settled also on the hedges and gardens, blackening all the vegetables where they alighted. My annuals were discoloured with them, and the stalks of a bed of onions were quite coated over for six days after. These armies were then, no doubt, in a state of emigration, and shifting their quarters; and might have come, as far as we know, from the great hop-plantations of Kent or Sussex, the wind being all that day in the easterly quarter. They were observed at the same time in great clouds about Farnham, and all along the vale from Farnham to Alton.*

* *For various methods by which several insects shift their quarters, see Derham's* Physico-Theology. ⟨G. W.⟩

LETTER LIV*

TO THE SAME

DEAR SIR,

When I happen to visit a family where *gold* and *silver fishes* are kept in a glass bowl, I am always pleased with the occurrence, because it offers me an opportunity of observing the actions and propensities of those beings with whom we can be little acquainted in their natural state. Not long since I spent a fortnight at the house of a friend where there was such a *vivary*, to which I paid no small attention, taking every occasion to remark what passed within it's narrow limits. It was here that I first observed the manner in which fishes die. As soon as the creature sickens, the head sinks lower and lower, and it stands as it were on it's head; till, getting weaker, and losing all poise, the tail turns over, and at last it floats on the surface of the water with it's belly uppermost. The reason why fishes, when dead, swim in that manner is very obvious; because, when the body is no longer balanced by the fins of the belly, the broad muscular back preponderates by it's own gravity, and turns the belly uppermost, as lighter from it's being a cavity, and because it contains the swimming-bladders, which contribute to render it buoyant. Some that delight in *gold* and *silver fishes* have adopted a notion that they need no aliment. True it is that they will subsist for a long time without any apparent food but what they can collect from pure water frequently changed: yet they must draw some support from animalcula, and other nourishment supplied by the water; because, though they seem to eat nothing, yet the consequences of eating often drop from them. That they are best pleased with such *jejune* diet may easily be confuted, since if you toss them crumbs they will seize them with great readiness, not to say greediness: however, bread should be given sparingly, lest, turning sour, it corrupt the water. They will also feed on the water-plant called *lemna* (*duck's meat*), and also on small fry.†

* This letter was first published in the *Gentleman's Magazine* for 1786 (Vol. LVI, p. 488) under "V", the same initial as describes the poet Collins. See *Life and Letters*.

† A favourite food of my goldfishes are mosquito larvæ.

When they want to move a little they gently protrude themselves with their *pinnæ pectorales*; but it is with their strong muscular tails only that they and all fishes shoot along with such inconceivable rapidity. It has been said that the eyes of fishes are immoveable: but these apparently turn them forward or backward in their sockets as their occasions require. They take little notice of a lighted candle, though applied close to their heads, but flounce and seem much frightened by a sudden stroke of the hand against the support whereon the bowl is hung; especially when they have been motionless, and are perhaps asleep. As fishes have no eyelids, it is not easy to discern when they are sleeping or not, because their eyes are always open.

Nothing can be more amusing than a glass bowl containing such fishes: the double refractions of the glass and water represent them, when moving, in a shifting and changeable variety of dimensions, shades, and colours; while the two mediums, assisted by the concavo-convex shape of the vessel, magnify and distort them vastly; not to mention that the introduction of another element and it's inhabitants into our parlours engages the fancy in a very agreeable manner.

Gold and *silver fishes*, though originally natives of China and Japan, yet are become so well reconciled to our climate as to thrive and multiply very fast in our ponds and stews. Linnæus ranks this species of fish under the genus of *cyprinus*, or *carp*, and calls it *cyprinus auratus*.

Some people exhibit this sort of fish in a very fanciful way; for they cause a glass bowl to be blown with a large hollow space within, that does not communicate with it. In this cavity they put a bird occasionally; so that you may see a goldfinch or a linnet hopping as it were in the midst of the water, and the fishes swimming in a circle round it. The simple exhibition of the fishes is agreeable and pleasant; but in so complicated a way becomes whimsical and unnatural, and liable to the objection due to him,

Qui variare cupit rem prodigialitèr unam.*

I am, &c.

* From Horace's *De Arte Poetica.*

LETTER LV

TO THE SAME

October 10, 1781.

DEAR SIR,

I think I have observed before that much the most considerable part of the *house-martins* withdraw from hence about the first week in October; but that some, the latter broods I am now convinced, linger on till towards the middle of that month: and that at times, once perhaps in two or three years, a flight, for one day only, has shown itself in the first week in November.

Having taken notice, in October 1780, that the last flight was numerous, amounting perhaps to one hundred and fifty; and that the season was soft and still; I was resolved to pay uncommon attention to these late birds; to find, if possible, where they roosted, and to determine the precise time of their retreat. The mode of life of these latter *hirundines* is very favourable to such a design; for they spend the whole day in the sheltered district, between me and the Hanger, sailing about in a placid, easy manner, and feasting on those insects which love to haunt a spot so secure from ruffling winds. As my principal object was to discover the place of their roosting, I took care to wait on them before they retired to rest, and was much pleased to find that, for several evenings together, just at a quarter past five in the afternoon, they all scudded away in great haste towards the south-east, and darted down among the low shrubs above the cottages at the end of the hill. This spot in many respects seems to be well calculated for their winter residence: for in many parts it is as steep as the roof of any house, and therefore secure from the annoyances of water; and it is moreover clothed with beechen shrubs, which, being stunted and bitten by sheep, make the thickest covert imaginable; and are so entangled as to be impervious to the smallest spaniel: besides, it is the nature of underwood beech never to cast it's leaf all the winter; so that, with the leaves on the ground and those on the twigs, no shelter can be more complete. I watched them on to the thirteenth and fourteenth of October, and found their evening retreat was exact and uniform; but after this they made no regular appearance. Now and then a straggler was seen; and, on the twenty-second of October, I observed two in the morning over the village, and with them my remarks for the season ended.

From all these circumstances put together, it is more than probable that this lingering flight, at so late a season of the year, never departed from the island. Had they indulged me that autumn with a November visit, as I much desired, I presume that, with proper assistants, I should have settled the matter past all doubt; but though the third of November was a sweet day, and in appearance exactly suited to my wishes, yet not a martin was to be seen; and so I was forced, reluctantly, to give up the pursuit.

I have only to add that were the bushes, which cover some acres, and are not my own property, to be grubbed and carefully examined, probably those late broods, and perhaps the whole aggregate body of the house-martins of this district, might be found there, in different secret dormitories; and that, so far from withdrawing into warmer climes, it would appear that they never depart three hundred yards from the village.

LETTER LVI

TO THE SAME

They who write on natural history cannot too frequently advert to *instinct*, that wonderful limited faculty, which, in some instances, raises the brute creation as it were above *reason*, and in others leaves them so far below it.* Philosophers have defined *instinct* to be that secret influence by which every species is impelled naturally to pursue, at all times, the same way or track, without any teaching or example; whereas *reason*, without instruction, would often vary and do that by many methods which *instinct* effects by one alone. Now this maxim must be taken in a qualified sense; for there are instances in which *instinct* does vary and conform to the circumstances of place and convenience.

It has been remarked that every species of bird has a mode of nidification peculiar to itself; so that a school-boy would at once pronounce on the sort of nest before him. This is the case among fields and woods, and wilds; but, in the villages round London, where mosses and gossamer, and cotton from vegetables, are hardly to be found, the nest of the *chaffinch* has not that elegant finished appearance, nor is it so beautifully studded with lichens, as in a more rural district: and the *wren* is obliged to construct it's house with straws and dry grasses, which do not give it that rotundity and compactness so remarkable in the edifices of that little architect. Again, the regular nest of the *house-martin* is hemispheric; but where a rafter, or a joist, or a cornice, may happen to stand in the way, the nest is so contrived as to conform to the obstruction, and becomes flat or oval, or compressed.

In the following instances *instinct* is perfectly uniform and consistent. There are three creatures, the *squirrel*, the *field-mouse*, and the bird called the *nut-hatch*, (*sitta Europæa*), which live much on hazle-nuts; and yet they open them each in a different way. The first, after rasping off the small end, splits the

* No comparison of instinct with intelligence—and there is a library of such—could be more apt than this single sentence.

shell in two with his long fore-teeth, as a man does with his knife; the second nibbles a hole with his teeth, so regular as if drilled with a wimble,* and yet so small that one would wonder how the kernel can be extracted through it; while the last picks an irregular ragged hole with it's bill: but as this artist has no paws to hold the nut firm while he pierces it, like an adroit workman, he fixes it, as it were in a vice, in some cleft of a tree, or in some crevice; when, standing over it, he perforates the stubborn shell. We have often placed nuts in the chink of a gate-post where *nut-hatches* have been known to haunt, and have always found that those birds have readily penetrated them. While at work they make a rapping noise that may be heard at a considerable distance.

You that understand both the theory and practical part of music may best inform us why *harmony* or *melody* should so strangely affect some men, as it were by recollection, for days after a concert is over. What I mean the following passage will most readily explain:

"Præhabebat porrò vocibus humanis, instrumentisque harmonicis musicam illam avium: non quod aliâ quoque non delectaretur; sed quod ex musicâ humanâ relinqueretur in animo continens quædam, attentionemque et somnum conturbans agitatio; dum ascensus, exscensus, tenores, ac mutationes illæ sonorum, et consonantiarum euntque, redeuntque per phantasiam:—cum nihil tale relinqui possit ex modulationibus avium, quæ, quod non sunt perinde a nobis imitabiles, non possunt perinde internam facultatem commovere."

Gassendus *in Vitâ Peireskii.*

This curious quotation strikes me much by so well representing my own case, and by describing what I have so often felt, but never could so well express. When I hear fine music I am haunted with passages therefrom night and day; and especially at first waking, which, by their importunity, give me more uneasiness than pleasure: elegant lessons still tease my imagination, and recur irresistibly to my recollection at seasons, and even when I am desirous of thinking of more serious matters.

I am, &c.

* Gimlet

LETTER LVII

TO THE SAME

A rare, and I think a new, little bird frequents my garden, which I have great reason to think is the *petttichaps*:* it is common in some parts of the kingdom; and I have received formerly several dead specimens from Gibraltar. This bird much resembles the *white-throat*, but has a more white or rather silvery breast and belly; is restless and active, like the *willow-wrens*, and hops from bough to bough, examining every part for food; it also runs up the stems of the *crown-imperials*, and, putting it's head into the bells of those flowers, sips the liquor which stands in the *nectarium* of each petal. Sometimes it feeds on the ground, like the *hedge-sparrow*, by hopping about on the grass-plots and mown walks.

One of my neighbours, an intelligent and observing man, informs me that, in the beginning of May, and about ten minutes before eight o'clock in the evening, he discovered a great cluster of *house-swallows*, thirty at least he supposes, perching on a willow that hung over the verge of James Knight's upper-pond. His attention was first drawn by the twittering of these birds, which sat motionless in a row on the bough, with their heads all one way, and, by their weight, pressing down the twig so that it nearly touched the water. In this situation he watched them till he could see no longer. Repeated accounts of this sort, spring and fall, induce us greatly to suspect that *house-swallows* have some strong attachment to water, independent of the matter of food; and, though they may not retire into that element, yet they may conceal themselves in the banks of pools and rivers during the uncomfortable months of winter.

One of the keepers of Wolmer-forest sent me a *peregrine-falcon*,† which he shot on the verge of that district as it was

* The country name does not distinguish between our two whitethroats, but the bird meant here is the lesser whitethroat.

† The only place in Hampshire where this falcon still breeds is the Isle of Wight. Several pairs also breed on the adjoining coast of Dorset. Four birds were observed at different periods over Hampshire in 1936. (*Papers and Proceedings of the Hampshire Field Club*, Vol. XIII, p. 275.)

devouring a wood-pigeon. The *falco peregrinus*, or *haggard falcon*, is a noble species of hawk seldom seen in the southern counties. In winter 1767 one was killed in the neighbouring parish of Faringdon, and sent by me to Mr. Pennant into North-Wales.* Since that time I have met with none till now. The specimen mentioned above was in fine preservation, and not injured by the shot: it measured forty-two inches from wing to wing, and twenty-one from beak to tail, and weighed two pounds and an half standing weight. This species is very robust, and wonderfully formed for rapine: it's breast was plump and muscular; it's thighs long, thick, and brawny; and it's legs remarkably short and well set: the feet were armed with most formidable, sharp, long talons: the eyelids and cere of the bill were yellow; but the irides of the eye dusky; the beak was thick and hooked, and of a dark colour, and had a jagged process near the end of the upper mandible on each side: it's tail, or train, was short in proportion to the bulk of it's body: yet the wings, when closed, did not extend to the end of the train. From it's large and fair proportions it might be supposed to have been a female; but I was not permitted to cut open the specimen. For one of the birds of prey, which are usually lean, this was in high case: in it's craw were many barley-corns, which probably came from the crop of the wood-pigeon, on which it was feeding when shot: for voracious birds do not eat grain; but, when devouring their quarry, with undistinguishing vehemence swallow bones and feathers, and all matters, indiscriminately. This falcon was probably driven from the mountains of North Wales or Scotland, where they are known to breed, by rigorous weather and deep snows that had lately fallen.

I am, &c.

* *See my tenth and eleventh letter to that gentleman.* ⟨G. W.⟩

LETTER LVIII

TO THE SAME

My near neighbour,* a young gentleman in the service of the East-India Company, has brought home a dog and a bitch of the Chinese breed from Canton; such as are fattened in that country for the purpose of being eaten: they are about the size of a moderate spaniel; of a pale yellow colour, with coarse bristling hairs on their backs; sharp upright ears, and peaked heads, which give them a very fox-like appearance. Their hind legs are unusually straight, without any bend at the hock or ham, to such a degree as to give them an aukward gait when they trot. When they are in motion their tails are curved high over their backs like those of some hounds, and have a bare place each on the outside from the tip midway, that does not seem to be matter of accident, but somewhat singular. Their eyes are jet-black, small, and piercing; the insides of their lips and mouths of the same colour, and their tongues blue. The bitch has a dew-claw on each hind leg; the dog has none. When taken out into a field the bitch showed some disposition for hunting, and dwelt on the scent of a covey of partridges till she sprung them, giving her tongue all the time. The dogs in South America are dumb; but these bark much in a short thick manner, like foxes; and have a surly, savage demeanour like their ancestors, which are not domesticated, but bred up in sties, where they are fed for the table with rice-meal and other farinaceous food. These dogs, having been taken on board as soon as weaned, could not learn much from their dam; yet they did not relish flesh when they came to England. In the islands of the *pacific* ocean the dogs are bred up on vegetables, and would not eat flesh when offered them by our circumnavigators.

* Charles Etty, son of the Vicar of Selborne, the Rev. Andrew. The reference in the letter must be subsequent to 1787, when he returned from a two years' voyage in the East Indies. The present letter is undated, and the nearest date to it is given six letters back, Sept. 9, 1781. This is an indication that the Selborne Letters are devoid of epistolary continuity and indeed of epistolary verisimilitude. In a letter to his sister, Mrs. Thomas Barker, dated 1784, the year of Andrew Etty's death, the author writes: "I miss poor Mr. Etty every day: he was a blameless man, without guile. His son Charles is in London making interest for an appointment to India. His escape off Ceylon was wonderful!"

We believe that all dogs, in a state of nature, have sharp, upright fox-like ears; and that hanging ears, which are esteemed so graceful, are the effect of choice breeding and cultivation. Thus, in the *Travels of Ysbrandt Ides from Muscovy to China*, the dogs which draw the Tartars on snow-sledges near the river Oby are engraved with prick-ears, like those from Canton. The Kamschatdales also train the same sort of sharp-eared peaked-nosed dogs to draw their sledges; as may be seen in an elegant print engraved for Captain Cook's last voyage round the world.

Now we are upon the subject of dogs, it may not be impertinent to add, that spaniels, as all sportsmen know, though they hunt partridges and pheasants as it were by instinct, and with much delight and alacrity, yet will hardly touch their bones when offered as food; nor will a mongrel dog of my own, though he is remarkable for finding that sort of game. But, when we came to offer the bones of partridges to the two Chinese dogs, they devoured them with much greediness, and licked the platter clean.

No sporting dogs will flush woodcocks till inured to the scent and trained to the sport, which they then pursue with vehemence and transport; but then they will not touch their bones, but turn from them with abhorrence, even when they are hungry.

Now, that dogs should not be fond of the bones of such birds as they are not disposed to hunt is no wonder; but why they reject and do not care to eat their natural game is not so easily accounted for, since the end of hunting seems to be, that the chase pursued should be eaten. Dogs again will not devour the more rancid water-fowls, nor indeed the bones of any wild-fowls; nor will they touch the fœtid bodies of birds that feed on offal and garbage: and indeed there may be somewhat of providential instinct in this circumstance of dislike; for vultures,* and kites, and ravens, and crows, &c. were intended to be messmates with dogs† over their carrion; and seem to be appointed by Nature as fellow-scavengers to remove all cadaverous nuisances from the face of the earth.

I am, &c.

* *Hasselquist, in his* Travels to the Levant, *observes that the dogs and vultures at Grand Cairo maintain such a friendly intercourse as to bring up their young together in the same place.* ⟨G. W.⟩

† *The Chinese word for a dog to an European ear sounds like* quihloh. ⟨G. W.⟩

LETTER LIX

TO THE SAME

The fossil wood buried in the bogs of Wolmer-forest is not yet all exhausted; for the peat-cutters now and then stumble upon a log. I have just seen a piece which was sent by a labourer of Oakhanger to a carpenter of this village; this was the but-end of a small oak, about five feet long, and about five inches in diameter. It had apparently been severed from the ground by an axe, was very ponderous, and as black as ebony. Upon asking the carpenter for what purpose he had procured it; he told me that it was to be sent to his brother, a joiner at Farnham, who was to make use of it in cabinet work, by inlaying it along with whiter woods.

Those that are much abroad on evenings after it is dark, in spring and summer, frequently hear a nocturnal bird passing by on the wing, and repeating often a short quick note. This bird I have remarked myself, but never could make out till lately. I am assured now that it is the *Stone-curlew*, (*charadrius oedicnemus*).* Some of them pass over or near my house almost every evening after it is dark, from the uplands of the hill and *North field*, away down towards Dorton; where, among the streams and meadows, they find a greater plenty of food. Birds that fly by night are obliged to be noisy; their notes often repeated become signals or watch-words to keep them together, that they may not stray or lose each the other in the dark.

The evening proceedings and manœuvres of the rooks are curious and amusing in the autumn. Just before dusk they return in long strings from the foraging of the day, and rendezvous by thousands over Selborne-down, where they wheel round

* The stone-curlew has long vanished from the Selborne neighbourhood, and is becoming increasingly rare in nearly all of its former breeding haunts, mainly because of the activities of the Forestry Commission in turning natural wastes into parade grounds of conifers. Extract from the *Papers and Proceedings of the Hampshire Field Club* (1937): "As usual, these birds assembled on Quarley Hill (in the extreme west of the county) prior to migration, always resorting to the same spots year after year: a root field, a fallow field and among junipers. They were fewer than usual this year (1936). Early in October the numbers usually reach 80 to 120."

in the air, and sport and dive in a playful manner, all the while exerting their voices, and making a loud cawing, which, being blended and softened by the distance that we at the village are below them, becomes a confused noise or chiding; or rather a pleasing murmur, very engaging to the imagination, and not unlike the cry of a pack of hounds in hollow, echoing woods, or the rushing of the wind in tall trees, or the tumbling of the tide upon a pebbly shore.* When this ceremony is over, with the last gleam of day, they retire for the night to the deep beechen woods of Tisted and Ropley. We remember a little girl who, as she was going to bed, used to remark on such an occurrence, in the true spirit of *physico-theology*, that the rooks were saying their prayers; and yet this child was much too young to be aware that the scriptures have said of the Deity—that "he feedeth the ravens who call upon him".

I am, &c.

* All the *Corvidae* in more or less degree, but especially the raven, exhibit the playfulness of disposition illustrated in this beautiful passage.

LETTER LXIII

TO THE SAME

As the frost in December 1784 was very extraordinary, you, I trust, will not be displeased to hear the particulars; and especially when I promise to say no more about the severities of winter after I have finished this letter.

The first week in December was very wet, with the barometer very low. On the 7th, with the barometer at 28—five tenths, came on a vast snow, which continued all that day and the next, and most part of the following night; so that by the morning of the 9th the works of men were quite overwhelmed, the lanes filled so as to be impassable, and the ground covered twelve or fifteen inches without any drifting. In the evening of the 9th the air began to be so very sharp that we thought it would be curious to attend to the motions of a thermometer: we therefore hung out two; one made by Martin and one by Dollond, which soon began to shew us what we were to expect; for, by ten o'clock, they fell to 21, and at eleven to 4, when we went to bed. On the 10th, in the morning, the quicksilver of Dollond's glass was down to *half a degree below zero*; and that of Martin's, which was absurdly graduated only to four degrees *above zero*, sunk quite into the brass guard of the ball; so that when the weather became most interesting this was useless. On the 10th, at eleven at night, though the air was perfectly still, Dollond's glass went down to *one degree below zero!* This strange severity of the weather made me very desirous to know what degree of cold there might be in such an exalted and near situation as Newton. We had therefore, on the morning of the 10th, written to Mr. ——, and entreated him to hang out his thermometer, made by Adams; and to pay some attention to it morning and evening; expecting wonderful phænomena, in so elevated a region, at two hundred feet or more above my house. But, behold! on the 10th, at eleven at night, it was down only to 17, and the next morning at 22, when mine was at ten! We were so disturbed at this unexpected reverse of comparative local cold, that we sent one of my glasses up, thinking that of Mr. —— must, some how, be wrongly constructed. But, when the instruments came to be confronted, they went exactly together: so that, for one night at least, the cold at Newton was 18 degrees less than at Selborne; and, through the whole frost, 10 or 12 degrees; and indeed, when we came to observe consequences, we could readily credit this; for all my laurustines, bays, ilexes, arbutuses, cypresses, and even my Portugal laurels,* and (which occasions more regret) my fine sloping laurel-hedge, were scorched up; while, at Newton,† the same trees have not lost a leaf!‡

We had steady frost on to the 25th, when the thermometer in the morning was down to 10 with us, and at Newton only to 21. Strong frost continued till the 31st, when some tendency to thaw was observed; and, by January the 3d, 1785, the thaw was confirmed, and some rain fell.

A circumstance that I must not omit, because it was new to us, is, that on Friday, December the 10th, being bright sun-shine, the air was full of icy *spiculæ*, floating in all directions, like atoms in a sun-beam let into a dark room. We thought them at first particles of the rime falling from my tall hedges; but were soon convinced to the contrary, by making our observations in open places where no rime could reach us.§ Were they watery particles of the air frozen as they floated; or were they evaporations from the snow frozen as they mounted?

We were much obliged to the thermometers for the early information they gave us; and hurried our apples, pears, onions, potatoes, &c. into the cellar, and warm closets; while those who had not, or neglected such warnings, lost all their stores of roots and fruits, and had their very bread and cheese frozen.

* *Mr. Miller,*|| *in his* Gardener's Dictionary, *says positively that the Portugal laurels remained untouched in the remarkable frost of* 1739-40. *So that either that accurate observer was much mistaken, or else the frost of December* 1784 *was much more severe and destructive than that in the year above-mentioned.* ⟨G. W.⟩

† Newton Valence, whose Vicar, Richard Yalden, cooperating with the author in these observations, died in this same year, to be succeeded by Edmund White.

‡ The reason is that the colder air on a still night of frost drifts like invisible vapour into the hollows and low-lying pockets. A plant or bush raised a couple of inches on a mound of soil will escape, while its neighbour of the same species will be, as White truly says, "scorched".

§ *Coleridge's Note.* "This is not uncommon in Westmorland and Cumberland. I have myself noticed it often in hard frosts."

|| Overseer of Chelsea Garden.

I must not omit to tell you that, during those two Siberian days, my parlour-cat was so electric, that had a person stroked her, and been properly *insulated*, the shock might have been given to a whole circle of people.

I forgot to mention before, that, during the two severe days, two men, who were tracing hares in the snow, had their feet frozen; and two men, who were much better employed, had their fingers so affected by the frost, while they were thrashing in a barn, that a mortification followed, from which they did not recover for many weeks.

This frost killed all the furze and most of the ivy, and in many places stripped the hollies of all their leaves. It came at a very early time of the year, before old November* ended; and yet may be allowed from it's effects to have exceeded any since 1739-40.

* Not because he was a-dying, but had been pushed back eleven days in 1752.

LETTER LXV

TO THE SAME

The summer of the year 1783 was an amazing and portentous one, and full of horrible phænomena;* for, besides the alarming meteors and tremendous thunder-storms that affrighted and distressed the different counties of this kingdom, the peculiar *haze*, or smokey fog, that prevailed for many weeks in this island, and in every part of Europe, and even beyond it's limits, was a most extraordinary appearance, unlike any thing known within the memory of man. By my journal I find that I had noticed this strange occurrence from June 23 to July 20 inclusive, during which period the wind varied to every quarter without making any alteration in the air. The sun, at noon, looked as blank as a clouded moon, and shed a rust-coloured ferruginous light on the ground, and floors of rooms; but was particularly lurid and blood-coloured at rising and setting. All the time the heat was so intense that butchers' meat could hardly be eaten on the day after it was killed; and the flies swarmed so in the lanes and hedges that they rendered the

* The cause of this "amazing and portentous" summer, described so pictorially, was a severe volcanic eruption in Iceland. Similar effects were noted as following the eruption of Krakatoa in Java in 1883.

horses half frantic, and riding irksome. The country people began to look with a superstitious awe at the red, louring aspect of the sun; and indeed there was reason for the most enlightened person to be apprehensive; for, all the while, Calabria and part of the isle of Sicily, were torn and convulsed with earthquakes; and about that juncture a *volcano* sprung out of the sea on the coast of Norway. On this occasion Milton's noble simile of the sun, in his first book of *Paradise Lost*, frequently occurred to my mind; and it is indeed particularly applicable, because, towards the end, it alludes to a superstitious kind of dread, with which the minds of men are always impressed by such strange and unusual phænomena.

— — — As when the *sun*, new risen,
Looks through the horizontal, *misty* air,
Shorn of his *beams*; or from behind the moon,
In *dim* eclipse, *disastrous twilight sheds*
On half the nations, and with *fear* of *change*
Perplexes monarchs — — — — — —

LETTER LXVI

TO THE SAME

We are very seldom annoyed with thunder-storms: and it is no less remarkable than true, that those which arise in the south have hardly been known to reach this village; for, before they get over us, they take a direction to the east or to the west, or sometimes divide into two, and go in part to one of those quarters, and in part to the other; as was truly the case in summer 1783, when, though the country round was continually harassed with tempests, and often from the south, yet we escaped them all;* as appears by my journal of that summer. The only way that I can at all account for this fact—for such it is—is that, on that quarter, between us and the sea, there are continual mountains, hill behind hill, such as Nore-hill, the Barnet, Butser-hill, and Portsdown, which some how divert the storms, and give them a different direction. High promontories, and elevated grounds, have always been observed to attract clouds and disarm them of their mischievous contents, which are discharged into the trees and summits as soon as they come in contact with those turbulent meteors; while the humble vales escape, because they are so far beneath them.

But, when I say I do not remember a thunder-storm from the south, I do not mean that we never have suffered from thunder-storms at all; for on June 5th, 1784, the thermometer in the morning being at 64, and at noon at 70, the barometer at 29—six tenths one-half, and the wind north, I observed a blue mist, smelling strongly of sulphur, hanging along our sloping woods, and seeming to indicate that thunder was at hand. I was called in about two in the afternoon, and so missed seeing the gathering of the clouds in the north; which they who were abroad assured me had something uncommon in it's appearance. At about a

* Cowper, however, did not escape them in northern Northamptonshire, as *The Task* (Book II) gives witness. See Harting's and Bowdler Sharpe's Editions.

quarter after two the storm began in the parish of Hartley, moving slowly from north to south; and from thence it came over Norton-farm, and so to Grange-farm, both in this parish. It began with vast drops of rain, which were soon succeeded by round hail, and then by convex pieces of ice, which measured three inches in girth. Had it been as extensive as it was violent, and of any continuance (for it was very short), it must have ravaged all the neighbourhood. In the parish of Hartley it did some damage to one farm; but Norton, which lay in the center of the storm, was greatly injured; as was Grange, which lay next to it. It did but just reach to the middle of the village, where the hail broke my north windows, and all my garden-lights and hand-glasses, and many of my neighbours' windows. The extent of the storm was about two miles in length and one in breadth. We were just sitting down to dinner; but were soon diverted from our repast by the clattering of tiles and the jingling of glass. There fell at the same time prodigious torrents of rain on the farms above-mentioned, which occasioned a flood as violent as it was sudden; doing great damage to the meadows and fallows, by deluging the one and washing away the soil of the other. The hollow lane towards Alton was so torn and disordered as not to be passable till mended, rocks being removed that weighed 200 weight. Those that saw the effect which the great hail had on ponds and pools say that the dashing of the water made an extraordinary appearance, the froth and spray standing up in the air three feet above the surface. The rushing and roaring of the hail, as it approached, was truly tremendous.

Though the clouds at South Lambeth, near London, were at that juncture thin and light, and no storm was in sight, nor within hearing, yet the air was strongly electric; for the bells of an electric machine at that place rang repeatedly, and fierce sparks were discharged.

When I first took the present work in hand, I proposed to have added an *Annus Historico-naturalis*, or The Natural History of the Twelve Months of the Year; which would have comprised many incidents and occurrences that have not fallen in my way to be mentioned in my series of letters;—but, as Mr. Aikin of Warrington has lately published somewhat of this sort, and as the length of my correspondence has sufficiently put your patience to the test, I shall here take a respectful leave of you and natural history together;

And am,

With all due deference and regard,

Your most obliged,

And most humble servant,

GIL. WHITE.

Selborne, *June* 25, 1787.

THE ANTIQUITIES OF SELBORNE

LETTER II

That Selborne* was a place of some distinction and note in the time of the Saxons we can give most undoubted proofs. But, as there are few if any accounts of villages before *Domesday*, it will be best to begin with that venerable record. "Ipse rex tenet *Selesburne*. *Eddid* regina tenuit, et nunquam geldavit. De isto manerio dono dedit rex *Radfredo* presbytero dimidiam hidam cum ecclesia. Tempore regis *Edwardi* et post, valuit duodecim solidos et sex denarios; modo octo solidos et quatuor denarios." Here we see that Selborne was a royal manor; and that Editha, the queen of Edward the Confessor, had been lady of that manor; and was succeeded in it by the Conqueror; and that it had a church. Besides these, many circumstances concur to prove it to have been a Saxon village; such as the name of the place itself,† the names of many fields, and some families,‡ with a variety of words in husbandry and common life, still subsisting among the country people.

* Bell says that the name means Great Brook. It was once, however, applied to the Oakhanger stream only and means Stream of the Sallows, from O.E. sealh = sallow.

† *Selesburne, Seleburne, Selburn, Selbourn, Selborne, and Selborn, as it has been variously spelt at different periods, is of Saxon derivation; for* Sel *signifies* great, *and* burn *torrens, a* brook *or* rivulet: *so that the name seems to be derived from the great perennial stream that breaks out at the upper end of the village.*—Sel *also signifies* bonus, *item,* fœcundus, fertilis. "Sel-ȝærſ-tun: fœcunda graminis clausura; fertile pascuum*: a meadow in the parish of Godelming is still called Sal-gars-ton.*"—*Lye's* Saxon Dictionary, *in the Supplement, by Mr. Manning.* ⟨G. W.⟩

‡ *Thus the name of* Aldred *signifies* all-reverend, *and that of* Kemp *means a* soldier. *Thus we have a* church-litton, *or enclosure for dead bodies, and not a* church-yard: *there is also a* Culver-croft *near the Grange-farm, being the enclosure where the priory pigeon-house stood, from* culver *a pigeon. Again there are three steep pastures in this parish called the Lithe, from* Hlithe, clivus. *The wicker-work that binds and fastens down a hedge on the top is called* ether, *from* ether *an hedge. When the good women call their hogs they cry* sic, sic,§ *not knowing that* sic *is Saxon, or rather Celtic, for a hog. Coppice or brush wood our countrymen call* rise, *from* hris, *frondes; and talk of a load of* rise. *Within the author's memory the Saxon plurals,* housen *and* peason, *were in common use. But it would be endless to instance in every circumstance: he that wishes for more specimens must frequent a farmer's kitchen. I have therefore selected some words to shew how familiar the Saxon dialect was to this district, since in more than seven hundred years it is far from being obliterated.* ⟨G. W.⟩

§ Σικα, *porcus, apud Lacones; un Porceau chez les Lacedemoniens: ce mot a sans doute esté pris des Celtes, qui diso*[*i*]*ent* sic, *pour marquer un porceau. Encore aujour*[*d*]*'huy quand les Bretons chassent ces animaux, ils ne disent point autrement, que* sic, sic.—Antiquité de la Nation, et de la Langue des Celtes, *par Pezron.* ⟨G. W.⟩

What probably first drew the attention of the Saxons to this spot was the beautiful spring or fountain called Well-head,* which induced them to build by the banks of that perennial current; for ancient settlers loved to reside by brooks and rivulets, where they could dip for their water without the trouble and expense of digging wells and of drawing.

It remains still unsettled among the antiquaries at what time tracts of land were first appropriated to the chase alone for the amusement of the sovereign. Whether our Saxon monarchs had any royal forests does not, I believe, appear on record; but the *Constitutiones de Foresta* of Canute, the Dane, are come down to us. We shall not therefore pretend to say whether Wolmer-forest existed as a royal domain before the conquest. If it did not, we may suppose it was laid out by some of our earliest Norman kings, who were exceedingly attached to the pleasures of the chase, and resided much at Winchester, which lies at a moderate distance from this district. The Plantagenet princes seem to have been pleased with Wolmer; for tradition says that king John resided just upon the verge, at Ward le ham, on a regular and remarkable mount, still called King John's Hill and Lodge Hill; and Edward III had a chapel in his park, or enclosure, at Kingsley.† Humphrey, duke of Gloucester, and Richard, duke of York, say my evidences, were both, in their turns, *wardens* of Wolmer-forest; which seems to have served for an appointment for the younger princes of the royal family, as it may again.

I have intentionally mentioned Edward III and the dukes Humphrey and Richard, before king Edward II because I have reserved, for the entertainment of my readers, a pleasant anecdote respecting that prince, with which I shall close this letter.

As Edward II was hunting on Wolmer-forest, Morris Ken, of the kitchen, fell from his horse several times; at which accidents the king laughed immoderately: and, when the chase was over, ordered him twenty shillings;‡ an enormous sum for those days!

* Well-head *signifies* spring-head, *and not a deep pit from whence we draw water. For particulars about which see Letter I to Mr. Pennant.* ⟨G. W.⟩

† *The parish of Kingsley lies between, and divides Wolmer-forest from Ayles Holt-forest. See Letter IX to Mr. Pennant.* ⟨G. W.⟩

‡ "*Item, paid at the lodge at Wolmer, when the king was stag-hunting there, to Morris Ken, of the kitchen, because he rode before the king and often fell from his*

Proper allowances ought to be made for the youth of this monarch, whose spirits also, we may suppose, were much exhilarated by the sport of the day: but, at the same time, it is reasonable to remark that, whatever might be the occasion of Ken's first fall, the subsequent ones seem to have been designed. The scullion appears to have been an artful fellow, and to have seen the king's foible; which furnishes an early specimen of that his easy softness and facility of temper, of which the infamous Gaveston took such advantages, as brought innumerable calamities on the nation, and involved the prince at last in misfortunes and sufferings too deplorable to be mentioned without horror and amazement.

---

horse, at which the king laughed exceedingly—a gift, by command, of twenty shillings."—A MS. in possession of Thomas Astle, esq. containing the private expenses of Edward II. ⟨G.W.⟩

LETTER V

In the church-yard of this village is a *yew-tree*, whose aspect bespeaks it to be of a great age: it seems to have seen several centuries, and is probably coeval with the church,* and therefore may be deemed an antiquity: the body is squat, short, and thick, and measures twenty-three feet in the girth, supporting an head of suitable extent to it's bulk. This is a male tree, which in the spring sheds clouds of dust, and fills the atmosphere around with it's farina.

As far as we have been able to observe, the males of this species become much larger than the females; and it has so fallen out that most of the yew-trees in the church-yards of this neighbourhood are males: but this must have been matter of mere accident, since men, when they first planted yews, little dreamed that there were sexes in trees.

In the yard, in the midst of the street, till very lately grew a middle-sized female tree of the same species, which commonly bore great crops of berries. By the high winds usually prevailing about the autumnal equinox, these berries, then ripe, were blown down into the road, where the hogs ate them. And it was very remarkable, that, though barrow-hogs and young sows found no inconvenience from this food, yet milch-sows often died after such a repast: a circumstance that can be accounted for only by supposing that the latter, being much exhausted and hungry, devoured a larger quantity.

While mention is making of the bad effects of yew-berries, it may be proper to remind the unwary that the twigs and leaves of yew, though eaten in a very small quantity, are certain death to horses and cows, and that in a few minutes. An horse tied to a yew-hedge, or to a faggot-stack of dead yew, shall be found dead before the owner can be aware that any danger is at hand: and the writer has been several times a sorrowful witness to losses

* "The largest yew I know of, said to be the largest in Hampshire, is that of Boarhunt Churchyard, 25 ft. 3 ins. in girth, or according to another measurement, 27 feet. Taking it at 26 feet, the above rate of growth would make it 1200 years old." J. P. Williams-Freeman, *Field Archaeology as Illustrated by Hampshire*.

of this kind among his friends; and in the island of Ely* had once the mortification to see nine young steers or bullocks of his own all lying dead in an heap from browzing a little on an hedge of yew in an old garden, into which they had broken in snowy weather. Even the clippings of a yew-hedge have destroyed a whole dairy of cows when thrown inadvertently into a yard. And yet sheep and turkies, and, as park-keepers say, deer, will crop these trees with impunity.

Some intelligent persons assert that the branches of yew, while *green*, are not noxious; and that they will kill only when *dead* and *withered*, by lacerating the stomach: but to this assertion we cannot by any means assent, because, among the number of cattle that we have known fall victims to this deadly food, not one has been found, when it was opened, but had a lump of *green* yew in it's paunch. True it is, that yew-trees stand for twenty years or more in a field, and no bad consequences ensue: but at some time or other cattle, either from wantonness when full, or from hunger when empty, (from both which circumstances we have seen them perish) will be meddling, to their certain destruction; the yew seems to be a very improper tree for a pasture-field.

Antiquaries seem much at a loss to determine at what period this tree first obtained a place in church-yards. A statute passed A.D. 1307 and 35 Edward I the title of which is "Ne rector arbores in cemeterio prosternat". Now if it is recollected that we seldom see any other very large or ancient tree in a church-yard but yews, this statute must have principally related to this species of tree; and consequently their being planted in church-yards is of much more ancient date than the year 1307.

As to the use of these trees, possibly the more respectable parishioners were buried under their shade before the improper custom was introduced of burying within the body of the church, where the living are to assemble. Deborah, Rebekah's nurse,† was buried under an oak; the most honourable place of interment probably next to the cave of Machpelah,‡ which seems to

* In 1746, when the author was at Thorney as executor to his uncle Thomas's property, left to Thomas White. Missel-thrushes eat yew-berries with impunity, but then the seed is expelled.

† *Gen.* xxxv, 8. ⟨G. W.⟩

‡ *Gen.* xxiii, 9. ⟨G. W.⟩

have been appropriated to the remains of the patriarchal family alone.

The farther use of yew-trees might be as a screen to churches, by their thick foliage, from the violence of winds; perhaps also for the purpose of archery, the best long bows being made of that material: and we do not hear that they are planted in the church-yards of other parts of Europe, where long bows were not so much in use. They might also be placed as a shelter to the congregation assembling before the church-doors were opened, and as an emblem of mortality* by their funereal appearance. In the south of England every church-yard almost has it's tree, and some two; but in the north, we understand, few are to be found.

The idea of R.C. that the *yew-tree* afforded it's branches instead of palms for the processions on *Palm-Sunday*, is a good one, and deserves attention. See Gent. Mag. Vol. L, p. 128.

* "My shroud of white, all stuck with yew."

LETTER XIV

"In the year 1373 Wykeham, bishop of Winchester, held a visitation of his whole diocese; not only of the secular clergy through the several deaneries, but also of the monasteries, and religious houses of all sorts, which he visited in person. The next year he sent his commissioners with power to correct and reform the several irregularities and abuses which he had discovered in the course of his visitation.

"Some years afterward, the bishop having visited *three several times* all the religious houses throughout his diocese, and being well informed of the state and condition of each, and of the particular abuses which required correction and reformation, besides the orders which he had already given, and the remedies which he had occasionally applied by his commissioners, now issued his injunctions to each of them. They were accommodated to their several exigencies, and intended to correct the abuses introduced, and to recall them all to a strict observation of the rules of their respective orders. Many of these injunctions are still extant, and are evident monuments of the care and attention with which he discharged this part of his episcopal duty."*

Some of these injunctions I shall here produce; and they are such as will not fail, I think, to give satisfaction to the antiquary, both as never having been published before, and as they are a curious picture of monastic irregularities at that time.

The documents that I allude to are contained in the *Notabilis Visitatio de Seleburne*, held at the Priory of that place, by Wykeham in person, in the year 1387.

This evidence, in the original, is written on two skins of parchment; the one large, and the other smaller, and consists of a *preamble*, 36 *items*, and a *conclusion*, which altogether evince the patient investigation of the visitor, for which he had always been so remarkable in all matters of moment, and how much he had at heart the regularity of those institutions, of whose efficacy in their prayers for the dead he was so firmly persuaded. As the

* *See Lowth's* Life of Wykeham. ⟨G. W.⟩

bishop was so much in earnest, we may be assured that he had nothing in view but to correct and reform what he found amiss; and was under no bias to blacken, or misrepresent, as the commissioners of Thomas Lord Cromwell seem in part to have done at the time of the reformation.* We may therefore with reason suppose that the bishop gives us an exact delineation of the morals and manners of the canons of Selborne at that juncture; and that what he found they had omitted he enjoins them; and for what they have done amiss, and contrary to their rules and statutes, he reproves them; and threatens them with punishment suitable to their irregularities.

This *visitatio* is of considerable length, and cannot be introduced into the body of this work; we shall therefore refer the reader to the Appendix, where he will find every particular, while we shall take some notice, and make some remarks, on the most singular *items* as they occur.

In the preamble the visitor says—"Considering the charge lying upon us, that your blood may not be required at our hands, we came down to visit your Priory, as our office required: and every time we repeated our visitation we found something still not only contrary to regular rules but also repugnant to religion and good reputation."

In the first article after the preamble—"he commands them on their obedience, and on pain of the greater excommunication, to see that the canonical hours by night and by day be sung in their choir, and the masses of the Blessed Mary, and other accustomed masses, be celebrated at the proper hours with devotion, and at moderate pauses; and that it be not allowed to any to absent themselves from the hours and masses, or to withdraw before they are finished."

Item 2d. He enjoins them to observe that silence to which they are so strictly bound by the rule of Saint Augustine at stated times, and wholly to abstain from frivolous conversation.

Item 4th. "Not to permit such frequent passing of secular people of both sexes through their convent, as if a thoroughfare, from whence many disorders may and have arisen."

Item 5th. "To take care that the doors of their church and

* *Letters of this sort from Dr. Layton to Thomas Lord Cromwell are still extant.* ⟨G. W.⟩

Priory be so attended to that no suspected and disorderly females, 'suspectæ et aliæ inhonestæ', pass through their choir and cloister in the dark"; and to see that the doors of their cloister between the nave and the choir, and the gates of their cloister opening into the fields, be constantly kept shut until their first choir-service is over in the morning, at dinner time, and when they meet at their evening collation.*

Item 6th mentions that several of the canons are found to be very ignorant and illiterate, and enjoins the prior to see that they be better instructed by a proper master.

Item 8th. The canons are here accused of refusing to accept of their statutable clothing year by year, and of demanding a certain specified sum of money, as if it were their annual rent and due. This the bishop forbids, and orders that the canons shall be clothed out of the revenue of the Priory, and the old garments be laid by in a chamber and given to the poor, according to the rule of Saint Augustine.

In *Item* 9th is a complaint that some of the canons are given to wander out of the precincts of the convent without leave; and that others ride to their manors and farms, under pretence of inspecting the concerns of the society, when they please, and stay as long as they please. But they are enjoined never to stir either about their own private concerns or the business of the convent without leave from the prior: and no canon is to go alone, but to have a grave brother to accompany him.

The injunction in *Item* 10th, at this distance of time, appears rather ludicrous; but the visitor seems to be very serious on the occasion, and says that it has been evidently proved to him that some of the canons, living dissolutely after the flesh, and not after the spirit, sleep naked in their beds without their breeches and shirts, "absque femoralibus et camisiis".† He enjoins that these culprits shall be punished by severe fasting, especially if they shall be found to be faulty a third time; and threatens the prior and sub-prior with suspension if they do not correct this enormity.

In *Item* 11th the good bishop is very wroth with some of the

* *A collation was a meal or repast on a fast day in lieu of a supper.* ⟨G. W.⟩

† *The rule alluded to in* Item 10*th, of not sleeping naked, was enjoined the Knights Templars, who also were subject to the rules of St. Augustine.*

See Gurtleri Hist. Templariorum.

⟨G. W.⟩

canons, whom he finds to be professed hunters and sportsmen, keeping hounds, and publicly attending hunting-matches. These pursuits, he says, occasion much dissipation, danger to the soul and body, and frequent expense; he, therefore, wishing to extirpate this vice wholly from the convent, "*radicibus extirpare*", does absolutely enjoin the canons never intentionally to be present at any public noisy tumultuous huntings; or to keep any hounds, by themselves or by others, openly or by stealth, within the convent, or without.*

In *Item* 12th he forbids the canons in office to make their business a plea for not attending the service of the choir; since by these means either divine worship is neglected or their brother-canons are over-burdened.

By *Item* 14th we are informed that the original number of canons at the Priory of Selborne was *fourteen*; but that at this visitation they were found to be let down to *eleven*. The visitor therefore strongly and earnestly enjoins them that, with all due speed and diligence, they should proceed to the election of proper persons to fill up the vacancies, under pain of the greater excommunication.

In *Item* 17th the prior and canons are accused of suffering, through neglect, notorious dilapidations to take place among their manerial houses and tenements, and in the walls and enclosures of the convent itself, to the shame and scandal of the institution; they are therefore enjoined, under pain of suspension, to repair all defects within the space of six months.

Item 18th charges them with grievously burthening the said Priory by means of sales, and grants of *liveries*† and *corrodies*.‡

* *Considering the strong propensity in human nature towards the pleasures of the chase, it is not to be wondered that the canons of Selborne should languish after hunting, when, from their situation so near the precincts of Wolmer-forest, the king's hounds must have been often in hearing, and sometimes in sight from their windows.—If the bishop was so offended at these sporting canons, what would he have said to our modern fox-hunting divines?* ⟨G. W.⟩

† "Liberationes, *or* liberaturæ, *allowances of corn, &c. to servants,* delivered *at certain times, and in certain quantities, as* clothes *were among the allowances from religious houses to their dependants. See the* corrodies *granted by Croyland abbey*."
Hist. of Croyland, *Appendix, N°* XXXIV.

"*It is not improbable that the word in after-ages came to be confined to the uniform of the retainers or servants of the great, who were hence called* livery servants."
Sir John Cullum's Hist. of Hawsted.

⟨G. W.⟩

‡ *A* corrody *is an allowance to a servant living in an abbey or priory.* ⟨G. W.⟩

The bishop, in *item* 19th, accuses the canons of neglect and omission with respect to their perpetual *chantry-services.*

Item 20th. The visitor here conjures the prior and canons not to withhold their original *alms,* "*eleemosynas*"; nor those that they were enjoined to distribute for the good of the souls of founders and benefactors: he also strictly orders that the fragments and broken victuals, both from the hall of their prior and their common refectory should be carefully collected together by their *eleemosynarius,* and given to the poor without any diminution; the officer to be suspended for neglect or omission.

Item 23d. He bids them distribute their *pittances,* "*pitancias*",* regularly on obits, anniversaries, festivals, &c.

Item 25th. All and every one of the canons are hereby inhibited from standing godfather to *any boy* for the future, "ne *compatres alicujus pueri* de cetero fieri presumatis", unless by express license from the bishop obtained; because from such relationship favour and affection, nepotism, and undue influence, arise, to the injury and detriment of religious institutions.†

Item 26th. The visitor herein severely reprimands the canons for appearing publicly in what would be called in the universities an *unstatutable manner,* and for wearing of boots, "caligæ de *Burneto,* et *sotularium*———in ocrearum loco, ad modum sotularium."‡

It is remarkable that the bishop expresses more warmth

* Pitancia, *an allowance of bread and beer, or other provision to any pious use, especially to the religious in a monastery, &c. for augmentation of their commons.*" *Gloss. to Kennett's* Par. Antiq. ⟨G. W.⟩

† "*The relationship between sponsors and their god-children, who were called* spiritual sons *and* daughters, *was formerly esteemed much more sacred than at present. The presents at christenings were sometimes very considerable: the connexion lasted through life, and was closed with a legacy. This last mark of attention seems to have been thought almost indispensable: for, in a will, from whence no extracts have been given, the testator left every one of his god-children a bushel of barley.* *Sir John Cullum's* Hist. of Hawsted.

"*D. Margaretæ filiæ Regis primogenitæ, quam* filiolam, *quia ejus in baptismo* compater *fuit, appellat, cyphum aureum et quadraginta libras, legavit.*"—*Archbishop Parker* de Antiquitate Eccles. Brit. *speaking of Archbishop Morton.* ⟨G. W.⟩

‡ *Du Fresne is copious on* caligæ *of several sorts.* "*Hoc item de Clericis, presertim beneficiatis:* caligis *scacatis* (*chequered*) *rubeis, et viridibus publice utentibus dicimus esse censendum.*" Statut. Eccles. Tutel. *The chequered boots seem to be the highland plaid stockings.*—"*Burnetum, i.e. Brunetum, pannus non ex lanâ nativi coloris confectus.*"—"Sotularium, *i.e. subtalaris, quia sub talo est. Peculium genus, quibus maxime Monachi nocte utebantur in æstate: in hyeme vero Soccis.*"

This writer gives many quotations concerning Sotularia, *which were not to be made too shapely; nor were the* caligæ *to be laced on too nicely.* ⟨G. W.⟩

against this than any other irregularity; and strictly enjoins them, under pain of ecclesiastical censures, and even imprisonment if necessary (a threat not made use of before), for the future to wear boots, "ocreis seu botis", according to the regular usage of their ancient order.

Item 29th. He here again, but with less earnestness, forbids them foppish ornaments, and the affectation of appearing like beaux with garments edged with costly furs, with fringed gloves, and silken girdles trimmed with gold and silver. It is remarkable that no punishment is annexed to this injunction.

Item 31st. He here singly and severally forbids each canon not admitted to a cure of souls to administer extreme unction, or the sacrament, to clergy or laity; or to perform the service of matrimony, till he has taken out the license of the parish priest.

Item 32d. The bishop says in this *item* that he had observed and found, in his several visitations, that the sacramental plate and cloths of the altar, surplices, &c. were sometimes left in such an uncleanly and disgusting condition as to make the beholders shudder with horror;—"quod aliquibus sunt horrori;"* he therefore enjoins them for the future to see that the plate, cloths, and vestments, be kept bright, clean, and in decent order: and, what must surprise the reader, adds—that he expects for the future that the sacrist should provide for the sacrament good wine, pure and unadulterated; and not, as had often been the practice, that which was sour, and tending to decay:—he says farther, that it seems quite preposterous to omit in sacred matters that attention to decent cleanliness, the neglect of which would disgrace a common convivial meeting.†

Item 33d says that, though the relics of saints, the plate, holy

* "*Men abhorred the offering of the Lord.*" 1 *Sam. chap. ii, v.* 17. *Strange as this account may appear to modern delicacy, the author, when first in orders, twice met with similar circumstances attending the sacrament at two churches belonging to two obscure villages. In the first he found the inside of the chalice covered with birds' dung; and in the other the communion-cloth soiled with cabbage and the greasy drippings of a gammon of bacon. The good dame at the great farm-house, who was to furnish the cloth, being a notable woman, thought it best to save her clean linen, and so sent a foul cloth that had covered her own table for two or three Sundays before.* ⟨G. W.⟩

† —— —— —— *ne turpe toral, ne sordida mappa*
Corruget nares; ne non et cantharus, et lanx
Ostendat tibi te—— —— ——

⟨G. W.⟩

vestments, and books of religious houses, are forbidden by canonical institutes to be pledged or lent out upon pawn; yet, as the visitor finds this to be the case in his several visitations, he therefore strictly enjoins the prior forthwith to recall those pledges, and to restore them to the convent; and orders that all the papers and title deeds thereto belonging should be safely deposited, and kept under three locks and keys.

In the course of the *Visitatio Notabilis* the *constitutions* of *Legate Ottobonus* are frequently referred to. Ottobonus was afterwards Pope Adrian V and died in 1276. His constitutions are in Lyndewood's *Provinciale*, and were drawn up in the 52d of Henry III.

In the *Visitatio Notabilis* the usual punishment is fasting on bread and beer; and in cases of repeated delinquency on bread and water. On these occasions *quarta feria*, et *sexta feria*, are mentioned often, and are to be understood of the days of the *week* numerically on which such punishment is to be inflicted.

1789

January 1. Snow thick on the ground. Timothy begins to sink his well at the malt-house.

January 3. Rime hangs on the trees all day. Turner's well-diggers have sunk his well about six feet. It is now about on a level with mine, viz. 63 feet deep. They came to-day to a hard blue rag,* & a little water.

January 4. Began the new hay-rick. Snow on the ground; but the quantity little in comparison with what has fallen in most parts. As one of my neighbours was traversing Wolmer-forest from Bramshot across the moors, he found a large uncommon bird fluttering in the heath, but not wounded, which he brought home alive. On examination it proved to be *Colymbus glacialis*, Linn. the great speckled Diver,† or Loon, which is most excellently described in Willughby's *Ornithology*. Every part & proportion of this bird is so incomparably adapted to it's mode of life, that in no instance do we see the wisdom of God in the Creation to more advantage. The head is sharp, & smaller than the part of the neck adjoining, in order that it may pierce the water; the wings are placed forward & out of the center of gravity, for a purpose which shall be noticed hereafter; the thighs quite at the podex, in order to facilitate diving; & the legs are flat, & as sharp backwards almost as the edge of a knife, that in striking they may easily cut the water; while the feet are palmated, & broad for swimming, yet so folded up when advanced forward to take a fresh stroke, as to be full as narrow as the shank. The two exterior toes of the feet are longest; the nails flat & broad, resembling the human, which give strength & increase the power of swimming. The foot, when expanded, is not at right angles to the leg or body of the bird; but the exterior part, inclining towards the head, forms an acute angle with the

* A chalky bed of the Upper Greensand. See Letter IV to Pennant.

† Probably the red-throated diver—*Colymbus stellatus*—which breeds in sparse numbers by the lochs of the Scottish islands. The great northern diver is still larger. Three of the former were reported in Hampshire in 1936, and one of the latter was seen in Bournemouth Bay. See *Papers and Proceedings of the Hampshire Field Club*, p. 276.

body; the intention being not to give motion in the line of the legs themselves, but by the combined impulse of both in an intermediate line, the line of the body. Most people know, that have observed at all, that the swimming of birds is nothing more than a walking in the water, where one foot succeeds the other as on the land; yet no one, as far as I am aware, has remarked that diving fowls, while under water, impell & row themselves forward by a motion of their wings, as well as by the impulse of their feet: but such is really the case, as any person may easily be convinced who will observe ducks when hunted by dogs in a clear pond. Nor do I know that any one has given a reason why the wings of diving fowls are placed so forward. Doubtless not for the purpose of promoting their speed in flying, since that position certainly impedes it; but probably for the encrease of their motion under water by the use of four oars instead of two; yet were the wings & feet nearer together, as in land birds, they would, when in action, rather hinder than assist one another. The *Colymbus* was of considerable bulk, weighing only three drachms short of three pounds averdupoise. It measured in length from the bill to the tail (which was very short) two feet; & to the extremities of the toes, four inches more; & the breadth of the wings expanded was 42 inches. A person attempted to eat the body, but found it very strong & rancid, as is the flesh of all birds living on fish. *Divers* or *loons*, though bred in the most northerly parts of Europe, yet are seen with us in very severe winters; & on the Thames are called *Sprat loons*, because they prey much on that sort of fish. The legs of the *Colymbi* & *mergi* are placed so very backward, & so out of all center of gravity, that these birds cannot walk at all. They are called by Linnæus *Compedes*, because they move on the ground as if shackled or fettered.

January 5. Turner's well-diggers advance slowly thro' a blue rag. Mr Churton left us, & went to Waverly.

January 6. Therm^r 25; 18. Fierce frost, sun, cutting wind. Severe day.

January 7. Salted-up a small hog in the pickling tub,—weight 8 scores, & 8 pounds: the meat was young, & delicate. The people at Froxfield fetch their water from Petersfield up Stoner hill.

January 8. A severe frost prevails all over the Continent.

January 9. The farmers are in pain about their turnips, both those on the ground, & those that are stacked under hedges. The people at Forestside drive all their cattle to be watered at a spring issuing out at Temple grounds at the foot of Temple hanger. Oakhanger ponds, & Cranmer ponds are dry. The frost has lasted now just seven weeks: it began Novr 23. T. Turner has sunk his well 9 feet without coming to water. He now desists on account of the expence. My well, I now find, has more than three feet of water; but the rope is too short to reach it.

January 12. Therm^r 8; at South Lambeth $2\frac{1}{2}$. This frost, as frosts usually do, went-off soon after the Therm^r was at the lowest.

January 13. Deep snow: snow drifted through every crevice. Swift thaw. Snow that had been driven in now melts & drips thro' the garret-ceiling.

January 14. The snow drifted in thro' the tiling now melts, & floats the ceiling. A *Gooseander* & a Dun diver,* a drake and a duck of the same species, *Mergus Merganser*, were brought me this morning. They are beautiful birds, never to be seen in the South but in hard frosts: were shot on the stream at Hedleigh.

January 15. Snow melts very fast. The frost, where a grave was dug, appeared to have ent'red the ground about 12 inches.

January 16. Now the rope is lengthened my well furnishes me with water.

January 17. Fine thaw, snow decreased.

January 18. A swan came flying up the Lythe, &, without regarding objects before it, dashed itself against Dorton-house, & fell down stunned. It recovered, & was sold to the miller at Hawkley.

January 22. Now the ice is melted on Hartley-park pond, many dead fish come floating ashore, which were stifled under the ice for want of air.

January 29. [Newton] Bantam-hens make a pleasant little note, expressive of a propensity towards laying. Fog so deep that we could not see the alcove in the garden.

January 31. [Selborne] Farmer Knight's wheat of a beautiful

* The goosander is still *Mergus merganser*. Dun diver is a name applied to both species of the "Saw-Bills", goosander and red-breasted merganser. Both visit inland waters in the winter.

colour. Children play at hop-scotch. Rain in Jan. 4 inc. 48h. I now see, that after the greatest droughts have exhausted the wells, & streams, & ponds, four or five inches of rain will completely replenish them.

February 1. Boys play at taw* on the plestor. Two of the Bantam hens lay each an egg.

February 4. Green rye† has a delicate soft tinge in its colour, distinguishable from that of wheat at a considerable distance.

February 5. As one of farmer Spencer's cows was gamboling, & frisking about last summer on the edge of the short Lythe, she fell, & rolled over to the bottom. Yet so far was she from receiving any injury by this dangerous tumble, that she fattened very kindly, & being killed this spring proved fine beef.

February 8. The open catkins illuminate the hazels; these are the male blossoms: the female are so minute as to be scarce discernible.

February 12. About this time Miss Chase, & Miss Rebecca Chase sailed for Madras in the Nottingham India-man.

February 13. Lined the hot-bed screen with reeds. Cucumbers come up well: bed works well.

February 19. A large bank in Burrant garden‡ covered with winter-aconites, which have been there more than 40 years. Missel thrush sings on one of the firs.

February 20. Dug a plot of ground for beans.

February 21. Yesterday I fixed some nuts in the chinks of some gate-posts in a part of my outlet where *Nut-hatches* used to haunt: & to day I found that several of them were drilled, & the kernels gone.

February 26. Our butcher begins to kill grass-lamb.

March 2. Sowed the great meadow with ashes; with 49 bushels bought of neighbours, & with 28 bushels of our own: total 77.

March 5. Male yew trees shed their farina in clouds.

March 6. Mr Richardson§ came.

* Marbles.

† As delicate as the observation.

‡ "Burhunt Farm". Ordnance Survey Map.

§ A friend who lived at Bramshot Place, near Liphook.

March 7. Mr Richardson left us.

March 9. Loud thunder at Hinckley in Leicestershire, & lightening that did some damage: it happened in the midst of snow.

March 10. Mr & Mrs Clement, & 3 children came.

March 13. Snow in the night: snow five inches deep. Snow melts on the roofs very fast: & runs thro' the ceiling of the garret.

March 15. Snow on the ground. Raw & cold. Mrs Clement left us.

March 16. Mended the cucumber frames.

March 17. Icicles hang in eaves all day. Snow melts in the sun.

March 19. Snow lies on the hill. Made the bearing cucumber-bed: the dung is full wet, but warm.

March 24. About this time sailed for Antigua Ned White,* aboard the Lady Jane Halliday, Captain Martin.

March 26. Icicles hang all day. Hot-bed smokes.

March 28. Snow did not lie. Apricots begin to blow. Earthed the nearing cucumber-bed. The plants in the seedling-bed grow, & want room. N. Aurora.

March 30. Sowed dwarf lark-spurs.

March 31. Sowed a crop of onions, lettuce, & radishes.

April 1. Rain in the night, spring-like. Crocus's make a gaudy show. Some little snow under the hedges.

April 3. Some wood-cocks are now found in Hartley-wood: as soon as the weather grows a little warm, they will pair, & leave us.

April 5. *Wry-neck* pipes. The smallest *uncrested wren* chirps loudly, & sharply in the hanger.

April 6. Timothy the tortoise heaves up the sod under which he is buried. Daffodil blows.

April 9. Brimstone butter-fly. The tortoise comes out. Dog violets blow. Summer like.

April 11. White frost†, sun. Timothy the tortoise weighs 6 ae. 14 oz. Dug several plots of garden ground & ground digs well. Sweet even.

* The author has mixed his years, for a similar entry occurs on March 25th of 1790. One of his host of nephews.

† The countryman distinguishes at least five different types of frost—white frost, black frost, ground frost, hedge frost and wind frost.

April 14. Pulled down the old forsaken martin's nests in some of which we found dead young. They grow fetid, & foul from long use. Redstart appears in my tall hedges.

April 17. Five gallons of french brandy from London. Cucumbers show fruit in bloom. Cuculus cuculat: the voice of the cuckoo is heard in Blackmoor woods. Sowed hollyhocks, columbines, snap-dragons, stocks, mignonette, all from S. Lambeth, in a bed in the garden: also sweet williams, & Canterbury bells.

April 19. The vines of John Stevens, which were trimmed late, not till March, bleed much: & will continue to do so untill the leaf is fully expanded. It is remarkable, that tho' this is the case while the trees are leafless, yet lop them as much as you please when the foliage is out, they will not shed one drop. Dr Hales* was not acquainted with this circumstance when he cut-off a large bough of his vine at Teddington late in the spring; & it was lucky for science that he was not. For his sollicitude for his vine, & his various attempts to stop the effusion of the sap, led him step by step to many expedients, which by degrees brought on abundance of curious experiments, & ended in that learned publication known by the name of *Vegetable Statics*, a work which has done much honour to the Author, & has been translated into many modern languages.

April 20. Apricots set very fast. The willows in bloom are beautiful. Men pole their hops: barley is sowing at the forest side. Several swallows, h. martins, & *bank-martins* play over Oakhanger ponds. The horses wade belly deep over those ponds, to crop the grass† floating on the surface of the water.

April 22. Young broods of goslings. Wood-sorrel, & anemony blow. The cuckoo cries along the hanger. Wheat thrives.

April 23. Swallows & martins do not yet frequent houses. Women hoe wheat.‡

* Rector of Faringdon from 1722 to 1761, a philosopher, social reformer and man of science of many curious enquiries. The author speaks of him in terms of warm affection, and Mr. Walter Johnson suggests, rather conjecturally, that his influence was largely responsible for the undertaking of the Journal. See Note on Letter XXIX to Barrington.

† *Glyceria fluitans* or manna grass.

‡ Probably the only cases to-day in England where women are seen frequently working in the fields are among the open fields of the Isle of Axholme (Lincs) and the small holdings of the Vale of Evesham.

April 26. This morning I saw a certificate from the town of Wymburn Minster in the country of Dorset to the parish of Selborne, acknowledging William Dewye to be parishioner of the said town.* This paper is dated Apr. 20, 1729: so that Will: Dewye, & wife, both still living, have been certificate people here exactly 60 years.

April 27. [Alton] Showers, windy. One beech in the hanger shows some foliage.

April 28. Timothy the tortoise begins to eat dandelion.

April 29. [Selborne] Scarce an hirundo has been seen about this village.

April 30. Brother Thomas White, & daughter, & little Tom came.

May 2. The long frost of last winter has proved very destructive to pond-fish the kingdom over, except in those pools & lakes thro' which passed a constant current of water: nor did the expedient of breaking holes in the ice avail. Mr Barker,† who has been writing an account of the late frost, thinks that it did mischief. A current of water introduces a constant current of fresh air, which refreshes continually the air of the pools & ponds, & renders it fit for respiration.

May 4. Beat the grass-banks in the garden. Put up the urns. Martins come into the old nests. Bat out. Nightingale in my outlet. Snails come out.

The *Fern-owl*, or *Goat-sucker* chatters in the hanger. This curious bird is never heard till warm weather comes: it is the latest summer bird except the fly-catcher.

May 8. Cut the first mesh of asparagus. The bloom of plums is very great. Peat-carting begins.

May 10. Nep. Ben came. The beeches on the hanger, now in full leaf, when shone down on by the sun about noon, exhibit most lovely lights & shades, not to be expressed by the most masterly pencil. The hops are infested by the *Chrysomela oleracea*, called by the country people the turnip-fly, or black dolphin, which eats holes in their leaves. This species is—"saltatoria, femoribus

* The certificate was issued by the Poor Law Authorities.

† Thomas Barker of Lyndon Hall, Rutland, married the author's sister, Anne. They were the parents of Sam Barker, a lively student of natural history and a consistent correspondent to his uncle. See p. 17.

posticis crassissimis":—"*chrysomelae saltatoriae* plantarum cotyledonibus, & tenellis foliis infestae sunt." Linn.

May 13. Nep. Ben & wife left us. Great tempest at Winchester.

May 15. Caught a mouse in the hot-bed: cut several cucumbers, but they are ill-shapen.

May 17. The mice have infested my garden much by nestling in my hot-beds, devouring my balsoms, & burroughing under my cucumber-basons: so that I may say with Martial...

Fines Mus populatur, & colono
Tanquam Sus Calydonius timetur.

Epigramm: XIX. lib: XI.

May 18. Very blowing all day.

May 19. *Stellaria holostea* greater stitchwort, blows: a regular, periodical plant.

May 20. Martins build briskly at the Priory, & in the street. Oaks show prodigious bloom.

May 22. Hirundines keep out in the rain: when the rain is considerable. Swifts skim with their wings inclining, to shoot off the wet.

May 23. *White thorn* blows. The air is filled with floating willow-down. Martins begin to build against the end of my brew-house. Columbines blow. N. Aurora. Timothy the tortoise begins to travel about, & be restless.

May 24. Dr Chandler* by letter dated Rolle en Suisse April 4th, 1789. "The *Swallows* disappeared here about the end of September, 1787, the weather being cold: but Octr 17th I saw a pair as we passed among the mountains towards Fort le Cluse on the road to Lyons; & my servant saw a pair on the 19th when we had got thro' the mountains into Bresse. Passing an islet of the Rhone Octr 23 near Pont St Esprit, again I saw a *swallow*, which dipped to drink. As we approached nearer Marseilles, we saw wasps, dragon-flies, butter-flies, & other summer-insects. I was ashore Novr 10 at Porto Longona, in the isle of Sr Elbe, off the coast of Italy, towards the evening. Philip declared that a *swallow*

* The traveller and antiquary (1738-1810) who gathered material for the *Antiquities of Selborne*. In 1763, he described the Oxford Marbles and he examined the monuments and inscriptions of parts of Asia Minor, the results of his researches being published in several volumes. He held the living of East Worldham from 1779 to 1800, and thus was White's neighbour until the latter's death.

had passed over his head, of which I doubted; but presently after saw three crossing the Port towards us. They flew almost strait, very swiftly; & I should have supposed were going to Italy, if the distance had been less, or the Sun not so near setting. Wasps were in full vigour, & numerous there. I was assured by a friend at Rome, March 16, 1788, that he had seen *swallows* at Naples six weeks before. Mr Morris informed me that *martins* had been busy under the eaves of the house, where he lodged, about a week. I saw there, two days after, four nests which they had begun to repair, & on the 26th a couple of the birds: but Mr M. declared that he had heard them twitter at least as early as the first of March. The first *swift* I observed was over the river Liris on my return from Naples April 27th: *Nightingales* sung there. On the 20th of last March Philip saw two *martins* about the lake of Geneva; & was assured by a man that he had seen them on the 18th. On the 25th he saw several swallows; & supposes the *martins* to have perished with the cold, as they have not been seen since, & the weather has been bad. They seem to have disappeared again, as I have not yet seen one. I remarked *bees*, & a *brimstone-butterfly*, March 15th; & about the same time magpies building in the trees opposite to my windows. I am told that a single *martin* commonly arrives first, as it were to explore; & again withdraws, as it were to fetch a colony. Mr Morris, who has lived several years at Rome, related, that the boys there angle for the *Swallows* with a line at the end of a reed, & instead of a hook, a noose baited with a feather, & hung out at the corners of the streets. Many are taken by this method, & carried home to be roasted & eaten; . . . or to supply the markets, where they are commonly sold in the season. At Chamberry in Savoy I observed in the evening a joyous croud, & a great bustle. My curiosity led me to see what was the matter. A net was spread from one house to an other across a street. These brutes tied the birds they intercepted (chiefly swifts) in pairs by two of their legs, & dismissed them from the windows to flutter down, & become the sport of the mob below. I turned away with horror, & disgust. The first *quail* that I have heard this year 1787 was near Rolle, on May 20th in the evening."

May 28. A fly-catcher has built a nest in the great apricot-tree, in which there is one egg.

June 1. Monks rhubarb seven feet high; makes a noble appearance in bloom.

June 5. Sowed some white cucumber-seeds from S. Lambeth under an hand-glass. Moon-shine.

June 6. *Aphides* begin to appear on the hops: in some places they are called smother-flies. Farmer Spencer's Foredown hops are much injured, & eaten by the chrysomēlae: while Mr Hale's adjoining are not much touched.

June 8. The bloom of hawthorns is vast: every bush appears as if covered with snow. Brother Thomas left us, & went to Fyfield.

June 9. Field-crickets shrill on the verge of the forest. Cuckoos abound there. Thinned the apricots, & took off many hundreds.

June 10—*July* 2. [South Lambeth.]

June 10. Rye in ear. Green pease at supper, a large dish. Young Cygnets on the Mole river at Cobham. Hay made, & carying at Wandsworth. Roses, & sweet-briars beginning to blow in my brother's outlet.*

June 11. Straw-berries cryed about.

June 12. Bro^{r} Benjn cuts his grass, clover & rye, a decent burden, but much infested with wild chamomile, vulg: margweed: may weed.

June 13. My brother's barley begins to come into ear. The squirrel is very fond of the cones of various trees. My niece Hannah's squirrel is much delighted with the fruit of the coniferous trees, such as the pine, the fir, the larch, & the birch; & had it an opportunity would probably be pleased with the cones of alders. As to Scotch firs, Squirrels not only devour the cones, but they also bark large boughs, & gnaw off the tops of the leading shoots; so that the pine-groves belonging to Mr Beckford at Basing-park are much injured & defaced by those little mischievous quadrupeds, which are too subtile, & too nimble to be easily taken, or destroyed. The Cypress-trees, & passion-flowers mostly killed by the late hard winter.

June 14. A patent machine, called a *Fire escape* (rather perhaps a '*Scape fire*) was brought along Fleet street. It consisted of a Ladder, perhaps 38 feet in length, which turned on a pivot, so as

* From June 10 to July 2, the author was staying with his brother, Benjamin, at South Lambeth.

to be elevated or depressed at will, & was supported on timber-frame-work, drawn on wheels. A groove in each rail of this ladder-like construction admitted a box or hutch to be drawn up or let down by a pulley at the top round & by a windlass at bottom. When the ladder is set up against a wall, the person in danger is to escape into the hutch, then drawn to the top. That the ladder may not take fire from any flames breaking out below, it is defended all the way by a sheathing of tin. Several people, it seems, had illiberally refused the Patentee the privilege of trying his machine against their houses: but Mr White, on application, immediately consented; when the ladder was applyed to a sash on the second story, & a man was hoisted up, & let down with great expedition, & safety, & then a couple of boys together. Some spectators were of opinion that the hutch or box was too scanty or shallow, & that for security it ought to be raised on the sides & lower end by a treillis of strong wire, or iron-work, lest people in terror & confusion should miss of their aim & fall over to the ground. This machine was easily drawn by four men only. The ladder, the owner told us, would reach to a third story, when properly elevated. The name of the Inventor is Moun^r^ Dufour.

June 17. [London] Cauliflowers. The Operahouse* in the Haymarket burnt down.

June 21. Vines begin to blossom: corn-flags blow. My brother trenched his field, & sowed it with barley: but the corn seems as if it would be too big, & begins already to lodge. [*Particulars added in another hand:* "one Acre & a Quarter" . . . "The Produce, when thrashed, was 9 Quarters one Bushel, & an half, viz. 73½ Bushels.]† My brother has set up a may-pole 55 feet in height: it is constructed out of two slender deal spars, & for support cramped to the corner of a garden wall.

June 23. Scarlet strawberries are cryed about at six pence the pottle: they are not finely flavoured.

June 24. Mazagan beans come in. The barley much lodged. No house-martins appear at S.L., a very few swallows, & only three

* The Queen's, opened in 1705; reopened in 1791.

† Mr. Walter Johnson gives the figures for the average yield of barley in 1929 as 34½ bushels. Thus, 150 years ago, rural Lambeth yielded double the crop of barley that the countryside as a whole yields to-day.

pairs of swifts that seem to belong to the place. No wonder then that flies abound so in the autumn as to become a nuisance.

June 25. Crop-gardeners sell their pease at market at 20^d the sack, & their cauliflowers at 18^d per dozen: pease abound, so as hardly to pay for gathering.

June 27. My brother cuts his first melon, a small cantaleupe. Barley in bloom, that which was lodged* rises a little.

June 28. Daws come on the cherry-trees, for the fruit. While Mrs J. White, & I were at S. Lambeth, we visited a Mrs Delhust of that place, the wife of an officer, who being at Gibraltar all the time of the siege, underwent all the horrors of that long blockade, & bombardment. Even at this distance of time, somewhat of terror, & uneasiness seem to be imprinted on her features, so as to occasion a lasting impression. Nor is there any room for wonder; for fear is a violent passion, which frequently repeated like other strong emotions, must leave traces behind. Thus, thro' the transports of inebriation, where men habituate themselves to excess in strong liquors, their faces contract an air of intoxication, even when they are cool & sober. This Lady, with many others, lodged for more than a twelve month in a cave of the rock to avoid the bombs & shot from the gun-boats, which annoyed the Southern part of the Istmus every night, as soon as it began to grow dark.

June 29. Marrow-fat pease come in.

July 1. [London] The price of wheat rises on account of the cold, wet, ungenial season. The wet & wind injures the bloom of the wheat.

July 2. [S. Lambeth] Cherries sold in the streets, but very bad. Young fly-catchers come out at Selborne.

July 3. [Alton] Young swallows on the top of a chimney. The western sun almost roasted us between Guildford & Farnham, shining directly into our chaise.

July 4. [Selborne] A cock red-backed butcher-bird, or flusher, was shot in Hartley-gardens, where it had a nest. My garden is in high beauty, abounding with solstitial flowers, such as roses, corn-flags, late orange-lillies, pinks, scarlet lychnises, &c. &c. The early honey-suckles were in their day full of blossoms, & so

* Flattened by the wind.

fragrant, that they perfumed the street with their odour: the late yellow honey-suckle is still in high perfection, & is a most lovely shrub; the only objection is that having a limber stem, & branches, it does not make a good standard.

July 5. My scarlet straw-berries are good: what we eat at S. Lambeth were stale, & bad. A peat-cutter brought me lately from Cranmoor a couple of snipe's eggs which are beautifully marbled. They are rather large, & long for the size of the bird, & not bigger at the one end than the other. The parent birds had not sat on them. These eggs, I find since, were the eggs of a Churn-owl: the eggs of Snipes, differ much from the former in size, shape & colour. The peat-cutter was led into the mistake by finding his eggs in a bog, or moor.

July 11. The fly-catchers in the vine bring out their young.

July 12. Wag-tails bring their young to the grass-plots, where they catch insects to feed them.

July 14. Benham skims the horse-fields. Rasps come in: not well flavoured. On this day a woman brought me two eggs of a *fern-owl* or *eve-jarr*, which she found on the verge of the hanger to the left of the hermitage, under a beechen shrubb. This person, who lives just at the foot of the hanger, seems well acquainted with these nocturnal swallows, & says she has often found their eggs near that place, & that they lay only two at a time on the bare ground. The eggs were oblong, dusky, & streaked somewhat in the manner of the plumage of the parent-bird, & were equal in size at each end. The dam was sitting on the eggs when found, which contained the rudiments of young, & would have been hatched perhaps in a week. From hence we may see the time of their breeding, which corresponds pretty well with that of the Swift, as does also the period of their arrival. Each species is usually seen about the beginning of May. Each breeds but once in a summer; each lays only two eggs.

July 15. We have planted-out vast quantities of annuals, but none of them thrive. Grapes do not blow, nor make any progress. The wet season has continued just a month this day. Dismal weather!

July 16. Wall-cherries are excellent. Lime-trees blossom, & smell very sweet. Mr & Mrs Sam. Barker, & Miss Eliz. Barker came from the county of Rutland.

July 19. When old beech-trees are cleared away, the naked ground in a year or two becomes covered with straw-berry plants, the seeds of which must have lain in the ground for an age at lest. One of the *slidders** or trenches down the middle of the hanger, close covered over with lofty beeches near a century old, is still called *strawberry slidder*, though no strawberries have grown there in the memory of man. That sort of fruit, no doubt, did once abound there, & will again when the obstruction is removed.

July 20. Began to cut my hay, a vast burden, but over-ripe.

July 21. *Anthericum ossifragum*, Lancashire asphodel† a beautiful plant, found by Mr Barker in bloom among the bogs of Wolmer forest. *Monotropa Hypopithys*‡ blossoms on the hanger. Thistles begin to blow. The naked part of the hanger is now covered with thistles; but mostly with the *carduus lanceolatus*.§ There are also the *carduus nutans*, the musk thistle; *carduus crispus*, the thistle on thistle; *carduus palustris*, the marsh-thistle. The seeds of these thistles may have lain probably under the thick shade of the beeches for many Years; but could not vegetate till the sun & air were admitted.

July 23. Farmer Knight sold two loads of wheat for 36 ae!|| Brisk gale. Hay makes well.

July 25. No garden-beans gathered yet. Threw the hay in the meadows into large cocks. The lime-trees with their golden tassels make a most beautiful show. Hops throw out their side branches, which are to bear the fruit. Cran-berries at bins pond not ripe. Hog pease are hacking at Oakhanger.

July 26. By observing two glow-worms, which were brought from the field to the bank in the garden, it appeared to us, that

* See note for Jan. 7, 1788.

† Viz. bog asphodel, now called *Narthecium ossifragum*. Not uncommon in peat bogs and on marshy ground.

‡ The bird's nest orchis. See note on Letter XLI to Barrington.

§ The spear thistle. What the author means by "thistle on thistle" is a problem. He may mean *C. acanthoides*, the welted thistle, where the clustered heads have somewhat the appearance described.

|| 72s. per quarter.

those little creatures put-out their lamps between eleven & twelve, & shine no more for the rest of the night.

July 27. Farmer Spencer & Farmer Knight are beginning to lime their respective farms at Grange & Norton.

July 28. Lapwings leave the bogs, & moors in large flocks, & frequent the uplands.

July 29. The land-springs have run for some time, & especially in the hollow lane that leads from the village to Rood.

July 30. John Hale brings home a waggon-load of woollen-rags, which are to be strewed on his hop-grounds in the spring, & dug in as manure. These rags weighed at ton weight & cost brought home near six pounds. They came from Gosport.

July 31. Louring, vast rain, blowing. This rain was very great at Malpas, in Cheshire.

August 1. Strong wind in the night which has injured the hops; & particularly farmer Spencer's in Culver croft. Trenched out several rows of celeri; but the plants are of a red ugly colour, & seem not to be a good sort. The seed came from the gardener at Alton.

August 2. The goose-berries are bent to the ground with loads of fruit.

August 3. Wheat reaped at Ropley. Ripening weather. Ant-flies begin to come forth on their business of emigration.

August 4. *Sedum Telephium*, orpine, & *Hypericum Androsaemum*, tutsan, growing in Emshot lane leading to Hawkley mill.

August 5. Mrs Brown* brought to bed of a daughter, who makes the number of my nephews & nieces 54. Forest-fuel brought in. Beechen fuel brought in. Wood-straw-berries are over.

August 6. *Rhus Cotinus*,† sive Coccygia blows; it's blossom is very minute, & stands on the extremities of it's filiform bracteols, which have a sort of feather-like appearance that gives the shrub a singular, & beautiful grace. This tree does not ripen it's berries with us. Is a native of Lombardy, & to be found at the foot of the Apennine, & in Carniola.

* The Barkers' daughter who married Edward Brown of Stamford.

† A sumach.

August 7. Mr & Mrs Barker, & Miss Eliz. Barker rode to Blackdown to see the prospect, & returned by three o'clock: they set out at six in the morning.

August 8. Two poor, half-fledged fern-owls were brought me: they were found out in the forest among the heath. Farmer Hewet of Temple cut 30 acres of wheat this week. This wheat was lodged before it came into ear, & was much blighted. It grew on low grounds: the wheat on the high malms at Temple is not ripe.

August 9. The country people have a notion that the *Fern-owl* or *Churn-owl*, or *Eve-jarr*, which they also call a *Puckeridge*, is very injurious to weanling calves* by inflicting, as it strikes at them, the fatal distemper known to cow-leeches by the name of *Puckeridge*. Thus does this harmless, ill-fated bird fall under a double imputation, which it by no means deserves; in Italy, of sucking the teats of goats, whence it is called *Caprimulgus*; & with us, of communicating a deadly disorder to cattle. But the truth of the matter is, the malady above-mentioned is occasioned by the *Oestrus bovis*, a dipterous insect, which lays it's eggs along the backs (chines) of kine, where the maggots, when hatched, eat their way thro' the hide of the beast into the flesh, & grow to a very large size. I have just talked with a man, who says he has more than once stripped calves who have dyed of the *puckeridge*; that the ail, or complaint lay along the chine, where the flesh was much swelled, & filled with purulent matter. Once myself I saw a large rough maggot of this sort taken (squeezed) out of the back of a cow. These maggots in Essex are called *wornils*. The least observation & attention would convince men, that these birds neither injure the goatherd, nor the grazier, but are perfectly harmless, & subsist alone, being night birds, on night-insects, such as *scarabaei* & *phalaenae*; thro' the month of July mostly on the *scarabaeus solstitialis*, which in many districts abounds at that season. Those that we have opened, have always had their craws stuffed with large night-moths & their eggs, & pieces of chafers: nor does it anywise appear how they can, weak & unarmed as they seem, inflict any harm upon kine, unless they possess the powers of animal magnetism, & can affect

* The fallacy is also rebutted both in the *Selborne* and the *Private Letters*.

them by fluttering over them. Mr Churton* informs me "that the disease along the chine of calves, or rather the maggots that cause them, are called by the graziers in Cheshire *worry brees*, & a single one *worry-bree*". No doubt they mean a *breese*, or *breeze*, one name for the gad-fly or *Oestrus*, which is the parent of these maggots, & lays it's eggs on the backs of kine. Dogs come into my garden at night, & eat my goose-berries. Levant weather.†

August 10. *Monotropa Hypopithys* abounds in the hanger beyond Maiden dance, opposite to coney-croft hanger.

August 11. Got-in forest-fuel in nice order. Farmer Knight begins wheat-harvest. Lovely weather.

August 12. The planters think these foggy mornings, & sunny days, injurious to their hops.

August 17. Cool air. Wheat gleaned.

August 18. Many pease housed. Harvest-scenes are now very beautiful! Turnips thrive since the shower.

August 19. Timothy Turner's brew-house on fire: but much help coming in & pulling off the thatch, the fire was extinguished, without any farther damage than the loss of the roofing. The flames burst thro' the thatch in many places. We are this day annoyed in the brown parlor by multitudes of flying ants, which come forth, as usual, from under the stairs.

August 22. Mrs Ben White came to us from Newton.

August 23. Boy brought me the rudiments of a hornet's nest, with some maggots in it. Every ant-hill is in a strange hurry & confusion; & all the winged ants, agitated by some violent impulse, are leaving their homes; &, bent on emigration, swarm by myriads in the air, to the great emolument of the hirundines, which fare luxuriously. Those that escape the swallows return no more to their nests, but looking out for new retreats, lay a foundation for future colonies. All the females at these times are pregnant. The males that escape being eaten, wander away & die.

* Many private letters were interchanged between the author and the Rector of Middleton Cheney, formerly a Brasenose don. Shakespeare also uses the country term of "breese" in a wonderful simile of Pompey's flying galley: "The breese upon her, like a cow in June, Hoists sail and flies".

† Weather causing the springs to rise.

August 24. A fern-owl sits about on my field walks.

August 25. Sweet harvest weather. Wheat ricked & housed. M^r^ & Mrs S. Barker, & Miss E. Barker left us.

August 27. Tho. Holt White* comes from Fyfield.

August 28. *Colchicum autumnale*, naked boys, blows. Wheat-harvest goes on finely.

August 30. Michaelmass daiseys begin to blow.

August 31. Gathered a *bushel-basket* of *well-grown* cucumbers, 238 in number. Molly White, & T. H. White left us, & went to London.

September 2. Bees feed on the plums, & the mellow goose-berries. They often devour the peaches, & nectarines.

September 3. Mr Charles Etty† returns from Canton.

September 4. Mr Thomas Mulso‡ comes from London. *Wry-necks*, birds so called, appear on the grass-plots & walks: they walk a little as well as hop, & thrust their bills into the turf, in quest, I conclude, of ants, which are their food. While they hold their bills in the grass, they draw out their prey with their tongues, which are so long as to be coiled round their heads.

September 6. Fog, sun, pleasant showers, moonshine. Rain in the night. Mushrooms begin to come. I see only now & then a wasp.

September 7. Mr Thomas Mulso left us & went to Winton.

September 8. Bro^r^ T. W. & Th. H. W.§ came from London.

September 9. Hops are not large. The *fly-catchers*, which abounded in my outlet, seem to have withdrawn themselves. Some grapes begin to turn colour. Men bind wheat. Sweet harvest, & hop-picking weather. Hirundines congregate on barns, & trees, & on the tower. The hops are smaller than they were last year. There is fine clover in many fields.

September 11. *Ophrys spiralis*, ladies traces, in bloom in the long Lythe, & on the top of the short Lythe. Wasps seize on butter-

* Nephew and son of Thomas White. He was brother to Molly White referred to in the entry of Aug. 31.

† See Note on Letter LVIII to Barrington.

‡ Son to John Mulso, the author's worldly-clerical friend who constantly reproached him for his lack of zeal as a pluralist.

§ Father and son.

flies, &, shearing off their wings, carry their bodies home as food for their young: they prey much on flies.

September 12. Some wheat is out. Trimming has a large field not cut. *Gentiana Amarella*, autumnal gentian, or fell-wort, buds for bloom on the hill. Sent 12 plants of *Ophrys spiralis* to M[r] Curtis of Lambeth marsh.

September 13. After a bright night, & vast dew, the sky usually becomes clouded by eleven or twelve o'clock in the forenoon; & clear again towards the decline of the day. The reason seems to be, that the dew, drawn-up by evaporation, occasions the clouds, which towards evening, being no longer rendered buoyant by the warmth of the sun, melt away, & fall down again in dews. If clouds are watched of a still, warm evening, they will be seen to melt away, & disappear. Several nests of gold-finches, with fledged young, were found among the vines of the hops: these nestlings must be second broods.

September 15. The hops at Kimbers grow dingy & lose their colour. T.H.W. left us, & went to Fyfield.

September 16. Timothy the tortoise is very dull, & inactive, & spends his time on the border under the fruit-wall.

September 17. No mushrooms on the down.

September 18. Began to light fires in the parlors. Some young martins in a nest at the end of the brew-house. Small uncrested wrens, chif-chaffs, are seen in the garden.

September 19. No mushrooms in the pastures below Burrant-hangers.* Here & there a wasp. The furze-seed which Bro. Tho. sowed last may on the naked part of the hanger, comes up well. Some raspberry-trees in the bushes on the common. Trees keep their verdure well.

September 20. Black-birds feed on the elder berries.

September 21. Myriads of Insects sporting in the sunbeams.

September 23. We find no mushrooms on the down, nor on Nore hill. Women continue to glean, but the corn is grown in the ears. Will. Trimming has wheat still abroad. Gathered-in the white pippins, a large crop.

September 24. M[r] & M[rs] Ben White came from London.

* See Note to entry of Feb. 19 of this year.

September 25. Men bag their hops; & house seed-clover. A fern-owl plays round the Plestor. As we were walking this day, Sept. 22nd: being the King's coronation, on Nore-hill at one o' the clock in the afternoon, we heard great guns on each side of us, viz. from the S. & from the N.E., which undoubtedly were the cannons of Portsmouth & Windsor; the former of which is at least 26 miles distant, & the latter 30. If the guns heard from the N.E. were not from Windsor, they must be those of the Tower of London.

September 26. Multitudes of Hirundines. Sweet Mich: weather.

September 27. A man brought me a *land-rail* or *daker-hen*, a bird so rare* in this district, that we seldom see more than one or two in a season, & those only in autumn. This is deemed a bird of passage by all the writers; yet from it's formation seems to be poorly qualifyed for migration; for it's wings are short, & placed so forward, & out of the centre of gravity, that it flies in a very heavy & embarrassed manner, with it's legs hanging down; & can hardly be sprung a second time, as it runs very fast, & seems to depend more on the swiftness of it's feet than on it's flying. When we came to draw it, we found the entrails so soft & tender, that in appearance they might have been dressed like the ropes of an woodcock. The craw or crop was small & lank, containing a mucus; the gizzard thick & strong, & filled with many shell-snails, some whole, & many ground to pieces thro' the attrition which is occasioned by the muscular force & motion of that intestine. We saw no gravels among the food: perhaps the shell-snails might perform the functions of gravels or pebbles, & might grind one another. *Land-rails* used to abound formerly, I remember, in the low, wet bean-fields of Xtian Malford† in North Wilts; & in the meadows near Paradise-Gardens at Oxford, where I have often heard them cry Crex, Crex. The bird mentioned above weighed seven ounces and an half, was fat & tender, & in flavour like the flesh of a woodcock. The liver was very large and delicate.

September 29. Swallows not seen: they withdraw in bad weather,

* Still rarer to-day. The earlier date of the hay-harvest and the close sitting of the bird are mainly responsible. The brooding bird is decapitated by the mechanical reaper.

† Where his relation, Francis White, had been rector.

& perhaps sleep most of their time away like dogs & cats, who have a power of accumulating rest, when the season does not permit them to be active.

October 3. Gathered in burgamot, & Creson burgamot pears. Gathered some grapes, but they are not good. B. Th. White sowed two pounds of furze-seed from Ireland on the naked part of the hanger. The furze-seed sown by him on the same space in May last is come-up well.

October 4. The breed of hares is great: last year there were few. Some have remarked that hares abound most in wet summers.

October 5. Gathered in Chaumontel pears: tied endive. Mr Ben, & Mrs Ben White left us.

October 6. Grapes do not ripen: they are as backward as in the bad summer 1782: the crop is large.

October 7. Many loads of hops set-out for wey hill.*

October 9. A bag of hops from Master Hale, weight 36 pounds, & an half.

October 10. Two hop-waggons return with loads of woollen rags, to be spread & dug in as manure for the hop-gardens.

October 11. A trufle-hunter called on us, having in his pocket several large trufles found in this neighbourhood. He says these roots are not to be found in deep woods, but in narrow hedge rows & the skirts of coppices. Some trufles, he informed us, lie two feet within the earth; & some quite on the surface: the latter, he added, have little or no smell, & are not so easily discovered by the dogs as those that lie deeper. Half a crown a pound was the price which he asked for this commodity. Some few bunches of grapes just eatable. Some of the latter nectarines well-flavoured. On this day, Dr Chandler saw several swallows, flying as usual, near Cologne: he had observed none at Rolle since the beginning of September, nor none on his way to Cologne. On the 12, in his way to Brussels, he saw more.

October 15. Mackarel sky. A wheat-ear seen on the down.

* Weyhill, near Andover, a great local mart for cheeses before the Machine Age. Weyhill Fair was famous all over southern England. *Piers Plowman*: "At Wey and at Winchester I went to the fair." Along the prehistoric Harroway that passes Weyhill came the sheep and the horses to the Fair, while at the ancient village-town the hops of the east met the cheeses of the west. See Letter XXII to Barrington and my Note.

October 16. Colchicums, a fine double sort, still in bloom. Ivy blows. Some mushrooms with thick stems, & pale gills.

October 19. [Newton] fierce, driving rain!

October 20. Gathered in nonpareils, & some royal russets.

October 21. *Woodcock* seen on the down, among the fern. Finished gathering the apples, many of which are fair fruit. Shoveled the zigzag.* Leaves fall. My wall-nut trees, & some ashes are naked.

October 22. Mended the planks of the zigzag. Bro. Tho. White sowed the naked part of the hanger with great quantities of hips, haws, sloes, & holly-berries.† In May last he sowed a pound of furze seeds on the same naked space; many of which appear to have grown: & lately he sowed two pounds more. Decembr 1790. As fast as any of these seeds have sprouted, they have constantly been brouzed off, & bitten down by the sheep, which lie very hard on them, & will not suffer them to thrive.

October 23. The quantity of haws is prodigious!

October 26. Bror Th. W. sows laburnum seeds on the hanger, & down. A wood-cock killed in the high wood.

October 27. Planted out many young laurustines, & Portugal laurels from the old stools.

October 28. The young men of this place found a stray fallow deer at the back of the village, which they roused, & hunted with grey hounds, & other dogs. When taken it proved to be a buck of three years old.

October 29. Bror Th. W. left us, & went to London.

October 30. My horses taken into the stable & not to lie out any more a nights. New coped the top of my kitchen-chimney, mended the tiling, & toached‡ the inside of the roofing to keep out the drifting snow.

* The Zig-Zag was constructed by John White up the Hanger to Selborne Common in 1753, and an obelisk now called the "Wishing Stone" was set on the top. The Bostal, an "inclining path" through the same beech-wood, was made many years later. A letter from John Mulso: "I fancy I shall like the alteration of your Hill better than the alteration of your verse"—refers to the Zig-Zag.

† The reason why Selborne Common is now bush instead of open ground!

‡ Torched. This is to point the inside joints with plaster, lime and hair. The term is still used among the older masons in remote parts of the country. In Gloucestershire, "torching" is mortaring the stone slates of the roof within, but only those at the intersections of the planes of the roofs. These slates are not pegged on to battens in order to get the effect of "swept valleys".

November 3. Planted 150 cabbages to stand the winter: dunged the ground. Grapes all very bad. Two swallows were seen this morning at Newton vicarage house, hovering & settling on the roofs, & out-buildings. None have been observed at Selborne since Octob^{r} 11. It is very remarkable, that after the hirundines have disappeared for some weeks, a few are occasionally seen again sometimes, in the first week of Novem^{r}, & that only for one day. Do they withdraw & slumber in some hiding-place during the interval? for we cannot suppose they had migrated to warmer climes, & so returned again for one day. Is it not more probable that they are awakened from sleep, & like the bats are come forth to collect a little food? Bats appear at all seasons through the autumn & spring months, when the Thermom^{r} is at 50, because then phalaenae & moths are stirring. These swallows looked like young ones.

November 4. The wind on Saturday last occasioned much damage among the shipping in the river, & on the E. coast.

November 5. Bro. & Sister Benjn came to us from Newton.

November 6. The hermitage capped with snow.

November 11. The tortoise is going under ground, but not quite buried: he is in motion, & pushing himself beneath the turf.

November 12. Bro^{r} & Sister Benjn left us, & went to Newton. Tortoise almost covered.

November 15. A flock of red-wings. Men have not finished their wheat season: some low grounds too wet to be sown.

November 16. Few woodcocks; & few pheasants left. Many hares have been found on our hill: the wetness of the season, it is supposed, induces them to leave the vales, & to retreat to the uplands. Reb. & Hannah White came from Newton.

November 17. D^{o} left us. Flood at Gracious street.

November 24. The miller supplies us with cold, damp flour, & says he can get no other: he adds, that the best wheat is at the bottom of the mows,* & will not come forth till the spring. The latter part of the wheat harvest was very wet.

November 28. Rime on the hanger.

* Corn left unthreshed in the barn.

November 29. Housed 8 cords* of beech billet,† which had taken all the rains of the late wet summer, & autumn; & is therefore of course in but indifferent order.

November 30. After the servants are gone to bed the kitchen-hearth swarms with minute crickets not so large as fleas, which must have been lately hatched. So that these domestic insects, cherished by the influence of a constant large fire, regard not the season of the year; but produce their young at a time when their congeners are either dead, or laid up for the winter, to pass away the uncomfortable months in the profoundest slumbers, & a state of torpidity.

December 3. Beautiful picturesque, partial fogs along the vales, representing rivers, islands, & arms of the sea! These fogs in London & other parts were so deep that much mischief was occasioned by men falling into rivers, & being over-turned into ditches, &c.

December 5. Mrs Ben White brought to bed of a Son, who makes my nephews & nieces 55 in number.

December 6. A bushel of American wheat, which Bro. Tho. sent last year to one of his tenants in the hundreds of Essex from Nore hill, produced this harvest 40 bushels of seed:—and is much admired in that district, because from the stiffness of it's straw it does not lodge. Wheat is so apt to lodge in these parts, that they are often obliged to mow it down in the blade about May, lest it should fall flat to the ground. This process they call swonging.

December 8. The Bramshot hounds kill a leash of hares‡ on the hill.

December 9. The Emshot hounds kill a leash of hares on the hill.

December 13. One of my neighbours shot a ring-dove on an evening as it was returning from feed, & going to roost. When his wife had picked & drawn it, she found its craw stuffed with the most nice & tender tops of turnips. These she washed & boiled, & so sate down to a choice & delicate plate of greens, culled & provided in this extraordinary manner. Hence we may see that granivorous birds, when grain fails, can subsist on the leaves of vegetables. There is reason to suppose that they would

* They measured 8 ft. by 4 ft. by 4 ft. (Walter Johnson's note).

† Faggots for burning.

‡ A set of three.

not long be healthy without; for turkies, tho' corn fed, delight in a variety of plants, such as cabbage, lettuce, endive, &c., & poultry pick much grass; while geese live for months together on commons by grazing alone.

> Nought is useless made; . . .
> . . . On the barren heath
> The shepherd tends his flock, that daily crop
> Their verdant dinner from the mossy turf
> Sufficient: after them the cackling *Goose*
> Close-grazer, finds wherewith to ease her want.
>
> Philips's *Cyder.**

December 19. Walked down to short heath: the sands were very comfortable, & agreeable to the feet: the grass grounds, & arable paths very wet, & unpleasant.

December 23. Dark & dismal. Mr Churton came from Oxford.

December 25. Our rivulets were much flooded; & the water at Oakhanger ran over the bridge, which in old days was called tun-bridge.

December 31. Storm in the night, that blew down my rain-measurer. The newspapers say that there are floods on the Thames.

* See Note to entry of July 26, 1788.

January 1. Frost, ice, sun, pleasant, moon-light. The hounds found a leash of hares on the hill.

January 3. The spotted Bantam lays a second time.

January 7. Mr Churton left us, & went to Waverley. Sweet weather: gnats play in the air. Paths dry.

January 8. Boys play at taw on the plestor.

January 9. Water-cresses come in.

January 10. A ripe wood-straw-berry on a bank, & several blossoms. Grass grows on the walks.*

January 11. The white spotted Bantam hen lays.

January 12. Snow-drops blow. We have in the window of the stair-case a flower-pot with seven sorts of flowers, very sweet & fragrant.

January 13. Driving rain all day.

January 14. A large *speckled diver* or *loon*† was sent to me from the Holt, where it was shot by one of Lord Stawell's servants as it was swimming & diving on a large lake or pond. These birds are seldom seen so far S. in mild winters.

January 16. Turnip-greens come in.

January 19. A trufle-hunter came with his dogs, & tryed my tall hedges, where, as he told us, he found only a few small bulbs, because the season was over: in the autumn, he supposes, many large trufles might be met with. He says, trufles do not flourish in deep woods, but in hedge-rows, & the skirts of coppices within the influence of the sun & air.

February 1. A fine young hog salted & tubbed; weight 7 scores, & 18 pounds.

February 6. The great *titmouse*, or *sit-ye-down*, sings. One crocus is blown-out. Insects abound in the air: bees gather much

* I have never seen any comparison between Gilbert White and Shakespeare, and yet these casual, clipped, brisk entries of the opening of the year give me just the feeling of "when icicles hang by the wall".

† See Note to entry of Jan. 9, 1789.

on the snow-drops, & winter-aconites. Gossamer* is seen streaming from the boughs of trees.

February 10. Bull-finches pick the buds of damson-trees.

February 11. Three gallons of best french brandy from London.

February 19. The moon & Venus in the S.W. & Jupiter & Mars in the E. make nightly a charming appearance.

February 20. As the Surveyor of Gosport-turnpike was mending the road in *Rumsdean bottom*, he found several Roman coins,† one of which was silver. Hence we may conclude that the remarkable entrenchments in that valley, whatever use may have been made of them since, were originally Roman. There is a tradition that they were frequently occupied during the grand rebellion in the time of Charles the first, a period in which many skirmishes happened in these parts, as at Cherriton, Alton, &c. These trenches must have been a post of consequence, because they are on a great road, & between large sloping woods. At the S.W. end of this valley, towards *Filmer-hill*, in a place called *Feather-bed-lane*, are three large contiguous barrows which seem to indicate that near the spot some considerable battle must have been fought in former times.‡

February 21. Frost, ice, bright, red even, prodigious white dew.

February 24. Dr Chandler came.

February 25. Cabbage sprouts come in. Both the pullets of last summer lay.

February 27. Daffodils begin to open. Dr Chandler left us.

February 28. Violets abound.

March 2. Sowed the meadow with ashes; of my own 22 bushels, bought 39: total 61.

March 3. Sheep turned into the wheat.

* See Letter XXIII to Barrington.

† Great numbers of Roman coins have been found on the site of Wolmer Pond since White's day. Correspondence between the Rev. Sewell, Rector of Headley, and the author exists (August, 1777) about the "pot of Medals" from Claudius Drusus to Commodus discovered there in 1774. Ridgehanger Camp, near Petersfield, an almost precipitous scarp falling to the Weald, is presumed to be Roman. A Roman bath was excavated on this site in 1855 with Samian and coarser ware. (See *Victoria History of Hampshire* and J. P. Williams-Freeman's *Field Archaeology as Illustrated by Hampshire*.)

‡ The old association between tumuli and battles has been an unconscionable time a-dying, but it is ashes at last.

March 4. Timothy the tortoise comes forth: he does not usually appear 'till the middle of April.

March 5. The tortoise does not appear. The trufle-man still follows his occupation; when the season is over, I know not.

March 6. A couple & an half of woodcocks, & several pheasants were seen in Hartley-wood.

March 7. The wheat in the N. field looks well: there has been no good crop since the year 1780.

March 10. About this time Charles Etty* sailed for Bengal direct, as second mate to the Earl Fitzwilliam India-man: Dundas captain.

March 11. Several hundreds of fieldfares on the hill: they probably congregate in order to migrate together.

March 13. Planted curran-trees. The garden hoed, & cleaned.

March 14. About this time Ned White† is to sail for Antegoa in the Lady Jane Halliday: Ross, Captain.

March 15. A vast snake‡ appears at the hot-beds.

March 16. Dog's toothed violets blow.

March 17. Timothy the tortoise lies very close in the hedge.

March 20. That noise in the air of some thing passing quick over our heads after it becomes dark, & which we found last year proceeded from the *Stone-curlew*,§ has now been heard for a week or more. Hence it is plain that these birds, which undoubtedly leave us for the winter, return in mild seasons very soon in the spring; & are the earliest summer birds that we have noticed. They seem always to go down from the uplands towards the brooks, & meads. The next early summer bird that we have remarked is the smallest *Willow-wren*, or *chif-chaf*; it utters two sharp, piercing notes, so loud in hollow woods as to occasion an echo, & is usually first heard about the 20th of March.

March 21. *Bombylius medius*, a hairy fly, with a long projecting

* See Note on Letter LVIII to Barrington; also entry of Sept. 3, 1789 and of Feb. 17, 1788.

† See Note on entry of March 24, 1789.

‡ The grass snake. These snakes often appear in my small pond and at my marrow heap.

§ There are numerous references to the habits, appearances and nidification of the stone-curlew in the *Selborne Letters*. See especially Letter LIX to Barrington. The same is true of the chiffchaff.

snout, appears: they are seen chiefly in Mar. & April. "Os rostro porrecto, setaceo, longissimo, bivalvi." A dipterous insect, which sucks it's aliment from blossoms. On the 21st of March a single *bank*, or *sand*-martin was seen hovering & playing round the sand-pit at short heath, where in the summer they abound. I have often suspected that *S. martins* are the most early among the hirundines.

March 25. Chaffinches pull-off the finest flowers of the polyanths. Ned White* sailed on this day.

March 28. Small birds, Tanner says green finches, pull off my polyanth blossoms by handfulls. A neighbour complained to me that her house was over-run with a kind of *black-beetle*, or, as she expressed herself, with a kind of *black-bob*, which swarmed in her kitchen when they get up in a morning before day-break. Soon after this account, I observed an unusual insect in one of my dark chimney-closets; & find since that in the night they swarm also in my kitchen. On examination I soon ascertained the Species to be the *Blatta orientalis* of Linnæus, & the *Blatta molendinaria* of Mouffet. The male is winged, the female is not; but shows somewhat like the rudiments of wings, as if in the pupa state. These insects belonged originally to the warmer parts of America, & were conveyed from thence by shipping to the East Indies; & by means of commerce begin to prevail in the more N. parts of Europe, as Russia, Sweden, &c. How long they have abounded in England† I cannot say; but have never observed them in my house 'till lately. They love warmth, & haunt chimney-closets, & the backs of ovens. Poda says that these, & house-crickets will not associate together; but he is mistaken in that assertion, as Linn. suspected that he was. They are altogether night insects, *lucifugae*, never coming forth till the rooms are dark, & still, & escaping away nimbly at the approach of a candle. Their antennae are remarkably long, slender, & flexile.

March 31. When h. crickets are out, & running about in a room in the night, if surprized by a candle, they give two or three shrill notes, as it were a signal to their fellows, that they may escape to their crannies & lurking-holes to avoid danger.

* See Note on entry of March 24, 1789.

† The cockroach was introduced from the East in the late seventeenth century (Walter Johnson's note).

April 1. Sharp, & biting wind. Some crude oranges were put in a hot cupboard in order that the heat might mellow them, & render them better flavoured: but the crickets got to them, & gnawing holes thro' the rind, sucked out all the juice, & devoured all the pulp.

April 2. *Nightingales* heard in honey-lane.

> The Nightingall, that chaunteth all the springe,
> Whose warblinge notes throughout the wooddes are harde,
> Beinge kepte in cage, she ceaseth for to singe,
> And mourns, bicause her libertie is barde.
>
> Geffrey Whitney's *Emblemes*: 1586, p. 81.

April 4. Sharp, cutting wind! Heath-fire in the forest makes a great smoke.

April 5. [Alton] Frost, sun & clouds, sharp wind.

April 6. [Reading] Young goslings on commons.

April 7-11. [Oxford] Thames very full & beautiful, after so much dry weather: wheat looks well; meadows dry, & scorched; roads very dusty.

April 11. Deep snow at Selborne: five inches deep! *Red-starts, Fly-catchers,* & *Black-caps* arrive. If these little delicate beings are birds of passage (as we have reason to suppose they are, because they are never seen in winter) how could they, feeble as they seem, bear up, against such storms of snow & rain; & make their way thro' such meteorous turbulencies,* as one should suppose would embarrass & retard the most hardy & resolute of the winged nation? Yet they keep their appointed times & seasons, & in spite of frosts & winds return to their stations periodically, as if they had met with nothing to obstruct them. The withdrawing & appearance of the *short-winged* summer birds is a very puzzling circumstance in natural History!

April 12. [Reading].

April 13. [Alton.]

April 14. [Selborne.]

April 18. A boy has taken three little young Squirrels in their

* One of White's rotund and magniloquent White-isms, evidently second nature to him, or they would not appear in the *Journals*. They are used sparsely and so very effectively.

nest, or *drey*, as it is called in these parts. These small creatures he put under the care of a cat who had lately lost her kittens, & finds that she nurses & suckles them with the same assiduity & affection, as if they were her own offspring. This circumstance corroborates my suspicion, that the mention of deserted & exposed children being nurtured by female beasts of prey who had lost their young, may not be so improbable an incident as many have supposed:—& therefore may be a justification of those authors who have gravely mentioned what some have deemed to be a wild & improbable story. So many people went to see the little squirrels suckled by a cat, that the foster mother became jealous of her charge, & in pain for their safety; & therefore hid them over the ceiling, where one died. This circumstance shews her affection for these foundlings, & that she supposes the squirrels to be her own young. The hens, when they have hatched ducklings, are equally attached to them as if they were their own chickens. For a leveret nursed by a cat see my Nat: History, p. 214. I have said "that it is not one whit more marvellous that Romulus, & Remus, in their infant & exposed state, should be nursed by a she wolf, than that a poor little suckling leveret should be fostered & cherished by a bloody grimalkin."*

April 20. Set the old Bantam speckled Hen with eleven eggs. My cook-maid desired there might be an odd egg for good luck: . . . numero Deus impare gaudet.

April 24. Planted potatoes & beans in the meadow garden. Much thunder & hail at Alton.

April 28. Full moon. Total eclipse.

April 29. Doctor Chandler, & lady came to the parsonage house.

May 6. Mrs Chandler brought to bed of a daughter at the parsonage-house.

May 8. Began to mow the orchard for the horses.

May 9. Master Trimming is taken with the small-pox. Timothy the tortoise eats dandelion leaves & stalks: he swallows his food almost whole.

May 10. The Bantam hen hatches seven chickens. Young red

* It is amusing to note that not only is this passage misquoted from the first edition in Harting's and other editions but that White himself has incorrectly copied it from his own text!

breasts. Made some tarts with the stalks of the leaves of the garden, or Monks rhubarb. Only three swifts; one was found dead in the church-yard.

May 12. The rhubarb-tart good, & well-flavoured.

May 13. Bro. Tho. came from London.

May 15. Timothy the tortoise weighs 6 ae 12 oz. 14 drs.

May 16. One polyanth-stalk produced 47 pips or blossoms. Mrs Edmund White* brought to bed of a boy, who has encreased the number of my nephews & nieces to 56. The bloom of apples is great: the white pippin, as usual, very full. It is a most useful tree, & always bears fruit. The dearling in the meadow is loaded with fruit: last year it produced only one peck of apples, the year before 14 bushels. This year it bore 10 bush. of small fruit. The white pippin produced a good crop again this year: the apples of this tree come in for scalding, & pies in August.

May 22. Monks rhubarb in full bloom.

May 25. Sowed a specimen of some uncommon clover from farmer Street. Sowed a pint of large kidney beans, white: also Savoys, Coss lettuces, & bore-cole.

May 27. Thunder: damage done in London.

May 30. John Carpenter brings home from the Plashet at Rotherfield some old chest-nut trees† which are very long. In several places the wood-peckers had begun to bore them. The timber & bark of these trees are so very like oak, as might easily deceive an indifferent observer, but the wood is very shakey, & towards the heart *cup-shakey*,‡ so that the inward parts are of no use. They were bought for the purpose of cooperage, but must make but ordinary barrels, buckets, &c. Chestnut sells for half the price of oak; but has some times been sent into the King's docks, & passed off instead of oak.

May 31. Bottled-out the port-wine which came here in October, but did not get fine.

June 4. *Ophrys nidus-avis*, and *ophrys apifera* blossom.§

* Née Anne Blunt and married to the Vicar of Newton Valence, one of the nephews, four years previously. See Note to entry of Feb. 22, 1788.

† Probably Spanish chestnuts.

‡ "Breaking into cup-like portions" (Walter Johnson).

§ The birds' nest and bee orchises. See Note to entry of July 21, 1789.

June 6.* Thus dogs smell *to* persons when they meet, when they want to be informed whether they are strangers or not. After sheep have been washed, there is the same confusion, for the reason given above.

June 7. [London] Went to London by Guildford & Epsom. Spring-corn & grass look well. Hay making near town.

June 17-*July* 1. [S. Lambeth.]

June 12. Cauliflowers abound. Pease sold for ten pence the peck.

June 13. Artichokes, & chardons,† come into eating. Cucumbers abound.

June 14. Sweet hay-making weather.

June 16. My Brother finishes a large rick of hay in very nice order.

June 20. Muck laid on a gardener's field poisons my Brother's outlet. A martin at Stockwell chapel‡ has built its nest against the window: it seems to stick firmly to the glass, and has no other support. In former summers I remember similar instances.

June 21. Scarlet-straw-berries good. A small praecox melon. The longest day:

> The longest daye in time resignes to nighte;
> The greatest oke in time to duste doth turne;
> The Raven dies; the Egle failes of flighte;
> The Phœnix rare in time herselfe doth burne;
> The princelie stagge at lengthe his race doth ronne;
> And all must ende that ever was begonne.
>
> Geffrey Whitney's *Emblemes*; p. 230, 1586.

June 22. Thermometer at Mr Alexander's—87 on a N. wall; a S. wall near. Fruit-walls in the sun are so hot that I cannot bear my hand on them. Bro^r^ Tho. therm^r^ was 89 on an E. wall in the afternoon. Much damage was done, & some persons killed by

* This entry on smell in animals is the tail of a longer observation recorded for August 1, 1777, and the end of it is by mischance lodged here.

† The silver-grey cardoon thistle that will grow in gardens up to 10 feet high, and is very decorative. The buds are cut off and cooked, each scale being detached for the eating.

‡ Now St. Andrew's Church, built in 1767 (Walter Johnson's note).

lightening on this sultry day. My Bro. Tho$^{s's}$ therm^{r} in Blackfriars road against an eastern wall in the afternoon was 89. My thermom^{r} after the sun was got round upon it, was 100: Thomas forgot to look in time.

June 27. Roses make a beautiful show. Orange-lillies blossom. Sr George Wheeler's tutsan* blows.

July 2. [Alton] Two heavy showers at Guildford with thunder.

July 3. [Selborne] My hay made into small cocks. Young swallows come out, & are fed on the wing. Wood straw-berries ripen.

July 4. The woman, who brought me two fern-owls eggs last year on July 14, on this day produced me two more one of which had been laid this morning, as appears plainly, because there was only one in the nest the evening before. They were found, as last July, on the verge of the down above the hermitage, under a beechen shrub on the naked ground. Last year those eggs were full of young, & just ready to be hatched. These circumstances point out the exact time when these curious nocturnal, migratory birds lay their eggs & hatch their young. Fern-owls, like snipes, stone-curlews, & some other birds, make no nest. Birds that build on the ground do not make much of nests.†

July 7. Grasshopper-lark whispers in my outlet. Turned the cocks of hay.

July 9. Gathered our first beans, long pods. Planted-out annuals.

July 11. Now the meadow is cleared, the brood-swallows sweep the face of the ground all day long; & from over that smooth surface collect a variety of insects for the support of their young.

July 14. Tempest, & much thunder to the N.W. Neither cucumbers, nor kidney beans, nor annuals thrive on account of the cold blowing season. Timothy the tortoise is very dull, & spends most of his time under the shade of the vast, expanded leaves of the monk's rhubarb.

July 15. Continual gales all thro' this month, which interrupt the cutting my tall hedges.

* One of the St. John's worts.

† Depending upon the protective coloration of their eggs.

July 17. M[r] Churton came. A nightingale continues to sing; but his notes are short & interrupted, & attended with a *chur*.* A fly-catcher has a nest in my vines. Young swallows settle on the grass-plots to catch insects.

July 18. M[rs] Clement & daughters came.

July 22. A man brought me a cuckoo, found in the nest of a water-wagtail among the rocks of the hollow lane leading to Rood. This bird was almost fledge.

July 24. Trenched four rows of celeri, good streight plants. Lime trees in full bloom. Large honey-dews on my great oak, that attract the bees, which swarm upon it. Some wheat is much lodged by the wind & rain. There is reason to fear from the coldness & wetness of the season that the crop will not be good. Windy, wet, cold solstices are never favourable to wheat, because they interrupt the bloom, & shake it off before it has performed it's function.

July 25. Lime trees are fragrant: the golden tassels are beautiful. D[r] Chandler tells us that in the south of France, an infusion of the blossoms of the lime-tree, tilia, is in much esteem as a remedy for coughs, hoarsenesses, fevers, &c., & that at Nismes he saw an avenue of limes that was quite ravaged & torn to pieces by people greedily gathering the bloom, which they dryed & kept for their purposes. Upon the strength of this information we made some tea of lime-blossoms, & found it a very soft, well-flavoured, pleasant, saccharine julep, in taste much resembling the juice of liquorice.

July 27. Honey-dews, which make the planters in pain for their hops. Hops are infested with aphides; look badly.

July 28 Children gather strawberries every morning from the hanger where the tall beeches were felled in winter 1788.

July 29. Some mushrooms, & funguses appear on the down. M[rs] J. White† made Rasp, & strawberry jam, & red curran jelly, & preserved some cherries.

* The nightingale ceases to sing in the middle of June, not in July, and the hoarse churring note is all that is heard after that date. Either this nightingale had lost its first nest—song comes to an end when the young are hatched—or mate, or the dates, as frequently happens in the *Journals*, are mixed.

† See Note to entry of July 7, 1788.

August 1. The circumference of trees in my outlet planted by myself, at one foot from the ground.

		f.	inch.
Oak by alcove in	1730	4	5
Ash by D° in	1730	4	6½
Great fir, bakers hill	1751	5	0
Greatest beech	1751	4	0
Elm	1750	5	3
Lime over at Mr Hale's planted by me in	1756	5	5
My single great oak in the meadow, age unknown		10	6½

The diameter of it's boughs three ways is 24 yards, or 72 feet: circumference of it's boughs 72 yards.

Mr White's* single great oak at Newton measures at one foot above the ground 12 feet 6 inch: the exact dimensions of that belonging to, & planted by Mr Marsham.† A vast tree must that be at Stratton to have been planted by a person now living!

August 3. Mr Churton left us.

August 5. Piled & housed all the cleft wood of eight cords of beech: the proportion of blocks was large.

August 6. The fern-owl churs still; grass-hopper lark has been silent some days.

August 7. Strawberries from the woods are over; the crop has been prodigious. The decanter, into which the wine from a cool cellar was poured, became clouded over with a thick condensation standing in drops. This appearance, which is never to be seen but in warm weather, is a curious phaenomenon, & exhibits matter for speculation to the modern philosopher. A friend of mine enquires whether the "*rorantia pocula*" of Tully in his "*de senectute*" had any reference to such appearances. But there is great reason to suppose that the ancients were not accurate philosophers enough to pay much regard to such occurrences. They knew little of pneumatics, or the laws whereby air is condensed, & rarifyed; & much less that water is dissolved in

* Nephew Edmund.

† Robert Marsham of Stratton Strawless, near Norwich, the naturalist and arboriculturist who wrote to and received a number of letters from the author. See p. 62.

air, & reducible therefrom by cold. If they saw such dews on their statues, or metal utensils, they looked on them as ominous, & were awed with a superstitious horror. Thus Virgil makes his weeping statues, & sweating brazen vessels prognostic of the violent death of Julius Caesar: . . . "maestum illacrymat templis ebur, aeraq sudant." Georgic 1st.

The phaenomenon in question is finely explained by the following quotation.—"If a bottle of wine be fetched out of a cool cellar in the hottest & driest weather in summer, it's surface will presently be covered with a thick vapour, which when tasted appears to be pure water. This watery vapour cannot proceed from any exudation of the wine thro' the pores of the bottle; for glass is impervious to water, & the bottle remains full, & when wiped dry is found to weigh as much as when taken out of the cellar. The same appearance is observable on the outside of a silver, or other vessel in which iced water is put in summer time; & it is certain, that the water which is condensed on the surface of the vessel does not proceed merely from the moisture exhaled by the breathing of the people in the room where this appearance is most generally noticed, because the same effect will take place, if the vessel be put in the open air." Watson's chemical essays, Vol. 3rd, p. 92.

August 10. A labourer has mown out in the precincts of Hartley-wood, during the course of this summer, as many pheasant's nests as contained 60 eggs! Bro. Thomas White came.

August 12. Sister Barker,* & nieces, Mary, & Eliz: came.

August 14. Young Hirundines cluster on the trees. Harvest-bugs† bite the ladies.

August 15. The last gathering of wood-straw-berries. Bull-finches & red-breasts eat the berries of the honey-suckles.

August 16. Cut 43 cucumbers. Wheat is binding. *Blackstonia perfoliata*, yellow centory, blossoms, on the right hand bank up the North field hill. The *Gentiana perfoliata* Linnaei. It is to be found in the marl-dell‡ half way along the N. field lane on the

* Anne, who married Thomas Barker in 1751.

† See Note to Letter XXXIV to Pennant.

‡ Pit from which marl was dug for dressing the fields. Marl-pits are still dug in Norfolk.

left; on the dry bank of a narrow field between the N. field hill, & the Fore down; & on the banks of the Fore down.

August 19. M[rs] Barker & her daughters Mary & Elizabeth, & M[rs] Chandler, & her infant daughter and nursemaid went all in a cart to see the great oak in the Holt, which is deemed by M[r] Marsham of Stratton in Norfolk to be the biggest in this Island.* Bro. Thos. & D[r] Chandler rode on horse-back. They all dined under the shade of this tree. At 7 feet from the ground it measures in circumference 34 feet: has in old times lost several boughs, & is tending towards decay. M[r] Marsham computes that at 14 feet length this oak contains 1000 feet of timber.

August 20. On this day farmer Spencer built a large wheat-rick near his house the contents of which all came from a field near West-croft barn at the full distance of a mile. Five waggons were going all day.

August 22. There is a covey of partridges in the North-field, seventeen in number.

August 23. John Hale made a large wheat-rick on a staddle.†

August 26. Planted out a bed of borecole,‡ & three long rows of curled endive. Bat comes out before the swallows are gone to roost.

August 27. Cold & comfortless weather.

August 30. Cut 152 cucumbers. A fine harvest day: much wheat bound,§ & much gleaning|| gathered.

August 31. Farmer Spencer's wheat-rick, when it was near

* Marsham's letter was written in the July of this year. The biggest tree in England is now and probably was in White's day the Spanish chestnut of Tortworth in the South Cotswolds. It is described in Strutt's *Sylva Britannica*, and, when I saw it in 1937, it had seventeen full-sized trees growing from the original bole. It was, according to tradition, planted by King Edgar in A.D. 800.

† A circular, mushroom-shaped, stone-block on a pyramidal base detached from it, formerly used as a foundation for wheat-ricks to keep the rats away. I have found it in use to-day, after extensive enquiries and explorations, in only one village.

‡ Broccoli.

§ Of course by hand, long before the days of the perfunctory self-binder which destroyed the beautiful and varied country craft of sheaf-knots.

|| Before mechanized farming, the poor (mostly women and children) gathered the gleanings for their families. The reason for the disuse of this immemorial custom is that the self-binder leaves hardly anything worth the gleaning in proportion to the labour expended.

finished, parted, & fell down. Charles,* & Bessy White came from Fyfield.

September 3. Some hop-poles blown down. Mr Prowting of Chawton begins to pick hops.

September 5. Boiled a mess of autumnal spinage, sown Aug. 3rd. Nep. J. White† left us, & returned to Sarum. There is a fine thriving oak near the path as you go to Combwood, just before you arrive at the pond, round which, at about the distance of the extremities of the boughs, may be seen a sort of circle in the grass, in which the herbage appears dry & withered, as if a fairy-ring was beginning. I remember somewhat of the same appearance at the same place in former years.

September 6. Hardly here & there a wasp to be seen.

September 9. Two stone-curlews in a fallow near Southington. A fern-owl flies over my House.

September 10. Cut 140 cucumbers. Hops light, & not very good. Sister Barker & Molly & Betsy left us, & went to London: Charles White also, & Bessy returned to Fyfield.

September 13. Cut 158 cucumbers. Nep. Ben White, & wife, & little Ben & Glyd came from Fyfield.

September 14. Onions rot. Barley round the village very fine.

September 16. Cut 100 cucumbers. Sweet autumnal weather.

September 17. Martins congregate on the weather-cock, & vane of the may-pole. The boys brought me their first wasps nest from Kimber's; it was near as big as a gallon. When there is no fruit, as is remarkably the case this year, wasps eat flies, & suck the honey from flowers, from ivy blossoms, & umbellated plants: they carry-off also flesh from butchers shambles.

September 18. My tall beech in Sparrow's hanger, which measures 50 feet to the first fork, & 24 afterwards, is just 6 feet in girth at 2 feet above the ground. At the back of Burhant house, in an abrupt field which inclines towards nightingale-lane, stand four noble beech trees on the edge of a steep ravin or water gully the largest of which measures 9 ft. 5 in. at about a yard from the ground. This ravin runs with a strong torrent in winter from

* Nephew and the son of Henry White. He was Rector of Shalden in Hampshire.

† Son of John White and at that time a surgeon in Salisbury.

nightingale-lane, but is dry in the summer. The beeches above are now the finest remaining in this neighbourhood, & carry fine heads.* There is a romantic, perennial spring in this gully, that might be rendered very ornamental was it situated in a gentleman's outlet.

September 19. On this day Lord Stawell sent me a rare & curious water-fowl, taken alive a few days before by a boy at Basing, near Basingstoke, & sent to the Duke of Bolton at Hackwood park, where it was put into the bason before the house, in which it soon dyed. This bird proved to be the *Procellaria Puffinus* of Linnæus, the *Manks puffin*, or *Shear-water* of Ray. *Shear-waters* breed in the Calf of Man, & as Ray supposes, in the Scilly Isles, & also in the Orknies: but quit our rocks & shores about the latter end of August; & from accounts lately given by navigators, are dispersed over the whole Atlantic. By what chance or accident this bird was impelled to visit Hants is a question that can not easily be answered.†

September 21. Mrs Clement, & six of her children, four of which are to be inoculated, & Mrs Chandler, & her two children the youngest of which is also to undergo the same operation, are retired to Harteley great house. Servants & all, some of which are to be inoculated also, they make 14 in family.

September 23. Coss-lettuce finely loaved & bleached! Nep. B. White‡ left us, & went to London.

September 24. Thomas cut 130 cucumbers.

September 25. A vast flock of lapwings, which has forsaken the moors & bogs, now frequents the uplands. Some ring-ouzels were seen round Nore-hill.

September 27. The inoculated at Harteley sicken.

September 30. Cut 81 cucumbers. On this day Mrs Brown was brought to bed at Stamford of twins, making my nephews & nieces 58 in number. The night following this poor, dear woman dyed, leaving behind her nine young children.

October 2. Bro. Thomas, & his daughter Mrs Ben White left us,

* See letter to Robert Marsham of Jan. 18, 1791, p. 227, Vol. II of *The Life and Letters of Gilbert White*, edited by Rashleigh Holt-White, 1901.

† A not very rare event. The birds are driven to land by sea-gales.

‡ Benjamin, son of Benjamin White, the publisher.

& went to London. Lord Stawell sent me from the great Lodge in the Holt a curious bird for my inspection. It was found by the spaniels of one of his keepers in a coppice, & shot on the wing. The shape, & air, & habit of the bird, & the scarlet ring round the eyes, agreed well with the appearance of a cock pheasant; but then the head & neck, & breast & belly, were of a glossy black: & tho' it weighed 3 ae 3$\frac{1}{2}$ oun., the weight of a large full-grown cock pheasant, yet there were no signs of any spurs on the legs, as is usual with all grown cock pheasants, who have long ones. The legs & feet were naked of feathers; & therefore it could be nothing of the Grous kind. In the tail were no long bending feathers, such as cock pheasants usually have, & are characteristic of the sex. The tail was much shorter than the tail of an hen pheasant, & blunt & square at the end. The back, wing-feathers, & tail, were all of a pale russet, curiously streaked, somewhat like the upper parts of an hen partridge. I returned it to the noble sender with my verdict, that it was probably a spurious or hen bird, bred between a cock pheasant, and some domestic fowl.* When I came to talk with the keeper who brought it, he told me, that some Pea-hens had been known last summer to haunt the coppices & coverts where this mule was found. Hen pheasants usually weigh only 2 ae 1 oun. My advice was that his Lordship would employ Elmer of Farnham, the famous game-painter, to take an exact copy of this curious bird. His Lordship did employ Elmer, & sent me as a present a good painting of that rare bird.

October 3. The row of ten weeks stocks under the fruit-wall makes a beautiful show.

October 4. Three martin's nests at Mr Burbey's are now full of young!

October 5. Cut 3 bunches of grapes: they were just eatable.

October 7. Timothy the tortoise came out into the walk, & grazed. Mr Edm^{d} White,† while he was at South Lambeth, this summer, kept for a time a regular journal of his Father's barometer, which, when compared with a journal of my own for the same space, proves that the Mercury at S. Lambeth at an average stands full *three* tenths of an inch higher than at Selborne.

* A hybrid between pheasant and blackcock. See entry of Aug. 5, 1789.

† The Vicar of Newton Valence.

Now as we have remarked that the barometer at Newton Valence is invariably three tenth lower than my own at Selborne, it plainly appears that the mercury at S. Lambeth exceeds in height at an average the mercury at Newton by six tenths at least. Hence it follows, according to some calculations, that Newton vicarage house is 600 feet higher than the hamlet of S. Lambeth, which, as may be seen by the tide coming-up the creek* before some of the houses, stands but a few feet above high water mark. It is much to be wished that all persons who attend to barometers would take care to use none but pure distilled Mercury in their tubes: because Mercury adulterated with lead, as it often is, loses much of it's true gravity, & must often stand in tubes above it's proper pitch on account of the diminution of it's specific weight by lead, which is lighter than mercury. The remarks above show the futility of marking the plates of barometers with the words—*fair*, *changeable*, &c., instead of *inches*, & *tenths*; since by means of different elevations they are very poor directions, & have but little reference to the weather. After the servants are gone to bed, the kitchen-hearth swarms with young *crickets*, *Blattae molendinariae*, of all sizes from the most minute growth to their full proportions. They seem to live in a friendly manner together, & not prey the one on the other.

"there the Snake throws her enamel'd skin."
Shakespear, Mids. night's dream.

About the middle of this month we found in a field near a hedge the slough of a large snake, which seemed to have been newly cast. From circumstances it appeared as if turned wrong side outward, & as drawn off backward, like a stocking, or woman's glove. Not only the whole skin, but scales from the very eyes are peeled off, & appear in the head of the slough like a pair of spectacles. The reptile, at the time of changing his coat, had intangled himself intricately in the grass & weeds, so that the friction of the stalks & blades might promote this curious shifting of his exuviae.

lubrica serpens
Exuit in spinis vestem.
Lucretius.

* The Effra by Vauxhall.

It would be a most entertaining sight could a person be an eye-witness to such a feat, & see the snake in the act of changing his garment. As the convexity of the scales of the eyes in the slough are now inward, that circumstance alone is a proof that the skin has been turned: not to mention that now the present inside is much darker, than the outer. If you look through the scales of the snake's eyes from the concave side, viz: as the reptile used them, they lessen objects much. Thus it appears from what has been said that snakes crawl out of the mouth of their own sloughs, & quit the tail part last; just as eels are skinned by a cook maid. While the scales of the eyes are growing loose, & a new skin is forming, the creature, in appearance, must be blind, & feel itself in an awkward uneasy situation.

October 11. Gathered the Cadillac pears, a bushel; the knobbed russets 2 bushels; the kitchen, ruddy apple at the end of the fruit-wall, near a bushel.

October 12. Gathered in near 4 bushels of *dearling* apples from the meadow tree: the crop is great, but the fruit is small.

October 13. Gathered in a bushel more of dearlings. Mrs Chandler returns home from the Harteley inoculation.

October 14. Gathered in more dearlings: the fruit is small, but the crop on that single tree amounts to nine bushels, & upwards.

October 15. Gathered in the royal russets, & the nonpareils, a few of each. Gathered the berberries.

October 16. *Red wings* return, & are seen on Selborne down. There are no haws this year for the redwings, & field fares.

October 17. Gracious street stream is dry from James Knight's ponds, where it rises, to the foot bridge at the bottom of the church litton closes. Near that bridge, in the corner, the spring is perennial, & runs to Dorton, where it joins the Well-head stream.

October 19. My well is very low, & the water foul.

October 20. Spring-keepers* come up in the well-bucket. How they get down there does not appear: they are called by Mr Derham†—*squillae aquaticae*.

* The freshwater shrimp.
† A Fellow of the Royal Society.

October 21. I conclude that the Holiburne trufler finds encouragement in our woods, & hangers, as he frequently passes along the village: he is a surly fellow, & not communicative. He is attended by two little cur-dogs, which he leads in a string.

October 24. Dr Chandler buys of the Holiburne trufle-man one pound of trufles; price 2s. 6d.

October 25. A flock of 46 ravens* over the hanger. Slipped-out pinks, & fraxinals; planted out dames violets from cuttings.

October 26. This morning Rear Admiral Cornish, with six ships of the line, & two smaller ships of war, sailed from St. Hellen's.

October 27. Grapes better.

October 28. Wet & uncomfortable.

October 29. Dug & cleansed the border in the orchard, & planted it with polyanths slipped-out.

October 30. Large *fieldfares*, a great flock, seen on the hill. Ravens on the down. Wild *wood-pigeons*, or *stock-doves*,† are seen at my wood at Holtham.

November 1. Bro^r^ Benjn & his wife came to us.

November 4. Green wheat comes up well. Stewed some trufles: the flavour of their juice very fine, but the roots hard, & gritty. They were boiled in water, then sliced, & stewed in gravy.

November 6. Very rough weather at Portsmouth: boats overset, & people drowned in coming from Spithead.

November 11. Two or three wood-cocks seen in the high wood: one was killed. Fyfield improves, & promises to make a good cock-dog.

November 13. Bro^r^ & Sister Benjn left us.

November 15. Timothy the tortoise gone under ground in the laurel-hedge. Paths very dry: boys play at taw on the plestor.

November 16. Paths greazy from the frost. Raked, & swept up the leaves in my outlet. The hanger naked.

November 20. The parish church of Calstock in Cornwall detroyed by lightening. The tempest was of vast extent, & in many

* If a contemporary bird-watcher saw one raven over the Hanger, he would write to the papers about it. It would be shot the next day, or the next.

† The stock-dove is, of course, a distinct species from the wood-pigeon or ring dove, and has no bar on the wing.

places mischievous, & awful! This village lies up the Tamer, above Saltash.*

November 21. A vast tempest at Sarum; & an house beat down. The mast of a man of war was struck at Spit-head by the lightening.

November 23. The water in my well is risen three or four rounds of the winch, viz. five or six feet: the spring that runs in may be seen, & heard. The water is now clear. Thus will three or four inches of rain replenish my well, deep as it is, after it has been very low, & foul, & almost dry for several months. I have made the same remark in former years. Our stream has been so low for many weeks that the miller at Kingsley could not grind; but was obliged to send his corn to Headleigh, where the Blackdown stream never fails. At Headleigh park-corner the Blackdown stream joins the Selborne rivulet: & at Tilford bridge they are met by the Farnham river, where together they form so considerable a body of water as within a few miles to become navigable, viz: at the town of Godalming; & there take the name of Wey.†

December 6. Mr Richardson‡ came.

December 9. Mr Richardson left us. Water-cresses come in.

December 13. Blowing, rough day.

December 16. Thatch torn by the wind.

December 23. Thunder, lightening, rain, snow! A severe tempest. Much damage done in & about London: damage to some ships at Portsmouth. Vast damage in various parts! Two men were struck dead in a wind-mill near Rooks-hill on the Sussex downs: & on Hind-head one of the bodies on the gibbet was beaten down to the ground. Harry & Ben Woods§ came.

December 25. H. & Ben Woods left us.

December 29. On this day Mrs Clements was delivered of a boy, who makes my nephews & nieces again 57 in number. By the death of Mrs Brown & one twin they were reduced to 56.

December 31. Total of rain in 1790, 32 inch. 27 h.

* White knew something of south-west England from his visits to his friend, Sampson Newbery, whose father was Rector of South Zele, near Taunton. See Note on Letter XXII to Barrington.

† See Letter I to Pennant.

‡ See Note to entry of March 6, 1789.

§ Nephews. Sons to Henry Woods, a London merchant who married the author's sister, Rebecca.

1791

January 1. Many horse-beans sprang up in my field-walks in the autumn, & are now grown to a considerable height. As the Ewel* was in beans last summer, it is most likely that these seeds came from thence; but then the distance is too considerable for them to have been conveyed by mice. It is most probable therefore that they were brought by birds, & in particular, by jays, & pies, who seem to have hid them among the grass, & moss, & then to have forgotten where they had stowed them. Some pease are also growing in the same situation, & probably under the same circumstances. Mr Derham has recorded that mice hide acorns one by one in pastures in the autumn; & that he has observed them to be hunted-out by swine, who discovered them by their smell.

January 5. The great oak in Harteley avenue, just as you enter the pasture-field, measures in girth 14 feet. It is a noble tree, & if sound worth many pounds. Why it was left at the general sale does not appear. The girth was taken at four feet above the ground.

January 11. Ten weeks stocks blow: crocus's sprout, & swell.

January 12. Mr Churton left us.

January 13. The earth is glutted with water: rills break out at the foot of every little hill: my well is near half full. The wind in the night blew down the rain-measurer.

January 14. Ivy berries swell, & grow: there have been no frosts to check them.—Tubbed, & pickled a good young fat pig:—weight—12 scores, & 4 pounds.

January 16. A disorder prevails among the horses: but has not reached this village yet.

January 17. Sam & Ned White came from Fyfield.

January 19. This morning the Baromr at Newton was only 28!

January 20. Rain & wind in the night. Thomas† says, that when he got-up the Baromr was down at 27-8!!

* One of the open fields as given in the Tithe Award Map at the end of this volume.
† The author's old servant who himself made some entries in the *Journals*.

January 21. Sam & Ned White left us. Late in the evening the planet Jupiter shines in the E.

January 27. One of the Bantam hens begins to lay. Mice devour the crocus's.

January 29. Three gallons of brandy from London.

January 30. [Seleburn] Dark, & harsh.

February 1. My apricot trees were never stripped of their buds before; & therefore seem to have suffered from a casual flight of gross-beaks* that came into these parts.

February 2. Prodigious high tide at London & in it's environs! it did much damage in various parts.

February 3. [Newton] Covered the asparagus beds, & the artichokes with muckle: † these were grown out very tall.

February 4. Benham finished mending the hedges.

February 5. [Selborne] Thaw, sun, grey. Hot-bed heats.

February 7. Bull-finches make sad havoc among the buds of my cherry, & apricot trees; they also destroy the buds of the gooseberries, & honey-suckles! Green-finches seem also to be concerned in the damage done: many neighbouring gardens have suffered. These birds were not observed at the time, nor do they seem to abound. It appeared afterward, that this damage was done by a flight of gross-beaks.

February 9. Sowed cucumber-seeds in pots plunged in the hotbed: bed heats well.

February 10. Brewed strong beer.

February 13. As there has been little frost, the antirrhinum cymb: flourishes, & blossoms thro' the winter.

February 14. Potted cucumbers: bed warm.

February 21. Chaffinches destroy the buds in the honey-suckles.

February 22. Men dig in the hop-gardens.

* Hawfinches, called "gross-beaks" from their massive beaks, much larger than those of any other native finches. See Note on Letter XI to Pennant. The entry of March 3 assumes them to be foreign immigrants like crossbills. But they are a resident species and frequently nest in garden orchards.

† "Muckle" is "long" cow-manure, manure, that is to say, with the straw not yet rotted into "short" manure. The term is still occasionally heard in remote country districts.

February 23. The farmers are very much behind in their plowings for a spring crop thro' the wetness of the season.

February 25. Mr Edm^d^ White took down my Barometer, & cleaned tube, & frame. It had not been meddled with for just 18 years, when my Bro^r^ John also took it down.

February 26. Deep snow, which damaged & broke my plum-trees, & hedges. This is much the greatest snow that we have seen this year. Some of the deep lanes are hardly passable.

February 27. Snow covers the ground. A large bough broken from the yew-tree, in the church yard, by the snow.

March 2. Seven cart-loads of hot dung carried in for the cucumber-bed: 5 loads from Hale, 1 from Parsons, & 1 of my own.

March 3. Sent me by Lord Stawell a *Sea-mall*, or *Gull*, & a *Coccothraustes*, or *Gross-beak*: the latter is seldom seen in England, & only in the winter.

March 5. Boys play at hop-scotch, & cricket. Some snow under hedges. The *wry-neck** returns, & pipes.

March 7. Coltsfoot blows. Stopped cucumbers. Sowed dwarf lark-spurs. Turned the dung.

March 9. Tapped the new hay-rick: the hay but moderate.

March 11. Sowed radishes, & parsley. Weeded the garden, & dug some ground.

March 12. No frost. Planted four rows of broad beans in the orchard. Some snow still under hedges.

March 13. Crocus's in high glory. Some snow under hedges. Vast halo round the moon.

March 14. Daffodil blows. Timothy the tortoise heaves-up the earth.

March 15. Sweet weather. Mackerel.†

March 17. The *Stone-curlew* is returned again: & was heard this evening passing over the village from the uplands down to the meadows & brooks. Planted ½ hundred of cabbages. Timothy comes out.

* If the hawfinch has increased, the wryneck has certainly decreased all over England since the eighteenth century, being to-day definitely a rare bird.

† Sky.

March 18. Snow lies deep in Newton-lane, & under hedges in the uplands. The hounds find no hare on all Selborne hill.

March 19. Sowed my own ashes on the great meadow. Timothy hides himself again. Men turn their sheep into the green wheat.* The hunters killed a female hare, which gave suck: so there are young leverets already. Dr Chandler's† labourer, in digging down the bank in the midst of the parsonage garden called the grotto, found human bones‡ among the rocks. As these lay distant from the bounds of the church-yard, it is possible that they might have been deposited there before there was any church, or yard. So again, in 1728, when a saw-pit was sunk on the Plestor under the wall of the court-yard, many human bones were dug-up at a considerable distance from the church-yard.

March 20. Mr Burbey§ shot a cock *Gross-beak* which he had observed to haunt his garden for more than a fortnight. Dr Chandler had also seen it in his garden. I began to accuse this bird of making sad havock among the buds of the cherries, goose-berries, & wall-fruit of all the neighbouring orchards. Upon opening its crop & craw, no buds were to be seen; but a mass of kernels of the stones of fruits. Mr B. observed that this bird frequented the spots where plum-trees grow; & that he had seen it with some what hard in it's mouth which it broke with difficulty; these were the stones of damasons. The latin Ornithologists call this bird *Coccothraustes*, i.e., *berry-breaker*, because with it's large horny beak it cracks & breaks the shells of stone-fruits|| for the sake of the seed or kernel. Birds of this sort are rarely seen in England, & only in winter. About 50 years ago I discovered three of these *gross-beaks* in my outlet, one of which I shot.

March 21. A hen gross-beak was found almost dead in my outlet: it had nothing in it's craw.

* Such husbandry was often practised before agriculture had declined to its present sickness. The sheep both manured the crop and browsed on the tops of the shoots, inducing them to break more abundantly lower down in the straw. Spring frosts, if not too late, will produce the same results in many different crops.

† At this time his home was at the Vicarage, Selborne.

‡ Perhaps a Saxon cemetery.

§ See Note to entry of May 11, 1788.

|| Fruit-stones are turned in the bill, so that by the pressure of these great crackers they are split in half, and the kernel is extracted. See Note to entry of Feb. 1.

March 23. Soft wind. The wood-pecker laughs.

March 25. Sowed onions, radishes, & lettuce: the ground harsh, & cloddy.

March 26. Cucumber-plants show bloom: but the bed is too hot, & draws the plants. We sow our seeds too soon, so that the plants want to be turned out of the pots before the great bed can be got to due temperament.

March 28. Sowed a large plot of parsnips, & radishes in the orchard. Crocus's fade & go off. Sowed also Coss lettuce with the parsnips.

March 30. Some rooks have built several nests in the high wood. The building of rooks in the High wood is an uncommon incident, & never remembred but once before. The Rooks usually carry on the business of breeding in groves, & clumps of trees near houses, & in villages, & towns. Timothy weighs 6 Li. 11 ou.

March 31. Made two hand-glasses for celeri. A gross-beak seen at Newton parsonage-house.

April 1. The bearing cucumber-bed becomes milder & more mellow; & the plants shoot & blow well. Daffodils make a show. Planted potatoes in the meadow-garden, ten rows.

April 2. Crown imperials begin to blow. Pronged the asparagus beds. Wheat looks well. Mrs B. White* & Hannah White come from London.

April 3. The *chif-chaf*, the smallest uncrested wren, is heard in the Hanger, & long Lythe. They are usually heard about the 21 of March. These birds, no bigger than a man's thumb, fetch an echo out of the hanger at every note.

April 4. Mary White† came from London.

April 6. The *cuckoo* arrives, & is seen, & heard.‡ The Apricots have no blossoms; they lost all their buds by birds. *Red start* returns, & appears on the grass-plot.

* The widow of the Rev. Richard Yalden, Vicar of Newton Valence, who married Benjamin White *en secondes noces*. Her stepson, Edmund White, succeeded Richard Yalden.

† Molly is the "little girl" of Letter LIX to Barrington, complacently reported as speaking of the rooks cawing at dusk as "saying their prayers". See Note to entry of Feb. 14, 1788.

‡ This entry was inserted under March 29, in the MS., but was erased (Walter Johnson's note).

April 8. Mary White left us.

April 10. The early beech in the long Lythe shows leaves fully expanded.

April 11. Timothy the tortoise marches forth on the grass-plot and grazes.

April 12. Mountain snow-drops blow. Black thorns blossom. Hannah White* walks up to the alcove before breakfast.

April 15. A nightingale sings in my outlet. Sowed sweet peas, candy-tuft, sweet alyssum, &c. A man brought me half a dozen good mushrooms from a pasture field! a great rarity at this season of the year!

April 18. Mr Ben White came from London.

April 19. Mr Chandler & son went away on a visit. Began to use the winter lettuce. Tho' a swallow or two were seen in the village as long ago as the 7th yet have they absconded for some time past! The house-martin is also withdrawn; no Swift has yet appeared at Selborne; what was seen was at Bentley.

April 20. Finished weeding, & dressing all the flower-borders. Several nightingales between the village, & comb-wood pond. Comb-wood coppice was cut last winter.

April 22. The merise,† or wild cherries in vast bloom. Grass grows, & clover looks very fine. Mr & Mrs B. White, & Hannah left us & went to Newton.

April 25. [Alton] Mowed some coarse grass in the orchard for the horses.

April 26-*May* 1. [Oxford.]

April 26. Some of the oaks, planted on the commons between Odiham & Reading about the time that I first knew that road, begin to be felled. Swallows. Goslings. Cherries, apples, & pears in beautiful bloom along the road: grass forward, & corn looks well.

May 1. A prodigious bloom of apple trees along the road.

May 2. [Alton] Swifts, & house-martins over the Thames at Pangbourn.

May 3. [Selborne] Dark & harsh.

* Benjamin White's daughter.

† See Note to entry of April 25, 1788.

May 4. Planted some tricolor violets, & some red cabbages sent from South Lambeth.

May 5. The bloom on my white apple is again very great. Set the middle Bantam hen with eleven eggs: the cook desired that there might be an odd one.

May 7. Vast bloom on my nonpareils. The orchard is mown for the horses. Cut the stalks of garden rhubarb to make tarts: the plants are very strong.

May 8. Mrs Clements & four children, & a nurse-maid came.

May 11. The down of willows floats in the air, conveying, & spreading about their seeds, & affording some birds a soft lining for their nests.

May 13. Ashen shoots injured by the late frosts, & kidney-beans & potatoe-sprouts killed.

May 15. Flesh flies get to be troublesome: hung out the meat-safe. Mrs Clements &c. left us.

May 16. Saw a *flie-catcher* at the vicarage, I think.

May 17. *Fly-catcher** returns. The *fern-owl,** or *eve-jar** returns, & is heard in the hanger. These birds are the latest summer-birds of passage: when they appear we hope the summer will soon be established.

May 20. The weather has been so harsh, that the swallows, & martins are not disposed to build. Found a hen redstart dead in the walks.

May 23. Brother Thomas White came.

May 24. *Ophrys nidus avis* blows in Comb-wood. Rain is wanted. Wheat looks yellow.

May 25. Mole-cricket jars. An old hunting mare, which ran on the common, being taken very ill, came down into the village as it were to implore the help of men, & dyed the night following in the street.

May 26. Finished sowing kidney-beans, having used one quart, which makes five rows, half white & half scarlet.

May 27. Garden red valerian blows: where it sows itself it soon becomes white.

* The flycatcher and eve-jar, nightjar, fern-owl or jenny-spinner (so called from the likeness of its churring to a spinning-wheel) are the latest of the summer migrants.

May 28. Bantam-hen brings out four chickens.

May 29. The race of field-crickets, which burrowed in the short Lythe, & used to make such an agreeable, shrilling noise the summer long, seems to be extinct. The boys, I believe, found the method of probing their holes with the stalks of grasses, & so fetched them out, & destroyed them.

May 30. Cinamon-roses blow.

May 31. Flowers smell well this evening: some dew.

June 1. Fern-owl, & chur-worm jar. Men wash their fatting sheep; & bay the stream to catch trouts. Trouts come up our shallow streams almost to the spring-heads to lay their spawn.

June 3. Myriads of tadpoles traverse Comb-wood pond in shoales: when rain comes they will emigrate to land, & will cover the paths & fields. We draw much water for the garden, so that the well sinks. Flowers are hurried out of bloom by the heat; spring-corn & gardens suffer.

June 4. Saint foin blows, & the S^{t} foin fly, *Sphinx filipendula*, appears. Rain at Emsworth. Fyfield sprung a fern-owl on the zig-zag which seemed confounded by the glare of the sun, & dropped again immediately. Mr Bridger sends me a fine present of trouts caught in the stream down at Oakhanger. The distant hills look very blue in the evenings.

June 5. Elder, & corn-flags begin to blow already. Thunder to the S.E., N.E., & N.W. Gardens, & fields suffer.

June 6. Wheat begins to come into ear: wheat, which was very yellow from the cold winds, by means of the heat has recovered it's colour without the assistance of rain. Dew, cloudless, sultry. Red even, dead calm. The lettuces, which stood under the fruit-wall thro' the winter, are just over. They have been of great service at the table now for many weeks.

June 7. Hops grow prodigiously, yet are infested with some aphides. Early cabbages turn hard, but boil well. Watered kidney-beans, which come-up well.

June 9. Summer-cabbages, & lettuce come in. Roses red & white blow. Began to tack the vines. Thomas finds more rudiments of bloom than he expected.

June 11. Male glow-worms, attracted by the light of the candles, come into the parlor. The distant hills look very blue. There was rain on Sunday on many sides of us, to the S. the S.E. & the N.W. at Alton & Odiham a fine shower, & at Emsworth, & at Newbury: & as near us as Kingsley. No may chafers this year with us.

June 12. Clouds, hail, shower, gleams. Sharp air, & fire in the parlor. Showers about. Garden-crops much retarded, & nothing can be planted. Farmer Bridger sends me three real snipe's eggs:* they are in shape, & colour exactly like those of the lapwing, only one half less. The colour of the eggs is a dull yellow, spotted with chocolate: they are blunt at the great end, & taper much till they become sharp at the smaller. The eggs, sent me for snipe's eggs last year, seem to have been those of a fern-owl.

June 13. Farmer Spencer mows his cow-grass.

June 14. White frost, dark & cold; covered the kidney beans with straw last night. My annuals, which were left open, much injured by the frost: the balsams, which touched the glass of the light, scorched. Kidney-beans injured, & in some gardens killed. Cucumbers secured by the hand-glasses but they do not grow. The cold weather interrupts the house-martins in their building, & makes them leave their nests unfinished. I have no martins at the end of my brew-house, as usual.

June 15. The kidney-beans at Newton-house not touched by the late frost.† Bro[r] Thomas left us.

June 16. Snails come out of hedges after their long confinement from the drought. A swallow in Tanner's chimney has hatched. The fern on the forest killed; but hardly touched by the frost on Selborne down, which is 400 feet higher than Wolmer.

June 17. Planted out my annuals from Dan. Wheeler. Pricked out some celeri, good plants. My crop of spinnage is just over: the produce from a pint of seed, sowed the first week in August, was prodigious.

June 18. Pricked out more celeri in my garden, & M[r] Burbey's. Planted some cabbages from D[r] Chandler's. Timothy hides himself during this wintry weather. The dry weather lasted just 3

* The slight difference is that the thick smears of chocolate are less settled at the blunt end of the snipe's egg than on the lapwing's.

† Probably because Newton Valence (600 feet) lies higher than Selborne.

weeks & three days; part of which was very sultry, & part very cold.

June 19. A flock of ravens about the hanger for many days.

June 20. [Bramshot place] Went round by Petersfield. *Foxgloves* blow. By going round by Petersfield we make our journey to Bramshot 23 miles. After we had been driven 20 miles we found ourselves not a mile from Wever's down, a vast hill in Wolmer forest, & in the parish of Selborne. Bramshot in a direct line is only seven miles from Selborne.

June 21. Mr Richardson's straw-berries very dry, & tasteless.

June 23. Went to visit Mr Edmund Woods Senr.* Swifts abound at Godalming.

June 24. Meadows not cut. *Nymphaea lutea* in bloom in a watry ditch. Went to see the village of Compton, where my father lived more than sixty years ago, & where seven of his children were born. The people of the village remember nothing of our family. Mr Fulham's conservatory richly furnished; & the grounds behind his house engaging, & elegant. The romantic grounds, & paddock at the west end of Godalming town are very bold & striking. The hanging woods very solemn, & grand; & many of the trees of great age & dimensions. This place was for many years inhabited by General Oglethorpe.† The house is now under a general repair being with it's grounds the property of Mr Godbold a quack Doctor. The vale & hanging woods round Godalming are very beautiful: the Wey a sweet river, & becomes navigable at this town. One branch of the Wey‡ rises at Selburne. At the entrance to the avenue leading to Bramshot-place are three great, hollow oaks, the largest of which measures 21 feet in girth. We measured this tree at about 5 feet from the ground, & could not come at it lower on account of a dry stone-wall in which it stands. We measured also the largest Sycamore in the front of the house, & found the girth to be 13. They are very tall, & are deemed to be 80 feet in height: but I should suppose they do not exceed 74 feet. I hear much of trees 80 or 90 feet high; but

* In the *Journals* of 1784 and 1786, the author records presents of more than ten gallons of French brandy from his Godalming friend.

† Founder of Georgia and M.P. for Haslemere (Walter Johnson's note).

‡ The Oakhanger stream as described in Letter I to Pennant.

have never measured any that exceed the supposed height of the Sycamores above.

June 25 to *July* 18. [South Lambeth.]

June 25. My brother's straw-berries well-flavoured. The vines here in bloom, & smell very sweet.

June 26. Fifteen Whites dined this day at my Bro. B. White's table; as did also a Mr Wells, a great, great, great grandson of the Revd John Longworth, in old times vicar of Selborne, who dyed about the year 1678.* D^r^ & Mrs Chandler returned to Selburne.

June 27. Timothy Turner cuts my grass for himself, a small crop. *Scarabaeus solstitialis* first appears in my brother's outlet: they are very punctual in their coming-out every year. They are a small species, about half the size of the *May chafer*, & are known in some parts by the name of *fern-chafer*.

June 28. When the Barom^r^ is 30 at S. Lambeth, it is 29-7 at Selborne, and 29-4 at Newton. My brother cut a good Romagna melon.

June 29. Some swallows in this district, & only two pairs of swifts, & no martins. No wonder then that they are overrun with flies, which swarm in the summer months, & destroy their grapes.

June 30. The Passion-flower buds for bloom: double flowering Pomegranade has had bloom.

July 1. Large American straw-berries are hawked about which the sellers call pine-strawberries. But these are oblong, & of a pale red; where as the true pine or Drayton straw-berries are flat, & green: yet the flavour is very quick, & truly delicate. The American new sorts of strawberries prevail so much, that the old scarlet, & hautboys are laid aside, & out of use.

July 3. My brother's cow, when there is no extraordinary call for cream, produces three pounds of butter each week. The footman churns the butter overnight, & puts it in water; in the morning one of my nieces beats it, & makes it up, & prints it.† Mr M. black cluster-grapes in his pine-house seem to be well ripened.

* A list of the Selborne Vicars is given in Letter II of the *Antiquities*, together with an account of John Longworth, Vicar in 1632.

† A futile question bubbles up from this anachronistic entry. If the author had lived in our century, would he have written a line?

July 5. [London] Rasps come in. Many Martins in the green park. In a fruit-shop near St. James were set out to sale black cluster-grapes, pine apples, peaches, nectarines, & Orleans plums.

July 6. Many martins in Lincolns inn fields.

July 7. [South Lambeth] Fine, showers, clouds.

July 8. Cut chardon-heads for boiling: artichokes dry, & not well flavoured. Roses in high beauty. My nieces make Rasp jam. Goose-berries not finely flavoured.

July 9. A cuckoo cries in my Bro^rs^ garden:* some birds of that sort have frequented this place all the summer. Young swallows at Stockwell. In Mr Malcolm's garden there is a bed of small silver firs, the tops of which are all killed by the frosts in June. The hothouses of this Gent: afford a most noble appearance; & his plantations are grand, & splendid. Passion-flower begins to blow in the open air. Cucumbers are scarce, & sell for $2\frac{1}{2}^{d}$ a piece. Crops of pease go off. Some celeri trenched out from the seedling bed.

July 10. Grapes swell. New potatoes.

July 11. Chardons† are usually blanched, & stewed like celeri: but my Brother boils the heads of his, which are very sweet, & in flavour like artichokes; the chief objection is, that they are very small, & afford little substance in their bottoms. The heads of chardons are sold in the markets & are thought to be a delicate morsel. Chardons are strong, vigorous plants, & grow six & seven feet high, & have strong sharp prickles like thistles.

July 12. On this day My Bro. Benj. White began to rebuild his house in Fleetstreet which he had entirely pulled to the ground. His grandson Ben White laid the first brick of the new foundation, & then presented the workmen with five shillings for drink. Ben, who is five years old, may probably remember this circumstance hereafter, & may be able to recite to his grandchildren the occurrences of the day.

July 13. My brother gathered a sieve of mush-rooms: they come up in the flower-borders, which have been manured with dung from the old hot beds.

* Benjamin White's at South Lambeth.
† See Note to entry of June 13, 1790.

July 14. A bat* of the largest sort comes forth every evening, & flits about in the front of my brother's house. This is a very rare species, & seldom seen. See my history of Selburne.

July 17. Small shower: heavy rain at Clapham, & Battersea. On this day M[rs] Edm[d] White was brought to bed of a daughter, who encreases my nephews & nieces to the number of 58.†

July 19. [Alton] Rye cut & bound at Clapham. Wheat looks well, & turns colour. Hay making at Farnham: pease are hacking near that town; hops distempered.

July 20. [Selborne] M[r] Budd's annuals very fine. Ground well moistened: after-grass grows.

July 21. My broad beans are but just come in.

July 22. Children bring wood-strawberries in great plenty. Made straw-berry jam. Gathered currans, & rasps for jam: my rasps are fair & fine. The farmers at Selborne had not half a crop of hay. Hops thrive at this place. Merise, wild cherries, over at the vicarage, ripen.

July 24. The foreign Arum in the vicarage court, called by my Grandmother Dragons, & by Linnæus *Arum dracunculus*, has lately blown. It is an Italian plant, & yet has subsisted there thro' all the severe frosts of 80 or 90 years; & has escaped all the diggings, & alterations that have befallen the borders of that garden. It thrives best under a N. wall, but how it is propagated does not appear. The spatha, & spadix are very long.

July 26. M[rs] Henry White,‡ & Lucy came from Fyfield.

July 29. A basket of mushrooms from Honey-lane. Gathered wall-nuts for pickling.

July 30. Made black curran-jelly. Finished cutting the tall hedges. Gathered some lavender.

July 31. "On the last day of this month my Fath[r] M[r] Ben. Wh. shot in his own garden at S. Lambeth, a *Loxia curvirostra*, or *Cross bill*, as it was feeding on the cones of his Scotch firs. There were six, four cocks, & two hens: what he shot was a cock,

* The noctule, first recorded by the author. See Letters XXII, XXVI and XXXVI to Pennant.

† Including, therefore, grand-nephews and grand-nieces.

‡ Née Miss Cooper of Oxford, a widow in this year, since her husband, the Rector of Fyfield, died three years before.

which was beautifully variegated with brown, & green, & a great deal of red: it answered very accurately to Willughby's description; & weighed rather more than 1 ounce & an half. In the evening, the five remaining birds were seen to fly over the garden, making a chearful note." Thus far Mrs Ben White.*

To which we add that flights of *Cross bills* used to frequent Mrs Snooke's† Scotch firs in the month of July only. Mr Ray says, "per autumnum interdum sed rarius *in Angliam* venit, non autem apud nos perennat aut nidificat." Synopsis.

August 1. Gathered our whole crop of apricots, being one large fine fruit.

August 2. Sowed white turnip radishes. Planted-out savoys, & other winter cabbages.

August 3. Somewhat of a chilly feel begins to prevail in the mornings and evenings. Sowed a pint of London prickly spinage seed to stand the winter. The same quantity last year produced an incredible crop. Trod & rolled in the seed. In Mr Hale's hop-garden near Dell are several hills containing male plants, which now shed their farina: the female plants begin to blow. Men hoe turnips, & hack pease. Men house hay as black as old thatch.

August 4. Farmer Tull begins to reap wheat. The hop-garden at Kimber's fails again, & looks black.

August 5. Mrs H. White, & Lucy left us. Two dobchicks in Combwood pond. Young martins, & swallows cluster on the tower, & on trees, for the first time. A pleasing circumstance mixed with some degree of regret for the decline of summer!

August 6. Boys bring wasp's nest. Codlings, & stewed cucumber come in. Housed, & piled 8 cords of beechen billet in fine order. Watered the cucumbers; well very low.

August 7. Received from Farnham, well packed in a box, a picture of a mule pheasant,‡ painted by Mr Elmer, & given me by Lord Stawell. I have fixed it in a gilt, burnished frame, & hung it in my great parlor, where it makes an elegant piece of furniture. The first broods of swallows, & house-martins, which con-

* Showing that natural history had become, by force of the author's genius, a family institution.

† The author's aunt, Rebecca, who had lived at Ringmer, near Lewes.

‡ See Note to entry of Oct. 2, 1790.

gregate on roofs, & trees, are very numerous: & yet I have not this year one nest about my buildings.

August 8. Some young broods of fly-catchers fly about.

August 11. Half hogshead of portwine from Southampton. Gleaners come home with corn.

August 12. Men bind their wheat all day.* The harvesters complain of heat. The hand-glass cucumbers begin to bear well: red kidney beans begin to pod.

August 13. Farmer Tull makes a wheat-rick at Wick-hill.

August 14. Hirundines enjoy the warm season. Late this evening a storm of thunder arose in the S. which, as usual, divided into two parts, one going to the S.W. & W. & the greater portion to the S.E. and E., & so round to the N.E. From this latter division proceeded strong, & vivid lightening till late in the night. At Headleigh there was a very heavy shower, & some hail at E. Tisted. The lightening, & hail did much damage about the kingdom. Farmer Spencer's char-coal making in his orchard almost suffocated us: the poisonous smoke penetrated into our parlor, & bed-chambers, & was very offensive in the night.

August 15. Lightening every moment in the W. & N.W. Cut 114 cucumbers. Harvesters complain of violent heat.

August 16. Colchicums, or naked boys† appear.

August 17. Holt White,‡ & Harry Woods came from Fyfield.

August 18. Timothy grazes. John White§ came from Salisbury. Cut 133 more cucumbers. Michaelmas daiseys begin to blow. Farmer Spencer, & Farmer Knight make each a noble wheat-rick: the crop very good, & in fine order.

August 19. The young men left us, & went to Funtington. A second crop of beans, long pods, come in. Sweet day, golden even, red horizon. Some what of an autumnal feel.

August 20. John White called in his way from Funtington to Salisbury. The whole country is one rich prospect of harvest scenery!! Fern-owl glances along over my hedges.

* The self-binder does it all now for them. It saves time but loses everything else worth having, the craftsmanly sheaf-knots being replaced by twine or wire, mechanically tied.

† Because the flower is leafless.

‡ Son of Thomas White, the eldest brother and author of *Fauna Calpensis*.

§ See Note to entry of Sept. 5, 1790.

August 21. Many creatures are endowed with a ready discernment to see what will turn to their own advantage & emolument; & often discover more sagacity than could be expected. Thus Benham's poultry watch for waggons loaded with wheat, & running after them pick up a number of grains which are shaken from the sheaves by the agitation of the carriages. Thus when my brother used to take down his gun to shoot sparrows, his cats would run out before him to be ready to catch up the birds as they fell.

August 24. Gathered kidney-beans, scarlet. Cut 80 cucumbers.

August 25. Holt White came back from Shopwick.

August 26. My potatoes come in, & are good.

August 27. Cut 179 cucumbers: in all this week—349. A large sea-gull went over my house.

August 29. Hop-picking begins in Hartley gardens. Cut 96 cucumbers.

August 30. Mr Hale begins his hops near the Pound field. Farmer Hoar says that during this blowing weather his well was raised some rounds of the rope.*

August 31. Cut 31 cucumbers. Fly-catcher still appears.

September 2. Cut 62 cucumbers. Holt White left us, & went to Newton.

September 3. Bad weather for the hops, & pickers. When the boys bring me wasps nests, my Bantam fowls fare deliciously; & when the combs are pulled to pieces, devour the young wasps in their maggot-state with the highest glee, and delight. Any insect-eating bird would do the same: & therefore I have often wondered that the accurate Mr Ray should call one species of buzzard *Buteo apivorus, sive vespivorus*, or the *Honey-buzzard*, because some combs of wasps happened to be found in one of their nests. The combs were conveyed thither doubtless for the sake of the maggots or nymphs, & not for their honey; since none is to be found in the combs of wasps.† Birds of prey occasionally feed on insects: thus have I seen a tame kite picking up the female ants, full of eggs, with much satisfaction.

* Due primarily to the heavy rainfall (as Walter Johnson suggests), but secondarily to the equinoctial gales.

† Linnæus, not Ray, named the Honey-Buzzard. The author is perfectly accurate in describing the food. The bird feeds on the larvae of wasps.

September 5. Cut 107 cucumbers. Nectarines are finely flavoured, but eaten by bees, & wasps. Churn-owl is seen over the village: fly-catchers seem to be gone.

September 6. Tyed up about 30 endives. A swift still hovers about the brew-house at Fyfield. About a week ago, one young swift, not half-fledged, was found, under the eaves of that building! The dam no doubt is detained to this very late period by her attendance on this late-hatched, callow young! The roof of my nephew's brew-house abounds with swifts all the summer.

September 7. Cut 125 cucumbers. Young martins, several hundreds, congregate on the tower, church, & yew-tree. Hence I conclude that most of the second broods are flown. Such an assemblage is very beautiful, & amusing, did it not bring with it an association of ideas tending to make us reflect that winter is approaching; & that these little birds are consulting how they may avoid it.

September 9. Gathered in the white apples, a very fine crop of large fine fruit, consisting of many bushels.

September 10. Young broods of swallows come out. Cut 171 cucumbers; in all 424 this week. Sweet moon light!

September 11. *Grey crow* returns, & is seen near Andover. Red even, sweet moon. Some nightly thief stole a dozen of my finest nectarines.

September 13. My well is very low, & the water foul! Timothy eats voraciously. Winged female ants migrate from their nests, & fill the air. These afford a dainty feast for the hirundines, all save the swifts; they being gone before these emigrations, which never take place till sultry weather in August, & September.

September 14. Hop-picking goes on without the least interruption. Stone-curlews cry late in the evenings. The congregating flocks of *hirundines* on the church & tower are very beautiful, & amusing! When they fly-off altogether from the Roof, on any alarm, they quite swarm in the air. But they soon settle in heaps, & preening their feathers, & lifting up their wings to admit the sun, seem highly to enjoy the warm situation. Thus they spend the heat of the day, preparing for their emigration, &, as it were consulting when & where they are to go. The flight about the church seems to consist chiefly of house-martins, about 400 in number: but there are other places of rendezvous about the village frequented at the same time. The swallows seem to delight more in holding their assemblies on trees.

When Autumn scatters his departing gleams,
Warn'd of approaching winter gathered play
The *Swallow people*; & toss'd wide around
O'er the calm sky in convolution swift,
The feather'd eddy floats: rejoicing once
Ere to their wintry slumbers they retire,
In clusters clung beneath the mouldring bank,
And where, unpierced by frost, the cavern sweats.
Or rather into warmer climes convey'd,
With other kindred birds of season, there
They twitter chearful, till the vernal months
Invite them welcome back:—for thronging now
Innumerous wings are in commotion all.*

September 15. The springs are very low: the water fails at Webb's bridge.

September 20. Some neighbours finish their hops. The whole air of the village of an evening is perfumed by effluvia from the hops drying in the kilns. Began to light a fire in the parlor.

September 24. Young martins, & swallows come-out, & are fed flying. Endive well blanched comes in. Bottled-off half hogsh: of port wine. The port ran eleven doz. & 7 bottles. Nep. Ben White & wife, & little Ben came.

September 25. Several wells in the village are dry: my well is very low; Burbey's, Turner's, Dan Loe's hold out very well.

September 26. Gathered in the pear-mains,† golden rennets, & golden pippins.

September 27. Strong cold gale.

September 28. Linnets congregate in great flocks. This sweet autumnal weather has lasted three weeks, from Septr 8th.

September 29. A gale rises every morning at ten o' the clock & falls at sunset.

* From Thomson's *Autumn*. It is evident that the poet, any more than the author himself, had not made up his mind between hibernation and migration.

† Worcester Pearmains, a ruddy, showy apple but a poor eater and cooker.

October 1. Nep. B. White left us, & went to London. It was with difficulty that we procured water enough for a brewing from my well.

October 2. Gathered one fine nectarine, the last. My double-bearing raspberries produce a good crop. Grapes very fine, endive good.

October 5. Arrived off the isle of Wight the Earl Fitzwilliams Captn Dundas from Madras. Charles Etty sailed in this India man as second mate about the 10th of March, 1790. Poor Charles Etty* did not come home in the Earl Fitzwilliams, having unfortunately broke his leg at Madras the evening before the ship sailed for Europe.

October 6. Received a bag of hops from Mr Hale, weight 61 pounds.

October 7. Gathered in Chaumontel, swans-egg, & Virgoleuse pears: the latter rot before they ripen. Gathered also the kitchen apples at the end of the fruit-wall, & the knobbed russetings: of both there is a great crop. Gathered the Cadillac pears, a small crop.†

October 8. Earthed up the celeri, which is very gross, & large.

October 9. It has been observed that divers flies, besides their sharp, hooked nails, have also skinny palms or flaps to their feet, whereby they are enabled to stick on glass & other smooth bodies, & to walk on ceilings with their backs downward, by means of the pressure of the atmosphere on those flaps; the weight of which they easily overcome in warm weather when they are brisk and alert. But in the decline of the year, this resistance becomes too mighty for their diminished strength; & we see flies labouring along, & lugging their feet in windows as if they stuck fast to the glass, & it is with the utmost difficulty they can draw one foot after another, & disengage their hollow caps from the slippery surface. Upon the same principle that flies stick,‡ & support themselves, do boys, by way of play, carry heavy weights by only a piece of wet leather at the end of a string clapped close

* See Note to Letter LVIII to Barrington.

See my *Introduction*.

‡ This theory is now abandoned: a sticky fluid is exuded from the pads. The "labouring" fly had been attacked by a fungus (Walter Johnson's note).

on the surface of a stone. Tho' the Virgoleuse pears always rot before they ripen, & are eatable; yet when baked dry on a tin, they become an excellent sweet-meat.

October 12. Gathered cucumbers for picklers. One of my Apricot-trees withers, & looks as if it would die. Hunter's moon rises early. Mrs Ben White left us, & took Tom with her, leaving Ben behind.

October 13. My beeches in the field shed ripe mast. Some of the Bantams sicken.

October 15. Bro. Ben, & wife, Hannah came. Wood-cock, & red wings return, & are seen.

October 17. Saw a wood-cock on the down among the fern: Fyfield flushed it.

October 22. One young martin in one of Burbey's nests, which the dams continue to feed. Gracious stream now runs a little.

October 24. The dams continue to feed the poor little martin in the nest at Burbey's with great assiduity!

October 25. There are two young martins in the nest.

October 26. No young martins to be seen in the nest, nor old ones round it.

October 27. Young martins, & their dams again. Wood-cock on the down. Bro. Ben, & wife, & Hannah left us, & went to Newton.

October 28. There are now apparently three young martins in the nest nearly fledged.

October 29. The young martins remain.

October 30. The young martins still in their nest; at least some of them. Dr Chandler saw four hawking round the plestor.

October 31. The young martins not seen in their nest: dams about.

November 1. The young martins are out: one was found dead this morning in the parsonage garden.

November 2. [Newton] The late rains have not had any influence yet on my well-water, which is very low, & foul. Snow on the Sussex downs.

November 4. [Selborne] Grey, gleams. Snow gone.

November 8. Planted one doz. of red hairy goose-berries, & one doz. of smooth amber, from Armstrong, in the quarters of the garden. Gathered-in the grapes: decaying. Two rills run now into my well, the water of which begins to get clear.

November 9. Planted a row of Hyacinths on the verge of the fruit-border; & tulips along the broad walk. Planted winter-cabbages. Potatoes dug up.

November 13. Thunder in the night. Thomas heard the Portsmouth evening gun.

November 25. Well rises very fast.

November 26. 3 gallons of brandy from London.

November 28. M^{r} & Mrs Edm^{d} White came.

November 29. Put a large cross on the hermitage.* A trufle-hunter tryed my tall hedges, & found some bulbs of those peculiar plants, which have neither roots, nor branches, nor stems.

December 1. M^{r} & M^{rs} Ed. White left us. The Hermitage, new capped with a coat of thatch, & embellished with a large cross, makes a very picturesq object on the hanger, & takes the eye agreeably.

December 3. Snow covers the ground, snow shoe deep.

December 5. Cut down, & covered the artichokes: covered the rhubarb plants; & the lettuces under the fruit-wall, & the spinage lightly with straw.

December 7. Ground very wet. Farmer Tull plants Butts-close with hops.

December 8. Timothy has laid himself up under the hedge against Benham's yard in a very comfortable, snug manner: a thick tuft of grass shelters his back, & he will have the warmth of the winter sun.

December 16. Swept-up the leaves in the walks.

December 17. Hard frost, very white, boys slide. Snipes come up from the forest along the meads by the sides of the stream. Hardly here & there a wood-cock to be seen.

* A little way up the hillside near the Bostal and opposite the Wakes. See Letter LX to Barrington in which the repercussions of the echoes heard at the Hermitage are described.

December 20. Saw lately a white, & a yellow wagtail* about the Well-head rivulet. No farther north than Rutland, wagtails withdraw, & are never seen in the winter.

December 21. [Newton] Dark & cold, frost.

December 23. [Selborne] Mr Churton came from Oxford.

* The pied and the grey wagtails. The yellow wagtail leaves us in autumn.

1792

January 6. Snow-drops, & crocus's shoot.

January 8. Mr Churton left us, & returned to Oxford.

January 13. Vast frost-work on the windows.

January 14. Lord Stawell sends me a cock & an hen brambling.*

January 17. The *Antirrhinum Cymb.* which flourished, & blossomed thro' all last winter, & the summer & autumn following, now killed by the frost. Hence it is probable that in milder regions it is at least a biennial,† if not a perennial. Before, it has always dyed every winter as soon as the hard frosts began to prevail.

January 19. The wood-men begin to fell beeches on the hanger.

January 23. Water-cresses come in.

January 27. The Swallow, Lord Cornwallis's advice sloop, arriv'd at Bristol from Madras, which it left on the 21st of Septem^{r}. The weather was so rough, that it could not get up the Bristol channel.

February 1. Turner's heifers feed down the dead grass in my great mead.

February 2. Grass-walks are very verdurous.

February 4. Spring like: crocus blows: gossamer floats: musca tenax comes forth: blackbird whistles.

February 6. Fairey-rings encrease on my grass-plot.

February 8. The hasels in my hedges are illuminated by numbers of catkins. Bantam lays.

February 9. Tubbed, & pickled a fat porker: weight nine scores, & eleven pounds: price 8^{s} & 4^{d}, from farmer Hoar.

February 10. Wood-cock killed in the shrubs above the Hermitage.

* A finch visiting us in the winter in small flocks and breeding in the forests of northern Europe. Several were noted in February, 1936, in the New Forest. (Hampshire Field Club.)

† White is correct, in spite of Walter Johnson's note to the contrary.

February 11. The *meadow* measures 2 *acres* & 19 *rods*, besides the dug ground.

February 13. Sowed the ashes of my own making in the great mead, where the grass is finest. Finished tacking the fruit wall-trees. Gossamer streams from the boughs of trees. Brimstone butterfly, Papilio rhamni.

February 15. Crown imperials sprout.

February 19. Frost comes within doors.

February 20. Snow about four inches deep. 3 Bantam hens lay.

February 21. Yellow wagtail* appears.

February 23. Began to drink tea by day light.

February 26. Rain in the night. Humble bee. Worms come out on grass plots: a great snail.

February 27. Mr Littleton Etty called. Long tailed titmouse. Crocus's blowing very much. Winter aconites fade.

March 1. The laurustines, & the young shoots of the honey-suckles are not hurt by the late frosts.

March 9. Much sharp March weather. Flights of snow, freezing all day.

March 10. Bror Benjamin, & wife, & Rebecca dined with us. White water-wagtail.†

March 12. Carted in 6 loads of hot dung for the cucumber bed; 1 of my own, & 5 from Kimbers.

March 15. Snow-drops are out of bloom. Rainbow.

March 16. Daffodil blows. . . .

it takes the winds of March
Before the Swallow dares.‡

March 17. Dog's toothed violets bud. Lord Stawell made me a visit on this day, & brought me a white wood-cock;§ it's head, neck, belly, sides, were milk-white, as were the under sides of the wings. On the back, & upper parts of the wings were a few spots of the natural colour. From the shortness of the bill I should sup-

* The grey wagtail. The yellow does not appear in our pastures from the Continent until the latter end of March.

† Pied wagtail.

‡ A curious misquotation for one of White's steady accuracy.
An instance of albinism.

pose it to have been a male bird. It was plump, & in good condition.

March 23. *Timothy* the *Tortoise* comes out. Crown imperials bud for bloom, & stink much.

March 25. Mrs Clement came with her three daughters.

March 26. Crocus's go off. The Kingsley miller assures me that he saw a *Swallow* skimming over the meadow near the mill. Hirundines are often seen early near mill-ponds, & other waters.

March 27. The ground in a sad wet condition, so that men cannot plow, nor sow their spring-corn. A wet March is very unkind for this district.

March 31. Mrs Chandler was brought to bed of a daughter.

April 1. Stormy, wet night. Mrs Clement, & daughters left us. Berriman's field measured contains 1 acre 3 qu. 25 rds.

April 3. Some players came hither from Alton.* A hand-glass of early celeri entirely eaten-up by the *Chrysomela oleracea saltatoria*, vulgarly called the *turnip fly*. Sowed more.

April 5. Wind damages the hedges. Some thatch torn by the wind. Mr White's tank at Newton runs over, & Capt. Dumaresque's is near full.

April 6. Players left us.

April 7. The cucumbers shoot out fibres down their hills: earthed them a little. Thomas mowed the dark green grass growing on the Fairy circles, & segments of circles in my grass plot, which encrease in number every year.

April 9. *Nightingale* sings. *Cuckoo* is heard. Timothy the tortoise weighs 6 ae 11½ oz.

April 10. [Wallingford] Hot sun. Goslins on commons. Black thorn blossoms.

April 11. [Oxford] Men hoe their wheat, which is very forward, & fine. Thomas in my absence planted beans, & sowed carrots, parsnips, cabbage-seed, onions, lettuce, & radishes.

April 12. Thermometer at Fyfield 72! in the shade.

April 13. A great thunder-storm at Woodstock, & Islip: the

* Local players are also recorded in the Log-Books of Henry White of Fyfield.

Charwel* much flooded, & discoloured. No rain at Oxford. Prodigious was the damage done about the Kingdom on this day by storms of thunder, lightening, & vast torrents, & floods, & hail. The town of Bromsgrove in Worcestershire was quite deluged, & the shops & sitting rooms filled with water. A house was burnt at some place; & in others many people hurt, & some killed.

April 16. [Alton] Great bloom of cherries, pears, & plums.

April 17. [Selborne] Saw a pair of swallows at Alton.

April 19. *Redstart* appears. Daffodils are gone: mountain-snow-drops, & hyacinths in bloom; the latter very fine: fritillaries going. Vast flood at Whitney in Oxfordshire, on the Windrush.

April 21. Planted 4 rows of my own potatoes in the garden. Mowed the terrace walk.

April 23. A nest of young blackbirds destroyed by a cat in my garden.

April 26. Two nightingales within hearing: cuckoos come round the village.

April 27. The middle Bantam hen sits in the barn. Planted four rows of potatoes in the home garden.

April 28. Planted in the mead-garden eleven rows of potatoes; four of which were potatoes from Liverpool, sent to Dr Chandler by Mr Clarke. Planted in the mead four rows of beans.

April 30. Men tye their hops. Dressing some of the borders. Heavy thundrous clouds. Tulips blow. On this beautiful evening came all at once *seven Swifts*, which began to dash & play round the church. *Chur-worm*† jars down at Dorton in swampy ground. Mrs Ben White, & her son Tom came from London.

May 1. Cut a good mess of asparagus.

May 2. Cut the leaves of Rhubarb for tarts: the tarts are very good. Sent some of the leaves of the crocus's to Edm^d^ White; they make good tyings for hops, being both tough, & pliant.

May 4. Began to use the lettuces under the fruit wall.

* The Cherwell is very liable to flood owing to its flat banks and easy valley. The same is true of the Windrush (see April 19) between Burford and Witney, where its valley widens.

† The mole-cricket.

May 6. During the severe winds it is not easy to say how the Hirundines subsist; for they withdraw themselves, & are hardly ever seen, nor do any insects appear for their support. That they can retire to rest, & sleep away these uncomfortable periods, as the bats do, is a matter to be suspected rather than proved: or do they not rather spend their time in deep & shelt'red vales near waters, where insects are more likely to be found?* Certain it is, that hardly any individuals of this Genus have been seen for several days together.

May 8. On this day 26 houses, besides a number of barns, stables, granaries, &c. were burnt down at Barton-Stacey near Winchester. Only ten or twelve houses were preserved, among which is the parsonage, a large farm house, & some others out of the line of the street. The people of Selborne subscribed 6 ae. 1s. 0d. on this occasion: the county collection was very large & ample.

May 9. Still for the first time since May 1st. Chalk cart.

May 10. Peat cart begins.

May 12. An army of caterpillars infest my young goose-berry trees, which were planted this spring: & the case is the same at Dr Chandler's. Thomas picked the trees carefully, & gave them a good watering.

May 13. Mrs Ben White came.

May 17. Sowed some Nasturtion seeds on the bank. Mr Charles Etty returns from Madras well in health, & not lame from the accident of breaking his leg; but thinner than he was. He went first to Bengal, & so home in a Danish India man.

May 18. The *fern-owl*, or *eve-jarr* is heard to chatter in the hanger. So punctual† are they!

May 19. The middle Bantam brought forth nine chickens.

May 20. The missel-thrush has a nest on the orchard pear-tree. The thunder of this evening burnt the barns, & out houses of a farm between Gosport & Titchfield, & destroyed eight fine horses.

May 21. The cock missel-thrush sings on the tops of the tall firs.

May 22. The Fly-catcher comes to my vines, where probably it

* This is so.

† The entry for 1791 occurs one day earlier.

was bred, or had a nest last year. It is the latest summer bird, & appears almost to a day! "Amusive bird,* say where your snug retreat?"!
The *white* apples are out of bloom, being forward: the *Dearling*, a late keeping apple, but just in bloom. So the earlier the fruit ripens the sooner the tree blossoms. The Dearling bears only once in two years, but then an enormous burthen. It has produced 10, & 13 bushels of fruit at a crop. The bloom this year is prodigious! the crop moderate, & the fruit small.

May 24. The old speckled Bantam sits on eight eggs. *Sorbus aucuparia*, the Quicken-tree, or mountain ash full of bloom. The bunches of red berries would make a fine appearance in winter: but they are devoured by thrushes, as soon as they turn colour. Tanner shot a hen Sparrow-hawk as she was sitting on her eggs in an old crow's nest on one of the beeches in the High wood. The bird fell to the ground, &, what was very strange, brought down with her one of the eggs unbroken. The eggs of Sparrow-hawks, like those of other birds of prey, are round, & blunt-ended, & marked at one end with a bloody blotch. The hen bird of this species is a fine large hawk; the male is much smaller, & more slender. Hawks seldom build any nest. This Hawk had in her craw the limbs of an unfledged lark.

May 27. The missel-thrush has got young.

May 30. My table abounds with lettuces, that have stood the winter; radishes; spinage; cucumbers; with a moderate crop of asparagus.

May 31. Grass grows very fast. Honey-suckles very fragrant, & most beautiful objects! Columbines make a figure. My white thorn, which hangs over the earth-house, is now one sheet of bloom, & has pendulous boughs down to the ground. One of my low balm of Gilead firs begins to throw out a profusion of cones; a token this that it will be a short-lived, stunted tree. One that I planted in my shrubbery began to decay at 20 years of age. Miller in his gardener's Dictionary mentions the short continuance of this species of fir, & cautions people against depending on them as a permanent tree for ornamental plantations.

June 1. M^r^ & Mrs Ben white left us, & went to Newton.

* From the author's own *The Naturalist's Summer Evening Walk*.

June 2. Mushrooms are brought to the door.

June 3. No may-chafers this year. The intermediate flowers, which now figure between the spring, & solstitial, are the early orange, & fiery-lily, the columbine, the early honey-suckle, the peony, the garden red valerian, the double rocket or dames violet, the broad blue flag-iris, the thrift, the double lychnis, spider-wort, monk's hood, &c.

June 4. Hay making about London.

June 5. One Fly-catcher builds in the Virginia Creeper, over the garden-door: & one in the vine over the parlor-window. Between Newton & us we heard three Fern-owls chattering on the hill; one at the side of the *High-wood,* one at the top of the *Bostal,* & one near the *Hermitage.* That at the top of the Bostal is heard distinctly in my orchard. Fern-owls haunt year by year the same spots.

June 6. The mare lies out. S^{t} foin begins to blow.

June 7. Heavy thundrous clouds, copious dew. Opened, & slipped-out the superfluous shoots of the artichokes.

June 8. Cut-off the cones of the *balm* of *Gilead fir* in such numbers that they measured one gallon & an half. So much fruit would have exhausted a young tree. The cones grow sursùm, upright; those of the Spruce, deorsùm, downward.

June 10. Began to use green goose-berries.

June 11. [Mareland, Alton] Went, & dined with my Brother Benjamin White at Mareland,* to which he & his wife were come down for two or three days. We found the house roomy, & good, & abounding with conveniences: the out-door accommodations are also in great abundance, such as a larder, pantry, dairy, laundry, pigeon-house, & good stables. The view from the back front is elegant, commanding sloping meadows thro' which runs the Wey (the stream from Alton to Farnham) meandering in beautiful curves, & shewing a rippling fall occasioned by a tumbling bay formed by Mr Sainesbury, who also widened the current. The murmur of this water-fall is heard from the windows. Behind the house next the turnpike are three good ponds, & round the extensive outlet a variety of pleasant gravel walks. Across the

* A village near Farnham, whither Benjamin White removed during this year from South Lambeth.

meadows the view is bounded by the Holt: but up & down the valley the prospect is diversifyed, & engaging. In short Mareland is a very fine situation, & a very pleasing Gentleman's seat. I was much amused with the number of Hirundines to be seen from the windows: for besides the several martins & swallows belonging to the house, many Swifts from Farnham range up & down the vale; & what struck me most were forty or fifty bank-martins, from the heaths, & sand-hills below, which follow the stream up the meadows, & were the whole day long busied in catching the several sorts of Ephemerae which at this season swarm in the neighbourhood of waters. The stream below the house abounds with trouts. Nine fine coach-horses were burnt in a stable at Alresford.

June 12. [Selborne] Mr Burbey has got eleven martins nests under the eaves of his old shop.

June 15. Beat the banks; & planted cabbages in the meadow-garden.

June 16. Planted some hand-glass plants in the frames of the fruiting cucumber-bed: cut down the lining, & worked it up with some grass-mowings. Some young fly-catchers are out, & fed by their dams.

June 17. When the servants are gone to bed, the kitchen-hearth swarms with minute crickets not so big as fleas. The Blattae* are almost subdued by the persevering assiduity of Mrs J. W.† who waged war with them for many months, & destroyed thousands: at first she killed some hundreds every night. The thermometer at George's fields Surrey 82: on the 21,—51. Saint foin fly, sphynx filipendulae, appears.

June 18. The spotted Bantam hen brings out seven chickens. Took a black birds nest the third time: the young were fledged, & flew out of the nest at a signal given by the old ones.

June 19. Pinks, scarlet-lychnis, & fraxinellas‡ blow. The narrow-leaved blue Iris, called Xiphium, begins to blow.

June 21. Put sticks to some of the kidney-beans. Longest day: a cold, harsh solstice! The rats have carried away six out of seven

* Cockroaches.

† Mrs. John White, living at The Wakes since the death of her husband in 1780.

‡ *Dirtamnus fraxinella*.

of my biggest Bantam chickens; some from the stable, & some from the brew-house.

June 24. Thunder, & hail. A sad midsum^{r} day. When the Blattae seem to be subdued, & got under; all at once several large ones appear: no doubt they migrate from the houses of neighbours, which swarm with them.

June 25. Timothy Turner sowed 40 bushels of ashes on Baker's hill: an unusual season for such manure! Tryed for rats over the stable, & brewhouse with a ferret, but did not succeed.

June 27. The late pliant sort of Honeysuckles, that do not make good standards, begin to show their yellow bloom: the more early are on the decline. Hung the net over the cherry-trees at the end of the house to keep off the magpies, which come to our very windows at three & four in the morning. The daws also from the church have invaded my neighbour's cherries. Pies, & daws are very impudent!

June 28. Glow-worms abound in Baker's hill.

June 29. Straw-berries from the woods are brought; but they are crude, & pale, as might be expected. Cut-off the large leaves of the *Colchicum*, or meadow-saffron, now decaying: towards the end of August the blossoms, called by some *naked boys*, will shoot out, & make a pleasing appearance.

June 30. The Saint foin about the neighbourhood lies in a bad way.

July 1. There is a natural occurrence to be met with upon the highest part of our down in hot summer days, which always amuses me much, without giving me any satisfaction with respect to the cause of it; & that is a loud audible humming of bees* in the air, tho' not one insect is to be seen. This sound is to be heard distinctly the whole common through, from the Money-dells, to Mr White's avenue-gate. Any person would suppose that a large swarm of bees was in motion, & playing about over his head. This noise was heard last week on June 28th.

> Resounds the living surface of the ground,
> Nor undelightful is the ceaseless *hum*
> To him who muses . . . at noon.

* Caused by minute dipterous and hymenopterous insects (note by Walter Johnson).

Thick in yon stream of light a thousand ways,
Upward, and downward, thwarting, & convolv'd,
The quivering nations sport.

Thomson's *Seasons.*

July 5. The Provost of Oriel,* & Lady came.

July 6. Mr Eveleigh says, that the churring of the fern-owl is like the noise of a razor-grinder's wheel.

July 7. Farmer Hoare's son shot at a hen *Wood-chat,*† or small *Butcher-bird* as it was washing at Well-head, attended by the cock. It is a rare bird in these parts. In it's craw were insects.

July 8. The Poet of Nature lets few rural incidents escape him. In his *Summer* he mentions the *whetting* of a *scythe* as a pleasing circumstance, not from the real sound, which is harsh, grating, & unmusical; but from the train of summer ideas which it raises in the imagination. No one who loves his garden & lawn but rejoices to hear the sound of the mower on an early, dewy morning.‡—

Echo no more returns the *chearful* sound
Of sharpening scythe.

Milton also, as a pleasing summer-morning occurrence, says,

. . . the mower whets his scythe.

L'Allegro.

July 9. The Provost & Lady left us. Thunder in the night, & most part of the day to the S. & S.E. Yellow evening.

July 10. Guns fire at Portsmouth.

July 13. Whortle-berries are offered at the door. Cherries have little flavour.

July 14. The double roses rot in the bud without blowing out: an instance this of the coldness, & wetness of the summer. Potatoes blossom.

July 16. Farmer Corps brought me two eggs of a *fern-owl,* which he found under a bush in shrub-wood. The dam was sitting on

* Dr. John Eveleigh who succeeded Dr. John Clarke in 1781. The author had now for many years been on good terms with his College.

† A black and white shrike with a chestnut crown which, though it nests in Normandy, is a rare visitor to south-eastern England.

‡ A sound that, except now and again in private gardens or along the roadside, will never, in our generation, be heard in England again.

the nest; & the eggs, by their weight, seemed to be just near hatching. These eggs were darker, & more mottled than what I have procured before.

July 18. Men cut their meadows. Mr Churton came.

July 19. My meadow is begun to be mowed.

July 20. Simeon Etty brought me two eggs of a *Razor-bill* from the cliffs of the Isle of Wight: they are large, & long, & very blunt at the big end, & very sharp & peaked at the small. The eggs of these birds are, as Ray justly remarks, "in omnibus hujus generis majora quàm pro corporis mole." One of these eggs is of a pale green, the other more white; both are marked & dotted irregularly with chocolate-coloured spots. *Razor-bills* lay but one egg, except the first is taken away, & then a second, & on to a third. By their weight these eggs seem to have been sat on, & to contain young ones.

July 21. Made rasp, & curran jam, & jelly.

July 22. Took the black bird's nest the fourth time: it contained squab young.

July 24. Preserved some cherries. My meadow-hay was carried, in decent order. As we were coming from Newton this evening, on this side of the Money-dells, a cock Fern-owl came round us, & showed himself in a very amusing manner, whistling, or piping as he flew. Whenever he settled on the turf, as was often the case, Mr Churton went, & sprung him, & brought him round again. He did not clash his wings over his back, so as to make them snap. At the top of the Bostal we found a bat hawking for moths. Fern-owls & Bats are rivals in their food, commanding each great powers of wing, & contending who shall catch the phalaenae of the evening.

July 26. This cool, shady summer is not good for mens fallows, which are heavy, & weedy. Lettuces have not loaved, or bleached well this summer.

July 29. Heavy showers. Apples fall much. The well at Temple is 77 feet deep: 60 to the water, & 17 afterward. My well measures only 63 feet.

July 30. Mr Churton left us, & went to Waverley.

July 31. The young Hirundines *begin* to congregate on the tower. How punctual are these birds in all their proceedings!

August 1. Floods out in several parts of the kingdom, & much hay & corn destroyed. Young buzzards* follow their dams with a piping, wailing noise.

August 5. The guns at the camp on Bagshot-heath were heard distinctly this evening.†

August 7. Several of my neighbours went up the Hill (this being the day of the great review at Bagshot heath) whence they heard distinctly the discharges from the ordnance, & small arms, & saw the clouds of smoke from the guns. The wind being N.E. they smelled, or seemed to smell, the scent of the gunpowder. Wickham bushes, the scene of action, is more than 20 miles from hence. The crouds of people assembled upon this occasion were great beyond anything seen at such meetings!

August 8. My lower wall nut tree casts it's leaves in a very unusual manner. No wall-nuts; the crop dropped off early in the summer.

August 12. The thermometer for three or four days past has stood in the shade at Newton at 79, & 80.

August 13. Goose-berries wither on the trees.

August 14. Housed two loads of peat.

August 18. Blackcaps eat the berries of the honey-suckles. M[rs] J. White, after long & severe campaign carried on against the *Blattae molendinariae*, which have of late invaded my house, & of which she has destroyed many thousands, finds that at intervals a fresh detachment of old ones arrives; & particularly during the hot season: for the windows being left open in the evenings, the males come flying in at the casements from the neighbouring houses, w[ch] swarm with them. How the females, that seem to have no perfect wings that they can use, can contrive to get from house to house, does not so readily appear. These, like many insects, when they find their present abodes over-stocked, have powers of migrating to fresh quarters. Since the *Blattae* have been so much kept under, the Crickets have greatly encreased in number.

* The day is far distant since buzzards nested in the neighbourhood of Selborne. Reports of them in Hampshire nowadays come from the New Forest, where they are sometimes seen on migration.

† A letter to Robert Marsham on the same subject was written on this very day.

August 19. My shrub, *Rhus cotinus*, known to the nursery-men by the title of *Coccygia*, makes this summer a peculiar shew, being covered all over with it's "bracteae paniculae filiformes", which give it a feathery plume-like appearance, very amusing to those that have not seen it before. On the extremities of these panicles appear about midsum̄er a minute white bloom, which with us brings no seeds to perfection. Towards the end of August the panicles turn red & decay.

August 20. Thomas, in mowing the walks, finds that the grass begins to grow weak, & to yield before the scythe. This is an indication of the decline of heat. Yucca filamentosa, silk grass, blows with a fine large white flower. It thrives abroad in a warm aspect. Habitat in Virginia.*

August 21. My large American Juniper, probably *Juniperus Virginiana*, has produced this summer a few small blossoms of a strong flavour like that of the juniper-berries: but I could not distinguish whether the flowers were male, or female; so consequently could not determine the sex of the tree, which is dioecious. The order is *dioecia monadelphia*.

August 22. The seeds of the lime begin to fall. Some wheat under hedges begins to grow.

August 23. Some wheat bound; & some gleaning. I have not seen one wasp.

August 24. John Berriman's hops at the end of the Foredown† very fine.

August 26. A fly-catcher brings out a brood of young; & yet they will all withdraw & leave us by the 10th of next month.

August 27. A fern-owl this evening showed-off in a very unusual, & entertaining manner, by hawking round, & round the circumference of my great spreading oak for twenty times following, keeping mostly close to the grass but occasionally glancing up amidst the boughs of the tree. This amusing bird was then in pursuit of a brood of some particular phalaena belonging to the oak, of which there are several sorts; & exhibited on the occasion a command of wing superior, I think, to that of the swallow itself. Fern-owls have attachment to oaks, no doubt on account of

* Not Virginia but North America. It is still a valued garden plant.

† Foredown had become Far Down by the time the Tithe Award was made in 1842.

food: for the next evening we saw one again several times among the boughs of the same tree; but it did not skim round it's stem over the grass, as on the evening before. In May these birds find the *Scarabaeus melolontha** on the oak; & the Scarabaeus solstitialis at Midsummer. These peculiar birds can only be watched & observed for two hours in the twenty-four; & then in a dubious twilight, an hour after sun-set & an hour before sun-rise.

August 28. Men make wheat-ricks. Mr Hale's rick fell. Vivid rain-bow.

August 29. Mr Clement begins to pick hops at Alton. *Clavaria's*† appear on the hanger.

August 31. Many moor-hens on Comb-wood pond.

September 1. Grass grows on the walks very fast. Garden beans at an end.

September 2. The well at Temple is 77 feet deep: 60 to the water, & 17 afterwards. My well measures only 63 feet to the bottom.

	yards	feet
Goleigh well to the water is	55½	166
,, ,, to the bottom	57½	172½
Heards well to the water is	70⅔	212
,, ,, to the bottom	83⅓	250

A stone was 4½ seconds falling to the bottom of Heards well; & 4 seconds to the water of Goleigh. The wells were measured accurately by the Revd Edmund White on the 25th of August 1792, in the midst of a very wet summer. Deep, & tremendous as is the well at Heards, John Gillman, an Ideot, fell to the bottom of it twice in one morning; & was taken out alive, & survived the strange accident many years. Only Goleigh & Heards wells‡ were measured by Mr E. White.

September 4. Hop-picking becomes general; & the women leave their gleaning§ in the wheat-stubbles. Wheat grows as it stands in the shocks.

* Cockchafer. † A club fungus.

‡ At Priors Dean and East Tisted, both on the chalk. Hence their difference in depth from the author's well in the Upper Greensand (Walter Johnson's note).

§ Like Ruth in the fields of Boaz. The time when the church-bells at 8.0 in the morning and 6.0 in the evening rang the gleaners into the cornfields vanished when the machines left nothing worth the gleaning. See also Note to entry of Aug. 30, 1790.

September 6. Gil. White left us. The flying ants of the small black sort are in great agitation on the zigzag, & are leaving their nests. This business used to be carryed on in August in a warm summer. While these emigrations take place, the Hirundines fare deliciously on the female ants full of eggs. Hop-picking becomes general; & all the kilns, or as they are called in some counties, *oasts*, are in use. Hops dry brown, & are pretty much subject this year to vinny, or mould.

September 8. Sowed thirteen rods, on the twelfth part of an acre of grass ground in my own upper Ewel close with 50 pounds weight of Gypsum; also thirteen rods in D° with 50 pounds weight of lime: thirteen rods more in D° with 50 pounds weight of wood & peat-ashes: and four rods more on D° with peat-dust. All these sorts of manures were sown by Bro[r] T. W.* on very indifferent grass in the way of experiment.

September 9. As most of the second brood of Hirundines are now out, the young on fine days congregate in considerable numbers on the church & tower: & it is remarkable that tho' the generality sit on the battlements & roof, yet many *hang* or cling for some time by their claws against the surface of the walls in a manner not practised at any other time of their remaining with us. By far the greater number of these amusing birds are house-martins, not swallows, which congregate more on trees. A writer in the Gent. Mag. supposes that the chilly mornings & evenings, at this decline of the year, begin to influence the feelings of the young broods; & that they cluster thus in the hot sunshine to prevent their blood from being benumbed, & themselves from being reduced to a state of untimely torpidity.

September 11. On this day my niece Anne Woods was married to M[r] John Hounsom, who encreases my nephews, & nieces to the number of 59. M[r] John White† came from Salisbury.

September 12. Began to light fires in the parlour. J.W. left us.

September 13. The stream at Gracious street, which fails every dry summer, has run briskly all this year; & seems now to be equal to the current from Well-head. The rocky channel up the

* Thomas White.

† Dr. John White of Salisbury, the author's nephew and one-time pupil.

hollow-lane towards Rood has also run with water for months: nor has my great water-tub been dry the summer through.

September 14. From London three gallons of French brandy, & two gallons of Jamaica rum.

September 15. Hop women complain of the cold.

September 16. Dr Chandler's Bantam sow brought him this last summer a large litter of pigs, several of which were not cloven-footed, but had their toes joined together. For tho' on the upper part of the foot there was somewhat of a suture, or division; yet below in the soles the toes were perfectly united; & on some of the hind legs there was a solid hoof like that of a colt. The feet of the sow are completely cloven. Mr Ray in his *Synopsis animalium quadrupedum* takes no notice of this singular variety; but Linnæus in his *Systema Naturae* says, "Varietas frequens Upsaliae Suis domestici semper *monunguli*: in ceteris eadem species."

September 17. Gathered-in the white pippins, about a bushel: many were blown down last week. Oats housed.

September 19. Rain. Hops become very brown, & damaged. The hop-pickers are wet through every day.

September 21. On this day Monarchy was abolished at Paris by the National Convention; & France became a Republic!*

September 22. As I have questioned men that frequent coppices respecting Fern-owls, which they have not seen or heard of late; there is reason to suspect that they have withdrawn themselves, as well as the fly-catchers, & black-caps, about the beginning of this month. Where timber lies felled among the bushes, & covert, wood-men tell me, that fern-owls love to sit upon the logs of an evening: but what their motive is does not appear.

September 23. My Bantam chickens, which have been kept in the scullery every night till now for fear of the rats, that carried away the first brood from the brew-house, went up last week to the beam over the stable. The earnest & early propensity of the *Gallinae* to roost on high is very observable; & discovers a strong dread impressed on their spirits respecting vermin that

* Most editors comment on the absence of national events from White's pages. Yet the editors of political bigwigs are not astonished that they have nothing to say about the first arrivals of the Hirundines.

may annoy them on the ground during the hours of darkness. Hence poultry, if left to themselves & not housed, will perch, the winter through on yew-trees & fir-trees; & turkies & Guinea-fowls, heavy as they are, get up into apple trees; pheasants also in woods sleep on trees to avoid foxes:—while pea-fowls climb to the tops of the highest trees round their owner's house for security, let the weather be ever so cold or blowing. Partridges, it is true, roost on the ground, not having the faculty of perching; but then the same fear prevails in their minds; for through apprehensions from pole-cats, weasels, & stoats, they never trust themselves to coverts; but nestle together in the midst of large fields, far removed from hedges & coppices, which they love to haunt*
frequent in the day; & where at that season they can skulk more secure from the ravages of rapacious birds. As to ducks, & geese, their aukward splay web-feet forbid them to settle on trees: they therefore, in the hours of darkness & danger, betake themselves to their own element the water, where amidst large lakes & pools, like ships riding at anchor, they float the whole night long in peace, & security.

September 25. Men begin to bag hops. Celeri comes in. Vine-leaves turn purple.

September 30. There is a remarkable hill on the downs near Lewes in Sussex, known by the name of Mount Carburn, which over-looks that town, & affords a most engaging prospect of all the country round, besides several views of the sea. On the very summit of this exalted promontory, & amidst the trenches of its Danish camp,† there haunts a species of wild Bee,‡ making its nest in the chalky soil. When people approach the place, these insects begin to be alarmed, & with a sharp & hostile sound dash, & strike round the heads & faces of intruders. I have often been interrupted myself while contemplating the grandeur of the scenery around me, & have thought myself in danger of being stung:—and have heard my Brother Benjamin say, that he &

* The MS. frequently places two alternate words one above another, each conveying a similar meaning.

† The fine camp on Mount Caburn was a Celtic hill-town of the Iron Age, about 100 B.C. Caburn is the only example of a Celtic place-name left in Sussex.

‡ *Bombus lapidarius*.

his daughter Rebecca were driven from the spot by the fierce menaces of these angry insects. In old days Mr Hay* of Glynd Bourn, the Author of *Deformity*, & other works, wrote a loco-descriptive poem on the beauties of Mount Carburn.

October 1. Wheat out at Buriton, Froxfield, Ropley, & other places.

October 2. Flying ants, male & female, usually swarm, & migrate on hot sunny days in August & Septem^r; but this day a vast emigration took place in my garden, & myriads came forth in appearance, from the drain which goes under the fruit-wall; filling the air & the adjoining trees & shrubs with their numbers. The females were full of eggs. This late swarming is probably owing to the backward, wet season. The day following, not one flying ant was to be seen. The males, it is supposed all perish: the females wander away; & such as escape from Hirundines get into the grass, & under stones, & tiles, & lay the foundation of future colonies.

October 3. Hirundines swarm around the Plestor, & up & down the street.

October 6. Many Hirundines: several very young swallows on the thatch of the cottage near the pound. The evening is uncommonly dark.

October 7. The crop of stoneless berberries is prodigious! Among the many sorts of people that are injured by this very wet summer, the peat-cutters are great sufferers: for they have not disposed of half the peat & turf which they have prepared; & the poor have lost their season for laying in their forest-fuel.† The brick-burner can get no dry heath to burn his lime, & bricks: nor can I house my cleft wood, which lies drenched in wet. The brick-burner could never get his last makings of tiles & bricks dry enough for burning the autumn thro'; so they must be destroyed, & worked up again. He had paid duty for them; but is, as I understand, to be reimbursed.

October 9. Master Hale houses barley that looks like old thatch. Much barley about the country, & some wheat. Some pheasants

* William Hay, a traveller, essayist and versifier of the first half of the eighteenth century, and deformed.

† This of course was written before the enclosure of the Selborne area. See Appendix.

found in the manour. The sound of great guns was heard distinctly this day to the S.E. probably from Goodwood, where the Duke of Richmond has a detachment from the train of artillery encamped in his park, that he may try experiments with some of the ordnance.

October 11. Dr Chandler mows the church-litton closes for hay. Farmer Parsons houses pease, which have been hacked for weeks. Barley abroad.

October 12. Gathered in the dearling apples: fruit small, & stunted.

October 19. Made presents of berberries to several neighbours. Ring-ouzel seen in the Kings field.

October 23. Dr Bingham & family left Selborne.

October 26. Hired two old labourers to house my cleft billet wood, which is still in a damp, cold condition, & should have been under cover some months ago, had the weather permitted.

October 27. Some few grapes just eatable: a large crop. Housed all the billet wood. Leaves fall in showers. A curlew is heard loudly whistling on the hill towards the Wadden.* On this day Mrs S. Barker was brought to bed of a boy, who advances my nepotes to the round & compleat number of 60.

October 28. Thomas saw a polecat run across the garden.

October 29. Finished piling my wood: housed the bavins: fallows very wet.

October 30. Planted 100 of cabbages, in ground well dunged, to stand the winter.

November 3. Men sow wheat: but the land-springs break out in some of the Hartley malm-fields.

November 5. Gossamer abounds. Vast dew lies on the grass all day, even in the sun.

November 8. Planted 3 quarters of an hundred more of cabbages to stand the winter: dug-up potatoes; those in the garden large, & fine, those in the meadow small, & rotting.

November 10. On this day Brother Benjamin quitted South Lambeth, & came to reside at His House at Mareland.

* Spelt "Wadding" in the Tithe Award of 1842.

November 12. Planted in the garden 2 codling-trees, 2 damson-trees, & 22 goose-berry trees, sent me by Bro^r T.W.

November 13. M^r Ed. White & man brought a good fine young white poplar from his out-let at Newton, & planted it at ye top of Parsons's slip behind the bench; where it will be ornamental.

November 15. Timothy comes out.

November 17. Baker's hill is planted all over with horse-beans, which are grown four or five inches high. They were probably sown by jays; & spring up thro' the grass, or moss. Many were planted there last year, but not in such abundance as now.

November 19. Water-cresses come in.

November 21. Sent 3 bantam fowls to Miss Reb. White at Mare-land, a cock & two pullets.

November 22. Timothy comes forth.

November 24. Saw a squirrel in Baker's hill: it was very tame. This was probably what Thomas called a pole-cat.*

November 26. Timothy hides.

November 29. This dry weather enables men to bring in loads of turf, not much damaged: while scores of loads of peat lie rotting in the Forest.

December 1. Thomas started a hare, which lay in her form under a cabbage, in the midst of my garden. It has begun to eat the tops of my pinks in many places. The land-springs, which began to appear, are much abated.

December 2. This dry fit has proved of vast advantage to the kingdom; & by drying & draining the fallows, will occasion the growing of wheat on many hundred of acres of wet, & flooded land, that were deemed to be in a desperate state, & incapable of being seeded this season.

December 4. Timothy is gone under a tuft of long grass, but is not yet buried in the ground.

December 5. Timothy appears, & flies come-out.

December 7. Took down the urns, & shut up the alcove.†

December 8. Dr Chandler brought a vast pear from the garden of

* If a sly dig at Thomas Hoar was not intended here, Gilbert White never wrote.
† A happy *vignette* of the eighteenth century.

his niece at Hampton, which weighed 20 ounces, & ¾, & measured in length 6 inches, & ¾, & in girth eleven inches. It is the sort known by the name of Dr Uvedale's great Saint Germain.

December 9. Damage by the wind in some places.

December 10. Mr Taylor brought me a pine-apple, which was, for the season, large, & well-flavoured.

December 14. [Newton] Grey, & mild, gleams.

December 15. [Selborne] Grey, sun, pleasant, yellow even.

December 16. The season has been so mild that the *Antirrhinum Cymb.* still flourishes, & continues in bloom.

December 20. Dark & wet. Shower, a short, but violent gust. Lightening.

December 24. Covered the artichokes, & rhubarb with litter, & the spinage, & the Yucca filimentosa with straw; & the few brown lettuces with straw. Mr Churton came.

December 26. Bramblings are seen: they are winter-birds of passage, & come with the hen-chaffinches. Nep. Ben. White & wife came.

December 29. B. White, & wife left us.

1793

January 4. Rain, rain, gleams. Venus is very resplendent.*

January 6. N. papers mention snow to the northward. On this day Mrs Clement was brought to bed of a boy, her ninth child. My nephews & nieces are now 61.

January 7. Nephew Holt White came.

January 10. Mr Churton left us.

January 11. On this day came my Nep. John White of Sarũm with his bride late Miss Louisa Neave, who encreased my Nep. & nieces to the number of 62.

January 12. Vast rain in the night, lightening. Great stream in the cart-way.

January 14. [Newton] Snow-drops bud, & winter-aconites blossom. John White, & wife, & Holt White left us.

January 16. [Selborne] dark, & sharp frost.

January 17. Turnip-greens come in.

January 20. Rime on the hanger. Mr Marsham, who lives near Norwich,† writes me word, that a servant of his shot a bird last autumn near his house that was quite new to him. Upon examination it appeared to him, & me to answer the description of the *Certhia muraria*, the *Wall-creeper*,‡ a bird little known, but some times seen in England. Ray, & Willughby never met with it, nor did I ever find it wild, or among the vast collections exhibited in London; but Scopoli had a specimen in his Museum, & says it is to be found in Carniola. It haunts towers, & castles, & ruins, some times frequents towns, running up the walls of tall houses, & searching the crannies, & chinks for spiders, & other insects. Some of the internal wing-feathers are beautifully marked on the inner web with two white, or pale yellow spots; & the middle of the outer web edged with red. Two of

* Like a song.

† At Stratton Strawless. One of the author's last correspondents.

‡ An example of White's extensive knowledge of birds, since he had never before seen a member of this species, which never visits England, though I have seen it in the Dordogne.

these quills, drawn in water-colours, by a young Lady, & charmingly executed, were sent me by Mr Marsham in a frank: the pencilling of these specimens is truly delicate, soft, & feathery. It is much to be regretted that she did not draw the whole bird. The claws of this bird are strong & large, say Linnæus, & Mr Marsham; & especially the hind claw.

January 21. Thrush sings, the song-thrush: the missle-thrush has not been heard. On this day Louis 16th late king of France, was beheaded at Paris, & his body flung into a deep grave without any coffin, or funeral service performed.

January 28. Bees come out, & gather on the snow-drops.

February 1. The Republic of France declares war against England & Holland.

February 3. A strong gust in the night blew down the rain-gage, which, by the appearance in the tubs, must have contained a considerable quantity of water.

February 4. Venus is very bright, & shadows.

February 5. [Newton] Mrs. J. White set out for Kingston on Thames.

February 8. [Selborne] War declared & letters of Marque granted against the french Republic.

February 10. Grey, sun, severe wind, with flights of snow, sleet, & hail.

February 11. Paths get dry. Sowed a bed of radishes, & carrots under the fruit-wall.

February 12. Mrs J. White returns.

February 15. Rain & hail in the night. Made a seedling-cucumber bed: mended the frame, & put it on.

February 16. Sent some winter-aconites in bloom to Dr Chandler; & received back some roots of *Arum dracunculus*. Tubbed, & salted-up a fine young hog, bought of Timothy Turner.

February 19. Sowed half a barrel of American Gypsum, which was sent for in the autumn by Bro. Tho. on the *fourth* ridge of Tim Turner's wheat, as you reckon from the walk in that field. The powder strewed about two thirds of the ridge from the Ewel S.E. ward.

February 20. Wheeled much dung into the garden.

February 21. Dug the garden-plot in the orchard, & in the meadow: but the ground is very wet, & heavy.

February 24. M[r] White of Newton sprung a pheasant in a wheat-stubble, & shot at it; when, notwithstanding the report of the gun, it was immediately pursued by the blue hawk, known by the name of the *Hen-harrier*, but escaped into some covert. He then sprung a second, & a third in the same field, that got away in the same manner; the hawk hovering round him all the while that he was beating the field, conscious no doubt of the game that lurked in the stubble. Hence we may conclude that this bird of prey was rendered very daring, & bold by hunger; & that Hawks cannot always seize their game when they please.* We may further observe that they cannot pounce their quarry on the ground, where it might be able to make a stout resistance; since so large a fowl as a pheasant could not but be visible to the piercing eye of an hawk, when hovering over a field. Hence that propensity of cowring & squatting till they are almost trod on, which no doubt was intended as a mode of security; tho' long rendered destructive to the whole race of *Gallinae*, by the invention of nets, & guns.

February 28. Planted 50 good cabbage-plants: mended the bed planted in the autumn, & eaten in part by the hares.

March 3. The wind last night blowed-off some tiles from my roof. This storm did much mischief about the kingdom.

March 4-15. [Mareland.]

March 4. We are much amused every morning by a string of Lord Stawell's Hunters that are aired, exercised, & watered in a meadow opposite to the windows of this house. There seem to be two sets, which appear alternatly on the days that they are not hunted. He has in all sixteen.

March 5. Herons haunt the stream below the house, where the Wey meanders along the meads. Lord Stawell sent me a curious water-fowl, shot on Frinsham pond, which proved to be the *Shoveler*, remarkable for the largeness of it's bill. It is a species of duck, & most exactly described by M[r] Ray. Large wood-pecker†

* Especially when a pheasant is several inches larger than a hen-harrier. Two pairs of Montagu's harriers bred in the New Forest in 1935 and one pair in 1936. But their status is extremely precarious. (Hampshire Field Club Papers.)

† The green woodpecker, yaffle, yaffingale or hewhole.

laughs very loud. My Brother's lambs frolick before the windows, & run to a certain hillock, which is their goal, from whence they hurry back; & put us in mind of the following passage in the Poet of nature:

Now the sprightly race
Invites them forth; then swift, the signal given,
They start away, & sweep the mossy mound
That runs around the hill.*

March 6. Dogs-tooth violets blow. Wag-tails on the grass-plots: they were here all this mild winter. Goldfinches are not paired.

March 7. Trouts begin to rise: some angling takes place in this month. My Brother's cucumbers are strong, & healthy. Lady Stawell tells Mrs White that they have seen more woodcocks & snipes at their table this winter than usual.

March 8. Many redwings feeding in the meadow.

March 10. The sweet bells at Farnham, heard up the vale of a still evening, is a pleasant circumstance belonging to this situation, not only as occasioning agreeable associations in the mind, & remembrances of the days of my youth, when I once resided in that town†:—but also by bringing to one's recollection many beautiful passages from the poets respecting this tuneable & manly amusement, for which this island is so remarkable. Of these none are more distinguished, & masterly than the following:—

Let the village bells as often wont,
Come swelling on the breeze, & to the sun
Half set, ring merrily their evening round.

. . . . . .

It is enough for me to hear the sound
Of the remote, exhilerating peal,
Now dying all away, now faintly heard.
And now with loud, & musical relapse
In mellow changes pouring on the ear.

The Village Curate.‡

* From Thomson's *Seasons* ("Spring").

† Gilbert White was probably at the Grammar School at Farnham in the days which the bells recalled to him in his age.

‡ It has been suggested that the author knew James Hurdis (1763-1801) who wrote these lines.

March 11. There is a glade cut thro' the covert of the Holt opposite these windows, up to the great Lodge. To this opening a herd of deer often resorts, & contributes to enliven & diversify the prospect, in itself beautiful & engaging.

March 12. Apricot begins to blow. Red-wings, & starlings abound in the meadow, where they feed in the moist, & watered spots.

March 13. During my absence Thomas parted-out my polyanths, & planted them in rows along the orchard walk, & up the border of Baker's Hill by the hot beds. My Brother has a pigeon-house stocked with perhaps 50 pairs of birds, which have not yet begun to breed. He has in the yard Turkeys, a large breed of ducks, & fine fowls. On the ponds are geese, which begin to sit.

March 14. Papilio rhamni, the brimstone butterfly, appears in the Holt. Trouts rise, & catch at insects. A dob-chick comes down the Wey in sight of the windows, some times diving, & some times running on the banks. Timothy the tortoise comes forth, & weighs 6 ae 5½ oz. Took a walk in the Holt up to the lodge: no bushes, & of course no young oaks: some Hollies, & here & there a few aged yews: no oaks of any great size. The soil wet & boggy.

March 17. On friday last my Brother and I walked up to Bentley church, which is more than a mile from his house & on a considerable elevation of ground. From thence the prospect is good, & you see at a distance Cruxbury hill, Guild down, part of Lethe hill, Hind-head, & beyond it to the top of one of the Sussex downs. There is an avenue of aged yew-trees up to the church: & the yard, which is large, abounds with brick-tombs covered with slabs of stone: of these there are ten in a row, belonging to the family of the Lutmans. The church consists of three ailes, & has a squat tower containing six bells. From the inscriptions it appears that the inhabitants live to considerable ages. There are hop-grounds along on the north side of the turn-pike road, but none on the south towards the stream. The whole district abounds with streams. The largest spring on my brother's farm issues out of the bank in the meadow, just below the terrace. Some body formerly was pleased with this fountain, & has, at no small expence bestowed a facing of Portland stone with an arch, & a pipe, thro' which the water falls into a stone bason, in a perennial stream. By means of a wooden trough this spring waters some part of the circumjacent slopes. It is not so copious as Wellhead.

March 20. Planted 30 cauliflowers brought from Mareland; & a row of red cabbages. The ground is so glutted with rain that men can neither plow, nor sow, nor dig.

March 21. Parted the bunches of Hepatica's, that were got weak, & planted them again round the borders.

March 24. This evening Admiral Gardner's fleet sailed from St Helens with a fair wind.

March 26. Snow, & rain, harsh. A sad wintry day!

March 28. Snow does not lie, ice, frost & icicles all day.

March 29. White sharp frost: thick ice: icicles. Apricots blow: peaches & nectarines begin to open their buds. Some thing again eats off the young celeri.

March 30. Made a new hand-glass bed for celeri in the garden. The crocus's still look very gay when the sun shines.

April 1. In the mid counties there was a prodigious snow; some people were lost in it, & perished.

April 3. The small *willow-wren*, or *chif-chaf*, is heard in the short Lythe. This is the earliest summer bird,* & is heard usually about the 20th of March. Tho' one of the smallest of our birds, yet it's two notes are very loud, & piercing, so as to occasion an echo in hanging woods. It loves to frequent tall beeches.

April 4. Timothy Turner ashed a great part of Baker's hill, & dunged one part. Wag-tail on grass-plots.

April 5. The air smells very sweet, & salubrious. Men dig their hop-gardens, & sow spring-corn. Cucumber plants show rudiments of fruit. Planted cuttings of currans, & goose-berries. Dug some of the quarters in the garden, & sowed onions, parsnips, radishes, & lettuces. Planted more beans in the meadow. Many flies are out basking in the sun.

April 6. On the 6th of last October I saw many swallows hawking for flies around the Plestor, & a row of young ones, with square tails, sitting on a spar of the old ragged thatch of the empty

* The wheatear is earlier.

house. This morning Dr Chandler & I caused the roof to be examined, hoping to have found some of these birds in their winter retreat: but we did not meet with any success, tho' Benham searched every hole & every breach in the decayed roof.

April 7. The chaffinches destroy the blossoms of the polyanths in a sad manner. Sowed a bed of carrots: the ground hard, & rough, & does not rake fine.

April 9. Thomas Knight, a sober hind, assures us, that this day on Wish-hanger Common between Hedleigh & Frinsham he saw several *Bank martins* playing in & out, & hanging before some nest-holes in a sand-hill, where these birds usually nestle. This incident confirms my suspicions, that this species of Hirundo is to be seen first of any; & gives great reason to suppose that they do not leave their wild haunts at all, but are secreted amidst the clefts, & caverns of these abrupt cliffs where they usually spend their summers. The late severe weather considered, it is not very probable that these birds should have migrated so early from a tropical region thro' all these cutting winds and pinching frosts: but it is easy to suppose that they may, like bats & flies, have been awakened by the influence of the Sun, amidst their secret latebrae, where they have spent the uncomfortable foodless months in a torpid state, & the profoundest of slumbers. There is a large pond at Wish-hanger which induces these sand-martins to frequent that district. For I have ever remarked that they haunt near great waters, either rivers or lakes. Planted in one of the quarters of the garden, in ground well dunged, 8 long rows of potatoes. Carted in hot dung for the cucumber-bed.

April 10. Dug the asparagus bed, & cleared away the straw laid on. Farmers wish for a gentle rain.

April 11. Hoed & cleaned the alleys.

April 12. The *Nightingale* was heard this harsh evening near James Knight's ponds. This bird of passage, I observe, comes as early in cold cutting springs, as mild ones!

April 13. Bat out. This is the twelfth dry day.

April 15. Sowed fringed bore-cole, & Savoys, & leeks.

April 16. Made a hot bed for the two-light frame with lapped glass.

April 19. Showers of hail, sleet. Gleams. Timothy, who has withdrawn himself for several days, appears.

April 20. The *Cuckoo* is heard on Greatham common.

April 23. Mowed the terrace. Cut the first cucumber. Pulled the first radishes. A swallow over my meadow.

April 24. When Thomas got-up to brew at four o' the clock, he heard some stone-curlews pass by over the house in their way to the uplands. In the evening they flie over the village downwards, towards the brook, & meadows, where they seem to spend the night.

April 27. Men begin to pole their hops. Mountain snow-drop blows.

April 28. Wall-flowers full of bloom, & very fine. Nightingale in my fields.

April 29. I have seen no hirundo yet myself. Sowed Columbines, two sorts; Scabius; Scarlet lychnis; Nigella; 10 weeks stocks; Mountain lychnis.

April 30. Saw two swallows at Gracious street.

May 2. Sad, blowing, wintry weather. I think I saw an house martin. There is a bird of the black-bird kind, with white on the breast, that haunts my outlet as if it had a nest there. Is this a ring-ouzel? If it is, it must be a great curiosity; because they have not been known to breed in these parts.*

May 3. Timothy eats. A pair of Missel-thrushes have made a nest in the apple-tree near the fruit-wall. One young half-fledged was found in the garden.

May 4. Some beeches begin to show leaves. Sowed some fine Savoy seed from Newton. Hen *red-start* appears.

May 5. Damson, sloe-trees, & wild Merise blow. *Cock Red start.* There has been so little frost, that the *Antirrhinum Cymb.* flourished & blossomed the whole winter thro', & is now very thriving, tho' it usually dies about Xmass. So that, in mild times, it is at least a biennial with us, & may be perhaps of longer duration in milder regions. James Knight has observed two large fieldfares† in the high wood lately, haunting the same part,

* It must surely have been a semi-white blackbird, no uncommon sight.

† Doubtless missel-thrushes. Fieldfares never breed in England.

as if they intended to breed there. They are not wild. A nest of this sort of bird would be a great curiosity.

May 9. The mag-pies, which probably have young, are now very ravenous, & destroy the broods of Missel-thrushes, tho' the dams are fierce birds, & fight boldly in defence of their nests. It is probably to avoid such insults, that this species of thrush, tho' wild at other times, delights to build near houses, & in frequented walks, & gardens.

May 10. M. thrushes do not destroy the fruit in gardens like the other species of turdi, but feed on the berries of missel toe; & in the spring on ivy berries which then begin to ripen. In the summer, when their young become fledge, they leave neighbourhoods, & retire to sheep walks, & wild commons.

May 12. The merise, or wild cherry in beautiful bloom.

May 13. Two nightingales sing in my outlet. Foliage of trees expands very fast. Peat begins to be brought in: it is in good condition. H. martins build. The old Bantam hen began to sit in the barn on eleven eggs. The *fern-owl*, or *churn-owl* returns, & chatters in the hanger.

May 14. Timothy travels about the garden.

May 16. Sowed in the three-light annual frame African & French marrigolds, China asters, pendulous Amaranths, Orange-gourds. Took the blackbird's nest the second time; it had squab young.

May 17. Set the second Bantam hen over the saddle cup-board in the stable with eleven dark eggs.

May 18. A man brought me a large trout weighing three pounds, which he found in the waste current at the tail of Bins pond, in water so shallow that it could not get back again to the Selborne stream. Made rhubarb tarts, & a rhubarb pudding, which was very good.

May 19. The white apple-tree shows again, as usual, much bloom.

May 20. Cut *two brace* of fine cucumbers; & left one for seed. The 10 weeks stocks, which stood the winter, make a fine show, & are very fragrant. Tulips blow.

May 21. Timothy eats much.

May 22. Nep. Ben. White, & wife came.

May 25. Cut down the greens of the crocus's; they make good tyings for hops; better than rushes, more pliant, & tough.

May 26. The white pippin is covered with bloom. Farmer Spencer's apple-trees blow well. Nep. Ben White, & wife left us.

May 28. The season is so cold, that no species of Hirundines make any advances towards building, & breeding. Brother Benjn & Mrs. White, & Mary White, & Miss Mary Barker* came.

May 28. My weeding-woman swept-up on the grass-plot a bushel-basket of blossoms from the white apple-tree: & yet that tree seems still covered with bloom.

May 30. Fyfield sprung a brace of pheasants in Sparrow's hanger. Hail-like clouds about.

May 31. My great oak abounds in bloom, which is of a yellowish cast: the young shoots usually look red. The house-martins at Mareland, in the few hot days, began to build, but when the winds became cold again immediately desisted.

June 1. Timothy is very voracious: when he can get no other food he eats grass in the walks.

June 2. Bro^{r} Benjn & I measured my tall beech in Sparrow's hanger, which, at five feet from the ground, girths six feet one inch, and three quarters.

June 3. The ground sadly burnt up. Royal russets show much bloom. Summer cabbage comes in.

June 4. Cinnamon rose blows.

June 5. Men's S^{t} foin burns, & dies away. The farmers on the sands complain that they have no grass.

June 6. Sowed two rows of large white kidney-beans: but the ground is so hard, that it required much labour to render it fit to receive the seed. The old Bantam brought out only three chickens.

June 7. Watered well the white poplar at the foot of the bostal. Cut the slope hedge in Bakers hill. Mrs Clement, & children came.

June 8. The young Bantam hen brought out only three chickens.

* Sister of Sam Barker and one of the author's nieces.

Showers that wetted the blades of corn, & grass, but did not descend to the root. Ground very hard.

June 9. Early orange-lilies blow. Few chafers. The water at Kingsley mill begins to fail. The land-spring in the stoney-lane, as you go to Rood, stops. We draw much water for the garden: the well sinks very fast.

June 10. Cut *five* cucumbers.

June 11. A man brought me a large plate of straw-berries, which were crude, & not near ripe. The ground all as hard as iron: we can sow nothing nor plant out.

June 12. Bright, sun, golden even. Cut *eight* cucumbers. Mrs Clement & children left us. Many swifts.

June 13. Cut *ten* cucumbers. Provence roses blow against a wall. Dames violets very fine, ten weeks stocks still in full beauty.

June 14. Cut four cucumbers. Mr John Mulso came.

June 15. Men wash their sheep. Mr J. Mulso left us.*

* Gilbert White was dead less than a fortnight after this entry. Few of the great writers of our literature have had an end so fortunate, none have more richly merited it.

THE PRIVATE LETTERS

TO THE REV. JOHN WHITE

Selborne, *June* 26, 1773.

DEAR BROTHER,

Your favour of the 17th reached me last Wednesday; and about the same time, I presume, you received my account about Jack's measles. My nephew continues perfectly well, and has not through the distemper nor since had the least cough. From the time that he came home he had somewhat of an hoarseness in his voice, which I took at first to be a cold; but upon considering the matter, it is owing no doubt to a cause incident to young men about his time of life.

It pleases me much to find that you have heard the sibilous, or shivering wren;* since now you know all the species; and that you have heard the sedge-bird; which for variety of notes, and swift transitions from the song of one bird to that of an other is, I think, a wonderful fellow, and was it not for the hurrying manner, would be an elegant warbler. It is plain Mr. Lever knows nothing of the grasshopper-lark;† if he did, he could not confound it with the sedge-bird, to which it bears not the least resemblance either in person, song, or manner of life. Did the

* The wood-warbler. See notes on Letters X and XVI to Pennant.

† The grasshopper-warbler. They breed nowadays mostly in the north-east of the county, but only in small numbers.

shivering wren make its noise in the tops of tall trees? Mr. Lever is, I perceive, a very adroit *natural* Naturalist; it is therefore pity he does not allow himself the advantage of books, and call in the assistance of system.

The sedge-bird sings all night when it is awake, therefore when you throw stones or dirt into the bushes, you rouse it from its slumbers, and set it to work again.

You will be very busy, no doubt, in your repairs, and will meet, I hope, with no disappointments. I thought a fortnight ago that I was going to build a chamber full speed. I had bespoke a mason in the room of Long, who was pre-engaged; and Jack was to have been the Comptroller general of my Majesty's works; but just as I was going to lay in all materials my Mason sent me word he had got an other job, and could not do mine 'til *after harvest.*

For these three days past we have had the king at Portsmouth; and have heard continual firings, which shook my house. My s^{t}foin is down; but the weather is unsettled. Mr. Lever has procured the *canne petiere** in Lancashire; Mr. Pennant mentions one shot in Cornwall. Some boys killed lately at Oakhanger-ponds some flappers or young wild-ducks; among the rest they took some young teals† alive; one I saw, and turned into James Knight's ponds. 'Til now I never knew that teals bred in England. So you see new information crowds in every day. Was not the sibilous bird that you heard the real grasshopper-lark; did it haunt the tops of the tallest trees, or low bush-hedges; did it sing by night or by day? Many children continue to die of the measles, among the rest the youngest of Mrs. Hale's this morning; and the whooping cough rather gets worse than better. Poor Nanny Woods's cough is very bad; and she is very weak, and mends very slowly.

Mr. Knight of Street house is dead.

With respects to my sister, I remain

Your affectionate, and obliged brother,

GIL. WHITE.

* The little bustard, long extinct as a breeding species and now a rare winter visitor, chiefly to the east coast.

† See Letter VI to Pennant.

TO THE SAME

Fyfield, *March* 9, 1775.

DEAR BROTHER,

As you have long experienced that I am not usually a tardy and negligent correspondent, you will, I suppose, conclude that something has happened to prevent my writing sooner, as really has been the case. I have had an heat and stiffness in my eyes from over much reading, that made writing very irksome for some time; they are now pretty well recovered again.

After your disappointment in town I was glad to hear by your last that you had a prospect of disposing of your son at Manchester; but now I understand that farther difficulties arise. The Scopoli from Mr. Pennant that you mention is at Selborne; and I will send it, if you desire it; but it affords no information.

As you rather complain of some reserve on Benjamin's side respecting your work, suppose you write to him, and ask him how much he will give you *downright* clear of the plates and printing for your copy; and then you will know your certain gain, and will run no risk. Anything in the naturalist way now sells well. Or if he chuses to go shares in profit or loss, enquire of him what proportion he should think would pay him for conducting the sale and publication. Booksellers have certainly a power of pushing books into the world; and it must be a work of great merit to obtain and make its way *invitis bibliopolis*. You mention also a want of books: might you not also apply to Benjamin to know on what terms he would furnish you with the *use* of books proper for your purpose 'til you had completed your Fauna? It is highly proper, it seems, to have a good many cuts. Mr. Curtis will superintend your engravings.

Mrs. Chapone* sold her two first vols. for £50. Now she has made up a third from essays, poems, adventures, &c. and sold

*John Mulso's sister, the lady who wrote such edifying works as *Letters on the Improvement of the Mind*. She also addressed some verses to Timothy to which he replied in very dignified fashion (p. 300). Holt-White adequately disposes of Bell's pretty fiction of the author's unrequited attachment to her.

† His son married the author's niece, Anne Woods, in 1792.

that to another for £250; so that it is expected the man will lose considerably by the purchase.

Many thanks for the copies of your *Gib. Letters*, which are very entertaining. You have the advantage of me now, since you have taken away my amanuensis. I am disturbed that Mr. Shaw takes no manner of notice of the *Hirundines*; nor how far the *melba* and *hyberna* extend, as might have been expected from his opportunities at Cadiz and elsewhere. Pray let Capt. Shaw know, that if he comes to Alton I should be glad to see him. The spirit for natural history that you left behind you is by no means evaporated; neither is your mantle worn out.

Lever has opened his museum at half a guinea per head. Harry has got a fine roomy kitchen indeed, and will have a fine parlor over. This addition shuts all his buildings finely together; and nothing is to be regretted but the expense. Sister Harry has got another fine boy, whose name is Edward. Nanny White is in a poor languishing way, still at lodgings near Vauxhall: Edmund White is gone on trial to Mr. John Hounsom,† linendraper in Fleet Street. The father is to advance with him a fee of £250; and the master makes a merit of taking so little, and says that from a stranger he should have demanded £300.

When opportunity serves, pray read Dr. Johnson's *Journey through Scotland*, and Dr. Burney's *Tour through Europe to make enquiries into the present state of musick*. Thanks for your information about cotton-cups.

Should you not produce in your work a short comparative table of weather at Gibraltar, Selborne, and N. America? Kalm will furnish you with the barom., thermom., &c. of America. I herewith send you my best account of the cobweb shower of 1741. What is said of spiders shooting webs, and flying &c. in Ray's Letters* is so much, that it cannot be transcribed. You should consult Ray's Letters.

When first I came I fully intended to have sent you my account of the cobweb shower; but this house is so full that I have no opportunity of being long enough alone to think accurately on any subject; so I must defer that part till I write again. We have continual wet weather; and farmers are sadly hindered in

* Author of *Historia Insectorum* and *Synopsis Methodica Avium*.

their spring crop: stormy and wet this day, March 11.

When Hesiod says that the chirping note of the *Cicada* comes from *under its wings*, he expresses himself thus—

> "ἤχετα τέττιξ
> Δενδρέῳ ἐφεζόμενος λιγύρην καταχεύετ' ἀοιδήν
> Πυκνόν ὑπό πτερύγων"—(*v*. 584).

Is there not a Frenchman who claims this discovery?

Sure insects have been more abroad this winter than usual: and lately, in our little interval of fine weather, many species of *Muscæ* came forth. *Chrysomela Gottingensis* begins to come forth.

Brother Thomas, Molly White, and myself came down to this place on Tuesday last; on Wednesday next Harry's boy is to be baptised; and on Friday we are to return to Selborne.

I have just dug away forty loads of earth from the end of my kitchen, and have now set my house above ground in all parts.

Mr. Halliday† behaves very well, and improves so much, that his friends are well pleased with the pains that have been taken with him. His parts, though somewhat backward, and slow, promise to be solid.

Building is very infectious and catching; I am so pleased with Harry's new parlour, that I want to go home and build one.

A certain plea of license against the incumbent's taking all the duty in person can avail him nothing. Every man may, if he chooses, do his own business himself, certainly.

A flock of Spoon-bills‡ was seen last winter near Yarmouth in Norfolk: one was shot and sent to Curtis,* who showed it to brother Thomas. This is a rare bird indeed in England, though common in Holland, and must have migrated across the German Ocean, no narrow frith, in spite of all that Mr. Barrington can say to the contrary. That gent. is got into some fracas with

† He married Ann, daughter of Henry White of Fyfield.

‡ I saw one on Breydon Water by Yarmouth in 1926. Sir Thomas Browne wrote of the breeding of the spoonbill in Norfolk in the seventeenth century. Never abundant, it was finished off as a native bird by the egg-collector. It is now a spring and autumn visitor to East Anglia in small numbers.

* William Curtis, the botanist and entomologist. He is also mentioned in the *Journals*, and it is possible that, as his birthplace was Alton, White was acquainted with him.

the R. S.: so that, I suspect, no more of my *Hirundines* will be "redde".

I will send you in my next what Chaucer says about gossamer; it is wonderful that so remarkable and prognostic a phenomenon should escape Thomson, the naturalist poet.

As America is at present the subject of conversation, it may be matter of some amusement to you to send you a quotation from the *Medea* of Seneca, prophetic of the discovery of that vast continent.

> veneant annis
> Secula seris, quibus *oceanus*
> *Pateat, tellus, Tiphysque novos*
> *Detegat* orbes; nec sit terra ultima Thule.

N.B. Tiphys was a pilot to the Argonautic expedition; and a type of Columbus.

All friends join in respects.

Yours affect.,

GIL. WHITE.

Sure your Fauna should sell outright for £100 clear of all deductions. Mr. Pennant gets that sum for his new edition of *British Zoology*; and your work will contain much more new, original information.† I want to see you the first of Faunists. With regard to anecdote and real natural history the less you borrow from books the better; you have a large fund of your own. Benjn will get very largely by Mr. P.'s Scotch tour.

† The author was very much more concerned with the fortunes of his brother's works than with those of his own. I have left out many letters whose subject is the same.

TO SAMUEL BARKER

[With a copy of the "Invitation to Selborne".]

Selborne, *Nov*. 3, 1774.

DEAR SAM,

When I sat down to write to you in verse, my whole design was to show you how easy a thing it might be with a little care for a nephew to excell his uncle in the business of versification; but as you have so fully answered that intent by your excellent lines, you must for the future excuse my replying in the same way, and make some allowance for the difference of ages.

However, when at any time you find your muse propitious, I shall always rejoice to see a copy of your performance, and shall be ready to commend, and, what is more rare and more sincere, even to object and criticise where there is occasion.

A little turn for English poetry is no doubt a pretty accomplishment for a young gentleman,* and will not only enable him the better to read and relish our best poets, but will, like dancing to the body, have an happy influence even upon his prose compositions. Our best poets have been our best prose writers; of

* These sentiments and reflections on poetry are highly characteristic of their age. The nineteenth century would have told him he was divinely inspired; the twentieth to put his verses in the fire.

assertion Dryden and Pope are notorious instances. It would be in vain to think of saying much here on the art of versification; instead of the narrow limits of a letter, such a subject would require a large volume. However, I may say in a few words that the way to excell is to copy only from our best writers. The great grace of poetry consists in a perpetual variation of your cadences: if possible no two lines following ought to have their pause at the same feet.

Another beauty should not be passed over; and that is, the art of throwing the sense and power into the third line, which adds a dignity and freedom to your expressions. Dryden introduced this practice, and carried it to great perfection; but his successor, Pope, by his over exactness, corrected away that noble liberty, and almost reduced every sentence within the narrow bounds of a couplet. Alliteration, or the art of introducing words beginning with the same letter in the same or following line, has also a fine effect when managed with discretion. Dryden and Pope practised this art with wonderful success. As, for example, where you say "the polished beetle," the epithet "burnished" would be better for the reason above. But then you must avoid affectation in this case, and let the alliteration slide in, as it were, without design; and this secret will make your lines bold and nervous. There are also in poetry allusions, similes, and a thousand nameless graces, the efficacy of which nothing can make you sensible of but the careful reading of our best poets, and a nice and judicious application of their beauties. I need not add that you should be careful to seem not to take any pains about your rhimes; they should fall in, as it were, of themselves. Our old poets laboured as much formerly to lug in two rhiming words as a butcher does to drag an ox to be slaughtered; but Pope has set such a pattern of ease in that way, that few composers now are faulty in the business of rhiming...

TO THE SAME

Seleburne, *Apr.* 17, 1786.

DEAR SIR,

Partly through idleness, and partly through infirmity I have too long neglected your late letter. My thanks are due for your curious account of the climate of *Zarizyn*,* and I feel myself the more obliged, because you know I love to study climates. Whether you translate or abridge Dr Pallas, I do not know; but should be glad to see the remaining part of the year, if the subject does not give you too much trouble. I believe all fervid regions afford instances of undulating vapours; that at a distance appear like water. Arabia, I know does; and the phenomenon is finely alluded to in the Koran. In what language does Pallas write?

The summer-like weather of last Friday fetched out Timothy. There is somewhat very forlorn and abject in that creature's first appearance after a profound slumber of five months. When a man first rouses himself from a deep sleep, he does not look very wise; but nothing can be more squalid and stupid than our friend, when he first comes crawling out of his hibernacula: so that some farther lines of Dryden's ode, (written he supposes on purpose to ridicule tortoises) may well be applyed to him:—

Has rais'd up his head,
As awak'd from the dead;
And amaz'd he stares around.

There was, as I remember, one Abdon, a judge of Israel, of whom there is nothing memorial, but that he had 40 sons and 30 nephews. As a father, this chieftain, I must acknowledge, exceeded me much: but as to the matter of *Nepotism*, I go much beyond him: for I had 42 nephews and nieces before; and now Mrs. Brown's little daughter makes the 43rd; and I have more at hand, if I do not reckon my chickens before they are hatched.*

* Pallas's Travels were published in St. Petersburg in 1776.

* The final number was 62.

Nephew John of Alton, now *Dr. White*, has met with an ugly accident: as he was descending from his hayloft, the ladder turned, and gave him a bad fall on the stones; by which he bruised his side, and dislocated his *left* wrist: but he was not confined one day, and is getting well. This young man has found employ, and much riding about: but he must have time to approve himself, before he can expect much prime business. On March 26th Mrs. and Miss Etty left us for some weeks: and on the 30th by permission, came Mr. Taylor, our vicar; and his bride Miss Lisle of Moyle's court near Ring-wood Hants. The lady is of a very good family in this county, and niece to Mr. Lisle of Crooke's-easton; the gentleman who stood and carried the grand contested election for this county in 1733; but it cost him £10,000. The lady was desirous of spending part of her honeymoon at her husband's parish. Charles Etty is expected home in June. Nephew Edm[d], for which I highly commend him, is parting with all kinds of farming whatsoever: he lets all his tithes, and all his glebe; reserving only to himself three or four fields for his horses and cows. He will now know what he has to depend on: whereas both his late uncles† were much imposed on; and were subject to all the rabble and hurry of common renters. Edmund I trust, some time hence, will make an excellent neighbour; but has been as yet a very bad one, for his time has been so taken up with various courtships, that he has never been at home yet for ten days together. He marries, I think, in June: but first keeps another term at Oxford. All my apricots were cut off by that violent weather in the beginning of March! So deep was the snow, and so starved the birds, that the poor ring-doves came into our gardens to crop the leaves and sprouts of the cabbages! Hay is become very scarce and dear indeed! My rick is now almost as slender as the waste of a virgin: and it would have been much for the reputation of the two last brides that I have married, had their wastes been as slender...

† Richard and Edmund Yalden, Vicars of Newton Valence, in succession to their father, Edmund.

TO THOMAS BARKER

Selborne, *Jan.* 10, 1787.

DEAR SIR,

I have herewith sent you the Selborne rain, an account of which, I think, has been kept very exactly: but know nothing of the Fyfield and S. Lambeth rain. There fell such a glut of rain in the beginning of October that men were in some pain about the wheat season: however, such lovely weather followed quite into November that the sowing time was unusually good. Again during the 14 first days of December there fell 5 inches of rain: this deluge washed our malm-grounds‡ sadly.

As to strong beer at Mr. Yalden's, I can say nothing about the management of it, because John Pullinger, who had the sole conducting of it, has left Edmund White: I only know that my strong beer is much admired by those that love pale beer, made of malt that is dryed with billet. My method is to make it very *strong*, and to hop very *moderately* at *first*; and then to put in it, at two or three times, half a pound at a time of *scalded* hops, before I tap it. This is the Wilts method, and makes the beer as fine as rock-water. As my family is small, I never brew more than *half a hogshead* at a time; but then I put malt at the rate of 13 bushels to the *hogshead*, and only 3 pounds and a half of hops at brewing. I tap my half-hogsheads at about 12 months old; and always brew with rain water, when I can. The tank at Newton is made of brick: their beer was, and is, often good; but their water, when drank by itself, has a filthy taste of lime and moss. Their table beer does not keep in summer.*

Please to present my best thanks to my sister for her kind charity which will be very acceptable to our numerous poor. Mrs. Etty is here, but will leave us soon, perhaps 'til midsummer.

Yr affectionate servant,

G. WHITE.

‡ See Note on Letter I to Pennant.

* Gilbert White kept *A Chronicle of Strong Beer and Raisin Wine* and of their brewings from 1772 to 1793, a fortnight before his death. How searchingly this letter reveals the plumbless gulf between the genuine country life of White's day and the poor thin ghost of it to-day!

The crop of beech-mast was prodigious, and of great service to men's hogs, which were half fat before they were shut up. Between mast and potatoes poor men killed very large hogs at little expense. Tom Berriman's hog weighed 16 scores; yet eat only seven bushels of barley-meal: whereas without the help above mentioned, he would have required 20 bushels.

Dame Berriman is much disordered in her mind, and very violent. I sent a woman to scatter some beech-seed in every bush on the down.†

Mrs. J. White joins in respects. Barometer has been very high for some days; on Monday it was 30.3.

† One of the reasons why Selborne Down is no longer downland.

TO MISS WHITE

Selborne, *Oct.* 19, 1778.

DEAR MOLLY,

Bating your account of your father's indisposition, which I hope will be very short, your letter was very agreeable to me; and particularly the circumstance which intimates your intention of coming down next Monday. Nothing, I hope, will prevent so agreeable an event; and I will take care to send Thomas* in time on that day to meet you at the inn at Chawton.

For some mornings past we have experienced severe frosts for the time of the year, which have stripped my vines of all their leaves, and left a fine crop of grapes naked, and forlorn on the walls; they used to be cloathed with foliage 'til the middle of next month! So you must come and eat grapes every day, or they will be spoiled.

A Selborne man was aboard the Porcupine sloop when she took the French India rich ship. I saw a letter from him this morning, in which he says that his share will come to £300. This will be some recompence to the poor fellow, who was kidnapped in an ale-house at Botley by a press-gang, as he was refreshing himself in a journey to this place. The young man was bred a carter, and never had any connection with sea-affairs.

Your hand-writing is very fair, and handsome: pray keep it up; and don't scribble it away. Nanny Barker is a very good correspondent; but spoils her hand by writing too fast. A little patience would make her also a good pen-woman.

Mr. Etty,† who is going suddenly to town, will take my letter with him. Mrs. Etty is well. I am with due affection,

Y^{r} loving Uncle,

GIL. WHITE.

I do not recollect any more errands. Respects over the way.‡

* The author's old servant, Thomas Hoar.

† When Andrew Etty died in 1784, he was buried by his "curate pro tempore", Gilbert White himself.

‡ Benjamin and Thomas were living opposite one another at South Lambeth.

TO THE SAME

Selborne, *Feb*. 20, 1783.

DEAR MRS. MARY,

I return you many thanks for your very entertaining letter; and for your method of making of mice; which is a receipt that no family ought to be without; and especially my family, as we have not had a mouse in the house for months.

We have had a strange wedding lately. A young mad-headed farmer out of Berks came to marry farmer Bridger's daughter, and brought with him four drunken companions. He gave two guineas and a crown to the ringers; and came and drank with them, and set all the village for two days in an uproar. Poor dame Butler, hearing that her son was fighting, fell into fits, and continued delirious two days. These heroes, after they had drank all the second day at the Compasses, while a dinner dressing at the great farm at Newton was spoiled, went up at last, and ranted and raved so, that they drove the two Mrs. Hammonds (one of whom is the bride's eldest sister) up into their chambers through fear. At six in the evening they took the bride (who wept a good deal) and carryed her away for Berks. The common people all agree that the bridegroom was the most of a gentleman of any they ever saw. He told the folks at the inn that whenever the next sister was married, he would come and spend ten guineas.

Our crocus's begin to look gaudy.

By the accident that happened to Miss Woods's suit of cloaths, which was entirely consumed, Geo. Fort's chamber and furniture sustained much damage, and his house was in danger.

In riding from Alton to Selborne Mrs. Etty had a fall; but being light, she was little hurt. The mare fell, having a stone in her foot. Poor Mrs. Hoar of Nore-hill dyed this morning!

Pray present my respects to your father, and tell him I was much concerned, on casting up our account, when I came to find that by the sudden rise of stock, he had overpurchased himself in my long ann., and had laid out more than £20 of his own money. If he pleases to have his money before I get to town, I will send him a draught on brother Ben...

SELBORNE HANGER

A WINTER PIECE

TO THE MISS BATTIES

The Bard, who sang so late in blithest strain
Selbornian prospects, and the rural reign,
Now suits his plaintive pipe to sadden'd tone,
While the blank swains the changeful year bemoan.
How fallen the glories of these fading scenes!
The dusky beech resigns his vernal greens,
The yellow maple mourns in sickly hue,
And russet woodlands crowd the dark'ning view.
Dim, clustering fogs involve the country round,
The valley and the blended mountain-ground
Sink in confusion; but with tempest-wing
Should Boreas from his northern barrier spring,
The rushing woods with deafening clamour roar,
Like the sea tumbling on the pebbly shore.
When spouting rains descend in torrent tides,
See the torn Zigzag weep its channel'd sides:
Winter exerts its rage; heavy and slow,
From the keen east rolls on the treasured snow;

Sunk with its weight the bending boughs are seen,
And one bright deluge whelms the works of men.
Amidst this savage landscape, bleak and bare,
Hangs the chill hermitage in middle air;
Its haunts forsaken, and its feasts forgot,
A leaf-strown, lonely, desolated cot!
  Is this the scene that late with rapture rang,
Where Delphy danced, and gentle Anna sang;
With fairy-step where Harriet tripped so late,
And on her stump reclined the musing Kitty sate?
  Return, dear Nymphs; prevent the purple spring,
Ere the soft nightingale essays to sing;
Ere the first swallow sweeps the freshening plain,
Ere love-sick turtles breathe their amorous pain,
Let festive glee th' enliven'd village raise,
Pan's blameless reign, and patriarchal days;
With pastoral dance the smitten swain surprise,
And bring all Arcady before our eyes.
Return, blithe maidens; with you bring along
Free, native humour, all the charms of song,
The feeling heart, and unaffected ease,
Each nameless grace, and every power to please.
  Nov. 1*st*, 1763.

A HARVEST SCENE

Waked by the gentle gleamings of the morn,
Soon clad, the reaper, provident of want,
Hies cheerful-hearted to the ripen'd field;
Nor hastes alone; attendant by his side
His faithful wife, sole partner of his cares,
Bears on her breast the sleeping babe; behind,
With steps unequal, trips her infant train:
Thrice happy pair, in love and labour join'd!
All day they ply their task; with mutual chat,
Beguiling each the sultry, tedious hours.
Around them falls in rows the sever'd corn,
Or the shocks rise in regular array.
But when high noon invites to short repast,
Beneath the shade of sheltering thorn they sit,
Divide the simple meal, and drain the cask:
The swinging cradle lulls the whimpering babe,
Meantime; while growling round, if at the tread
Of hasty passenger alarm'd, as of their store
Protective, stalks the cur with bristling back,
To guard the scanty scrip and russet frock.

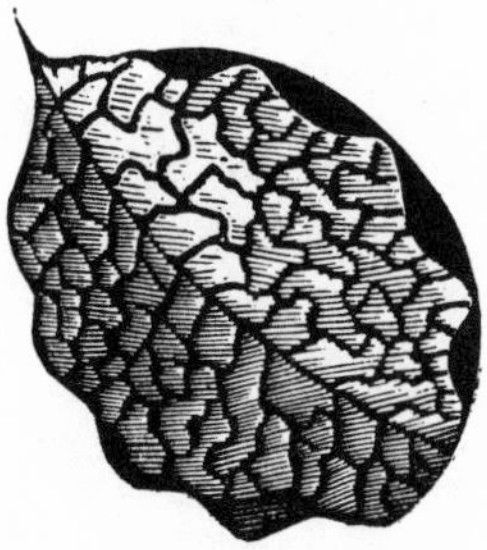